This is an introduction to the phonology of Present-day English. It deals principally with three varieties of English: 'General American', Southern British 'Received Pronunciation' and 'Scottish Standard English'. It offers a systematic and detailed discussion of the features shared by these major accents, and explains some major differences. Other varieties of English – Australian and New Zealand English, South African English and Hiberno-English – are also discussed briefly. Without focussing on current phonological theory and its evolution, the author demonstrates the importance of 'theory', in whatever shape or form, in phonological argumentation. The book also includes a helpful introductory section on speech sounds and their production, and detailed suggestions for further reading follow each chapter.

This clear and helpful textbook will be welcomed by all students of English language and linguistics.

CAMBRIDGE TEXTBOOKS IN LINGUISTICS

*General Editors:* J. BRESNAN, B. COMRIE, W. DRESSLER, R. HUDDLESTON, R. LASS, D. LIGHTFOOT, J. LYONS, P. H. MATTHEWS, R. POSNER, S. ROMAINE, N. V. SMITH, N. VINCENT

# ENGLISH PHONOLOGY

# ENGLISH PHONOLOGY

## An introduction

HEINZ J. GIEGERICH

DEPARTMENT OF ENGLISH LANGUAGE
UNIVERSITY OF EDINBURGH

CAMBRIDGE
UNIVERSITY PRESS

Published by the Press Syndicate of the University of Cambridge
The Pitt Building, Trumpington Street, Cambridge CB2 1RP
40 West 20th Street, New York, NY 10011-4211, USA
10 Stamford Road, Oakleigh, Victoria 3166, Australia

First published 1992

Printed in Great Britain at the University Press, Cambridge

*A catalogue record for this book is available from the British Library*

*Library of Congress cataloguing in publication data*

Giegerich, Heinz J.
English phonology: an introduction / Heinz Giegerich.
  p.  cm. – (Cambridge textbooks in linguistics)
Includes bibliographical references.
ISBN 0–521–33303–2 (hardback). – ISBN 0–521–33603–1 (paperback)
1. English language – Phonology.  I. Title.  II. Series.
PE1133.G47  1992
421′.5 – dc20  92–2744 CIP

ISBN 0 521 33303 2 hardback

ISBN 0 521 33603 1 paperback

# CONTENTS

# PREFACE

This is a textbook intended to introduce students of English, of English linguistics and of linguistics to the phonology of Present-day English. It is not a reference manual on the subject; nor is it an introduction to current phonological theory (in relation to English or otherwise).

To qualify for the former, it would have to be less selective in its coverage. In particular, the coverage of different accents of English is highly selective, for the ones treated here (Southern British 'Received Pronunciation', 'General American' and 'Scottish Standard English') can hardly be claimed to form a 'representative sample', whatever such a sample may be representative of. While this choice of reference accents is advantageous in many respects (not least in practical terms), it covers only part of the typological spectrum. Some of the rest, which is neither small nor, in typological terms, insignificant, is dealt with on a mere handful of pages appended to chapter 3. I do not pretend to do justice to those other varieties of English; I merely hope to make the reader aware of the fact that varieties of English exist which are different from those that I focus on, and that those differences are of considerable phonological interest.

Perhaps the most glaring omission in this book is intonation. This topic might have warranted an at least chapter-long treatment; but such a treatment (especially if it had been of a formal-analytical rather than merely descriptive kind, in line with my assumptions regarding the proper nature of phonological study) would have necessitated formalised input into the phonology from a variety of other areas of linguistics: from syntax (to a greater extent than is suggested in chapter 9), and also from semantics and pragmatics. The subject of intonation is in this sense too different from the rest of the phonology to be easily incorporated in what is intended to be a reasonably homogeneous analytical framework. Moreover, a satisfactory treatment of intonation would have required a more detailed phonetic grounding than is given here – especially one in acoustic phonetics; and if one also considers the fact that the three reference accents display marked differences in their intonation patterns then my reasons become clear for excluding the topic, with some reluctance, rather than merely scratching its surface. I do believe, however, that chapter 9 lays the foundations for the study of intonation; and I make suggestions there for further reading on the subject.

The selectivity of my approach to English phonology is even more evident on the theoretical side. There I am making a deliberate attempt at minimalism: the phonological theory used in most of this book is an extremely simple one – so simple, indeed, that it cannot be taken seriously as a contender in the ongoing and ever-intensifying theory debate in phonology. It is phonemicist and as such open to criticism from most theory-sensitive quarters; and it allows itself no access to nonphonological information – a limitation that phoneme theory itself has long since abandoned. I nevertheless take this theoretical stance in most of this book, for the following reasons.

First: being avowedly introductory, this book is concerned with a range of phonological phenomena of English that I view as central to the subject, uncontroversial and amenable to analysis in terms of a simple theory such as this one. Such phenomena make no great demands on one's theoretical machinery; and since the development of such machinery is not the main concern of this book, its relative lack has few – if any – adverse effects on my treatment of the subject.

Second: the simplicity of this theory enables me to be explicit about it at this level – and it is the responsibility of the writer on a subject such as this one to preach methodological rigour, and to make the reader aware of his dependence on specific theoretical assumptions in whatever he says about 'facts'.

Third: it follows from the theory's simplicity that it has scope for development – development whose possible directions are to some extent mapped out in the final chapter, but which are also to a large extent left to the reader (and especially to the teacher). I merely try to set the stage for further study. By presenting phoneme theory as a simple derivational framework I hope to prepare the reader for the study of more sophisticated derivational theories: Generative and Lexical Phonology are seen as developments, perhaps as necessary ones, that may evolve from the core of derivationalism introduced here. Moreover, the theory of Contrastive Underspecification is but the logical consequence of a view of the phoneme as a redundancy-free underlying unit. To understand the attraction of such theories the reader must first grasp the basic principles behind them; and, in my view, a simple phonemic theory (albeit one with the derivational bias that I impose on it) embodies all these basic principles. As for the representational side of phonological theory, this too is in my view best introduced in a framework that keeps derivational devices to a minimum; and my relative emphasis on (suprasegmental) representations is in part driven by personal interest (which will of course determine the shape of anybody's book) and in part by the recognition, by now a fairly widespread one, that this is where phonological theory is going and perhaps has already gone.

Finally, I must record my gratitude to John Anderson, Linda van Bergen, Derek Britton, Karen Corrigan, Edmund Gussmann, Bob Ladd, Roger Lass, April McMahon, Donka Minkova and Jørgen Staun. They have helped me write this book by commenting on parts or all of it in the earlier stages of its long history; and they have corrected more errors than I can admit to without embarrassment. The remaining ones are my responsibility, not theirs. Ginny Barnes typed most of the manuscript; she decided to move to the Middle East shortly after this experience.

*Innerleithen, November 1991*                    HEINZ GIEGERICH

# 1
# Speech sounds and their production

## 1.1 Organs and processes

Most speech is produced by an air stream that originates in the **lungs** and is pushed upwards through the **trachea** (the windpipe) and the **oral** and **nasal cavities**. During its passage, the air stream is modified by the various organs of speech. Each such modification has different acoustic effects, which are used for the differentiation of sounds. The production of a speech sound may be divided into four separate but interrelated processes: the **initiation** of the air stream, normally in the lungs; its **phonation** in the larynx through the operation of the vocal folds; its direction by the velum into either the oral cavity or the nasal cavity (the **oro-nasal** process); and finally its **articulation**, mainly by the tongue, in the oral cavity. We shall deal with each of the four processes in turn. (See figure 1.1.)

### 1.1.1 *The initiation process*

The operation of the lungs is familiar through their primary function in the breathing process: contraction of the intercostal muscles and lowering of the diaphragm causes the chest volume to increase and air is sucked into the lungs through the trachea. When the process is reversed, air will escape – again through the trachea. Apart from recurring at regular intervals as breath, this air stream provides the source of energy for speech. In speech, the rate of the air flow is not constant; rather, the air stream pulsates as the result of variation in the activity of the chest muscles. Major pulses are associated with stress – as in the second syllables of *A'merica, ma'chine* etc.; and syllables may to some extent be manifestations of minor chest pulses.

In English (and most other languages), all speech sounds require a **pulmonic** (lung) **air stream** for their production; alternative means of producing an air stream are occasionally used in certain languages, but need not concern us here. Moreover, the air stream used for speech in English is always **egressive**, that is, moving out of the lungs and up the trachea. Again,

1

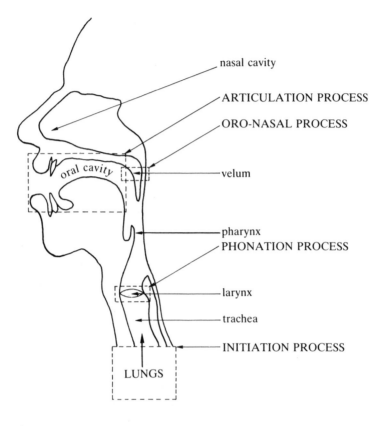

Figure 1.1    The organs of speech

some languages have sounds in which the air stream takes the opposite (ingressive) direction, but we need not concern ourselves with those. For our purposes, it is sufficient to state that in English, *speech sounds are initiated by a pulmonic egressive air stream.*

### 1.1.2   *The phonation process*

At the upper end of the trachea, the air stream passes through the **larynx**, a cartilage casing whose forward part (the Adam's Apple) can be felt just below the chin. The larynx contains two horizontal folds of tissue, which protrude into the passage of air from the sides: the **vocal folds**. The gap between the vocal folds, through which the air stream passes upwards into the pharynx and the mouth, is called the **glottis**. This is where the process of phonation takes place. The vocal folds can be manipulated by the speaker and brought into a variety of different positions, thus altering the shape of the glottis. At least three such positions are linguistically significant.

1   *Closed glottis.* The vocal folds are brought close together so that no air can pass between them. The speech sound resulting from this closure of the glottis and subsequent release is called **glottal stop**, sometimes heard in English preceding a forcefully pronounced vowel (as in *Out!*). In many accents of English, the glottal stop can replace [t] in words such as *football, bottle, bit.*

2   *Narrow glottis.* When the vocal folds are brought together in such a way that only a narrow gap is left for the air stream to pass through, the passage of air makes them vibrate. This vibration of the vocal folds in turn causes vibration on the part of the air column above the glottis. The resulting sound waves characterise **voiced sounds** of speech. The vibration of the larynx can usually be felt by laying a finger on (or just above) the Adam's Apple when producing a sound like [v] (as in *vine*) – contrast this with [f] (as in *fine*), a voiceless but otherwise very similar sound. All vowel sounds are voiced, as are sounds like [m], [l], [v], [b] etc.

3   *Open glottis.* This is the state that the glottis assumes in normal breathing as well as in the production of **voiceless sounds**. The vocal folds are spread and do not vibrate; the glottis is sufficiently wide open so as to allow the air stream to pass through without obstruction. Voiceless sounds are, for example, the [st] sequence in *stone* – the rest of the word is voiced – the [k] in *kill* etc.

Once again, there are a few more states of the glottis that are linguistically significant in certain languages. We ignore these here, as in English and related languages only the three-way distinction made above is systematically used: the closed glottis for the glottal stop, the narrow glottis (with vibrating vocal folds) for voiced sounds and the spread glottis for voiceless sounds (see figure 1.2).

### 1.1.3   *The oro-nasal process*

Having passed through the larynx and the back of the throat (the **pharynx**), the air stream can go either into the **nasal cavity** or into the **oral cavity**. In normal breathing, it will usually pass through the nasal cavity and emerge at the nostrils; in many – but by no means all – speech sounds, the nasal cavity is blocked off in the back of the throat and the air stream is

Front ('Adam's Apple')

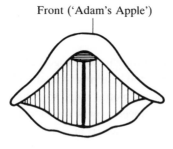

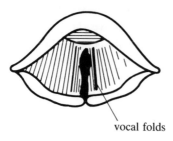

vocal folds

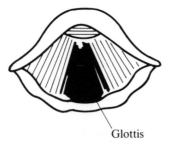

Glottis

Figure 1.2   Three positions of the glottis
(a) closed for glottal stop
(b) narrow (vocal folds vibrating) for voiced sounds
(c) open for voiceless sounds

directed into the oral cavity. This is done by the **velum**, a soft flap of muscle and tissue in the back of the roof of the mouth. Its end (the **uvula**) is visible in a wide-open mouth. The velum can be manipulated by the speaker. It has two linguistically significant positions.

1   *Raised velum*. Raised and pressed against the back of the pharynx, the velum prevents the entry of air into the nasal cavity; the air stream emerges through the oral cavity. Speech sounds produced with a raised velum are therefore called **oral sounds**. Examples are English vowels as well as sounds such as [v], [f], [l] etc.

Note that, in addition to this blockage of the nasal cavity, the oral cavity may also be blocked off somewhere further forward in the mouth, so that the air stream can proceed neither through the nose nor through the mouth. Examples are [p], [t], [k] etc. This temporary complete stoppage can be easily observed, for example, in a slow pronunciation of the word *happy*. We shall deal with such additional processes of obstruction, occurring in the oral cavity, in section 1.1.4.

2   *Lowered velum*. When the velum is not raised against the back of the pharynx the air stream has access to the nasal cavity. If at the same time the oral cavity is blocked somewhere further forward in the mouth – the entire air stream therefore passing through the nose – the result will be a **nasal sound**. Examples are [m] and [n] (as in *might* and *night*), where slow pronunciation demonstrates how the air stream passes entirely through the speaker's nose.

Some languages have sounds in which the velum is lowered as in [m] and [n] but, unlike in those sounds, the oral passage is not independently blocked. In such cases, exemplified by certain French vowels (as in *vin*), the air stream is divided in two, passing through both the oral and the nasal cavity. Such speech sounds are called **nasalised oral sounds;** they occur in English occasionally in certain contexts; but for the time being we may ignore this particular setting.

We note simply the following two positions of the velum; raised, where the nasal cavity is blocked off and oral sounds result; and lowered, with a concomitant stoppage somewhere in the mouth, resulting in nasal sounds (see figure 1.3).

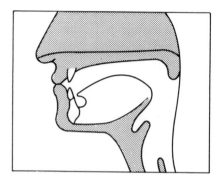

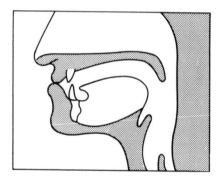

Figure 1.3    Settings of the velum
(a) raised for oral sound (here: *pie*)
(b) lowered for nasal sound (here: *my*)

### 1.1.4 *The articulation process*

Most of the differentiation of the various speech sounds of a language takes place in the mouth, in a process called **articulation**. Due to the mobility of the lips and the tongue, the size and shape of the oral cavity as well as of the exit passage of the air stream can be greatly modified. The oral cavity acts as a resonator in speech production; any modification of its shape will produce different acoustic properties on the part of the speech sounds produced.

Consider, for comparison, the way in which a trombone works. As in human speech, its sound is initiated by pulmonic air. The air stream sets the player's lips in vibration – this corresponds in speech to the phonation process, taking place in the larynx. Lip vibration in turn sets the body of air inside the trombone in vibration; the metal body of the trombone thus acts as a resonator as the oral cavity does in speech. And by sliding the front part of the trombone backwards and forwards, the musician modifies the volume of the body of resonating air and thereby the sound. The speaker does the same through the process of articulation in various places of the mouth.

By closing and subsequently opening the lips, for example, [p] and [b] are produced (the difference between the two being one of voicing: in [b], the vocal folds vibrate). Raising the tip of the tongue towards the roof of the mouth just behind the upper teeth produces [s] and [z] or, if the contact is made complete, [t] and [d]. Closing off the air stream by bringing the back part of the tongue in contact with the velum produces [k] and [g], and so forth.

The parts of the mouth that are used to produce such narrowing or closure of the oral cavity are called **articulators**. The **active articulator** – that is, the one that moves – is always the lower lip or (some part of) the tongue; the **passive articulator** is some part of the roof of the mouth.

Speech sounds are described and classified by referring to the articulators involved; some familiarity with the anatomy of the mouth is therefore essential (see figure 1.4). We shall refer to the principal articulators by the following names. Starting from the front, the **upper** and **lower lips** and the **upper** and **lower teeth** (more precisely, incisors) are used for articulation. The **tongue** is usefully divided into **tip**, **blade**, **front** and **back**. On the roof of the mouth we distinguish, as passive articulators, the **alveolar ridge** (a hard ridge that can be felt behind the upper incisors), the **palate** (a hard bony structure in the front part of the roof) and the **velum** (the soft continuation of the palate in the back of the mouth). Recall that apart from acting as a passive articulator, the velum also functions in the oro-nasal process.

After this brief description of the principles of articulation and of the active and passive articulators, we are now in a position to characterise more precisely how differences in articulation lead to differences among speech sounds.

### 1.2 Articulation in detail

As we have seen in the preceding section, articulation can take place in various different places in the oral cavity – this differentiation is

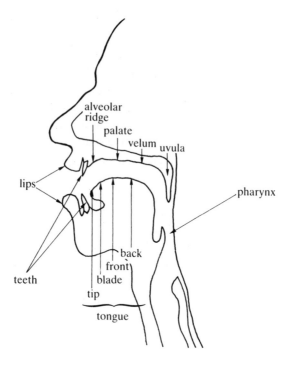

Figure 1.4    The oral cavity, with principal articulators

crucial to speech, as it produces the different phonetic effects that make one speech sound distinct from another. We have also touched on another, equally important variable: it was mentioned that [t] and [s], for example, differ in the **manner** in which the tongue is brought towards the roof of the mouth rather than in the precise place in the mouth where this happens. Speech sounds are distinct from one another, then, in terms of their **place of articulation** as well as their **manner of articulation**. As in the previous sections, we shall here discuss only such places and manners of articulation as are relevant to the description of English, bearing in mind that different languages do make different and additional articulatory distinctions.

Before we proceed, we make – at this point for reasons of exposition only – an important distinction: that between vowels and consonants. Most readers will have some idea of this distinction; we make it only slightly more precise for the moment by stating that the articulation of a consonant involves some audible obstruction in the oral cavity while the articulation of a vowel involves no such obstruction. In phonetic terms, this is a viable definition. However, we shall see later that it raises some important and difficult questions about the classification of certain English speech sounds.

### 1.2.1 *Consonants: places of articulation*

It is in many (but not all) cases possible to characterise the place of articulation of a consonant in terms of the passive articulator involved – recall the names of the passive articulators listed in section 1.1.4 above. Starting from the front, we may distinguish the following places of articulation for English.

(a) **Bilabial.** The lips are brought together, as in *pie, buy, my*; the first two of these are oral and the last one nasal, the first one voiceless and the last two voiced.

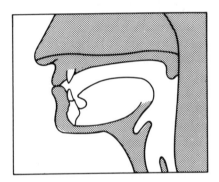

Figure 1.5    Bilabial articulation: *pie*

(b) **Labiodental.** The lower lip is raised against the upper incisors, as in *fat* and *vat*. The former word begins with a voiceless labiodental consonant, the latter with a voiced one.

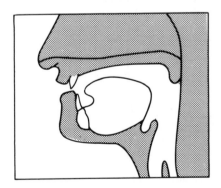

Figure 1.6    Labiodental articulation: *fat*

9

(c) **Dental**. The tip of the tongue is raised against the upper incisors, or inserted between the upper and lower incisors, as in *thigh* and *thy*. Again the former is voiceless and the latter voiced.

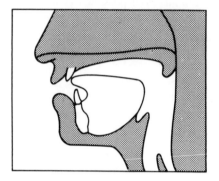

Figure 1.7    Dental articulation: *thigh*

(d) **Alveolar**. The tip of the tongue is raised against the alveolar ridge. English has many alveolar consonants; examples are *nigh*, *lie*, *tie*, *die*, *sue* and *zoo*. Voicing and nasality distinguish these further from one another, but notice that the characteristics of place, voicing and nasality do not suffice to make each of these sounds distinct from all others: both *tie* and *sue*, for example, have voiceless oral alveolar consonants. These need to be further distinguished in terms of their manners of articulation.

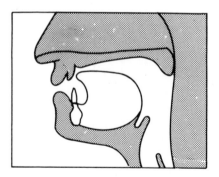

Figure 1.8    Alveolar articulation: *sue*

(e) **Palato-alveolar**. The front of the tongue – and not just the tip – is raised towards the back of the alveolar ridge and the front of the palate, as in *she* and, rather rarely in English, the second consonant in *leisure*.

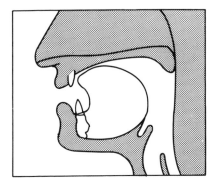

Figure 1.9    Palato-alveolar articulation: *she*

(f) **Palatal**. The front of the tongue is raised towards the palate, slightly further back than in a palato-alveolar sound. Example: *you*.

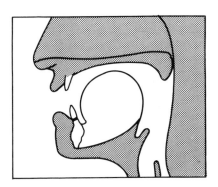

Figure 1.10    Palatal articulation: *you*

(g) **Velar**. The back of the tongue is raised towards the velum, as in *cool* and the final consonants in *back*, *bag* and *bang*. Voicing and nasality distinguish these further.

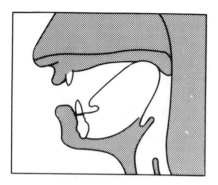

Figure 1.11   Velar articulation: *cool*

The relation between the active and passive articulators has in these cases been a rather simple one: in most cases, the active articulator is automatically the one directly below the passive articulator. Only in two cases is an active articulator involved in two different places of articulation: the lower lip can produce bilabial and labiodental sounds, and the tip of the tongue acts in both dental and alveolar articulations. There is one further place of articulation where the active articulator is displaced along the horizontal dimension; this occurs in the pronunciation of [r] in some English accents. The articulation of this sound varies greatly from one accent to another; in some English West Country and American pronunciations the tip of the tongue is curled back and brought near the roof of the mouth behind the alveolar ridge – with some speakers further back than with others. Such an articulation is called **retroflex**; in terms of its location on the roof of the mouth, this kind of [r] can be characterised broadly as a post-alveolar retroflex consonant.

### 1.2.2   *Vowels*

Vowels can differ from one another quite radically – compare those in *feed* and *food*, *cat*, *cot* and *kite*, to give just a few examples. What they all have in common is that their articulations do not involve any audible obstruction of the air stream – this was stated earlier as the main phonetic difference between vowels and consonants. We are in this section concerned with the differences in articulation that lead to such differences in vowel quality as are exemplified by the words given above. A discussion of such differences and others will enable us to describe the characteristics, in terms of articulation, of any given vowel.

Differences between vowels are brought about by the raising of different parts of the tongue as well as by differences in the extent of such raising. Additionally, the posture of the lips may vary; we shall deal with this third variable later. For the time being, we switch our attention from the roof of the mouth to the tongue. This switch of focus is done for convenience of description and does not imply, of course, that vowel and consonant articulations are radically different from each other – we shall see the similarities between vowel and consonant articulations more clearly in section 1.2.3 below. Indeed, we shall see there that the distinction between the two categories of speech sounds is not as sharp as it seems here.

One of the difficulties in establishing the principal features of vowel sounds lies in the fact that exemplification with 'real-life' English vowels is of little help, for two reasons. Firstly, the vowel in almost any given English word will vary greatly from one accent of the language to another – in fact, much more so than most consonants would. Secondly, vowel sounds in English tend not to be as 'pure' as we would like the examples to be that we use to show the different dimensions of articulation. English vowels almost always display a complex – and at this point unhelpful – mixture of these dimensions. Exemplification from English will therefore, in the paragraphs that follow, only provide very rough guidelines.

To start with, produce a vowel such as the one in *feed*. Notice that your tongue is pushed forward and raised towards the roof of your mouth, and that your lips are spread. Now exaggerate these qualities so that your tongue is pushed forward inside your mouth as far as possible and raised towards the roof of the mouth to such an extent that it only just fails to produce audible friction. Let us denote the resulting sound with the symbol [i]. For most speakers, [i] is actually rather different from the vowel in *feed* in that it is of much sharper and brighter quality.

Next, retract your tongue as far as possible, keeping it at the same time in its position of extreme raising. Purse your lips and produce a vowel. The result is not really like any English vowel; if you have produced something like the one in *food* then you probably have not retracted your tongue as far as is required in this exercise. The desired vowel may be symbolised as [u].

The difference between [i] and [u] is one of **backness**: [i] is a front vowel, [u] a back vowel. Front vowels are produced with the front of the tongue raised, back vowels with the back of the tongue raised. We shall return to the spreading of the lips in [i] and their rounding in [u] later: this variable of articulation will require separate attention.

As the next step, produce [i] and then lower your jaw as far as possible, leaving your tongue in the extreme front position. The result is not unlike the vowel in *lad*, but again it is a rather exaggerated version of this vowel (which for most speakers will have less opening of the mouth and less fronting of the tongue). We denote the front vowel with extreme opening of the mouth as [a]. Similarly, return to [u] and, keeping your tongue in the extreme back position, lower your jaw again as far as possible. Spreading your lips, you will produce a vowel similar to the one in *palm* in certain (southern English) accents. We shall symbolise this vowel as [ɑ].

The vowels [a] and [ɑ] have in common that they are produced with a maximally open mouth, therefore with maximal distance between the tongue and the roof of the mouth. They differ in this respect from [i] and [u]. We shall call this difference a difference in **height**, referring to the position of the tongue in the vertical dimension. [i] and [u] are high vowels, [a] and [ɑ] low vowels. The four vowel sounds that we have just produced represent the extreme points of the principal dimensions of vowel articulation: height and backness. [i] is a high front vowel, [u] a high back vowel, [a] a low front vowel and [ɑ] a low back vowel.

'Real-life' vowels, in English and most other languages, are not usually quite as extreme in their articulation as these four reference vowels are: high vowels in English are not quite as high, front vowels not quite as front etc. as the four reference vowels.

Figure 1.12 is a schematic representation of the places that the high point of the tongue can occupy in the oral cavity during vowel articulation. In that sense the diagram is a very much simplified representation of part of the oral cavity (excluding the dental and alveolar regions, which do not figure in vowel articulation). The four reference vowels that we have just established occupy the four corners of the diagram; this must be so because each of the four represents an extreme point of articulation. All vowels that occur in speech can now be plotted within this trapezium and no 'real-life' vowel can – by definition, given the way we have defined the corner points – ever occur outside the trapezium.

To make our framework of reference more detailed, we may now fill in some of the intermediate points. Both backness and height are, of course, gradual scales rather than binary oppositions. It is customary to define intermediate height points on the trapezium as follows. Divide the height ([i]–[a]) scale into four points that are equidistant from each other. This equidistance is not really objectively verifiable in terms of physical distance measurements inside the mouth; we rely on the impressionistic reality of vowel height descending in equal steps. These 'equidistant' vowels may be symbolised as [i]–[e]–[ɛ]–[a] in the diagram. Again, it is impossible to identify these points in the diagram with vowel sounds of English; suffice it

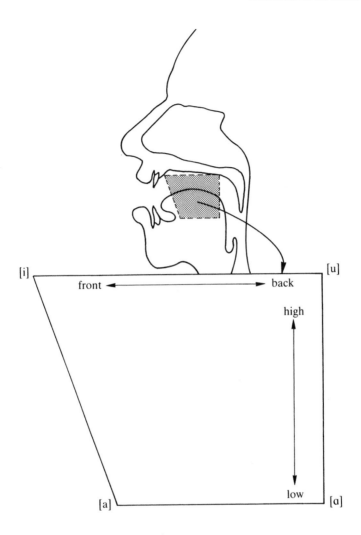

Figure 1.12 The vowel trapezium

to say that [e] is similar to the vowel in *bait* in Scottish pronunciation – other accents tend not to have a pure vowel in this position – and that [ɛ] is similar to the vowel in *bet*, for many accents of English. But here again, neither of the two examples is quite as far forward as the reference vowels [e] and [ɛ] and their height identification is not precise.

For the back series, we may fill in the corresponding intermediate vowels as [o] and [ɔ], so that [u]–[o]–[ɔ]–[ɑ] represents the set of back reference vowels with decreasing height in equal steps. At the same time, lip rounding decreases in equal steps. Very roughly, [o] corresponds to *coat* in Scottish pronunciation – other accents rarely have a pure vowel in this area – and [ɔ] to *caught*. The set of eight reference vowels can now be plotted on the trapezium, as in figure 1.13.

Confirm, finally, your pronunciation of this set of eight reference vowels by first repeating the corners [i], [a], [ɑ], [u], ensuring that they represent the extreme points as which they have been defined. Repeat the front series [i]–[e]–[ɛ]–[a], ensuring that they are impressionistically equidistant and that their qualities are pure. Then repeat the back series, again ensuring equidistance, and gradual spreading of the lips: [u]–[o]–[ɔ]–[ɑ]. And finally, check the height correspondence of opposite vowels by running through [i]–[u], [e]–[o], [ɛ]–[ɔ], [a]–[ɑ].

We have now established height and backness as the two principal parameters of vowel articulation, both referring to the position of the tongue. Also, we have established – in the form of the vowel trapezium (figure 1.13) – a reference grid on which all the vowels that occur in speech can be plotted for description.

The additional parameter of **lip rounding** has been complicating our description of the reference vowels somewhat. Now that we have established our system of eight vowels, the following picture of rounding emerges. The front reference vowels 1 to 4 are unrounded, the back reference vowels

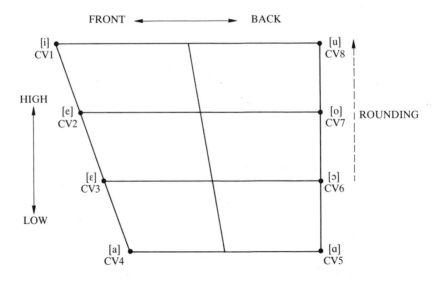

Figure 1.13 The cardinal vowel scale

5 to 8 are increasingly rounded as they increase in height; starting with no. 5, which is unrounded. Given the essentially artificial nature of our system of reference vowels, such a distribution of rounding is, of course, as arbitrarily defined as their other features are. The reason why these vowels are defined for rounding in this way lies in the fact that the basic vowel systems of the world's languages, including English, tend to behave just like that. In English, for example, the front vowels are unrounded, as in *beat – bait – bet – bat*. In the back series (*calm – caught – coat – coot*), the first (*calm*) is unrounded and the last three increase in rounding just as the back reference vowels do, although rounding (as well as actual backness) is here subject to considerable accent variation.

The system of reference vowels in figure 1.13 is known as the **cardinal vowel (CV) scale**, devised by the English phonetician Daniel Jones. The cardinal vowel scale is an important tool for phoneticians in the difficult task of describing vowel sounds that they have heard. Given that there is a good deal of objectivity in the definition of the reference points, one phonetician will be able to pinpoint a vowel on the trapezium and another phonetician will be able to reproduce its quality at a glance. We shall, in future chapters, use the cardinal vowel scale for similar purposes in the analysis of vowels in various accents of English. But more importantly, the purity of these reference vowels has made them useful examples in this introductory exposition of the articulatory qualities that make up and distinguish vowel sounds.

As has already been pointed out, 'real-life' vowels such as those found in English do not display the dimensions of height, backness and rounding as purely as the cardinal vowels do. Their tongue position will never actually reach the extreme points of highness, lowness, backness and frontness. Moreover, they are not always of constant quality throughout their duration – in fact, they seldom are. Cases of vowel quality that changes during the pronunciation of the vowel are exemplified by English words like *now*, *boy* and *buy*; we use the term **diphthong** for such vowels. Vowels of constant unchanging quality are called **monophthongs**. While the latter can be plotted as points in the trapezium, the former are plotted as arrows pointing from starting to finishing point.

It is not easy to find monophthongs, in the precise phonetic sense, in English: many English vowels are at least slightly diphthongised in some or even most accents. The vowel in *bed* is usually a monophthong, as is the one in *bud*. The first vowel in *father* is usually a monophthong but with some speakers it ends slightly higher and less back than it begins. Similarly, the vowel in *feed* is often a monophthong, but for many speakers it is slightly diphthongised, ending higher than it begins. *Go* and *day* are diphthongs in many accents but in Scottish pronunciation they are almost pure monophthongs. (See figure 1.14.)

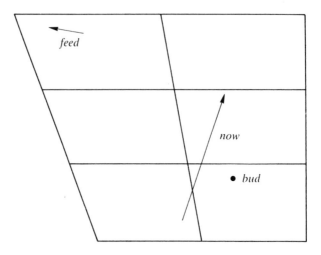

Figure 1.14   The *feed*, *now* and *bud* vowels in a Southern English pronunciation

### 1.2.3   *Manners of articulation*

Consider the range of English consonants whose place of articulation is the alveolar ridge. In section 1.2.1, this set was exemplified with the words *tie*, *die*, *nigh*, *lie*, *sue* and *zoo*. We have already seen that sounds such as these are differentiated in terms of phonation (some are voiced, others voiceless), in terms of the oro-nasal process (the consonant in *nigh* is nasal, the others oral) and in terms of their place of articulation, which in this case happens to be the same for all of them. What we have not so far characterised is the nature of the action that the tongue performs in this (or any other) place of articulation. This additional variable in phonetic description is called **manner of articulation**.

In the case of English alveolar consonants, the need for such further specification is a particularly pressing one: the variables that we have been discussing – voicing, oro-nasality and place – do not suffice to tell the members of this set apart. *Tie* and *sue*, for example, both begin with a consonant that we characterise as voiceless, oral and alveolar – but in what respect do they differ? In this set, then, the manner of articulation feature has a classificatory as well as a descriptive function: it is needed not only for the purpose of a precise phonetic description of what happens in the production of a given sound, but also for the purpose of telling two different sounds apart. In the case of other consonants, this may not be so. Consider, for example, the dental consonants in English, as in *thigh* and *thy*. As English only has these two dental sounds, we can tell them apart by simply calling them the voiceless and voiced dental consonant respectively; these characteristics alone set them apart from each other and from all other English consonants. For their classification, the manner of articulation is not needed (nor is, incidentally, the oro-nasal characterisation) – but nevertheless, we still wish to complete our phonetic description of these sounds by specifying their manner of articulation, even if this specification is, for the purpose of identifying a sound within the whole sound system of English, redundant.

To characterise different manners of articulation, we may first draw the fairly straightforward distinction between **stops** and **continuants**. *A stop is a sound that involves complete closure of the oral cavity*. The articulators come so close together that no air can escape between them. Stops are found in words like *tie, die, pie, buy* etc. as well as in *my, nigh* etc. These two kinds of stops differ from each other in terms of the oro-nasal process: in the former, the velum is raised so that the air stream escapes through neither the oral cavity nor the nasal cavity; in the latter (*my* etc.) the air stream escapes through the nose, due to the lowering of the velum, but not through the mouth. In terms of our definition, both kinds of sounds are stops.

In continuants, on the other hand, the air stream is not totally blocked in the oral cavity – it can escape continuously through the mouth. The consonants in *sue, zoo, lie, you, thigh* etc. are continuants. So are vowels: we note at this point that there is nothing to prevent us from including vowels in our description of manners of articulation.

Note that our definitions of stops and continuants are mutually exclusive: any sound that is not a stop is a continuant, and vice versa. We may therefore simplify our terminology and talk about continuants and noncontinuants (where a noncontinuant is automatically a stop), or, simpler still, we may distinguish speech sounds in terms of the binary feature [+ continuant] vs [− continuant]. Example (1) below gives some examples of this phonetic distinction:

(1)  [+ continuant]          [− continuant]

   rye, lie, you, woo        pea, tea, key
   thigh, thy, sue, zoo, etc.   buy, die, guy
   *all vowels*              my, nigh, etc.

Obviously, this distinction alone does not suffice to characterise manners of articulation in precise phonetic terms. In the [+ continuant] category, for example, we find sounds of quite radically different manners of articulation. Let us therefore make an additional distinction between **sonorants** and **obstruents**. *A sonorant is a sound whose phonetic content is predominantly made up by the sound waves produced by its voicing.*

In other words, sonorants are characterised by 'periodic acoustic energy'. We assume here that there are no voiceless sonorants because, simply speaking, the removal of voicing from a sonorant makes it nondistinct from other members of this set and practically inaudible. The consonants in *my*, *nigh*, *rye*, *lie* and all vowels are sonorants – remove the voicing from them and the result will be simple breathing, practically soundless.

In contrast, *obstruent articulation involves an obstruction of the air stream that produces a phonetic effect independent of voicing.* In a word such as *tie*, for example, the initial stop is audible although it is voiceless, and it is distinct from the equally voiceless stop in *pie*. Similarly, the consonants in *sue* and *zoo* are obstruents, the latter voiced. It follows from this definition that obstruents can typically occur in voiced and voiceless variants. Sonorants are, at least for the purposes of our slightly idealised description, always voiced.

Again, the two categories sonorant and obstruent have been defined in a mutually exclusive way: any nonsonorant is automatically an obstruent and vice versa. We may again simplify our terminology and characterise speech sounds as either [+ sonorant] or [− sonorant]. The list in (2) below gives some English examples of both.

(2)  [+ sonorant]             [− sonorant]

    my, nigh                    pea, tea, key
    lie, rye                     buy, die, guy
    you, woo                     thigh, sue, etc.
    *all vowels*                 thy, zoo, etc.

It is not immediately obvious how these features help in defining manners of articulation: the definition of neither feature clearly refers to the posture of an articulator; yet we have been assuming that a manner of articulation is essentially a matter of such a posture. The status of the two features is in fact a more fundamental one than that of a 'manner of articulation' is: together, the two features make up manners of articulation or, to put it the other way around, what we refer to as manners of articulation are combinations of the basic properties that the two features describe.

Two features, each of them binary, can be combined with each other in four different ways. In the case of the features [Sonorant] and [Continuant], the four combinations given in (3) below are possible; any given sound will fit into one of these four categories:

(3)

a. $\begin{bmatrix} - \text{ continuant} \\ + \text{ sonorant} \end{bmatrix}$  b. $\begin{bmatrix} - \text{ continuant} \\ - \text{ sonorant} \end{bmatrix}$  c. $\begin{bmatrix} + \text{ continuant} \\ - \text{ sonorant} \end{bmatrix}$  d. $\begin{bmatrix} + \text{ continuant} \\ + \text{ sonorant} \end{bmatrix}$

These four possible combinations reflect exactly the four major manners of articulation that we shall need to distinguish. We shall deal with each of them in turn.

a. $\begin{bmatrix} - \text{ continuant} \\ + \text{ sonorant} \end{bmatrix}$

Any sound so specified has, by virtue of the definitions of the two features, complete closure at some point of the oral cavity and, at the same time, a steady air stream whose phonetic effect is predominantly characterised by voicing. To allow these two characteristics to occur together, the sound must involve lowering of the velum so that the air stream, which is blocked in the mouth, can escape through the nose. Such a sound must therefore be nasal. Members of this category are called **nasal stops** (or, since all English nasals are stops, simply **nasals**). All nasals are voiced. Examples are found in *my*, *nigh* and *hang*.

b. $\begin{bmatrix} - \text{ continuant} \\ - \text{ sonorant} \end{bmatrix}$

Like nasal stops, these sounds have total closure in the oral cavity due to being noncontinuants; but being nonsonorants, they do not have a nasal air stream either. The velum is raised so that for a brief period the air stream is completely blocked. Pressure builds up in the mouth and is suddenly – audibly – released when the articulators are separated. Such sounds are usually labelled **oral stops** or, referring to their audible release, **plosives**. As nonsonorants, oral stops may be voiced or voiceless. Examples are *pie*, *buy*, *tie*, *die* etc.

c. $\begin{bmatrix} + \text{ continuant} \\ - \text{ sonorant} \end{bmatrix}$

These sounds are continuants in that the air stream is not totally blocked in the oral cavity; but being nonsonorants, they do have an obstruction of the air stream that produces a phonetic effect independent of voicing. This phonetic effect is a hissing noise, produced by turbulence in the air stream as it is forced through the narrow gap between the articulators. Referring to this hissing noise, or friction, such sounds are usually called **fricatives**. Being nonsonorants, fricatives may be voiced or voiceless. Examples are *fie*, *vie*, *thigh*, *thy*, *sue*, *zoo* and some others.

$$\text{d.} \quad \begin{bmatrix} + \text{ continuant} \\ + \text{ sonorant} \end{bmatrix}$$

Such sounds have a steady air stream through the oral cavity, which is not obstructed in such a way as to produce friction. Like all other sonorants, they are voiced. This definition fits all vowels as well as a range of consonants, including those in *rye* (if produced as a retroflex), *lie*, *you* and *woo*. None of these has any radical obstruction of the air stream, although in *lie* it will be noticed that the tongue does make contact with the roof of the mouth. Sounds of this feature composition are referred to by the cover term **approximants**. Since there are some major and so far unexplained differences within this category, we have to investigate them in some more detail.

Before we do so, we must note a fifth manner of articulation: that of the initial consonants in *chin* and *gin*. In such consonants, an oral-stop phase is followed by a phase of friction: the release of the stop is not sudden as in [t] but gradual, so that a brief fricative period follows the closure. Note how the initial consonant in *chin* is similar to both the one in *tin* (the corresponding oral stop) and the one in *shin* (the corresponding fricative). Sounds like this are called **affricates**.

This manner of articulation is not a 'basic' one like the four discussed earlier; it combines characteristics of two of those – in fact, it may well be argued that, in purely phonetic terms, an affricate should be analysed as a sequence of two sounds, a stop plus a fricative.

### 1.2.4   *Approximants in detail: vowels revisited*

As we have seen, certain consonants – namely those in *rye*, *lie*, *you* and *woo* – as well as all vowels, are members of the manner of articulation category 'approximant'. This raises some questions. Firstly, how do we distinguish these consonants from each other, given such rather obvious manner of articulation differences as the tongue contact in *lie* and the absence of such contact in *rye* (if pronounced as a retroflex)? 'Approximant' as a manner of articulation is evidently not detailed enough. And secondly, what precisely is the difference between vowels and the consonants in this set, given that they are all approximants? We shall deal with the first question first.

Let us review what has been said about the phonetic characteristics of these consonants in the course of this chapter. Example (4) below summarises the results of their previous description.

(4)

| | Phonation process | Oro-nasal process | Place | Manner |
|---|---|---|---|---|
| *rye* | voiced | oral | post-alveolar | approximant |
| *lie* | voiced | oral | alveolar | approximant |
| *woo* | voiced | oral | bilabial/velar | approximant |
| *you* | voiced | oral | palatal | approximant |

If we were merely interested in the classification of these sounds, labelling each one most economically in such a way that it is different from all others, then we would have accomplished our task already: the place of articulation column makes the necessary distinctions. However, classification is not our aim here: before we can attempt such a classification we have to establish precisely what the whole set of English speech sounds is. And although we have already collected quite a few examples of English speech sounds, we do not yet have a definitive list.

What we are here concerned with is the precise phonetic description of speech sounds, and in that respect the information given in (4) is less than satisfactory. The consonant in *lie* obviously differs from the others in terms of manner of articulation.

The consonant [l] in *lie* is produced with a steady voiced air stream through the mouth. The tip (or blade) of the tongue is raised and touches the alveolar ridge quite firmly. What makes this sound a continuant sonorant rather than a stop (despite the firm tongue contact) is the fact that this tongue contact does not produce closure of the oral cavity. The contact only takes place in the middle of the mouth and the air stream escapes freely along the sides. Compare the [t] in *tie*, where the tip and sides of the tongue make contact with the alveolar ridge and molars respectively, so that the air stream is completely blocked. [t] is therefore a stop. In [l], the sides of the tongue are not raised. Such sounds, in which contact only takes place along the centre line of the mouth (and the air stream escapes along the sides of the contact), are called **laterals.** [l] is a **lateral approximant** because the air stream escapes without friction. Some languages, for example Welsh, have lateral fricatives; these have some degree of obstruction in the lateral air stream. Sounds which do not have the lateral articulation of [l] are called **central** (or simply nonlateral). All sounds of English other than [l] are central.

Next, what characterises the consonant in *rye* in many accents of English is the more or less retroflex posture of the tongue. Its manner of articulation is, like that of the consonants in *woo* and *you*, that of a central approximant and not radically different from those. [r] is, however, subject to considerable variation in the accents of English. Some Scottish speakers, for example, pronounce [r] as a series of rapid contacts of the tip of the tongue with the back of the alveolar ridge (a so-called trill) or, occasionally, with a single tap in that place of articulation. As these realisational differences are of no further consequence for the sound system of English, we shall disregard them and, simplifying matters, keep referring to [r] as a postalveolar approximant.

We finally turn to the question of differentiating the consonants in *you* and *woo* from vowels, noting in particular that the vowel in *woo* is rather similar to the consonant preceding it. A comparable situation arises in *ye*: again, the vowel and the consonant are remarkably similar. Let us first review our phonetic description of the four sounds in question and see how these similarities arise. Afterwards we shall ask the more basic question of how we can maintain the distinction between vowels and consonants in the face of such rather striking similarities.

According to our analysis of vowel sounds in section 1.2.2, the vowel in *woo* is a rather high back rounded vowel, although not as high and back as cardinal vowel no. 8. This means that the back of the tongue is raised quite high towards the velum and the lips are pursed. The consonant in *woo* has narrowing of the oral cavity both by the lips and – perhaps less obviously – by the back of the tongue towards the velum. Notice that the two descriptions really express the same fact: narrowing in the bilabial and velar areas. Notice also that in the case of both sounds, the obstruction of the air stream produces neither closure nor friction: they are both approximants. Clearly, then, the similarities of the two sounds are borne out by our phonetic description.

The same can be said for the vowel and the consonant in *ye*. Both are again approximants; as for place of articulation, the vowel is characterised as high front unrounded and the consonant as palatal. In both cases, then, the lips are spread and the front of the tongue is raised towards the palate without producing closure or friction. Again our phonetic analysis of the two sounds would predict that their qualities are rather similar.

Other vowels are, of course, less similar to the consonants in *ye* and *woo* than these vowels are. The low vowels [a] and [ɑ], for example, have a degree of approximation between the tongue and the roof of the mouth that is much less close than that of the high vowels.

(5)  Consonants | Vowels

| | |
|---|---|
| Plosives | / / / / / / / / / / / / / |
| | / / / / / / / / / / / / / |
| Fricatives | / / / / / / / / / / / / / |
| Approximants | high |
| | . |
| / / / / / / / / / / | . |
| / / / / / / / / / / | . |
| / / / / / / / / / / | low |

degree of narrowing

As (5) shows, what we have been calling height for vowels and the closeness of approximation for consonants are really just different sections on the same scale of narrowing of the oral cavity. Plosives have complete closure; fricatives have narrowing with friction; approximants have less narrowing without friction. The height scale for vowels reflects different degrees of frictionless approximation: the high vowels and approximant consonants have about the same degree of narrowing of the oral cavity while low vowels have less narrowing than any consonants have.

What, then, is the difference between vowels and consonants if their manner of articulation provides no reliable distinction, at least not in borderline cases such as approximant consonants and high vowels? The phonetic distinction that was suggested at the beginning of section 1.2, referring to audible obstruction in the oral cavity, does not work for approximant consonants: like vowels, these have no audible obstruction. We have to invoke here a nonphonetic criterion, one that does not refer to the phonetic qualities of sounds but to their function in the structure of the language. A vowel must constitute the peak of a syllable, while any sound that occurs in the margin of a syllable is a consonant. We say that *vowels are syllabic while any nonsyllabic sound is a consonant*. In *ye*, for example, the difference between the two sounds is merely that the first one is nonsyllabic – it occurs in the left margin of the syllable – while the second one is syllabic: it is the peak of the syllable. The first one is therefore a consonant and the second one a vowel, despite the fact that they are both approximants with (near-)identical phonetic characteristics. We shall have to say more about the distinction between vowels and consonants in chapter 6 below, where we discuss the syllable in detail; for the moment, we shall continue to rely on our rather simple definition.

### 1.3 Conclusion

It has been the concern of this chapter to provide the phonetic grounding for the description of speech sounds and to some extent also for their classification. In our phonetic description, we have enquired into the properties and positions of the vocal organs that are responsible for the production of different speech sounds. Such an enquiry is in principle universal: all speech sounds of all languages are produced with the same equipment. It was only for practical reasons that we chose to restrict our investigation to sounds found in English.

The classification of speech sounds is in some respects a different and less universal matter. The question is, what is the **inventory** of the speech sounds of English, or, more ambitiously, what is the **sound system** of English and how do its members **function** in it? As we shall see, establishing such a sound system implies establishing a list of sounds as well as the properties of each member. For this classification, whose aim it is to express relevant sound distinctions in an economical way, we shall draw heavily on the phonetic foundations laid in this chapter. But we shall go further in a direction in which we have already taken a first step: we shall have to devise a set of features that enables us to differentiate each member of the sound system from all other members, thus characterising each sound in the system precisely and as economically as possible.

The initial step in this direction consisted in defining the features [Continuant] and [Sonorant]: as we have seen, the four basic manners of articulation are merely combinations of these two features. Rather than using a separate feature for each manner of articulation, we need only these two. Moreover, the two features can be applied to vowels and consonants alike. What is rather less satisfactory is the fact that, apart from these two features, we have been referring to different sets of characteristics in our description of vowels and consonants: to the active articulator in the case of vowels (high, low etc.) and to the passive articulator in the case of consonants (alveolar, palatal etc.). Our eventual set of features, if it is to be useful in differentiating every sound from every other one, must be a unified set and cover both vowels and consonants – especially since we have seen that the difference between vowels and consonants is not in each case, in phonetic terms, a principled one and in some cases nonexistent.

Our programme for the next chapters, then, is this. We shall first establish the inventory of speech sounds in English – consonants first and then vowels. For this, we shall have to investigate various accents of English; the characterisation of different accents will be a by-product of this investigation. From there we shall return to the question of distinctive features and see how the items on our list of sounds constitute a system, where each element is distinct from all others but also, in a systematic way, related to all others. Then we shall study phonetic units that are larger than single sound segments: syllables and feet (the units within which stress is defined). And finally, we shall turn to the actual phonetic behaviour of sound segments in connected speech, to see how their behaviour may vary in different contexts and how such variation can be explained.

### Suggested reading to chapter 1

The account of articulatory phonetics given here is intended to give sufficient phonetic backing to the following chapters; nevertheless, further reading on phonetics is strongly recommended. The following introductory phonetics textbooks are particularly useful for this purpose: Abercrombie (1967) as general background reading; Ladefoged (1982) and Catford (1988) for both reading and specific reference. Catford (1977) is a more advanced treatment of phonetics that is to some extent superseded by Catford (1988). Below are references to these books in more detail.

> Section 1.1.1  On initiation see Ladefoged (1982: chs. 1, 9), Catford (1988: chs. 1, 2), Catford (1977: ch. 5).
> Section 1.1.2  On phonation see Ladefoged (1982: ch. 6), Catford (1988: ch. 3), Catford (1977: ch. 6).
> Section 1.1.3  On the oro-nasal process see Ladefoged (1982: chs. 1, 3), Catford (1988: sect. 5.1), Catford (1977: ch. 8).
> Section 1.1.4  On articulation in general see Ladefoged (1982: ch. 1).
> Sections 1.2.1, 1.2.3  On place and manner of articulation see Ladefoged (1982: ch. 7), Catford (1988: chs. 4, 5), Catford (1977: chs. 7, 8).

Section 1.2.2   On vowel articulation and cardinal vowels see
Ladefoged (1982: chs. 1, 9), Catford (1988: chs. 7, 8),
Catford (1977: ch. 9).

An important aspect of phonetics, which is not covered in this book, is
acoustic phonetics. See Ladefoged (1982: ch. 8) for an introduction; for a
full textbook treatment see, for example, Fry (1979).

# 2
# Towards a sound system for English: consonant phonemes

## 2.1 Phonetics and phonology, or how many speech sounds does English have?

Consider a casual pronunciation of the word *tenth* and of the phrase *on fire*. In chapter 1, we came across three nasal stops in English: a bilabial one (as in *my*), an alveolar one (*nigh*) and a velar one (*hang*) – here, we are faced with two more. The nasal in *tenth* is, on closer inspection, not alveolar as in *ten* but dental, and the one in *on fire* is often pronounced at a labiodental place of articulation. This means, then, that nasals can be pronounced with at least five different places of articulation; and there may well be more.

Among oral stops, we have similarly noted bilabial, alveolar and velar places of articulation (as in *pool – tool – cool* respectively) – but again, if we observe more carefully we find that more than these three places of articulation may be involved. Before a front vowel – in *keel*, for example – the stop is not as far back as it is in *cool*; for most speakers the former may not be velar at all but, rather, palatal. Moreover, in *width* the stop is not usually alveolar, as one would expect (why?) but dental. Note that in all these cases – *tenth, on fire, keel, width* – the consonant that we are looking at is clearly influenced by the following sound, anticipating its place of articulation. Do we, then, have to recognise the existence of palatal and dental oral stops, too?

Next, consider what we called 'the English lateral': [l]. We stated that it is voiced – but note that in *play* it may not be. (Contrast here *play* and *atlas*: the latter is much more clearly voiced than the former.) And finally, for many speakers the two lateral sounds in *lilt* will be quite different from each other: the second one will be 'dark' in quality, pronounced with the back of the tongue raised somewhat towards the velum in addition to the alveolar lateral articulation that it shares with the first, 'clear' [l] in *lilt*. How many different laterals, then, does English really have?

The problem is that the more carefully we listen to the way people speak, the more different speech sounds of English we find. In fact, our little sample goes some way towards showing that, on the level of precise phonetic description, the number of different sounds of English is practically infinite. Speech sounds will always differ in different contexts; no two speakers pronounce the same word in exactly the same way; and even the same speaker rarely pronounces the same word twice in precisely the same way. How can we then realistically hope to establish a manageable inventory of English sounds?

It can be argued that there is another level of analysis, on which the number of speech sounds in a language is not infinite and actually rather small. Let us say that it is the function of speech sounds to express the different meaning units of a language – for simplicity's sake, let us assume these meaning units to be words. Different speech sounds are used in a language to make different words sound different, so that each meaning is connected with a different phonetic form. Obviously, this connection of meaning and sound ('form') is rather basic to the way language works. In terms of this basic function of distinguishing words, some phonetic differences between sounds are relevant in a given language and others are not. Returning to our initial example, *tenth*, the difference between alveolar and dental articulation of the nasal does not give rise to different words, nor does it anywhere else in English. This place of articulation difference therefore has no **contrastive function** in English nasals. Note, however, that exactly the same place differentiation does have contrastive function among English fricatives: if the place of articulation of the final fricative in *tenth* is changed from dental to alveolar, we get a different word: *tense*. English, then, uses the phonetic difference between dental and alveolar fricatives for the differentiation of words but not the one between dental and alveolar nasals.

This argument has given rise to a second and more abstract level on which speech sounds are represented: on the **concrete level**, we observe and describe what speech sounds 'exist'; on the **abstract level**, we only recognise such differences between elements as have contrastive function in the language. Thus, on the contrastive level dental and alveolar nasals in English are represented by one and the same element, while dental and alveolar fricatives are represented by two different contrastive elements (actually by four, since they are also contrastively differentiated in terms of voicing: *sue – zoo* etc.).

We are now in a position where we can draw a clear distinction between the **phonetic description** discussed in chapter 1 and the **phonological analysis** that the title of this book promises. The phonetic description takes stock, with more or less sophisticated scientific means, of what speech sounds exist, how they are produced and perceived and what their acoustic properties are. Phonetics is, in that sense, a natural science. Phonological analysis, on the other hand, establishes a system of sound distinctions relevant to a particular language (where 'relevance' is here defined as 'having contrastive function') and seeks to determine how the elements of this abstract system behave in actual speech. To return, once more, to our example of *tenth*, the phonetic investigation reveals that the nasal is dental, while in a phonological analysis we may say that it is 'underlyingly' not distinct from the alveolar nasals in *ten*, *nigh* etc. and that it is here realised as a dental nasal due to the influence of the following dental fricative. Phonology, then, investigates the regularities that govern the phonetic realisations of sounds in the words of a language – similar to the way in which, for example, the study of syntax is concerned with the regularities that govern the behaviour of words and phrases in the sentences of a language. In terms of the traditional division of academic subjects into 'faculties', phonology is a branch of the 'humanities' while phonetics is a 'natural science'. That neither can be successful without the other goes without saying.

### 2.2  Phones, phonemes and allophones

As we have seen, a phonological analysis entails two levels of representation – a concrete (phonetic) one and an abstract (underlying) one – as well as statements on how the units on one level are connected with corresponding units on the other level. These statements have the form of realisation rules; they will be discussed in detail in chapter 8 below. Let us call the underlying representation of a speech sound a **phoneme**; units on the abstract level of representation are phonemes, those on the concrete phonetic level are simply speech sounds, often referred to as **phones**. Once a speech sound has been identified as a realisation of a certain phoneme, it is called an **allophone** of this phoneme. Thus, we say that the dental nasal phone in *tenth* is an allophone of the alveolar nasal phoneme. Before we begin to establish the phonemes of English, we must define more precisely what a phoneme is, what methods we use to determine phonemes and how they relate to the phones of the phonetic level.

We define a phoneme as a *minimal contrastive sound unit of a language*. Phonemes are **minimal units** in that they cannot be broken up into smaller successive units: each phone in a string of phones corresponds to exactly one phoneme on the underlying level. This statement is not as trivial as it seems:

31

it implies an important assumption and raises, in some cases, rather difficult questions. The assumption is that the phones on the concrete phonetic level are discrete units with clearly defined boundaries, marking precisely where one phone ends and the next one begins. In reality, this is not strictly speaking the case: the transitions from the phonatory, oro-nasal and articulatory processes of one phone to those of the next one do not necessarily all happen at the same time. In a word such as *pan*, for example, the voicing of the vowel does not begin exactly where the plosive is released but rather later; the tongue starts moving towards the alveolar ridge half-way through the vowel and the lowering of the velum takes place rather earlier than the oral closure is formed for the nasal, making the vowel at least partially nasalised. Nevertheless, we assume in this word the succession of exactly three phones. What seems to be a straightforward phonetic operation of segmentation in reality involves phonological reasoning: segmentation is the first one in the series of abstractions that constitutes a phonological analysis. At times, it raises questions that have no phonetic answers: is an affricate, for example, a single segment with changing manner of articulation or a sequence of a stop plus a fricative? Do we, consequently, divide a word like *judge* into three or five phones? And is a diphthong a single vowel or a sequence of two? Any answer to such questions has consequences for the phonological analysis of the language.

Phonemes are **contrastive units** in that they distinguish words, thus representing differences in meaning. If a sound difference gives rise to a meaning difference in at least one pair of words in a language then this sound difference is phonemic in that language. Thus, as we have seen, the difference between voiceless dental fricatives and voiceless alveolar fricatives serves to distinguish *tenth* and *tense* (and, of course, many others); the two sounds are therefore different phonemes of English. Although phonemes distinguish words, they do not in themselves have meaning; we may say that phonemes bear information but no meaning – we shall return to this

The method for establishing the phonemes of a language follows from their contrastive function: to find out whether two phones are allophones of the same phoneme or of different phonemes we simply have to find out whether they are contrastive in the language. If a pair of words exists that differs in one sound only – a so-called **minimal pair** – then that sound difference is phonemic and the two sounds involved are different phonemes. *Tenth* and *tense*, for example, are a minimal pair, differing only in their final sounds. Similarly, the minimal pair *bat – pat* proves the phonemic status of the initial consonants, while *bat – bit* proves that the two different vowels are different phonemes.

One final point, before we proceed to determine the phonemes of English (beginning, in this chapter, with the consonant phonemes). It follows from our definition of the phoneme that none of the allophones of a phoneme can be in a contrastive relationship with each other – if they were then they would be allophones of different phonemes. The converse is not true, however: two phones that do not contrast – that is, that do not make a minimal pair – are not necessarily allophones of the same phoneme. Consider the voiceless fricative [h] represented by the letter *h* and the velar nasal symbolised as [ŋ], in spelling represented, for example, by *ng* (*hang*). Both have rather restricted distributions in English words: [h] can only occur before a vowel, the velar nasal only after a vowel. Due to this complementary distribution, the two sounds cannot possibly figure in a minimal pair. Are they therefore allophones of the same phoneme? The problem with such a conclusion would be that it would make no sense. Given that the two sounds in question have, in phonetic terms, virtually nothing in common, it would be impossible to define a common underlier for them: a putative phoneme realised as either [h] or [ŋ] would be incapable of a nonarbitrary characterisation. Phonemes are representations of sets of sounds that are phonetically similar and whose differences can be explained, for example, by their different contexts – recall our explanation of the dental realisation of the nasal in *tenth*.

We have to impose the condition on phonemic analysis, then, that the allophones of a phoneme must be phonetically similar. The allophones of a phoneme can then be defined like this: *phonetically similar sounds that do not contrast with each other are allophones of the same phoneme*. Under this definition, [h] and [ŋ] cannot be allophones of the same phoneme but the dental and alveolar nasals can be. Phonetic similarity is a somewhat tricky notion: when are two phones phonetically similar and when are they not? We return to this problem in chapter 8, when we discuss the rules of allophony in detail; for the moment, such methodological questions need no further elaboration.

### 2.3 The consonant phonemes of English

#### 2.3.1 *The basic inventory*

Phoneme inventories vary not only from language to language but also from one accent to another. Table 2.1 below lists those consonant

Table 2.1 *English consonant phonemes: basic inventory*

| | | | | | | |
|---|---|---|---|---|---|---|
| /p/ | pie | Pooh | leap | rip | ripe | |
| /t/ | tie | two | | writ | write | mitten |
| /k/ | kye | coo | leak | rick | | |
| /b/ | buy | boo | | rib | | |
| /d/ | die | do | lead | rid | ride | |
| /g/ | guy | goo | league | rig | | |
| /tʃ/ | | chew | leech | rich | | Mitchum |
| /dʒ/ | | jew | | ridge | | pigeon |
| /m/ | my | moue | | rim | rhyme | |
| /n/ | nigh | gnu | lean | | Rhine | |
| /ŋ/ | | | | ring | | |
| /f/ | fie | | leaf | riff | rife | |
| /θ/ | thigh | | Leith | | | |
| /s/ | sigh | sue | lease | | rice | |
| /ʃ/ | shy | shoe | leash | | | mission |
| /v/ | vie | | leave | | | |
| /ð/ | thy | | | | writhe | |
| /z/ | | zoo | | | rise | mizzen |
| /ʒ/ | | | | | | vision |
| /l/ | lie | loo | | | rile | |
| /r/ | rye | rue | leer | | | |
| /w/ | Wye | woo | | | | |
| /j/ | | you | | | | |
| /h/ | high | who | | | | |

phonemes that are – with one possible exception – common to all accents of English; accent-specific variation in the consonantal inventory will be discussed in section 2.3.2. Affricates (*chew – jew*) are here treated as single phonemes rather than stop-plus-fricative sequences.

First, a word about the notation used in the left-hand column. This column gives a different symbol for each different phoneme – we shall from now on use these symbols in referring to phonemes. This method of transcription will be discussed in section 2.3.3 below. Symbols referring to phonemes are enclosed in slanted brackets /.../; symbols referring to allophones of phonemes, or simply to phones, are enclosed in square brackets [...]. Thus we write, for example, that the alveolar nasal phone [n] in *nigh* is an allophone of the phoneme /n/. This notational distinction is important: by putting a symbol into slanted brackets we imply the claim that it represents a phoneme of the language and is therefore an element of the abstract underlying system rather than a concrete speech sound. As we have seen, such a claim may well be false. For example, we noted in section 2.1 that a voiceless palatal plosive, symbolised usually by [c], may occur in

English words like *keel* but that it is an allophone of the voiceless velar plosive rather than a separate phoneme. Thus, English may have [c] but it has no /c/.

Further columns in the table give examples of the occurrence of phonemes in word-initial, word-final and word-medial position. These examples serve two purposes: firstly, they illustrate the typical phonetic realisations of each phoneme and should enable the reader to transcribe the consonant phonemes of English words with the appropriate symbols; secondly, the examples are chosen in such a way as to prove the phonemic status of each of the consonants listed.

Each column (except for the right-hand one) contains words that differ only with respect to one consonant sound – the columns therefore contain sets of minimal pairs, proving the phonemic status of the consonants by which they differ. The right-hand column does not, strictly speaking, give such conclusive proof of the phonemic status of the word-medial consonants: *vision* and *mission*, for example, differ with respect to two sounds rather than just one and the word-medial consonants are not alone responsible for the expression of the meaning difference between the two words. However, it can be said with reasonable certainty that this pair of words does establish the medial sounds as different phonemes although it is not a true minimal pair: there just happens to be no minimal pair because English happens not to have the words *\*vission* or *\*mision*. If one considers how rarely the /ʒ/ phoneme occurs then such accidental gaps in the vocabulary are hardly surprising. In cases of rare phonemes such as /ʒ/, phonologists may have to resort to 'near-minimal pairs' like *vision – mission*, although their use in establishing phonemes has some obvious dangers and should, if possible, be avoided: strictly speaking, a near-minimal pair constitutes no proof. Some minimal pairs involving /ʒ/ do exist: *lesion – legion, leisure – ledger* (but note that the latter is again only a near-minimal pair for those American speakers who rhyme *leisure* with *seizure*).

The gaps in the table are actually not without interest. In some cases, these are accidental, caused only by the fact that English does not happen to have words like *\*leeb, thoo, rish* etc. Such words are possible in English but do not exist. On the other hand, some further gaps are systematic rather than accidental: English not only does not but cannot have words such as *\*ngoo* because /ŋ/, spelt *ng*, can only occur after a vowel. Speakers of the language normally have clear intuitions about this distinction between accidental and systematic gaps; we shall return to those later (in ch. 6) when we investigate syllable structure and the constraints that govern the distributions of phonemes within the syllable.

### 2.3.2 *Some regional modifications*

Some accents of English have slightly modified inventories of consonant phonemes. Thus, it is well known that Scottish speakers do not pronounce *loch* and *lock* in the same way. For these speakers, *loch* and *lock* are a minimal pair: the latter ends in /k/, the former in a voiceless velar fricative /x/, which is therefore an additional phoneme in Scottish English. /x/ occurs in Scots dialect words and names (*dreich, Rannoch, Auchtermuchty*) and in the Scottish pronunciations of non-native words such as *parochial, Munich*; it is usually associated with *ch* spellings and may occur, more or less sporadically, in other accents of English as well.

Moreover, for most Scottish, many Canadian and US as well as some English speakers *Wye* and *why* are a minimal pair, the latter being pronounced with what is usually a voiceless bilabial fricative /ʍ/. This additional phoneme is also found in *which* (vs. *witch*), *whine* (vs. *wine*), *what* (vs. *Watt*). Words that can have /ʍ/ are usually spelt with *wh*.

Finally, consider the velar nasal /ŋ/. This sound has a rather limited distribution: it occurs only after vowels before /k/ (*rank, sink*) as well as – in most accents – syllable-finally (*rang, sing*), where it contrasts with both /m/ (*ram*) and /n/ (*ran, sin*). For that reason, it is obviously a phoneme for those speakers. However, many speakers from the English North and West Midlands pronounce *rang, sing, singing* etc. with [ŋg] clusters rather than single [ŋ]. This may appear as a minor difference between accents but it has consequences for the phoneme inventory of such speakers. They do not have the phoneme /ŋ/ because *sin – sing, ram – rang* are not minimal pairs: they differ not only in the quality of the nasal but also in the presence or absence of /g/. More precisely, the distribution of the velar nasal in such accents is like this: [ŋ] occurs before velar plosives (/g/, /k/) and nowhere else; moreover, there can be no nasal other than the velar one in these contexts: the velar nasal, for these speakers, never contrasts with the other nasals. It must therefore be an allophone of one of the other nasal phonemes rather than a phoneme in its own right. Our condition that the allophones of a phoneme have to be phonetically similar suggests that [ŋ] is an allophone of /n/ rather than /m/: the velar nasal is clearly more similar, in terms of articulation, to the alveolar one than it is to the bilabial one.

What is worth noting about this case of accent differentiation is the way in which a difference in the phonemic inventory is brought about by different distributional behaviour of phonemes rather than by differences in individual phones. Both Southern and Midlands English speakers have phonetic [ŋ] and [g]; nevertheless, Southern speakers have the phoneme /ŋ/ while for Midlands speakers [ŋ] is an allophone of /n/. The other two cases of inventory differences that we have discussed are in this respect much more straightforward: a speaker who does not differentiate the pronunciations of *loch* and *lock*, for example, does not have the phoneme /x/, and one who does not distinguish *why* and *Wye* does not have /ʍ/. In these cases, the presence or absence of a phoneme is determined simply by the occurrence of certain phones.

### 2.3.3 *Phonemic transcription and information*

The phonemic inventory of a language has exactly as many members as the language has linguistically relevant sound distinctions. Any further members of the inventory would fail to express phonological contrast; for example, if we proposed different abstract sound elements for the nasals in *tenth* and *nigh* then these two elements would not meet the requirement of being contrastive. Our definition of the phoneme makes it impossible to assign the two nasal sounds in question to different phonemes. If, on the other hand, we decided to assign the fricatives in *tenth* and *tense* to one and the same phoneme then we would be ignoring the fact that they function contrastively in English. Indeed, our definition of allophones forbids us to treat the two fricatives as allophones of the same phoneme. The phonemic level, then, expresses all and only relevant sound differences; it expresses no redundant sound differences, that is, differences that have no function in the differentiation of words.

Our set of phonemic symbols, laid out in table 2.1, expresses the redundancy-free nature of the phonemic representations in that it contains a different symbol for each phoneme. The need for such a special spelling system – and that is what our set of phonemic symbols essentially is – is obvious: the conventional spellings of English words cannot perform this task because in many cases they fail to correspond one-to-one to phonemes. A phoneme may in English spelling be represented by different letters in different words; two phonemes may in different words be represented by the same letter; or a single phoneme may be represented by a sequence of two letters, each of which may elsewhere denote a different phoneme. Here are some examples:

the phoneme /ŋ/, spelt as *ng* (*sing*) or *n* (*sink*)
the phonemes /θ/ and /ð/, both spelt as *th* (*thigh*, *thy*)
the phoneme /ʃ/, spelt as *sh* (*shy*), *ss* (*mission*), *ti* (*friction*) or *ce* (*ocean*)
the phoneme /dʒ/, spelt as *g* (*gin*), *dg* (*edge*), *j* (*Jim*), *ge* (*pigeon*)

Many more examples can be found, each of them showing that the spelling of English, with its idiosyncrasies, is not suitable for the expression of phonemic distinctions in a clear one-to-one way.

Our transcription of the phonemic level of representation is, in this respect, the ideal representation of English speech, containing as it does all and only the linguistically relevant detail of the phonetic form of words. Phonemes, while having no linguistic meaning, bear **relevant phonological information**.

As we shall see in more detail in later chapters, the phonetic information given in the actual pronunciation of a word – that is, the information transmitted in phones – consists of two kinds:

1 **Phonologically relevant information**, needed to distinguish one word from another. This aspect of the form of a word is **unpredictable:** *tenth* and *nigh* just happen to contain the nasal /n/ and there is no actual reason why they should not contain any other phoneme or phonemes in its place. The choice between saying *nigh* rather than *my* is up to the speaker, depending entirely on what word he or she wishes to utter. This is the information expressed on the phonemic level; note that dictionary entries usually give the spelling, the meaning and (some form of) a phonemic transcription of a word. Dictionaries give no redundant information – none of the three components of a lexical entry can be derived by any kind of rule.

2 The phones of speech also contain **redundant information**, not needed to distinguish one word from another. This information is redundant for two reasons: it is *not needed for phonological contrast* and it is (largely) **predictable**. In *tenth*, for example, the nasal is realised as dental due to a general rule that predicts the 'assimilation' of the place of articulation of the nasal to that of the next consonant. And, unlike the choice of the phoneme /n/ in this word, the selection of the dental allophone of this nasal is involuntary on the part of the speaker: rules that determine particular realisations of phonemes are applied entirely automatically, involving no decisions (and not even any awareness) on the part of the speaker. For both reasons, redundant information is systematically excluded from the phonemic representation of a word.

This is just another way of looking at the distinction between the phonemic and phonetic levels of representation. The phonemic level contains a skeleton of information crucial to the identification of words, no more and no less. The phonetic level is richer in information in that it additionally contains all the phonetic detail that is linguistically redundant: not needed for contrast and predicted by realisation rules. These two aspects of redundancy are, of course, logically connected: information that is predicted by an automatic rule cannot be needed for contrast; an automatic rule cannot possibly introduce any nonredundant information. We shall discuss the properties of the allophonic level of representation in chapter 8 below.

### 2.3.4 *The phonetic content of phonemes*

In the first chapter and the first part of this one we have pursued two rather different lines of enquiry, which it is now time to reconcile. We first described the phonetic processes involved in the production of speech sounds, aiming for a precise phonetic description of the phones that occur in English. Then, in the first half of this chapter, phonemes were discussed. Phonemes, we saw, are abstract units defined purely in terms of their contrastive function. Phonemes are not physical (phonetic) units but mental abstractions on the part of the phonologist and, presumably, the speaker. Our inventory of consonant phonemes in section 2.3.2 was drawn up without reference to the precise phonetic description of speech sounds: we establish phonemes by means of **commutation tests** – finding minimal pairs – but need not for this purpose refer directly to phonetic properties.

It might, in fact, be argued that phonemes do not have any phonetic properties because they are not units of the phonetic level of representation: phonemes, one might say, have nothing to do with phonetics because they are abstract nonphonetic units. While this statement is certainly true it also requires some qualification.

Recall our condition on allophones stated in section 2.2 above: the allophones of a phoneme must be phonetically similar. Clearly, it makes sense to encode in the phoneme itself all those properties that are shared by its allophones. If all the realisations of a phoneme are, for example, alveolar nasals then the simplest way of stating this is by characterising the phoneme itself as an alveolar nasal. Informally, we have already been referring to phonemes in this way – but were we methodologically justified in doing so?

Attributing phonetic properties like 'alveolar' and 'nasal' to abstract phonemes would have at least two advantages. It would, firstly, allow for a more precise statement of our so far rather impressionistic notion of 'phonological contrast': the contrast between /m/ and /n/, for example, could be characterised as a bilabial vs. alveolar contrast among nasals. Our listing of phonemes in section 2.3.1 contained no such precision; table 2.1 is, in principle, an unstructured collection of phonemes in random order.

Secondly, characterising /n/, for example, as an alveolar nasal phoneme would suggest a possible range of allophones: they would all have to be alveolar nasals, differing only in other respects.

Things are not quite so simple. Consider the case of the 'alveolar nasal' phoneme in more detail. This phoneme can, as we have seen, be realised as a dental nasal in words such as *tenth*. Is the phoneme, then, to be characterised underlyingly as alveolar or dental? The most plausible answer, clearly, is alveolar: /n/ is realised as an alveolar nasal in *nigh*, *ten*, *penny* and many other cases, the dental realisation obviously being the less common one, caused by the special circumstance of being followed by a dental fricative. We see, then, that the underlying characterisation of a phoneme as 'alveolar', 'nasal' etc. is rather abstract and nonphonetic in nature: it is, unsurprisingly, just as abstract as the phoneme itself. An alveolar phoneme may have nonalveolar allophones. A voiced phoneme, as we shall see, may have voiceless allophones, an approximant phoneme may be realised with friction, and so forth. The features that we use for the underlying characterisation of phonemes are of the same kind as the ones employed in the concrete phonetic description of phones; but what they express is rather different: phonological generalisations rather than information about their precise phonetic implementation.

Table 2.2 gives the (proposed) underlying characterisation of the consonant phonemes of English, with places of articulation along the horizontal dimension and manners of articulation along the vertical one. The features employed in this table for the characterisation of phonemes draw on the phonetic description of speech sounds that we developed in chapter 1. Recall that this description entailed the following five dimensions:

1 the place of articulation
2 the manner of articulation
3 the phonation process (voiced vs. voiceless)
4 the oro-nasal process (oral vs. nasal)
5 lateral vs. central

All five of these dimensions are also relevant on the phonemic level under discussion here, although some more so than others. Our bidimensional table 2.2 is in this respect a somewhat simplified exposition of the phonological specification of phonemes: in each column, voiced phonemes are on the right and voiceless ones on the left (this is the third dimension); all nonnasals are oral (the fourth dimension); all nonlaterals are central (the fifth dimension).

Table 2.2 *The English consonant phonemes*

|  | Bilabial | Labiodental | Dental | Alveolar | Post-alveolar | Palato-alveolar | Palatal | Velar | Glottal |
|---|---|---|---|---|---|---|---|---|---|
| Nasal (stop) | m |  |  | n |  |  |  | ŋ |  |
| Oral stop | p  b |  |  | t  d |  |  |  | k  g |  |
| Affricate |  |  |  |  |  | tʃ  dʒ |  |  |  |
| Fricative | (ʍ) | f  v | θ  ð | s  z |  | ʃ  ʒ |  | x  m | h |
| Approximant | (w) |  |  |  | r |  | j | w |  |
| Lateral (approximant) |  |  |  | l |  |  |  |  |  |

That it is possible to condense our exposition in this way is in itself rather illuminating, in that it shows how many redundancies there are in a full phonetic description. Since all nasals are stops, any nonstop will automatically be oral. Since the only English lateral is an approximant, any nonapproximant will be central. Approximants and nasals (recall: sonorants) are by definition voiced. Evidently, there are some regularities hidden in table 2.2 that, since they lead to a better understanding of the consonant system of English, are worth exploring.

Some features of phonemes, while relevant to the phonetic description of the phoneme's realisations, are redundant when we aim for the mere identification of the members of the phoneme system, such that the specification of each one merely has to be different from that of each of the others without necessarily being fully explicit. Since, for example, English has no lateral fricative phonemes, the specification as 'central' is redundant for fricatives (although, of course, in phonetic terms English fricatives are central). And since English, in fact, only has one lateral phoneme, we may refer to it as 'the lateral phoneme', although in phonetic terms it is, of course, not only lateral but also voiced, oral and an approximant. We are faced here again with the distinction between the descriptive and classificatory uses of features. This distinction was mentioned in chapter 1. We see now more clearly in which direction our discussion of phoneme systems and features is going.

This discussion will not leave the features themselves unquestioned. In table 2.2, we have simply used those place of articulation features that earlier proved helpful in our phonetic description of phones. Purely for the sake of simplicity, these features were here used for classificatory purposes also – but do we really need them all, for classification and even for description? Or can our set of features be simplified? Recall that most of the manner of articulation labels in the vertical dimension of the table have already been shown to be somewhat overcomplicated: they are simply combinations of the two basic features [Sonorant] and [Continuant]. Perhaps the same can be done where the place of articulation features are concerned? Notice that some of the place categories in table 2.2 are rather poorly used; this may well indicate that for the sake of phonetic precision we have been rather overprecise in phonological terms. We shall return to this question in chapters 4 and 5 below, where our feature system will be rather radically revised.

### Suggested reading to chapter 2

Sections 2.1, 2.2   The phonetics–phonology distinction as well as the phoneme concept are discussed in practically every phonology textbook. For detailed discussion, see in particular Lass (1984: chs. 1, 2), also Sommerstein (1977: ch. 1), Hawkins (1984: ch. 1), Hyman (1975: chs. 1, 3). On the evolution of phoneme theory see again Hyman (1975: ch. 3), in more detail Fischer-Jørgensen (1975), Anderson (1985).

Section 2.3   Most textbooks on English phonology contain accounts of the consonant phonemes of English (e.g. Knowles 1987; Kreidler 1989); reading the relevant chapters may illuminate points that have here remained unclear. The detailed exposition of the English consonant phonemes and their typical realisations given in Gimson (1989: ch. 8) is strongly recommended as accompanying reading to this chapter.

# 3
# Some vowel systems of English

## 3.1 A choice of reference accents

As we have seen, the consonant system of English is relatively uniform throughout the English-speaking world; accents of English differ mainly in terms of their vowel systems as well as in the phonetic realisations of vowel phonemes. The aim of this chapter is the discussion of three of the vowel systems of English: one from (Southern) England, one from Scotland and one from the United States. All three of them are 'standard' systems in that they are used by speakers of Standard English rather than by speakers of nonstandard regional dialects. They therefore reflect accents of such speakers who have the syntax, morphology and vocabulary of the variety of Standard English spoken in England, Scotland and the United States respectively.

Needless to say, these three accents are not the only ones to go with whatever variety of Standard English may be spoken in various parts of the world: for example, Canada, Australia, New Zealand, South Africa, Northern and Southern Ireland and not least the West of Britain and certain parts of the United States have different accents, which may to a greater or lesser extent also be standardised. None of these accents will be systematically covered in this book (but see section 3.7 below, where the characteristics of some of them will be briefly summarised). Why, then, make this particular choice of three standard accents? Apart from the fact that all three accents are interesting in their own right – a fact that hardly distinguishes these from others – there are several reasons for choosing these three for detailed and systematic treatment.

Firstly, each of the three differs from the others – at times quite radically – in a phonologically interesting way: the discussion and comparison of the three systems will reveal general properties of the vowel phonology of English – probably more readily so than the choice of any other three systems would do. Secondly, most (and possibly all) of the standard systems not discussed are historically related to one or more of the ones chosen here and are therefore similar to those; our choice will, it is hoped, enable the reader to analyse any other vowel system of Standard English. A third and more pragmatic reason follows from the second one: it is hoped that the majority of readers will find a vowel system here that is sufficiently similar to their own so as to allow the easiest possible access to the rather complex set of problems that the vowel phonology of English presents.

The chapter is organised as follows. Section 3.2 gives brief introductions to the three reference accents and establishes their inventories of vowel phonemes in tabular form. In section 3.3 we attempt to characterise the basic aspects of the three inventories as structured systems of vowel contrasts, noting in each case any major variants of the systems as well as the systematic differences between the three reference accents. Section 3.4 focusses on vowels in the context of (actual or historic) /r/, as in *hear*, *there*, *sure* etc. These constitute separate subsystems of vowels and reveal further important differences between the reference accents. In section 3.5 we look at the subsystems of unstressed vowels in the three accents; and section 3.6 concludes this chapter with a discussion of the phonetic content of our phonemic symbols.

### 3.2   Three inventories

#### 3.2.1   *The Southern British Standard vowel phonemes*
Most areas of Southern Britain (that is, excluding Scotland and to some extent the North of England) share a standard vowel system that is subject to little regional variation. What variation occurs within this geographical area is found mainly on the level of the phonetic realisations of vowel phonemes and only to a small extent in the number and systematic behaviour of the phonemes themselves. The best-known manifestation of this Southern British Standard is the one referred to as **Received Pronunciation (RP)**, an accent that no longer has any regional definition (although it originates historically in the South-East) but is, instead, defined in social terms. RP is the accent spoken, throughout England, by the upper-middle and upper classes; it is widely used in the private sector of the education system and spoken by most newsreaders of network BBC. RP is also, along with 'General American' (to be discussed in section 3.2.3 below), the most common model accent in the teaching of English as a foreign language. Given its social stratification, this accent carries as much prestige as it attracts social prejudice. We base our discussion of the Southern British accent(s) on RP not because of its prestige or any assumptions about its supposed 'correctness', or for any other nonphonological reasons (except,

Table 3.1 *Vowel phonemes of Received Pronunciation*

|  | Closed syllables | Open syllables |
|---|---|---|
| /i/ | beat  peel  dean  seem | bee  knee  tea |
| /ɪ/ | bit  pill  din  bid | |
| /e/ | bait  pale  Dane  same | bay  Tay  hay |
| /ɛ/ | bet  den  pet  bed | |
| /ɑ/ | Bart  darn  bath  psalm | Shah  bra  car |
| /a/ | bat  Dan  pal  Sam | |
| /u/ | boot  pool  Luke  fool | shoe  coo  two |
| /ʊ/ | put  pull  look  full | |
| /o/ | boat  pole  both  foal | show  know  toe |
| /ʌ/ | butt  done  putt  some | |
| /ɔ/ | bought  caught  dawn  short  sport | Shaw  shore  paw |
| /ɒ/ | cot  don  lock  stop  cough | |
| /aɪ/ | bite  pile  dine  like | shy  buy  nigh |
| /aʊ/ | bout  down  fowl  lout | cow  now  brow |
| /ɔɪ/ | noise  voice  coin  joist | coy  boy  joy |
| /ɪə/ | beard  weird  fierce | beer  fear  idea |
| /ɛə/ | Baird  laird  scarce | bear  fare  hair |
| /ʊə/ | gourd | pure  tour  sure |
| /ɜ/ | bird  heard  word  work | burr  fur  her |
| /ə/ | bottom  hammock | butter  China  comma |

perhaps, the fact that it is particularly well documented), but simply because its vowel system is a near-universal Southern British one. In any case, in our discussion of the vowel system the realisation characteristics of RP are of comparatively little interest – and it is mainly those that set RP apart from other Southern British accents, as well as being socially distinctive or diagnostic.

Table 3.1 sets out the vowel phonemes of RP, together with examples of their occurrence in syllables closed by a consonant and in open syllables, that is, syllables ending in a vowel. Both sets of examples contain sufficient minimal pairs to prove the phonemic status of each of the vowel sounds listed. Note at this point the systematic gaps that occur in the right-hand category of examples: these restrictions on the occurrence of certain vowel phonemes will play an important part in our discussion of the basic vowel system which will follow in section 3.3.2 below. The typical phonetic content of the symbols used here will be explained in section 3.6.

### 3.2.2  *The vowel phonemes of Scottish Standard English*
**Scottish Standard English (SSE)**, the variety of Standard English spoken in Scotland, has few lexical and syntactic characteristics that set

Table 3.2 *Vowel phonemes of Scottish Standard English*

| | Closed syllables | Open syllables |
|---|---|---|
| /i/ | beat peel dean seem here | bee knee tea |
| /ɪ/ | bit pill din bid bird | |
| /e/ | bait pale Dane same hair | bay Tay hay |
| /ɛ/ | bet pet den bed heard | |
| /a/ | Sam psalm darn bath car | Shah bra |
| /u/ | pool pull fool full sure | shoe coo two |
| /o/ | boat pole both shore sport | show know toe |
| /ʌ/ | butt done some word fur | |
| /ɔ/ | caught cot dawn don cough short | Shaw paw |
| /aɪ/ | bite pile dine like | shy buy nigh |
| /aʊ/ | bout down fowl lout | cow brow now |
| /ɔɪ/ | noise coin joist | boy coy joy |
| /ə/ | butter bottom hammock | China comma |

it apart from the Standard English used in England. In this respect, SSE is very different from the **Scots** spoken in the non-Gaelic-speaking part of the country. Scots is a group of dialects (or, as has been argued, a language) in its own right, with many lexical, syntactic, morphological and phonological features that distinguish it from Standard English.

SSE is, however, spoken with accents that are quite radically different from any other accent of Standard English. Most of these differences are due to the influence of Gaelic (in the Highlands and Islands) and Scots (in the non-Gaelic-speaking areas). These two kinds of interference give rise to two different accents: the former, Gaelic-influenced one usually referred to as Highland English; and the latter simply called the Scottish Standard English accent (although this term is, strictly speaking, inaccurate: there are (at least) two different SSE accents). It is this latter accent that we shall deal with here.

The SSE accent is in a sense an analysts' artefact: there is no single accent in Scotland that has the sociolinguistic status of a 'standard'. But it can be localised at least to some extent. SSE is, roughly, spoken by the middle class of Central Scotland, notably in Edinburgh and Glasgow. Surrounding areas – the Borders and the North of Scotland – share many but not all of the characteristics of the SSE accent. The vowel inventory set out in table 3.2, with examples providing minimal pairs, is the one shared by most varieties

Table 3.3 *Vowel phonemes of General American*

|        | Closed syllables              | Open syllables    |
|--------|-------------------------------|-------------------|
| /i/    | beat  peel  dean  seem  here  | bee  knee  tea    |
| /ɪ/    | bit  pill  din  bid           |                   |
| /e/    | bait  pale  Dane  same  scarce| bay  Tay  hay     |
| /ɛ/    | bet  den  pet  bed            |                   |
| /ɑ/    | car  psalm  cot  stop  don    | Shah  bra         |
| /a/    | bat  Sam  Dan  bath           |                   |
| /u/    | boot  pool  Luke  fool  sure  | shoe  coo  two    |
| /ʊ/    | pull  put  look  full         |                   |
| /o/    | boat  foal  both  sport       | show  know  toe   |
| /ʌ/    | putt  butt  done  some        |                   |
| /ɔ/    | caught  dawn  short  cough    | Shaw  paw         |
| /aɪ/   | bite  dine  like  file        | shy  buy  tie     |
| /aʊ/   | bout  down  fowl  lout        | cow  brow  now    |
| /ɔɪ/   | noise  voice  coin  joist     | boy  coy  joy     |
| /ɜ/    | bird  heard  burr  fur        |                   |
| /ə/    | butter  bottom  hammock       | China  comma      |

of SSE. Some varieties have additional phonemic contrasts, a few of which will be discussed in section 3.3.3. The phonetic content of the symbols used in the table will be discussed in section 3.6.

### 3.2.3  The vowel phonemes of General American

**General American (GA)** is a cover term used for the group of accents in the United States that do not bear the marked regional characteristics of either the East (more precisely, Eastern New England and New York City) or the South (mainly ranging from Virginia, the Carolinas and Georgia to Louisiana and Texas). These two areas are easily perceived as linguistically distinct from the rest of the United States, while the rest – the GA area – appears to be the variety that has no marked regional characteristics, except the negative ones of being noneastern and non-southern. GA is, then, one of (at least) three 'standard accents' found in the United States; it is by far the most widespread one. It has the largest geographical spread and is the accent most commonly used in the television networks covering the whole of the United States.

Covering as it does a vast area of the country, GA is not, of course, a single and totally homogeneous accent. But since its internal variation is mainly a matter of differences in the phonetic realisations of a system of phonemes that is by and large shared by all GA speakers, the generalisation

47

expressed in the notion 'General American' is useful in phonological terms
– perhaps more so than in dialectological and sociolinguistic terms.

The vowel phonemes of GA are listed, with examples, in table 3.3; the
symbols used in the table will be explained in section 3.6. In section 3.3.4,
we shall investigate how this unstructured inventory can be interpreted as a
structured vowel system. At that point, some regional variation of the basic
GA system will also be noted.

### 3.3   Three basic vowel systems

#### 3.3.1   *Pairs of phonemes*

Our previous displays of the three vowel inventories – the three
tables in section 3.2 – have been rather unstructured and do not really lend
themselves to a concise comparison between the three reference accents.
The question we have to ask is this: do the vowel phonemes of an accent (or
of a language) come in random sets, or do they have any kind of internal
**structure**? In other words, are there recurrent and systematic relationships
between the members of each set, such that we can speak of **vowel systems**
rather than just inventories? The mere fact that this question is being asked
would suggest that the answer is yes. In its pursuit we shall see, more clearly
than we have so far, how the three accents differ and what they have in
common. On closer inspection, some patterns emerge from our displays in
section 3.2.

Consider the phonemic contrast /i/–/ɪ/, a contrast that occurs in all three
inventories. It can be argued that these two phonemes are not an arbitrary
subset of their respective inventory but a pair whose members are more
closely related to each other than to any other members of the inventory.
Below are some arguments.

1   They are similar in quality (although not exclusively so: /ɪ/ is also
    rather similar to /e/. Clearly, the notion of 'similarity in quality'
    requires further discussion.
2   In most accents of English (though not in SSE), they form a
    long–short opposition. In such accents, /i/ is in comparable
    contexts longer than /ɪ/: compare, for example, *beat* and *bit* in
    RP and GA.
3   Their distribution follows a semi-complementary pattern: /i/ can
    occur in open and closed syllables (*bee, beat*) while /ɪ/ can occur
    in closed syllables only: *bit*.

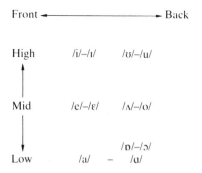

Figure 3.1    Pairs of English vowel phonemes

These observations do not on their own provide conclusive evidence for a particularly close relationship between /i/ and /ɪ/. Given that the first criterion is not entirely reliable as it stands, the other two could equally be used to pair, for example, /i/ and /ʌ/, or /e/ and /ɪ/. However, what makes the /i/–/ɪ/ pairing particularly promising in our attempt to uncover the structure of the vowel inventories is this:

4    Similar pairs occur, with remarkable symmetry, throughout the system: our criteria 1–3 can be used to pair, in RP, /e/ and /ɛ/, /ɑ/ and /a/, /u/ and /ʊ/, /o/ and /ʌ/, as well as /ɔ/ and /ɒ/. In each such pair, the members are phonetically similar (although less so in the case of /o/–/ʌ/ than in the others); they form long–short oppositions in RP and GA; and the second member is restricted to closed syllables.

5    And finally, even the way in which certain accents – SSE in particular – do *not* have certain vowel phonemes is rather telling: what is a pair in one accent is collapsed into a single phoneme in another. *Pool – pull*, for example, are a minimal pair in RP (/pul/ – /pʊl/), but in SSE both are pronounced identically as /pul/. In distributional terms, the phoneme that is absent is in all such cases the one with the more restricted occurrence: the one that cannot occur in open syllables – compare here in particular the RP and SSE inventories (tables 3.1 and 3.2 respectively). The absence of certain vowel phonemes in some accents can be viewed, then, as the collapse of certain pairwise oppositions and thereby reinforces our notion of pairs.

In figure 3.1, the pairs that we have just established are arranged along the dimensions of high–low and front–back familiar from chapter 1. The third dimension established there – that of roundness – is disregarded. As a comparison of the phoneme tables in section 3.2 above shows, only RP has the full system given in figure 3.1. GA lacks /ɒ/, and SSE lacks /a/, /ɒ/ and /ʊ/. This variation among the three reference accents will be discussed further on in this chapter. Disregarding such accent-specific gaps, figure 3.1 demonstrates that our pairs of vowels lend themselves to a classification in terms of the high–low and front–back dimensions: /i/–/ɪ/ is a high front pair, /e/–/ɛ/ a mid front pair and so forth. We shall continue this classification in chapter 4 below, where the additional dimension of roundness will also be put to classificatory use. (There, we shall also discuss the characterisation of /ʌ/, which is here – perhaps somewhat hastily – classed as 'mid back'.) For the moment we merely note that vowel pairs may be classified along the dimensions given in figure 3.1 (plus the roundness dimension): English vowel phonemes constitute a system not only by being pairwise related but also by having recurrent relationships *among* pairs. /i/–/ɪ/ as a high front pair corresponds to /u/–/ʊ/ as a high back pair and so forth. What remains to be discussed, apart from the less straightforward cases that seem to cluster in the bottom-right corner of figure 3.1, is the (presumably also recurrent) feature that distinguishes the members of each pair: in phonetic terms we have only so far only stated that each pair contains similar yet somewhat different vowels. This discussion, too, will have to wait until chapter 4.

Not all the members of the inventories in tables 3.1–3.3 take part in such a formation of pairs. Among the ones that do not are, first of all, the phonemes /ɪə/, /ɛə/, /ʊə/, /ɜ/ and /ə/ (not all of which occur in all three reference accents): these will be discussed further in sections 3.4 and 3.5 below. More notably, the diphthongs /aɪ/, /aʊ/ and /ɔɪ/ are not members of pairs. In distributional terms, these are on a par with /i/, /e/ etc. in that they occur in open as well as closed syllables (*buy*, *bite* etc.), as well as being relatively long in RP and GA; but they do not have counterparts comparable to /ɪ/, /ɛ/ in any of the three systems. We shall refer to /aɪ/, /aʊ/ and /ɔɪ/ as the **true diphthongs** of English, thereby distinguishing them in particular from /e/ and /o/, which in RP and GA also have diphthongal realisations: [eɪ] and [oʊ] respectively. The reason why we do not treat /e/ and /o/ as diphthongs on the phonemic level is threefold. Firstly, similar diphthongal realisations can also be found, if to a lesser extent, in other 'first members of pairs' – hence /i/ is frequently realised as [ɪi] and /u/ as [ʊu]. The behaviour of /e/ and /o/ is therefore not radically different from that of /i/ and /u/. Secondly, the realisations of /e/ and /o/ are not invariably diphthongal in all accents of English: in SSE they are monophthongs – [e] and [o]. And thirdly, even outside SSE monophthongal realisations of [e] and [o] occur, for example in GA *hair* [her] and *sport* [sport]. The true diphthongs, on the other hand, are invariably of a diphthongal quality in all three reference accents; and this difference in behaviour is borne out by our attempt to structure the three vowel systems: /e/, /o/ are members of pairs (as /i/, /u/ etc. are) and therefore treated as phonemic monophthongs on a par with all other 'paired' vowel phonemes, while the true diphthongs /aɪ/, /aʊ/ and /ɔɪ/ are kept separate.

### 3.3.2 England

#### 3.3.2.1 The basic vowel system of RP

Following the criteria established in section 3.3.1 above, we may structure the RP vowel inventory in terms of the pairs in (1a), along with the true diphthongs (1b).

(1) a.  

| | | |
|---|---|---|
| bee, beat | /i/–/ɪ/ | bit |
| bay, bait | /e/–/ɛ/ | bet |
| Shah, psalm | /ɑ/–/a/ | Sam |
| shoe, pool | /u/–/ʊ/ | pull |
| show, boat | /o/–/ʌ/ | butt |
| Shaw, caught | /ɔ/–/ɒ/ | cot, cough |

b. /aɪ/  bite, buy  
/aʊ/  bout, brow  
/ɔɪ/  coin, boy

Recall from figure 3.1 that these pairs can be further structured in terms of the high–low and front–back dimensions. This we shall pursue in detail in chapter 4 below; for the moment, the only structure that we impose on the RP inventory is that of a set of pairs, as in (1).

The members of each pair are phonetically similar to each other (in some cases more so than in others). Moreover, the left-hand member of each pair is realised longer than its right-hand counterpart is in comparable contexts; and the left-hand member can occur in open syllables while the right-hand one can only occur in closed syllables.

#### 3.3.2.2 Some variation

The basic vowel system of RP is shared by the majority of Southern British speakers. But there is some amount of variation among the accents of this linguistic area that is worth noting, especially since it is useful for a brief demonstration of what types of variation are possible among accents.

1 *Realisational variation.* This type of variation, where the number and systematic relationship of the phonemes are the same and only their phonetic realisations differ from one accent to another, is extremely common. Here are two examples. Firstly, London speakers commonly pronounce /i/ as [ɪi] (*see*), /e/ as [ʌɪ] (*say*), /aɪ/ as [ɒɪ] (*sigh*), and /ɔɪ/ as [oɪ] (*boy*) – notice that this deviation from the standard RP realisations follows a certain pattern (which?). The second example is the variable realisation of the phoneme /ʌ/ in the accents of England. /ʌ/ is realised as a low vowel in RP but as a considerably higher one in the Midlands and South-West – roughly between /ə/ and /ʊ/. Neither of the two examples of variation have any consequences for the vowel system, which is for both London and Midland speech the same as that given in table 3.1 (although one might wish, in the interest of phonetic explicitness, to replace certain symbols).

2 *Phonemic variation.* The variability of /ʌ/ – as we have seen, a purely realisational matter in the Midlands and South-West – does have phonemic consequences in the more northern parts of England: North Midlands and Northern English accents make no distinction between /ʌ/ and /ʊ/, so that words like *putt, luck, buck* have the phoneme /ʊ/ just like *put, look* and *book*. These accents, then, do not have /ʌ/. *putt – put, buck – book* etc. are 'homophones', that is, different words with identical pronunciation. The absence of the /ʌ/–/ʊ/ contrast is one of the best-known 'shibboleths' of Northern speakers.

3 *Lexical variation.* Two accents may share the same system of phonemes, and even their principal realisations, but they may use different phonemes in different words. Here again are two examples. Firstly, some of the Northern English speakers that do not have the /ʌ/–/ʊ/ contrast pronounce *book* and *look* in such a way that they rhyme with *Luke*. Such speakers have both /u/ and /ʊ/ (though not normally /ʌ/), but in certain words they use /u/ where non-Northern speakers would have /ʊ/. Such variation is purely a matter of the lexical incidence of phonemes and has no consequences for the phoneme system itself. Example (2) below summarises the accent variation found in connection with /ʌ/, /ʊ/ and /u/ in England; note the phonemic difference between the RP and North Midland (NMl) columns – two NMl phonemes correspond to three RP ones – and the lexical difference between

the NMl and North columns, both of which have the same two phonemes which differ only in terms of their lexical incidence:

| (2) | | RP | NMl | North |
|---|---|---|---|---|
| | luck | /ʌ/ | /ʊ/ | /ʊ/ |
| | look | /ʊ/ | /ʊ/ | /u/ |
| | Luke | /u/ | /u/ | /u/ |

The second example is again a well-known shibboleth of non-Southern speech. Midland and Northern English speakers have *bath* as /baθ/ and similarly *past, fast, cast, laugh* etc. with /a/ rather than /ɑ/. Such speakers do have the /ɑ/ phoneme in *father, darn, psalm* etc. – again, it is merely the lexical incidence of the two phonemes /a/ and /ɑ/ that varies. This pattern of lexical variation is summarised in (3):

| (3) | | RP | Non-South |
|---|---|---|---|
| | darn | /ɑ/ | /ɑ/ |
| | psalm | /ɑ/ | /ɑ/ |
| | bath | /ɑ/ | /a/ |
| | Sam | /a/ | /a/ |

Lexical variation is, strictly speaking, of little phonological interest, although it is, wherever it occurs, a particularly noticeable aspect of accent variation. It concerns the dialectologist more than it does the phonologist because the real object of phonological enquiry, namely the phoneme system with its realisations, is unaffected by this type of variation.

### 3.3.3 *Scotland*

#### 3.3.3.1 *The basic Scottish Standard English vowel system*

It was argued in section 3.3.1 above that the vowel inventories of English can be systematised by arranging vowel phonemes in pairs. The main arguments for such pairing were the similar qualities of the members of such pairs as well as their, in some ways, complementary behaviour: /i/ can, for example, occur in open and closed syllables, while /ɪ/ can occur in closed syllables only. Moreover, /i/ is in many accents (though not, as we shall see, in SSE) of longer duration than /ɪ/.

The reader will have noticed already that SSE has a considerably smaller inventory of vowel phonemes than, say, RP has. This hampers our attempt at arranging vowel phonemes in pairs; but it does so in a rather interesting way.

(4) a.

|  |  |
|---|---|
| bee, beat | /i/–/ɪ/ bit |
| bay, bait | /e/–/ɛ/ bet |
| Shah, psalm, Sam | /a/ |
| shoe, pool, pull | /u/ |
| show, boat | /o/–/ʌ/ butt |
| Shaw, caught, cot, cough | /ɔ/ |

b. /aɪ/ bite, buy
/aʊ/ bout, brow
/ɔɪ/ coin, boy

As in our treatment of RP in section 3.3.2 above, we do not attempt to structure this inventory any further for the moment; but recall the remarks on the high–low and front–back dimensions made in section 3.3.1 above.

In the SSE vowel system, /a/, /u/, /ɔ/ and the true diphthongs are not members of pairs of phonemes: these phonemes can all occur in open as well as closed syllables and they do not have counterparts – comparable to /ɪ/ – that are phonetically similar but can occur in closed syllables only. A look at the RP system given in figure 3.1 shows that the two systems compare in a rather interesting way: the gaps in the SSE system (compared to RP) are not random but systematic.

### 3.3.3.2 *Comparison with Received Pronunciation*

1 *Phonemic differences.* In three instances, SSE lacks a pairwise opposition found in RP and has a single phoneme instead. The rest of the basic SSE system corresponds one-to-one to that of RP. The basic systems are compared in table 3.4. The gaps in the SSE system, compared to that of RP, have the following pattern: in no case is a complete pair of RP vowel phonemes absent in SSE; it is always just one member of a pair. Moreover, the phoneme that SSE lacks is in each case the one with the more restricted distribution, namely the one that cannot occur in open syllables: in each of the depleted pairs, the member that SSE retains is free to occur in open and closed syllables.

These phonemic differences between RP and SSE are, in the broader framework of accent variation in mainland Britain, rather surprising in that they are unparalleled by differences between RP and Northern English accents. In (part of) the North of England, the Southern (RP) /ʌ/ phoneme is absent. This phoneme is maintained further north in SSE, while the contrasts that SSE does collapse are all undamaged south of the Scottish border. This observation shows that the Scottish border is a rather sharp

Table 3.4 *Scottish Standard English – Received Pronunciation correspondences*

| SSE | | RP | | SSE | | RP | |
|---|---|---|---|---|---|---|---|
| /i/ | —— | /i/ | beat | /aɪ/ | —— | /aɪ/ | bite |
| /ɪ/ | —— | /ɪ/ | bit | /aʊ/ | —— | /aʊ/ | bout |
| /e/ | —— | /e/ | bait | /ɔɪ/ | —— | /ɔɪ/ | boy |
| /ɛ/ | —— | /ɛ/ | bet | | | | |
| /a/ | ⎰— | /ɑ/ | psalm | | | | |
| | ⎱— | /a/ | Sam | | | | |
| /u/ | ⎰— | /u/ | pool | | | | |
| | ⎱— | /ʊ/ | pull | | | | |
| /o/ | —— | /o/ | boat | | | | |
| /ʌ/ | —— | /ʌ/ | butt | | | | |
| /ɔ/ | ⎰— | /ɔ/ | caught | | | | |
| | ⎱— | /ɒ/ | cot | | | | |

linguistic divide: deviations from the RP vowel system that are found in Scotland are not a continuation of deviations already found in the North of England but form a pattern in their own right.

2   *Realisational differences*. Some of these have been noted already; and fuller comments will be given in section 3.6 below as part of a discussion of the phonetic content of our phonemic symbols. But it will be useful at this point to note the following, most salient realisational differences between RP and SSE:

> /e/ and /o/ have diphthongal realisations in RP – [eɪ] and [oʊ] – while in SSE they are pure monophthongs.
> The low vowel /a/, while corresponding in systemic terms to RP /ɑ/ (since it can occur in open syllables), is usually produced further front than its RP counterpart is.
> The SSE phoneme /u/ is considerably further forward than its RP counterpart but as rounded.
> The true diphthongs /aɪ/ and /aʊ/ of SSE have higher and more central starting points than their RP counterparts and are usually realised as [ʌɪ], [ʌʊ] respectively. Moreover, the former is subject to allophonic variation, such that *rice*, for example, is pronounced [rʌɪs] and *rise* [raˑɪz] (the '·' symbol meaning 'half-long'). This variation is part of the Scottish

Vowel-Length Rule, to be discussed in the following paragraphs and in full detail in chapter 8 below.

A major realisational difference between RP and SSE concerns the length of vowels. In each of the RP pairs of vowels, one member is significantly longer than the other in comparable contexts: recall such pairs as RP *beat – bit, bait – bet* etc. SSE has no such length differentiation among its vowels – not even within the pairs that it retains: the vowels in *beat* and *bit, bait* and *bet* etc. are all of the same length; compared to RP vowels, they are all short. In SSE, the members of such pairs are distinct in terms of quality alone while in RP they differ in terms of quality as well as length.

The readiness of SSE to collapse certain contrasts is in part explained by the absence of phonemic length distinctions in SSE. Given that vowel phonemes can be distinct, as they are in RP, in terms of quality and quantity (length), the absence of the latter kind of distinction in SSE goes half-way towards the collapse of pairs of phonetically similar vowels into one. /i/ and /ɪ/, /e/ and /ɛ/, /o/ and /ʌ/ are in SSE distinct in terms of quality alone. And given that such quality differences are not great – this is why they constitute pairs in the first place – they can easily disappear. This is what has happened in the case of some SSE pairs.

However, matters concerning vowel length in SSE are not quite as simple as they may appear from what has just been said. It is not actually the case that all SSE vowels are, wherever they occur, of the same length: many (but not all) SSE vowel phonemes have long and short allophones. We shall discuss the rule responsible for this variation, which is not in this form found in either RP or GA, in chapter 8 below. But here is a preliminary description.

/i/, to take just one example, is realised long in the top series of contexts and short in the bottom series:

(5)  /i/  →  $\begin{cases} \text{[i:]} & \text{breathe, sneeze, leave, hear, bee} \\ \text{[i]} & \text{Keith, lease, leaf, feed, leap etc.} \end{cases}$

(The colon in [i:] indicates a long realisation.) The same allophonic variation is found in a number of other SSE vowels: they are realised long before voiced fricatives, /r/ and in word-final position; elsewhere, they are short. This rule, known as the **Scottish Vowel-Length Rule**, governs vowel length in all members of the basic system except /ɪ/, /ʌ/ and (in most varieties of SSE) /ɛ/, which are short in all contexts.

Note that these vowel-length differences are allophonic rather than phonemic in SSE: given the distinctness of the contexts in which long and short vowels can occur, the two kinds of vowels – [i] and [iː], for example – can never constitute minimal pairs. Where [i] occurs [iː] cannot occur and vice versa. In RP, on the other hand, the long/short distinction does occur in minimal pairs: recall *beat* – *bit*. But here length is never the only feature that distinguishes two vowel phonemes: there is always a quality difference as well, which, as we shall see, is in fact the more important one. While length distinctions are properties of RP phonemes, then, they are redundant properties in that they go together with quality distinctions. SSE has no length distinctions among vowel phonemes at all. Vowel length is entirely determined by neighbouring sounds.

### 3.3.3.3 *Some modifications*

Some SSE speakers, especially middle-class speakers from Edinburgh and Glasgow, have phonemic contrasts not present in the basic SSE system laid out in (4) above. Such speakers have some or all of the modifications shown below:

| (6) | Basic SSE | | Modified SSE | |
|---|---|---|---|---|
| | /a/ | { | /ɑ/ | psalm |
| | | | /a/ | Sam |
| | /ɔ/ | { | /ɔ/ | caught |
| | | | /ɒ/ | cot |
| | /u/ | { | /u/ | pool |
| | | | /ʊ/ | pull |

It has been claimed that these modifications are likely to occur in the order in which they are given here: SSE speakers who have the /ɔ/–/ɒ/ contrast usually have the /ɑ/–/a/ contrast as well, and those who have the /u/–/ʊ/ contrast are likely also to have both others. It is hard to explain why the acquisition of additional contrasts should take place in this order; however, the overall pattern of modification lends itself to a simple explanation. The additional contrasts of modified SSE are precisely the RP contrasts missing in the basic SSE system. It makes sense in sociolinguistic terms to predict that middle-class SSE speakers are subject to English influence and are likely to acquire features of the RP vowel system. As long as speakers with modified SSE systems maintain the other characteristics of SSE – the Vowel-Length Rule and the monophthongal realisations of /e/ and /o/, for example – their accents remain distinctly Scottish, if not in systemic terms.

### 3.3.4  *The United States*

#### 3.3.4.1  *The basic General American vowel system*

The third of the reference accents introduced in section 3.2 was the General American one. Let us now return to the vowel inventory of this accent, displayed in table 3.3, and see what its structure is. By structure we mean the relationships – more precisely, the nature of the contrasts – that hold between the members of the inventory: are the vowel phonemes in table 3.3 just in random contrast to each other, or are there recurrent differences between pairs, or sets, of phonemes?

It was argued in section 3.3.1 that the vowels in the vowel systems of English can be organised into pairs – in some vowel systems more extensively so than in others: many of the vowel phonemes that can occur in open syllables have counterparts in the system that are phonetically similar but cannot occur in open syllables. Thus, /i/ can occur in open syllables but its counterpart /ɪ/ cannot. /bi/ is a possible English word but */bɪ/ is not. In many accents – in RP and GA but not in SSE – the vowels that can occur in open syllables are also longer than the ones that cannot: the /i/ in *beat* is longer than the /ɪ/ in *bit*. Applying the criteria for the formation of pairs that we established in section 3.3.1, we can now replace the unstructured inventory of GA vowel phonemes by the following structured system:

(7)a.       bee, beat       /i/–/ɪ/       bit
            bay, bait       /e/–/ɛ/       bet
   Shah, psalm, cot       /ɑ/–/a/       Sam
           shoe, pool       /u/–/ʊ/       pull
           show, boat       /o/–/ʌ/       butt
   Shaw, caught, cough       /ɔ/
  b.           bite, buy       /aɪ/
            bout, brow       /aʊ/
             coin, boy       /ɔɪ/

In each of the pairs, the left-hand member is in comparable contexts longer than its phonetically similar counterpart on the right and can occur in open syllables. /ɔ/ and the true diphthongs are not members of pairs: all of these can occur in open syllables and none has a phonetically similar counterpart that can occur in closed syllables only.

The vowel system of GA can be further structured than was done above: it can be shown that the pairs (and /ɔ/) are systematically related to each other in terms of height and backness (as well as roundness). Their rather symmetrical distribution over the vowel trapezium gives a first impression of these relationships (see figure 3.2), which will be discussed in detail in chapter 4 below. (Recall also some remarks made on this issue in section 3.3.1 above.) For the moment, we content ourselves with the structure expressed by the pairing of vowels in (7), without even attempting to define the features that distinguish the members of each pair. This amount of structure is sufficient for a first characterisation of the system. It also enables us to draw some comparisons with the Southern British (RP) system.

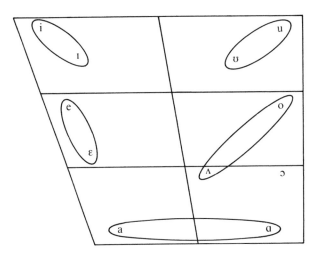

Figure 3.2   GA vowel phonemes

### 3.3.4.2   *Comparison with Received Pronunciation*

In our discussion of RP and its modifications in England (section 3.3.2.2), three different types of accent variation were noted: realisational variation, phonemic variation and lexical variation. The reader is referred back to that section for the details of this distinction.

1   The *realisational differences* between GA and RP will be listed in section 3.6 below. None of these is of particular importance here and we may postpone their statement until then.

2   There is one major *phonemic difference*, relating to the number and systematic relationship of phonemes, between GA and RP: RP has /ɒ/, which constitues a pair with /ɔ/. GA does not have this phoneme. Words that have /ɒ/ in RP have either /ɔ/ or /ɑ/ in GA:

| (8) | | GA | RP |
|---|---|---|---|
| salt, cough | | /ɔ/ | |
| cot, stop | | /ɑ/ | /ɒ/ |

As RP also has the /ɑ/ and /ɔ/ phonemes, the following pattern of distribution is caused by the absence of /ɒ/ in GA:

| (9) | GA | RP |
|---|---|---|
| psalm | /ɑ/ | /ɑ/ |
| cot | /ɑ/ | /ɒ/ |
| cough | /ɔ/ | /ɒ/ |
| caught | /ɔ/ | /ɔ/ |

3   *Lexical differences*. In addition to the difference in the lexical incidence of /ɑ/ caused by the absence of /ɒ/ in the GA system, there is a difference in the lexical distribution of /ɑ/ and /a/ between GA and RP. Both accents have /ɑ/ and /a/ but some words that have /ɑ/ in RP have /a/ in GA. Thus, *bath*, *fast*, *cast*, *laugh* and many other words have /a/ in GA but /ɑ/ in RP:

| (10) | GA | RP |
|---|---|---|
| Sam | /a/ | /a/ |
| bath | /a/ | /ɑ/ |
| psalm | /ɑ/ | /ɑ/ |

We noted in section 3.3.2.2 that a similar lexical difference occurs in the comparison of RP with non-Southern English accents: the distribution of /a/ in GA is roughly the same as that found in the English Midlands and North, different only in that the spread of /a/ extends slightly further into words with RP /ɑ/: *banana* and a few other words have /ɑ/ in RP and non-Southern English but /a/ in GA.

There are a number of further lexical differences between GA and RP; but unlike the one just discussed, they are sporadic and largely resist generalisation. Nevertheless, they are well known and the reader will undoubtedly be able to name more. Some of the best-known examples are: *tomato* (/e/ in GA, /ɑ/ in RP), *leisure* (/i/ for many GA speakers, /ɛ/ in RP), *neither* (/i/ in GA, /aɪ/ for most RP speakers), *lever* (/ɛ/ for many GA speakers, /i/ in RP), *progress* (/ɑ/ in GA, /o/ in RP), *compost* (/o/ in the second syllable in GA, /ɒ/ in RP), *wrath* (/a/ in GA, /ɒ/ in RP).

### 3.3.4.3  *Some variation*

The phonemic contrast of /ɔ/ and /ɑ/ is not as clear-cut in GA as the other contrasts in the vowel system are. With some speakers, the lexical incidence of /ɔ/ and /ɑ/ varies; other speakers do not have the contrast at all.

Variation of the lexical incidence of the two phonemes is not governed by a general rule of geographical distribution or even by obvious tendencies. But here are some examples. *Dog* has generally /ɔ/ but *cog* generally /ɑ/. Similar words, such as *fog, log, hog* etc., tend to have /ɑ/ in the North and /ɔ/ in the Midlands of the United States, and the same holds for *ma* and *pa*. *Water* has /ɑ/ in the South and /ɔ/ elsewhere.

Describing such cases in terms of variation in lexical incidence implies obviously that the speakers concerned have both phonemes, /ɔ/ and /ɑ/, and that the use of these phonemes in individual words varies from one speaker to another. Such variation is, then, not really a phonological problem, as it operates among speakers who share the same vowel system – that of basic GA, which contains both /ɔ/ and /ɑ/.

For some GA speakers, however, /ɔ/ and /ɑ/ are not separate phonemes. For such speakers, many of whom are found in the West of the United States, *cot* and *caught* are homophones and all the words listed under /ɔ/ and /ɑ/ in (8) have the same vowel phoneme. The phoneme replacing /ɔ/ and /ɑ/ in such accents is usually best described as /ɑ/ (although in some cases it may be more appropriately characterised as /ɔ/ or, possibly, /ɒ/). This modification of the basic GA system – the only one we note here, although some others exist – can be stated as follows, disregarding possible variation in the quality of the vowel resulting from the merger:

| (11) | | Basic GA | Modified GA |
|------|--------|----------|-------------|
| | caught | /ɔ/ | /ɑ/ |
| | cot | /ɑ/ | |

### 3.4  Vowels and /r/

#### 3.4.1  *Rhotic and nonrhotic accents*

In the preceding sections we have dealt with the 'basic systems' of vowel phonemes in stressed syllables (mostly in stressed monosyllabic words). We now turn to a secondary system of vowels in such stressed syllables: that of stressed vowels before /r/. We shall see that in this context, which we shall presently define more precisely, different sets of vowels occur in the three accents, which are in turn different from those of the basic systems. More precisely, not all members of the basic system occur in this context, and not all of the ones that do occur are members of the basic system.

Referring to the vowels in question as 'vowels before /r/' is inaccurate in two respects. Firstly, we are not primarily interested in the pre-/r/ vowels in *hurry, herring, lyrics, Tory* etc., but rather in those exemplified by *here, sure, sport, short, word* and so forth. Defining the contexts of these vowels accurately, we cannot therefore simply speak of 'postvocalic /r/'; instead, we have to identify the position of the /r/ within the syllable. Syllable structure will be discussed in detail in chapter 6 – here we simplify matters somewhat and divide syllables into two parts: the onset, comprising any consonant(s) before the vowel, and the rhyme, containing the vowel and any following consonant(s):

(12)

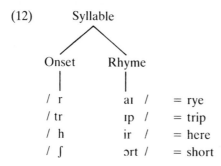

| Onset | Rhyme | | |
|-------|-------|---|--------|
| / r   | aɪ /  | = | rye    |
| / tr  | ɪp /  | = | trip   |
| / h   | ir /  | = | here   |
| / ʃ   | ɔrt / | = | short  |

The /r/ in *hurry, herring* etc. begins a new syllable – it is therefore in the syllable onset – while in the words that we are here dealing with, *here, short* etc., the /r/ is positioned in the rhyme: it follows the vowel within the same syllable.

Secondly, not all accents of English actually have rhyme-/r/ – and it is those accents that are, in many ways, of particular interest here. In RP, for example, /r/ cannot occur in this context, yet it has vowel phonemes in *here, sure, hair* and *bird* that are not part of the basic RP system discussed in section 3.3.2. Defining the contexts in which these additional vowel phonemes occur in RP, we may either speak of vowel phonemes occurring in such words that in other accents (for example, SSE and GA) have rhyme-/r/, or we may refer to the context as one of historic /r/. Speaking in purely historical terms, the peculiarities of the RP vowel system in this context were caused by the loss of rhyme-/r/ – note that this earlier stage of the language is reflected in the spelling, which is therefore useful for the

Table 3.5 *Vowels before (actual or historic) /r/*

| | SSE | GA | RP |
|---|---|---|---|
| here | /ir/ | /ir/ | /ɪə/ |
| hair | /er/ | /er/ | /ɛə/ |
| car | /ar/ | /ɑr/ | /ɑ/ |
| sure | /ur/ | /ur/ | /ʊə/ ⎤ |
| sport | /or/ ⎤ | /or/ ⎤ | /ɔ/ ⎥ /ɔ/ |
| short | /ɔr/ ⎦ | /ɔr/ ⎦ /ɔr/ | /ɔ/ ⎦ |
| word | /ʌr/ ⎤ | | ⎤ |
| bird | /ɪr/ ⎥ /ʌr/ ⎤ /ɜr/ | /ɜr/ | /ɜ/ |
| heard | /ɛr/ ⎦ ⎦ | /ɜr/ ⎦ | ⎦ |

identification of relevant examples. It is important to bear in mind, however, that present-day RP simply does not have /r/ in words like *here*, *sure*, *sport* etc.

Accents of English that have /r/ in syllable rhymes – often referred to as the 'postvocalic' position, although this is, as we have seen, somewhat inaccurate – are called **rhotic** accents; accents that do not have /r/ in this context are **nonrhotic**. RP is nonrhotic, as are the Australian, New Zealand, South African and some East Coast and Southern American accents. GA, SSE and some English West Country accents, to name a few, are rhotic.

Table 3.5, which will be discussed in the next sections, lists the vowel phonemes of SSE and GA before rhyme-/r/. The right-hand column gives the RP vowels that occur in the same set of words. The words used here are drawn from the tables listing the full inventories of the three accents in section 3.2. We omit the true diphthongs.

### 3.4.2 Scottish Standard English

In SSE, the vowel phonemes occurring before rhyme-/r/ are the same as those found in the basic SSE system. However, the phonemes /ʌ/, /ɪ/ and /ɛ/ are unstable in this context: some speakers rhyme *word* and *bird* (having /ʌ/ in both), and in addition some SSE speakers have no phonemic contrast between these two and *heard*. In phonetic terms, the result of this /ʌ/–/ɪ/–/ɛ/ collapse is a central vowel, here symbolised as /ɜ/. This vowel is an addition to the basic SSE system, present only in the speech of such SSE speakers who do not have the /ʌ/–/ɪ/–/ɛ/ contrast before rhyme-/r/.

This decision to introduce a new phoneme is not really justified by the criteria for phonemic status that were discussed in chapter 2: /ɜ/ does not stand in phonemic opposition with /ʌ/, /ɪ/ and /ɛ/ before /r/ – simply because the speakers that have /ɜ/ do not have any of the other three in the same context. We would in phonemic terms be justified – strictly speaking, even required! – to denote the result of the /ʌ/–/ɪ/–/ɛ/ collapse with one of these three symbols instead of introducing a new one. The reason why we choose /ɜ/ nevertheless is phonetic rather than phonemic: again, we are faced with the conflict between being phonemically systematic, on the one hand, and phonetically explicit, on the other. The vowel here denoted as /ɜ/ does not contrast with /ʌ/, /ɪ/ or /ɛ/ but it is phonetically different from those in that it is a central vowel. Thus, compromising our principles of phonemic analysis, we use /ɜ/ here for the sake of the phonetic explicitness of our transcription. A less explicit and more rigorously systematic phonemic transcription might well disregard the phonetic difference (it is, after all, not a greater one than that found between the allophones of other phonemes) and analyse the central vowel as a pre-/r/ realisation of /ʌ/, /ɪ/ or /ɛ/. We shall come across more instances of the same problem shortly. In terms of phoneme theory, the problem is one whose surface we have only just scratched: if we had decided against the use of /ɜ/, then which symbol would we have used for this vowel, /ʌ/, /ɪ/ or /ɛ/? This question has theoretical implications to which we shall return in a later chapter.

### 3.4.3 *General American*

In GA, *word*, *bird* and *heard* rhyme (as in the variant of SSE just discussed). Again we use the symbol /ɜ/ for the central vowel present in all three words – and again we are faced with the same problem: /ɜ/ does not contrast with the GA phonemes /ʌ/, /ɪ/ and /ɛ/ in this context. We choose /ɜ/ for reasons of phonetic explicitness, once more noting the theoretical problem that this decision raises. Note, incidentally, that our choice of /ir/ for *here* (and some other choices) is equally unjustified in terms of contrast: given that /i/ and /ɪ/ do not contrast in this context, how can we be sure that the phoneme in question is /i/ rather than /ɪ/?

Few GA speakers have the /ɔr/–/or/ contrast in *sport – short*; many rhyme these two words but may nevertheless maintain the contrast in *morning – mourning*. For those who do not have the contrast at all, we assume the lower one of the two phonemes – /ɔ/ – in both. (But note again the same problem!) Comparing SSE and GA, we notice that the suspension of phonemic contrasts before /r/ follows a regular pattern: SSE speakers may have no /ʌ/–/ɪ/–/ɛ/ contrast; GA speakers never have this contrast and in addition may collapse /o/ and /ɔ/. As we shall see, this pattern is continued in RP.

A note, finally, on the realisation of the vowel-plus-/r/ sequences in GA. Due to the frequently retroflex character of /r/ in GA with comparatively open approximation, the vowel and /r/ are often merged into what may well appear to be a single sound segment: an *r*-coloured vowel. This is particularly apparent in the case of /ɜ/ plus /r/, where the *r*-coloured vowel is often transcribed as [ɝ]; several other vowels behave in the same way.

### 3.4.4 *Received Pronunciation*

As we saw in section 3.4.1 above, RP in nonrhotic: it does not permit /r/ to occur in syllable rhymes. This property gives rise to several phonemes in addition to the basic RP system; but also, it reduces the number of basic vowel contrasts in this context. The problems that such absence of contrasts raises in terms of phoneme theory were discussed in connection with SSE and GA; this discussion will not be repeated here.

In addition to the basic vowel system, RP has the following vowel phonemes: /ɪə/ in *here*, *beer* (contrast *bee* /i/), /ɛə/ in *hair*, *bear* (contrast *bay* /e/), /ʊə/ in *sure*, *cure* (contrast *shoe* /u/). As the second elements of these diphthongs are central vowels, these phonemes are referred to as the **centring diphthongs** of RP. In historical terms, these originate in most instances from the loss of rhyme-/r/ and are therefore often associated with *r*-spellings; but there are also instances of these phonemes that are not connected with historic /r/: *idea*, *diarrhoea* /ɪə/, *Eritrea* /ɛə/, *skua* /ʊə/. In such words, the diphthong is the result of the contraction of two syllables, which is more common in some words than it is in others: while very few RP speakers have three syllables in *idea* ([aɪ.di.ə], where dots mark syllable boundaries), preferring instead the bisyllabic pronunciation [aɪ.dɪə], most speakers will resist, for example, the contraction of *skua* [skju.ə] to monosyllabic [skjʊə] anywhere but in casual speech. Centring diphthongs not associated with (historic) /r/ result from such contraction; in noncontracted forms, where the two vowel segments are in separate syllables, we analyse these as two separate vowel phonemes in sequence: a member of the basic system (/i/, /e/ or /u/) plus /ə/.

Like GA and a variant of SSE, RP rhymes *word*, *bird* and *heard*. The vowel is /ɜ/, as in GA, but without following /r/ or *r*-colouring. *Sport* and *short* rhyme; the vowel phoneme in both is the same as that in *Shaw* (/ɔ/ of the basic system). *Car* rhymes with *Shah* – again a member of the basic system. Many RP speakers do not have the centring diphthong /ʊə/. For those speakers, *Shaw*, *shore* and *sure* are homophones: /ʃɔ/.

When we compare SSE, GA and RP we note that a tendency towards the suspension of certain vowel contrasts, already present in SSE and even more in GA, is continued in RP: GA has no contrast of /ʌ/, /ɪ/ and /ɛ/ before rhyme-/r/ and the additional tendency also to collapse /o/ and /ɔ/. RP goes a step further in the same direction: as in GA, the /ʌ/–/ɪ/–/ɛ/ contrast is suspended; suspension of the /o/–/ɔ/ contrast is compulsory; and in addition, there is the tendency to collapse /ʊə/ and /ɔ/.

As was stated in section 3.4.1, nonrhotic accents do have postvocalic /r/ if it is at the same time part of a syllable onset rather than a rhyme; in other words, if it is intervocalic. Thus, words such as *hearing, herring, hurry* etc. contain /r/ in RP as they do, of course, in all other accents. We shall not go into the details of the vowel system in this particular context; a few remarks will suffice.

The vowel phonemes that occur in this context are essentially those of the basic system rather than the ones of the secondary system given in table 3.5. Thus we can get /ɪr/ (*lyrics*), /ɛr/ (*herring*), /ʌr/ (*hurry*), /ar/ (*marry*) etc. But not all contrasts of the basic system occur before /r/ – there is no /o/–/ɔ/–/ɒ/ contrast, only /ɔ/ (*boring*). The centring diphthongs of the secondary system tend to occur in *hearing, Mary* and *jury*.

Intervocalic /r/ occurs in RP not just in the middle of words; in connected speech, it is also found in word-final position if the next word begins with a vowel. In *far and wide*, for example, /r/ occurs in connected speech: /fɑr/; similarly, /r/ occurs in *here and there, sure of* etc. In such cases, /r/ forms a syllable with the following vowel in connected speech and therefore occurs in a syllable onset – such syllabification across word boundaries is a general feature of the phonology of connected speech in English, discussed in detail in chapter 9 below. The phenomenon of /r/ occurring in this context is usually referred to as **linking** /**r**/.

In addition, /r/ can be inserted intervocalically where it is not for historical reasons expected; that is, where it is not present in the spelling. Such **intrusive** /**r**/ is found in word-final position in phrases such as *Shah of Persia* /ʃɑr/, *law and order* /lɔr/, *the idea is* /aɪdɪər/; word-medially it can occur in *drawing* /drɔrɪŋ/. Note that rhotic accents have the equivalent of linking /r/ as a matter of course (simply because such accents realise every /r/ present in the spelling); but intrusive /r/ is very rare in such accents. We shall return to linking and intrusive /r/ in section 9.3.2 below.

### 3.5 Unstressed and low-stressed syllables: schwa and some other vowels

Our study of English vowel phonemes has so far been entirely concerned with vowels occurring in fully stressed syllables: most of our examples have been drawn from monosyllabic nouns, verbs or adjectives, all of which bear full stress under normal circumstances. However, when a word consists of more than one syllable, only one syllable will bear full stress: consider *'animal, ca'lamity, 'little* and such like (where the stressed syllable is marked by a preceding '''). It is only in such stressed syllables that we may expect the full set of vowel phonemes discussed above to occur; in unstressed syllables, the range of vowel contrasts is severely restricted. We deal in this section with this restricted set of vowels.

Stress will be discussed in some detail in chapter 7 below; but (anticipating some of this discussion) we may note now that this is not a strictly binary phenomenon: syllables may have different degrees of stress. Consider words such as *'nightin,gale, ,intro'duction, ,kanga'roo*. Each of these contains one fully stressed syllable, one syllable with lower stress (marked ',') and one or more totally unstressed syllables. This three-way stress differentiation in words is not only easily perceived; it is also relevant to the range of vowels that may be expected to occur in any given syllable. As we shall see, syllables with lower ('secondary') stress may contain the same, full range of vowel phonemes that occurs in syllables with full ('primary') stress; but in unstressed syllables most vowel contrasts are absent. We begin by exemplifying the RP vowel phonemes that occur under secondary stress and then turn to unstressed syllables.

| | |
|---|---|
| /i/: | *'necta,rine, 'mezza,nine, 'gaber,dine* (for those speakers who do not have the opposite, secondary–primary, stress pattern in such items) |
| /ɪ/: | *'aste,risk, 'pia,nist* |
| /e/: | *'nightin,gale, 'caba,ret, 'Tro,pez, 'tou,pee* |
| /ɛ/: | *'palimp,sest, 'may,hem, 'con,tent* (noun), *'pro,test* (noun) |
| /ɑ/: | *'El,gar, 'samo,var, 'camou,flage* |
| /a/: | *'alma,nac, 'mani,ac, 'gym,nast* |
| /u/: | *'came,roon, 've,nue, 'me,nu* |
| /ʊ/: | *'mush,room* |
| /o/: | *'came,o, 'mot,to, 've,to, 'bin,go* |
| /ʌ/: | *,un'even, ,un'fair* etc., *'cor,puscle, ,ump'teen* |
| /ɔ/: | *'ven,dor* |
| /ɒ/: | *'alco,hol, 'e,thos, 'ther,mos* |
| /aɪ/: | *'rab,bi, 'ali,bi, 'cac,ti* |
| /aʊ/: | *'Mat,thau, 'Lin,dau* |
| /ɔɪ/: | *'al,loy, 'tan,noy* |

The vowel phonemes listed here as occurring under secondary stress constitute the full range that we established in primary-stressed syllables. Note that in the case of /aʊ/, a gap could only be avoided by resorting to proper names: some of the basic vowel phonemes are poorly attested under secondary stress. We conclude that there is no reason to suppose that under secondary stress the inventory of vowel phonemes is systematically restricted. As we shall see, entirely unstressed syllables present a different picture.

The most common vowel in unstressed syllables – indeed, probably the most common vowel of the language – is the central vowel /ə/, often referred to as **schwa**. Schwa is, in terms of its articulation, neither high nor low, neither front nor back. It is a vowel produced with a neutral setting of the articulators and is in this respect a 'minimal' vowel, involving, as it does, no displacement of the articulators from the neutral position. Schwa can occur in open and closed syllables (*sofa, China, London, hammock*), word-initially (*about, oblige, affect*), word-medially (*pedestal*) and word-finally (again *sofa, China*). It may be the only vowel of an unstressed word: *the, a, an*. In some contexts – before word-final sonorant consonants – it is rather elusive: *button, little* etc. either have schwa in their final syllables – /bʌtən/ – or the final syllables contain syllabic consonants – that is, consonants making up the peak element of the syllable – instead of having vowels in that position: /bʌtn̩/.

The realisation of /ə/ is subject to some variation in all accents. On the whole, it is lower in word-final position (*sofa*) than it is word-medially (*purest, pedestal*). This is especially true for SSE, where the final vowels in *sofa, China*, as well as the initial vowels in *about, alert* etc. have a phonetic quality rather similar to [ʌ]. Note, however, that [ə] and [ʌ] never contrast in unstressed syllables: no accent of English has minimal pairs of the form [sofə] – [sofʌ]. The [ʌ]-like vowel found in SSE *sofa* etc. is clearly a realisation of /ə/. This is not to say that the phonemic status of /ə/ is without problems – we shall discuss those below.

Schwa does contrast, in all accents of English, with /ɪ/ where it occurs in word-final position: *sofa – Sophie, pitta* (bread) *– pity* etc. In some accents the contrast is also found before consonants, as in *purest – purist, affect – effect, accept – except*. But in many words, the lexical distribution of the two phonemes is variable in this context: *bracelet, goodness, duchess* and many others may well have either /ə/ or /ɪ/ in their final syllables. *Family* may have /ɪ/ before the /l/ (like *homily*) or schwa. Especially SSE and younger RP speakers, as well as all speakers in casual speech, seem to prefer /ə/ in many cases where conservative RP speakers, or more formal speech, would favour /ɪ/. In GA the /ə/–/ɪ/ contrast before consonants is all but obliterated: any occurrence of /ɪ/ in this context is highly sporadic and speaker-specific.

Given that the full vowel phonemes discussed earlier in this chapter occur only in stressed syllables and schwa only in totally unstressed syllables, the phonemic status of the latter raises some questions. Taking stress into account, schwa is in complementary distribution with all other vowels (except /ɪ/): where schwa can occur, no other vowel can, and vice versa. There are no minimal pairs contrasting schwa with any vowel other than /ɪ/. We are therefore, strictly speaking, not entitled to call schwa a phoneme of English: schwa occurs where all vowel contrasts (except the one with /ɪ/) are suspended. Recall that we came across the same problem – the suspension of certain vowel contrasts – in section 3.4 above, when we were studying vowels before /r/. This is a major issue in phoneme theory, to which we shall return in chapter 8 below; for the moment, we take a methodological short-cut and continue to call schwa a phoneme, /ə/, bearing in mind that we have not been able to justify this decision.

Let us return finally (and briefly) to the notion of stress. We have established that under secondary stress all vowel phonemes can occur, while in unstressed syllables only schwa and /ɪ/ are possible. The question is, how reliable is our perception of this difference in nonprimary stress? Can we be certain that, as we have been assuming, the last syllables in *almanac* and *asterisk* have secondary stress while those in *purest*, *purist* are unstressed? Is it possible at all, in a bisyllabic word, to determine whether the syllable that does not bear primary stress has secondary stress or no stress at all? Our analysis has been based on the assumption that it is; but we have to acknowledge that the argument is in danger of circularity. The range of possible vowels is not only determined by stress, the perception of stress is also determined by vowel quality. Hence we say, on the one hand, that a full vowel such as /o/ is permitted in the second syllable in *veto* because that syllable has secondary stress; and on the other hand, we perceive that syllable as having secondary stress because it contains a full vowel. What this clearly calls for is a fuller discussion of what we mean by 'stress'. This discussion will have to wait until chapter 7.

### 3.6 Phonemic symbols and phonetic content

We conclude this chapter with a brief review of the phonemic symbols that have been introduced in it. This review will consist of a defence of the choice of symbols made here, as well as of a description of their typical phonetic content in the three reference accents.

Given our definition of the phoneme, an adequate phonemic transcription must follow three principles. First, such a transcription must be **phonemically systematic** by having a separate symbol for every phoneme and, of course, by using the same symbol for each occurrence of a given phoneme. This, as we saw in chapter 2, follows from the nature of the phonemic level of representation. Second, an adequate phonemic transcription should be **free of redundancies** in its symbol inventory. This characteristic also reflects the nature of phonemic representations: given that in our understanding such representations contain no predictable information, it would follow that the notational devices used for such representations should be similarly redundancy-free. And third, a phonemic transcription attempts to be as **phonetically explicit** as possible, for example by using symbols in accordance with established phonetic conventions (such as the principles of the International Phonetic Association) – without, however, needlessly complicating the symbols that it employs. The last two principles are in conflict: the second one may be compromised by the third one, and vice versa. Different authors use different transcriptions depending on whether they come down in favour of simplicity (that is, lack of redundancy) or of explicitness.

To exemplify this point, let us return to the pairs of vowel phonemes that were suggested in section 3.3.1, such as those in RP/GA *beat – bit, pool – pull*. Given that in RP and GA the members of each such pair are distinct in terms of length as well as quality, the following methods of transcription come to mind:

(13)  a.  /i/–/ɪ/     b.  /iː/–/i/     c.  /iː/–/ɪ/
          /u/–/ʊ/         /uː/–/u/      /uː/–/ʊ/

All three of these methods are found in the phonological literature of English (and more exist, which need not concern us at this point). Example (13a) is the method used in this book. It avoids redundancy by utilising, in the transcription, only one of the two features that differentiate the members of such pairs: (13a) expresses differences in vowel quality through the use of different symbols for the members of any given pair, but it makes no statement of the accompanying length differences. Example (13b) takes the opposite approach: here, the length difference is utilised to express the contrast – the symbol ':' indicates 'long' – but no mention is made of the quality differences among the members of pairs. Note that this method is even more economical, in terms of symbol inventories, than that exemplified in (13a): three symbols ('i', 'u' and ':') are used here to identify the four members of the two pairs, while (13a) needs four symbols ('i', 'ɪ', 'u' and 'ʊ'), two of which are somewhat exotic. Example (13c), finally, is a combination of the other two, in that it expresses both the length distinction and the quality distinction in each pair. This method is maximally (perhaps, depending on the writer's objectives, optimally) explicit in phonetic terms; but since it is clearly not redundancy-free it is inconsistent with our understanding of phonemic representations. This leaves us with (13a, b) as serious candidates for the phonemic-transcription method to be used in this book. Why, then, are we using (13a) rather than (13b), even at the cost of having to introduce more symbols than (13b) would necessitate?

The reason lies in a fourth principle pursued in the phonemic transcriptions of this book: an attempt is made here to avoid, as far as possible, differences in phonemic transcription between the three reference accents RP, GA and SSE – and, as we saw above, method (13b) is unusable in SSE simply because no phonemic length differences can possibly be posited among the vowels of that accent. And using (13a) for SSE while transcribing RP/GA vowel phonemes in terms of (13b) would be somewhat inconvenient; moreover, we shall see in chapter 4, where this theme will be taken up again from a phonological rather than merely notational perspective, that vowel-length differences can in RP and GA just as easily be derived from underlying differences in vowel quality as they can be in SSE. This is not to say, however, that differences in vowel quality must in *all* accents be treated as the underlying ones, and length differences as redundant: as we shall see in section 3.7 below, the vowel-pair distinctions found in some accents of English are clearly length-based. Indeed, an alternative, length-based phonemic analysis of vowel pairs in RP and GA would not be unreasonable: the vowel systems of these two accents constitute a border-line case in a typology of length-based vs. quality-based English systems. The economy requirement forces us to come down on one side or the other; and we come down on the quality side for convenience, as well as for other reasons that will be discussed in chapter 4.

A similar argument was anticipated in section 3.3.1 above with regard to our representation of /e/ and /o/. These two phonemes have diphthongal realisations in RP and (in most contexts) in GA; but in SSE they are monophthongs. We saw that there are various systemic reasons for treating them as underlyingly monophthongal in all three accents; but our transcription principles of economy and cross-accent uniformity alone require us to adopt the notations /e/ and /o/ throughout. The only alternative would be to adopt /eɪ/ and /oʊ/ throughout; and in terms of symbol economy it clearly makes more sense to say '/e/ has a diphthongal realisation in RP' than it does to say '/eɪ/ has a monophthongal realisation in SSE'.

We must bear in mind, then, that economy of symbols (especially when it is applied across accents) may seriously compromise the phonetic explicitness of phonemic transcriptions. We have to spell out more details regarding the actual pronunciation of any given phoneme in different accents than we would have to if our transcriptions already contained more such phonetic detail (thereby being not only more cumbersome but also less uniform across the three reference accents).

Below are some guidelines for the phonetic interpretation of our phonemic vowel symbols. For the phonetic description of vowel sounds in general, the reader is referred back to section 1.2.2.

/i/   is a high front unrounded vowel similar to CV [i] but neither as high nor as front as the CV. It may be slightly diphthongised as [ɪi] in GA and RP.

/ɪ/   is similar to /i/ but less high and less front, on the whole more centralised. In GA and RP it is also of shorter duration than /i/ in comparable contexts (compare *beat* and *bit*). In SSE it can be considerably lower than in other accents.

/e/   is similar to CV [e] but not quite as front. As was discussed above, the phoneme so denoted is realised as the diphthong [eɪ] in RP and GA although in the latter not before rhyme-/r/ (*hair, scarce*). Recall the discussion of this symbol earlier in this section.

/ɛ/   is lower than /e/, similar to CV [ɛ] but more central. In RP and GA, it is also shorter than /e/ in comparable contexts (compare *bait – bet*).

/ɑ/   of RP and GA is low back unrounded, similar to CV [ɑ] (although the degree of backness varies).

/a/   is a low front unrounded vowel in the vicinity of CV [a]. It may vary considerably in height, however: conservative RP speakers may have realisations only slightly lower than CV [ɛ], while in Northern English speech it is very low and often slightly backed. In GA it is somewhat higher than CV [a] but less high than in conservative RP. The alternative symbol /æ/ is often used in descriptions of RP and GA to indicate a typical realisation that is higher than CV [a]; but for reasons of simplicity and cross-accent uniformity, this symbol is not adopted here. In GA and RP, /a/ is shorter than /ɑ/ in comparable contexts (*Sam – psalm*).

In SSE, /a/ denotes the phoneme that replaces the /a/–/ɑ/ contrast of other accents. It is a low unrounded vowel, often half-way between front and back but subject to considerable variation along the front–back dimension.

/u/   is a high back rounded vowel though not as far back as CV [u]. Especially in SSE, it may be considerably fronted while retaining its rounding, while in RP it is increasingly centralised. Slight diphthongisation to [ʊu] is common, though not in SSE.

/ʊ/   of GA and RP is also classed as a high back rounded vowel but it is less round, much lower and more central than /u/. It is shorter than /u/ in comparable contexts (*pool – pull*). SSE does not have this phoneme.

/o/   Classed as a mid back rounded vowel similar to CV [o], this phoneme is always diphthongal in RP, ranging from (conservative) [oʊ] to (more modern) [əʊ]. In GA its realisation is diphthongal [oʊ] except before rhyme-/r/ (*short*); and in SSE it is invariably monophthongal. Recall the discussion of this symbol at the beginning of this section.

/ʌ/   This phoneme has a wide range of realisations in the accents of English. All of these are unrounded and slightly more back than front. In RP it is almost fully low (and, especially for conservative speakers, back) while in other accents, especially in the English Midlands, it may be considerably higher.

/ɔ/   is a low-to-mid back rounded vowel, similar to CV [ɔ]. In (especially modern) RP it tends to be higher than in other accents, half-way towards CV [o].

/ɒ/   is part of the RP inventory only. It is slightly lower and less rounded than RP /ɔ/. In comparable contexts it is also shorter than /ɔ/ (*caught – cot*).

/ɜ/   is part of the inventories of RP, GA and a variety of SSE. It is almost exactly central (neither high nor low, neither front nor back) and neutral with respect to rounding.

/ə/,   often referred to as 'schwa', is a central vowel of almost identical quality to /ɜ/; but it occurs in unstressed syllables only. (For a discussion of its phonemic status see section 3.5 above.) It is shorter than /ɜ/ and may, in words such as *button, little*, be entirely dropped.

/aɪ/   in RP and GA begins as a low vowel, slightly retracted from CV [a] and ends somewhat below the position identified for /ɪ/ above. In SSE, this phoneme has two allo-phones governed by the Scottish Vowel-Length Rule (see sect. 3.3.3 above and, more fully, ch. 8 below): a 'short' one best described as ranging from [aɪ] to [ʌi], and a 'long' one: [aˑɪ].

/aʊ/ in RP and GA glides from a low rather back position to a point somewhat short of that associated above with /ʊ/. In London speech as well as the Southern and East Coast United States the first element may be front and the second element reduced or lost. In SSE the typical realisation of /aʊ/ is [ʌʊ].

/ɔɪ/ glides from low-to-mid back rounded towards mid-to-high front unrounded. The starting point may be higher – [oɪ] – in SSE and some varieties of GA.

The phonetic qualities of the centring diphthongs /ɪə ɛə ʊə/ may be derived from the interpretations of the symbols given above.

We conclude this section by plotting the vowel phonemes (more prec-isely: their typical realisations) on the vowel trapezium familiar from section 1.2.2. In figure 3.3 is one such diagram for each of the three reference accents.

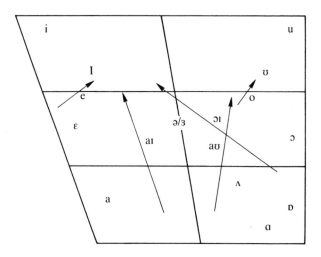

Figure 3.3a   Typical realisations of Received Pronunciation vowel phonemes

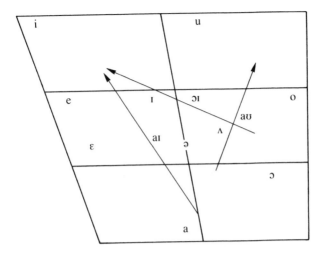

Figure 3.3b   Typical realisations of Scottish Standard English vowel phonemes

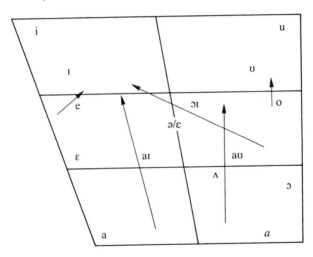

Figure 3.3c   Typical realisations of General American vowel phonemes

### 3.7   *Appendix:* Some more accents of English

To conclude this introduction to some of the vowel systems of English we turn briefly to some further accents: to those spoken in **Australia, New Zealand, South Africa** and **Southern** and **Northern Ireland**.

These will here be only briefly, and somewhat superficially, described; they will not serve as 'reference accents' in the chapters that follow – in fact, nothing further will be said about them beyond this chapter.

Why, then, are these accents brought into the discussion at all, and why these particular ones? There are several reasons. Firstly, the native speaker of one of these accents – and, for mainly geographical reasons, particularly one of *these* accents – will undoubtedly have encountered some problems in relating his or her own vowel inventory to those of RP, GA or SSE discussed in the main part of this chapter. While, for example, a speaker from the English West Country can be safely assumed to have at least a passive familiarity with RP, and one from Canada to have a good deal of acquaintance with GA, there is no particular reason why a South African speaker should readily relate to RP, GA or SSE, if only for the purpose of learning about the phonology of English: in purely geographical terms, that speaker is rather remote from all of these accents.

Secondly, RP, GA and SSE are in no way more 'central' to the phonology of English than other accents are. They serve here as *types* of English, representing different points in an accent typology that can be drawn up within this rather heterogeneous linguistic entity that we conventionally – and conveniently – call 'English'. Other accents not only deserve a mention in a book of this kind for completeness' sake; their discussion will also provide a background against which the typological status of the reference accents will become evident.

### 3.7.1 *Australian, New Zealand and South African English*

These three accents may be grouped together in that all three of them are typologically closer to RP than to GA or SSE in one sense, and closer to RP *and* GA than to SSE in another sense. Firstly, all three of them are **nonrhotic** like RP but unlike GA and SSE. And secondly, in all three accents, pairs of vowel phonemes such as the ones in *beat – bit, bait – bet* etc. display **distinctive vowel length**, which makes them conform with the RP/GA type but not with the type represented by SSE: as we saw earlier, RP and GA have distinctive vowel length as well as distinctive vowel quality, while in SSE such pairs of vowel phonemes are distinct in terms of quality alone. We shall return to such typological matters later in this appendix.

We shall deal here exclusively with the systems of stressed vowels found in the accents under discussion, disregarding unstressed vowels and also those (stressed or unstressed) vowels occurring in the vicinity of (historic or

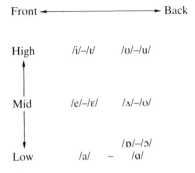

Figure 3.4   The RP system

actual) /r/. The RP basic system (excluding the 'true diphthongs') is repeated in figure 3.4 for comparison.

### 3.7.1.1   *Australian and New Zealand English*

There are no major phonemic differences between these accents and RP: both the Australian and – with one possible exception – the New Zealand basic vowel system are the same as the RP one, if only in terms of the number of phonemes they contain. But there are notable realisational differences, which warrant a different transcription of phonemes and also in some cases a different classification in terms of the high–low and front–back dimensions. We deal with the 'long' vowels (*beat, bait, boot* etc.) first and then turn to their 'short' counterparts in the system.

All nonlow 'long' vowels have typically diphthongal realisations – a feature that may also be observed as a tendency (albeit as a slighter one) in RP. The typical realisations of these phonemes are, roughly, as follows:

(14)  /i/ → [ɪi] ~ [əi]          /u/ → [u] ~ [əʊ]
     /e/ → [ɛɪ] ~ [ʌɪ]          /o/ → [əu] ~ [ʌʊ]

These typical realisations highlight the rather abstract nature of the qualities denoted by our phonemic symbols, as well as of our assumption that these vowels are 'underlyingly' monophthongs: their diphthongal realisation is as invariable, and the quality difference between first and second elements in some cases as great, as that of the 'true diphthongs'. The latter are rather more similar to their RP counterparts than those given above are:

(15)  /aɪ/ → [ɑɪ]
     /aʊ/ → [aʊ] ~ [æo]
     /ɔɪ/ → [ɔɪ]

Of the 'long' low vowels, /ɔ/ displays no notable difference from its RP counterpart, but the Australian/New Zealand counterpart of RP /ɑ/ requires comment. It is a low vowel, as in RP, but it is front rather than back. Below are the typical realisations – we retain for the moment the underlying characterisations.

(16)  /ɔ/ → [ɔː]
     /ɑ/ → [aː]

Of the 'short' vowels, the back series /ʊ ʌ ɒ/ (*put, putt, pot*) are not significantly different in their typical realisations from their RP counterparts – note that the phonemic status of the *pot* vowel is the same as that of its RP counterpart: distinct from the *port/caught* vowel (unlike in SSE) and from the *part/psalm* vowel (unlike in GA).

But the realisations of the front series (*bit, bet, bat*) require some discussion. The last two of these are significantly higher than they are in RP:

(17)  /a/ → [æ] ~ [ɛ]
     /ɛ/ → [e]

The *bit* vowel constitutes what is perhaps the most important difference between the Australian and New Zealand accents: while in the former variety this vowel too is realised higher than in RP, thus following the pattern established for *bet* and *bat* above, its New Zealand counterpart is a central rather than high vowel which fails to contrast with (unstressed) schwa – an analytical problem that we here ignore. Hence the typical realisations of this phoneme are as follows (where the 'umlaut' sign '¨' indicates centralisation):

(18)  /ɪ/ →  { [i] (Aus.)
              { [ə] ~ [ï] (NZ)

These observations cast some doubt on the appropriateness of our phonemic symbols in the transcription of Australian and New Zealand vowels: there are severe discrepancies between what is standardly denoted by our phonemic symbols and the typical realisations of these phonemes in these varieties of English. If we maintain those symbols then we uphold the systematic and economical nature of our transcription; but we compromise severely on the side of its phonetic explicitness – recall what was said on this topic in section 3.6. We might, of course, alter our transcription strategy radically at this point and opt for maximal phonetic explicitness, simply enclosing the symbols used for the 'typical realisations' in phonemic brackets:/ɪi/, /ɛɪ/, /ʌʊ/ etc. But as we saw in section 3.6, such a radical change would be inconsistent with the rather abstract notion of the phoneme assumed here. Instead, we continue to operate with a phonemic transciption that is biased towards systematicity and symbol economy. Consider the following preliminary solution:

(19)   'Long' vowel phonemes        'Short' vowel phonemes

| /i/ | /u/ | /ɪ/ | /ʊ/ |
|-----|-----|-----|-----|
| /e/ | /o/ | /ɛ/ | /ʌ/ |
| /a/ | /ɔ/ | /æ/ | /ɒ/ |

As a minor adjustment, the *Sam* vowel is now represented as /æ/ rather than /a/, expressing its typically higher realisation than in (most of) our reference accents. The only major adjustment is that the *psalm* vowel is appropriately classed as low front /a/. Note that this symbol is available for this vowel since its short counterpart (*Sam*) is now denoted /æ/.

What is less than attractive about this solution is that it entails a rather strikingly inconsistent use of symbols on the two different levels of representation: for example, /æ/ may be realised as [ɛ], while /ɛ/ is typically [e] and /e/ something else in turn. This problem may be overcome by using a quantity-based transcription, of the kind exemplified in (13b) above, instead: then, we would get the following picture:

(20)   'Long' vowel phonemes        'Short' vowel phonemes

| /iː/ | /uː/ | /i/ | /u/ |
|------|------|-----|-----|
| /eː/ | /oː/ | /e/ | /ʌ/ |
| /aː/ | /ɔː/ | /æ/ | /ɔ/ |

Note that this solution is still rather economical – and somewhat abstract – in that it disregards the diphthongal qualities with which some of the 'long' phonemes typically surface. Such a solution is, perhaps, the ideal compromise in respect of our particular expectations of a phonemic transcription system; however, it poses an interesting problem. This transcription suggests that there is a major typological difference between RP/GA and Australian/New Zealand English with respect to precisely that feature which above was said to be shared by RP/GA and Australian/New Zealand English: above we said that these varieties of English (but not SSE) have distinctive vowel length in common; now it emerges that this feature is expressed, as the underlying dichotomiser, in the Australian/New Zealand systems but *not* in the RP/GA ones.

The problem clearly rests with our transcription of the RP/GA vowel systems. These systems make use of length *and* quality distinctions in their vowel pairs, those of Australian/New Zealand English, as we have just seen, of length alone (and that of SSE of quality alone). RP/GA, then, are typologically ambiguous; and a decision has to be made as to which of the two features, length or quality, is the more basic one in RP/GA vowel contrasts. Our choice of a quality-based transcription has anticipated this decision, which will be discussed in more detail in chapter 4 below: we shall see there that the quality distinctions within vowel pairs are indeed the more basic ones, as the transcription suggests. For the moment, then, we acknowledge that RP/GA belong with both the 'quality type' and the 'length type' in that their vowel contrasts express both features; but they will be shown in chapter 4 to have a closer affinity with the 'quality type' (and therefore with SSE), thus vindicating our choice of transcription.

### 3.7.1.2 *South African English*

South African English shares with Australian/New Zealand English the feature of **nonrhoticness**, as well as that of **distinctive vowel length**. As we saw above, RP and GA also share the latter feature; but those accents are – *unlike* Australian/New Zealand and South African English – also characterised by **distinctive vowel quality** in pairs such as *beat – bit* etc.

In the subsystem of 'long' vowel phonemes, two features distinguish South African English from other systems with distinctive vowel length. Firstly, the high vowels (*beet, boot*) are diphthongised to a far lesser extent than they are in Australian/New Zealand English and perhaps even in RP. Secondly, the *psalm* vowel is extremely back (unlike in Australian/New Zealand, where it is front, and more so than in RP/GA) and for many 'broad' speakers slightly rounded. The other members of this subsystem are similar in their realisations to their RP counterparts: the mid vowels (*bait, boat*) are invariably diphthongised; and the *caught* vowel is mid rather than low, approximating [oː] for some speakers similar to modern RP. It is therefore distinct from the vowel in *psalm, cart* even where that vowel is rounded. The typical realisations of the members of this subsystem are (roughly) as those in (21) below; note that the phonemic representations carry length marks similar to the ones devised for Australian/New Zealand English in section 3.7.1.1 above. The reasons for this will become clear presently.

(21)   'Long' vowel phonemes
        /iː/ → [iː]        /uː/ → [uː]
        /eː/ → [əɪ]       /oː/ → [əʊ]
                         /ɔː/ → [ɔː] ~ [oː]
                         /ɑː/ → [ɑː] ~ [ɒː]

In the subsystem of short vowel phonemes, the back series (*put, putt, pot*) is unremarkable, similar in realisation to that found in RP and Australian/ New Zealand English. In the front series, both the vowel of *bat, Sam* and that of *bet* are comparatively higher than in RP, similar to Australian/New Zealand English. But the *kit/bit* vowel – or vowels – constitute what is probably a unique feature of South African English.

As we saw in section 3.7.1.1, *kit/bit* are pronounced with an extremely high front vowel [i] in Australian English and with a central vowel [ə] ~ [ï] in New Zealand – this was noted as the most reliable distinguishing feature of those two varieties. In South African English, the *kit* vowel is likely to be [i] and the *bit* vowel [ï]. The phonemic status of these two South African English vowels is not altogether clear; and it certainly cannot be established without reference to the subsystem of unstressed vowels. Recall from section 3.5 above that the phonemic status of unstressed /ɪ/–/ə/ in RP is far from unproblematical. Confining ourselves to stressed vowels, it seems safe to state that [i] occurs in the vicinity of velar consonants (*kit, pick, sing*) as well as after /h/ (*hit*) and word-initially (*inn*), while in complementary contexts [ə] ~ [ï] is likely to occur: *bit, lip, slim*. This would make [i] and [ə] allophones of the same phoneme: these two sounds do not contrast (in stressed syllables), given their complementary distribution – where [i] occurs [ə] cannot occur, and vice versa. In stressed positions, [i] and [ə] do not contrast. Bearing in mind the possibility that problems may occur in the phonemicisation of unstressed vowels, we may state the (stressed) sub-system of vowel phonemes in South African English as follows:

(22)  '*Short*' *vowel phonemes*

| /ɪ/ → | { | [i] | /ʊ/ → [ʊ] |
| | | [ə] | |
| /e/ → | | [e] | /ʌ/ → /ʌ/ ~ [ä] |
| /æ/ → | | [æ] ~ [ɛ] | /ɒ/ → [ɒ] |

The South African English counterparts of the 'true diphthongs' found in other accents (*bite, bout, boy* etc.) are listed below:

(23)  '*True (?) diphthongs*'
  /aɪ/ → [aɪ] ~ [a:]
  /aʊ/ → [ɑʊ] ~ [aʊ]
  /ɔɪ/ → [ɔɪ]

Notably, the *bite* vowel frequently has a monophthongal low front realisation in 'broad' South African English; for such speakers, this vowel is perhaps better grouped, like /a:/, with the long monophthongs ((21) above), where it contrasts with low back /ɑ:/. The term 'true diphthong' is therefore inaccurate for South African English if applied to the whole class of three vowel phonemes.

### 3.7.2 *Hiberno-English: Southern and Northern*

The accents of English spoken in Ireland fall into two distinct groups: Southern and Northern Hiberno-English ('Ulster English'). In geographical terms, this division is related to the political division between the Republic of Ireland and the UK province of Northern Ireland; however, accents associated with the Northern Irish group are also spoken in certain areas of the Republic (namely, in those formerly part of the historic province of Ulster, which includes present-day Northern Ireland as well as some parts of the Republic). The linguistic division into Southern and Northern accents is a sharp one. Although both are **rhotic**, the two groups of accents are rather far apart in typological terms. The former is historically derived from Southern (or perhaps South-Western) British accents and is, consequently, of the type here represented by RP (and, in view of its rhoticness, GA): its vowel pairs are distinct in terms of length and quality. The latter group is historically more closely related to Scots and is typologically on a par with Scottish Standard English in terms of its basic vowel system and also in the sense that vowel length has no phonemic status, pairs of vowels being distinct in terms of quality alone. We shall deal with each accent group in turn, paying little attention, however, to variation within each group.

### 3.7.2.1 *Southern Hiberno-English*

The South, exemplified here by what can be roughly characte-rised as the Dublin accent, has by and large the same vowel system as RP does (excluding, of course, those vowel phonemes of RP that are directly associated with its nonrhoticness – recall sect. 3.4.4). Differences between RP and Southern Hiberno-English are largely realisational; but in some cases such differences affect the choice of appropriate phonemic symbols and the classification of phonemes in terms of the High–Low and Front–Back dimensions.

The vowel phonemes that can only occur in closed syllables are appropriately transcribed as in (24) below, where their typical realisations are also listed:

(24)  /ɪ/ → [ɪ]                    /ʊ/ → [ʊ]
      /ɛ/ → [ɛ]                    /ʌ/ → [ʌ] ~ [ɔ̈]
      /æ/ → [æ] ~ [a]              /ɒ/ → [ɒ] ~ [ɑ]

There are two phonemes in this subsystem whose realisations can differ markedly from those of their RP counterparts. Firstly, the vowel in *putt, cut* – phonemically, as in RP, /ʌ/ – may be realised as a mid back vowel that is centralised and slightly rounded, here transcribed as [ɔ̈]. The alternative realisation as [ʌ] is found in more conservative Dublin speech. Secondly, the vowel of *pot, cot*, while phonemically transcribed /ɒ/ and possibly pronounced in that way, may be unrounded to [ɑ] in 'broad' Dublin speech. Recall from the discussion of GA (sect. 3.3.4) that this accent similarly has an unrounded low back vowel in *pot, cot*; unlike in Southern Hiberno-English, however, the /ɒ/ phoneme is entirely absent from the GA system. Compared to RP, the two phonemes /ʌ/ and /ɒ/ appear to be 'swapped over' in that the RP unrounded phoneme is rounded in broad Dublin speech and vice versa. Note, finally, that the *Sam* vowel is here transcribed /æ/. The typical realisation of this phoneme is little or no higher than it is in RP or GA; the symbol /æ/ rather than /a/ is here chosen for practical reasons: as we shall see, the /a/ symbol will be used elsewhere in the system.

As in RP, the members of the familiar pairs of vowel phonemes are distinct in Southern Hiberno-English in terms of quality as well as length: those phonemes that can occur in both open and closed syllables – and we turn to those now – are not only different in quality from their closed-syllable counterparts but also, if occurring in comparable contexts, consistently longer. Hence we get the following subsystem (again with typical realisations):

(25)  /i/ → [iː] ~ [ɪi]            /u/ → [uː] ~ [ʊu]
      /e/ → [eː]                   /o/ → [oː]
      /a/ → [aː]                   /ɔ/ → [ɔː] ~ [ɑː]

The first notable feature of this set is the monophthongal realisation of the *bait* and *boat* vowels /e/ and /o/; /i/ and /u/ (*beet, boot*) may, however, be slightly diphthongised. Secondly, /ɔ/ (*caught, thought*) is frequently unrounded to low back [ɑː], similar to the possibly unrounded realisation of /ɒ/; but in Dublin the rounded, RP-like realisation [ɔː] is said to be quite common. And finally, the *psalm* vowel is low front, distinct from the *caught* vowel even where the latter is unrounded. By transcribing the *psalm* vowel as /a/ (rather than /ɑ/) we express its frontness; the *psalm–Sam* contrast is expressed through our choice of /æ/ for the latter, whose realisation tends to be not only shorter but also somewhat higher than that of the former.

Similar to RP and GA – but rather different from the accents discussed earlier in this appendix – Southern Hiberno-English displays clear quality distinctions among the members of vowel pairs, as well as employing vowel length for the expression of these contrasts. The decision as to whether to view length or quality as the basic dichotomising feature in this accent is somewhat arbitrary; we adopt here the quality-based phonemic transcription familiar from our treatment of RP/GA simply in order to avoid the suggestion of a typological difference where there is none.

The 'true diphthongs', of *bout*, *bite*, *boy* respectively, are typically realised as follows:

(26)  /aʊ/ → [aʊ] ~ [ʌʊ]
      /aɪ/ → [ɛɪ] ~ [ʌɪ]
      /ɔɪ/ → [ɔɪ] ~ [ʌɪ]

What is remarkable about this set is that certain (archaic or rural) varieties of Southern Hiberno-English do not have the /aɪ/–/ɔɪ/ contrast; more modern (urban) varieties have introduced the distinction – without, however, necessarily following the pattern of lexical incidence found in those varieties of English where the contrast is of long standing.

### 3.7.2.2  *Ulster English*

As was noted above, the group of Northern varieties of Hiberno-English is historically related to Scots. As a result, it not only has its basic vowel system in common with SSE; it also depends entirely on **vowel quality** in its expression of pairwise vowel contrasts (of which there are considerably fewer in this system than there are in RP). Moreover, the regularities governing vowel length on the phonetic level bear a close resemblance to those of SSE.

Figure 3.5 gives the basic vowel system that Ulster English shares with SSE; we shall discuss the typical realisations of these phonemes below. Pairs such as *Sam – psalm*, *cot – caught* as well as *pull – pool* are homophones in Ulster English as they are in SSE; the phonemes /a/, /ɔ/ and /u/ take the places of the RP contrasts /a/–/ɑ/, /ɒ/–/ɔ/ and /ʊ/–/u/ respectively.

Vowel length is entirely allophonic, governed by a version of the **Scottish Vowel-Length Rule** (recall section 3.3.3.2 above): all vowel phonemes of the basic system shown in figure 3.5 except /ɪ/ and /ʌ/ are long before voiced fricatives, /r/ and at the ends of words, and short in other contexts. /ɪ/ and /ʌ/ are invariably short. Ulster English differs here from SSE in that /ɛ/ takes

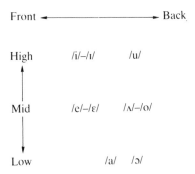

Figure 3.5   The Scottish Standard English/Ulster system

part in the Length Rule – in SSE it does so only partially, with a geographical distribution that is not fully understood. (See section 8.4.2 below for a fuller discussion of the Scottish Vowel-Length Rule.)

In addition to the long-vowel realisations predicted by the Scottish Vowel-Length Rule, the vowel phonemes /e ɛ a ɔ/ are realised long, in Ulster English, in monosyllabic words closed by consonants other than /p t k/. Examples are [bɛːd] (*bed*), [laːd] (*lad*), [kɔːd] (*cod*) – the 'long' realisation of /e/ will be discussed below. This allophonic rule, which constitutes an Ulster-specific widening of the range of 'long' contexts of the Scottish Vowel-Length Rule, overlaps with the latter in a rather complex way, which, however, need not concern us here. Suffice it to say that on the underlying (phonemic) level, all Ulster English vowel phonemes are (equally) short, and that /i u e ɛ o ɔ a/ have long allophones in one class of contexts and /e ɛ a ɔ/ in another class, where both the context classes and the class of lengthening vowels partially overlap. What Ulster English has in common with SSE, despite differences in detail, is that the familiar pairs of vowels are underlyingly distinct in terms of quality alone – not in terms of length *and* quality, as in RP, GA and Southern Hiberno-English, and not in terms of length alone, as in the accents discussed in section 3.7.1 above.

To substantiate this claim of persistent quality distinctions, let us look at the typical realisations of the phonemes given in figure 3.5, bearing in mind the length differences that may occur, in some cases, on the phonetic level. The realisations given in table 3.6 are, roughly, those found in Belfast.

The picture is further complicated by variation in the lexical incidence of phonemes – where *bull*, for example may have /ʌ/ rather than /u/, and *water* /a/ rather than /ɔ/, etc. – and by certain phonemes failing to contrast in certain contexts: for example, /a/ and /ɛ/ do not contrast before /k/, *neck* and

Table 3.6 *Ulster English vowel phonemes and their realisations*

| /i/ | → | [i:] ~ [ɪi] | long | *sneeze, see* |
| | | [i] | short | *seat* |
| /ɪ/ | → | [ï] ~ [ë] | (always short) | *bit* |
| /e/ | → | [e:] ~ [ɛ:] | long in open syllables | *way* |
| | | [e:ə] | long elsewhere | *same, save* |
| | | [eə] | short | *state* |
| /ɛ/ | → | [ɛ:] ~ [ɛə] | long | *bed* |
| | | [ɛ] | short | *bet* |
| /u/ | → | [ü:] | long | *choose* |
| | | [ü] | short | *doom* |
| /ʌ/ | → | [ʌ̈] ~ [ö] | (always short) | *putt* |
| /o/ | → | [o:] | long | *grove* |
| | | [o] | short | *boat* |
| /ɔ/ | → | [ɔ:] | long | *cause, saw* |
| | | [ɒ] ~ [ɑ] | short | *cot, stock* |
| /a/ | → | [a:] ~ [ɑ:] | long | *have, car* |
| | | [a] | short | *cat* |

*knack* being [nɛk]. Disregarding such details, we may make the following general observations concerning the Ulster English vowel system and its realisations.

First, vowel length is of no phonemic relevance in this system but is governed by allophonic rules. This has been noted already; it is confirmed by the typical realisations listed in table 3.6: while there are individual phonemes whose allophones are distinct in terms of length alone, distinctions *among* phonemes always involve quality. Second, the basic system is (as was also noted before) identical with that of SSE to the extent that not only the number of contrasts is shared but also, conveniently, the same range of phonemic symbols may be employed. Third, Ulster English shares with SSE and Southern Hiberno-English the failure to realise /e/ and /o/ as [eɪ] and [oʊ] respectively; however, the centring diphthongisation of /e/ and /ɛ/ (as [eə] and [ɛə] respectively) is Ulster-specific. And fourth, Ulster English shares with Southern Hiberno-English the possibility of rounding /ʌ/ and, conversely, of unrounding /ɔ/.

The realisations of two of the 'true diphthongs' are diagnostic of Ulster (especially Belfast) speech:

(27)  /aɪ/ → [æɪ] ~ [eɪ]
      /aʊ/ → [ɑï] ~ [eï]
      /ɔɪ/ → [ɔɪ]

The *bite* vowel, denoted /aɪ/, may have a rather strikingly high first element similar to that of the RP pronunciation of *bait* – note that the /e/–/aɪ/ contrast is preserved in Ulster speech through the absence of RP-like diphthongal realisations of the former. The *bout* vowel has realisations that differ quite sharply from what is suggested by the phonemic transcription /aʊ/: the first element of this diphthong may, especially in broad Belfast speech, be considerably higher than [a] and the second element is typically unrounded and centralised front.

**Suggested reading to chapter 3**

Sections 3.1, 3.2 Bailey and Görlach (1982), a collection of essays discussing the different varieties of English found in the world, will be interesting background reading to this chapter. On accents and dialects in the British Isles see Hughes and Trudgill (1987). On 'standard' pronunciations see Mobärg (1989). Wells (1982: ch. 1) gives a detailed introduction to phonological variation. RP is defined and discussed in Wells (1982: sects. 2.1.2, 4.1), GA in Wells (1982: sects. 2.1.3, 6.1), SSE in Wells (1982: sect. 5.2) and in Abercrombie (1979). Pronouncing dictionaries are useful for readers who are not thoroughly familiar with the reference accents: Jones (1977) and Wells (1990) for RP, Kenyon and Knott (1953) for GA. (There is no SSE pronouncing dictionary.)

Section 3.3 On the vowel systems of the three reference accents, see the following: RP – Wells (1982: sects. 2.1.2, 4.1), Gimson (1989); Northern modifications – Wells (1982: sects. 4.4.2, 4.4.3); GA – Wells (1982: sects. 2.1.3, 6.1), Kenyon (1958), Bronstein (1960), Prator and Robinett (1972), Bauer *et al.* (1980); SSE – Wells (1982: sect. 5.2), Abercrombie (1979).

Section 3.4   On vowels before (historic and actual) /r/ see the references to RP, GA and SSE given above; also Romaine (1978) on SSE.

Section 3.6 On problems of phonemic/phonetic transcription see Abercrombie (1964) and Abercrombie (1967: ch. 7). Pullum and Ladusaw (1986) is a guide to the phonetic symbols currently in use; all symbols used in this book are discussed there. See also IPA (1949).

Section 3.7   For background reading to the varieties of English discussed in this section, see Lass (1987: ch. 5) and again Bailey and Görlach (1982). On the specific accents consult the following: Australian/New Zealand/South African English – Wells (1982: ch. 8); Hiberno-English – Wells (1982: sect. 5.3); specifically on Ulster (Belfast) English see Milroy (1981).

# 4
# Phonological features, part 1: the classification of English vowel phonemes

## 4.1 The role of features in phonology

Any serious scientific enquiry, if it is to yield objectively valid results, requires a strict methodology: it needs to define its terms, the precise nature of the units denoted by these terms, as well as the operations through which such units are established. One such unit of phonological analysis is the **phoneme**, defined (in sect. 2.2) as the minimal contrastive sound unit of a language. This definition has furnished us with a simple and entirely objective method of establishing phonemes: the **commutation test**. Two phones are realisations of different phonemes if they produce phonological contrast; that is, if they figure in at least one minimal pair. Recall that this is not, strictly speaking, the whole story: we had to provide an additional definition of the allophone in section 2.2 to ensure that /h/ and /ŋ/ are different phonemes; and in section 3.4 we encountered some methodological problems that are so far unresolved. But we can conclude that the central unit of our analysis – the phoneme – is based on sound methodological principles. The problems of section 3.4 will eventually be resolved.

We also noted at various points of the preceding investigation that phonemes are not unanalysable ('atomic') elements, but that they can be analysed further. While a phoneme cannot by definition be broken up into shorter **successive** units, it can be viewed as a bundle of **simultaneous** units called **phonological features**: individual properties whose sum makes up the phoneme. These features, and not the phonemes, are the smallest and most basic units of phonological analysis. They have to be spelled out and defined in order to make a phonological analysis methodologically sound.

Dealing as it does with the basic units of analysis, feature theory is an important part of phonological theory, and not the least controversial one at that. As in the case of other phonological units, the use of any particular feature is not directly dictated by the physical (phonetic) facts but has to be decided on by the analyst. Features are, like phonemes, theoretical constructs rather than 'facts': there are many ways of analysing a given set of phonemes in terms of sets of features, and feature theory is concerned with finding and defining the most suitable set. We shall see in the next chapter, for example, that the features used for the classification of consonants in section 2.3.4 are unsatisfactory in several ways, and we shall replace them with a more suitable set of features.

What tasks do we expect a set of phonological features to perform? Firstly, we expect it to express the phonemic contrasts of a language fully and economically. Assuming that features are binary, that is, of the form [+ X] vs. [− X] like the ones already introduced in section 1.2.3 above, it is our aim in this and the following chapter to devise a set of features that expresses phonemic contrasts in the following way:

(1)   Phoneme A    Phoneme B    Phoneme C    Phoneme D

$$\begin{bmatrix} + X \\ + Y \end{bmatrix} \qquad \begin{bmatrix} + X \\ - Y \end{bmatrix} \qquad \begin{bmatrix} - X \\ + Y \end{bmatrix} \qquad \begin{bmatrix} - X \\ - Y \end{bmatrix}$$

That is, given a set of phonemes and a set of features, we want each phoneme to differ from every other phoneme in terms of at least one of the 'plus/minus' specifications of the features. This function of features was earlier referred to as the **contrastive function**. Of course, we need a single set of features for this task, one that can handle the entire sound system of a language and not, for example, separate sets of features for vowels and consonants; and we want our set of features to be as small and economical as possible.

Secondly, the **descriptive function**: on the concrete (phonetic) level of representation, the feature specification of every sound must describe accurately the phonetic nature of that sound. Recall here what was said in section 2.3.4: the difference between the two levels of representation is that on the abstract (phonemic) level, sound segments are specified only by means of those features that are needed to express phonemic contrast, while on the concrete (phonetic) level, sound segments are fully specified. That is, on the phonetic level we need all those features that serve in the physical (phonetic) description of a sound, even those features that are not necessary for the expression of contrast. Some features, then, may well be relevant on the phonetic level but redundant on the phonemic level. We shall return to this difference between the two levels of representation in chapter 8 below, where we shall also see that on the phonetic level, feature specifications are not necessarily binary: the binarity of features is a characteristic of the phonemic level only. Here, we only need to conclude that features are used on both levels of phonological analysis and that, because of their descriptive use on the phonetic level, they must themselves be phonetic in nature: all features must have a phonetic definition; otherwise they would be of no use in the phonetic definition of a sound. We shall return to this requirement presently.

Thirdly, phonological features serve in the expression of generalisations in the phonology of a language. We want our set of features to be such that it enables us to say that 'all sounds specified as [+ X], or [+ X, − Y] etc. behave in such-and-such a way in such-and-such a context'. Such generalisations form an important part of the phonology of a language, and one that we have not touched on so far. We shall see in chapter 8 below that phonemes fall into classes with respect to their behaviour, and we want such classes – that is, the phonemes that have a certain form of behaviour in common – to be defined in terms of features. Phonological features, then, have a **classificatory function**: they define classes of phonemes. Again, since we have not discussed phonological generalisations in any detail, we cannot do full justice to this third function of features in this and the following chapter, having to rely instead mainly on the contrastive and descriptive functions. But here is an example that will illustrate several of the points made above.

We saw in chapter 3 that the basic vowel systems found in the accents of English tend to be organised into pairs, such that one member of each pair can occur in open and closed syllables and the other can only occur in closed syllables. The basic vowel system consists, then, of two subsystems: one containing vowels allowed in open syllables and the other containing vowels not allowed in such contexts. In many cases, a member of one subsystem corresponds one-to-one to a member of the other subsystem; we discussed this pairwise correspondence and its limitations in the various accents of English in chapter 3. It would be desirable, clearly, to have a feature in our phonology that expresses this important restriction on the contexts of certain vowels, such that 'all vowels with the feature [+ X] can occur in open syllables but all vowels specified as [− X] cannot'. The question is whether such a feature can be found.

Suppose we introduce the feature [+ open syllable] vs. [− open syllable], so that, for example, /i/ is [+ o.s.] and /ɪ/ [− o.s.]. What would this achieve? As for the contrastive function, this feature would express the /i/–/ɪ/ contrast by specifying the former as 'plus' and the latter as 'minus': even if the two phonemes agree in terms of all other features, the feature [O.s.] makes the necessary distinction.

The feature would, however, fail in its descriptive function. Given that [Open syllable] tells us nothing about the phonetic characteristics of a sound specified 'plus' or 'minus' – the feature simply has no phonetic definition – it would be quite useless on the phonetic level of analysis.

Moreover, this feature would not enable us to make a true generalisation: the statement 'all vowels specified as [+ o.s] can occur in open syllables and all [– o.s.] vowels cannot' is obviously circular, given that the feature itself is defined by nothing other than the regularity for whose expression it is used. Features like this have to be rejected, then, due to their failure to perform the second and third functions given above.

If, however, we find a phonetically definable feature that distinguishes the two sets of vowel phonemes, we are in a quite different position: we would still, of course, be able to characterise contrasts such as the /i/–/ɪ/ one; but in addition we would be able to use such a feature, unlike [O.s], for the phonetic characterisation of sounds and also we would be able to make a true generalisation. If X is a phonetic quality that /i/, /u/, /e/ etc. have and /ɪ/, /ʊ/ and /ɛ/ etc. lack, then we would be making a rather interesting statement in saying 'all [+ X] vowels can occur in open syllables'. Such a rule would link two seemingly quite unrelated phenomena: a phonetic quality of a sound and a property of the structure of syllables. Generalisations in linguistic (and, generally, scientific) enquiry are of exactly this nature: they establish links between phenomena that are in other respects quite independent of each other, such that 'all X are also Y'. It is obvious that such a generalisation is only meaningful if X and Y are not the same thing.

But the question still is, can such a feature, with a phonetic definition, be found? We shall return to this question in section 4.2.2 below.

### 4.2  Phonological features and the basic vowel system

We begin our study of phonological features by looking at those features that characterise the English vowel system. Additional features needed to classify the consonant phonemes will be studied in chapter 5 below. Only the basic vowel system, as discussed in section 3.3, will have to be analysed in terms of features – a feature analysis of the secondary systems, containing vowels such as /ɜ/ and /ə/, would raise a number of rather complex questions to which we would, at this point, not be able to find satisfactory answers.

The features, and many of their combinations, will be common to all three of the basic systems discussed in section 3.3: it has already become evident that these three systems bear many similarities. As a by-product of our investigation, a single basic vowel system will soon emerge, which occurs in more or less modified form in the three reference accents and is further modified in the regional variants of the three accents.

### 4.2.1  *Major classes: [Sonorant], [Continuant] and [Consonantal]*

Before we embark on our task, let us recapitulate briefly what was said in chapter 1 about the definition of the notion 'vowel'. This definition, it will be recalled, has so far involved two binary features; we retain these features and incorporate them without revision in our set of phonological features:

> [Sonorant]:   A sonorant is a sound whose phonetic content is predominantly made up by the sound waves associated with voicing.

Approximants and nasals are [+ sonorant], fricatives and oral stops [− sonorant]. Members of the latter category are referred to as 'obstruents': all such sounds have in common that, unlike sonorants, they are produced with an obstruction of the air stream that results in friction or closure. Voicing is not essential in such sounds: as we shall see, obstruents may be voiced or voiceless (while sonorants are always voiced).

> [Continuant]:   A continuant is a sound during whose production the air stream is not blocked in the oral cavity.

Approximants and fricatives are [+ continuant], nasal and oral stops (that is, 'stops' in general) are [− continuant].

The four possible combinations of these two binary features express four major classes of sounds; the two features are for that reason often referred to as 'major class features'. Here are the four classes:

$$
(2) \quad \begin{bmatrix} +\text{sonorant} \\ +\text{continuant} \end{bmatrix} \quad = \text{'approximants'}
$$

$$
\begin{bmatrix} -\text{sonorant} \\ +\text{continuant} \end{bmatrix} \quad = \text{'fricatives'}
$$

$$
\begin{bmatrix} +\text{sonorant} \\ -\text{continuant} \end{bmatrix} \quad = \text{'nasal stops'}
$$

$$
\begin{bmatrix} -\text{sonorant} \\ -\text{continuant} \end{bmatrix} \quad = \text{'oral stops'} \\ \text{('plosives')}
$$

It was noted in section 1.2.4 that this classification does not draw a distinction between vowels and approximant consonants. It may seem odd that vowels do not constitute a major class of their own; however, we also saw in section 1.2.4 that there are good reasons for not making such a distinction on phonetic grounds: certain vowels and certain approximant

93

consonants are phonetically too similar to merit their differentiation in terms of phonetically based features – recall here our discussion of *ye* and *woo*.

What makes /j/ and /w/ consonants and /i/ and /u/ vowels is their function in syllables rather than their phonetic characterisation: vowels constitute syllable peaks while any sound occurring in the margin of a syllable is a consonant. We return to this question in chapter 6; here we conclude that all vowels have the feature specification [+ sonorant, + continuant]; they share this specification with the class of approximant consonants. That class, however, is in itself rather heterogeneous in that it comprises the subclass of 'semivowels' /j w/ – which, as we saw, are in phonetic terms rather vowel-like – and the subclass /l r/, sometimes referred to as 'liquids'. Unlike semivowels (and vowels, of course), liquids are clearly consonantal in phonetic terms: their production involves a degree of obstruction in the vocal tract that is clearly audible: radical narrowing in the case of /r/, and central contact in the case of /l/. This obstruction is a feature that liquids have in common with stops and fricatives, although in those the degree of narrowing is so great that they merit the feature [−sonorant]. Here is a definition of the feature [Consonantal]:

> [Consonantal]: Consonantal sounds are produced with a radical obstruction in the vocal tract.

Vowels as well as j w/ are [- consonantal], all other sounds are [+ consonantal]. [Consonantal] is the third of the major class features; it subdivides the class of approximants as demonstrated in table 4.1.

It follows from the definitions of [Sonorant] and [Consonantal] that a sound specified as [− sonorant] cannot be [− consonantal]; in other words, any [− sonorant] sound is redundantly [+ consonantal]. This three-way feature classification is not as economical, then, as our previous two-way one was in that not all combinations of 'plus' and 'minus' values are actually used. We return to the notions of feature economy and redundancy below; what is more important at this point is the fact that the three features define four major classes, of which the class of 'approximant' is further divided into two subclasses – two because 'vowels' and 'semivowels' are not distinct. This reflects precisely the result of our earlier discussion: what distinguishes vowels from semivowels is their position in the syllable rather than their phonetic make-up. This resolves the apparent contradiction in classifying /j w/ as [− consonantal] while at the same time calling them 'consonants' (albeit 'semivowels'): the term 'consonant' is not a phonetic one – it refers to a sound's function in the syllable – while the feature [Consonantal] does have a phonetic definition. A phonetically nonconsonantal sound may still

Table 4.1 *The major class features*

| | Nasal stop | Oral stop | Fricative | Approximant Liquid | Semivowel | Vowel |
|---|---|---|---|---|---|---|
| [Sonorant] | + | − | − | + | + | + |
| [Continuant] | − | − | + | + | + | + |
| [Consonantal] | + | + | + | + | − | − |
| Examples | m n ŋ | p b t d | f v θ ð | l r | j w | i u |

function as a consonant in a syllable. We shall come back to this problem in chapter 6. For the remainder of this chapter we shall deal with the further classification of phonemes characterised as [+ sonorant, + continuant, − consonantal], calling these 'vowels' and ignoring the fact that /j w/ also fall into this category.

### 4.2.2 *Pairs of vowels revisited: the feature [Tense]*

We turn now to the feature responsible for the quality distinction between, for example, /i/ and /ɪ/ in our reference accents RP, GA and SSE. The discussion will be confined to these accents; specifically, accents where pairs of vowels are predominantly distinguished in terms of length (for example, South African, Australian and New Zealand English – see sect. 3.7 above) are excluded from the discussion.

Recall from section 3.3 the English vowel phonemes, shown in figure 4.1. All these pairs occur in the basic RP system; the GA and SSE systems do not contain all of them.

In section 3.3.1, various reasons were given for organising vowel phonemes into such pairs. Firstly, the members of each pair are phonetically similar (but not identical). Secondly, one member is in most accents (but not in SSE) longer, in comparable contexts, than the other: compare *beat* and *bit*. And thirdly, the phoneme that is in most accents the longer one can in all accents (including SSE) occur in open syllables while the other one can only occur in closed syllables: *\*/bɪ/, *\*/bɛ/ etc. are impossible in English.

Is there a phonetically defined feature that can be held responsible (solely or in conjunction with other features) for these differences between the members of each pair, such that one member is [+ X] and the other [− X]? Such a feature would be extremely useful in our analysis of the English vowel system. One use was discussed in section 4.1: the feature would enable us to state in a simple way the restriction of /ɪ/, /ɛ/, /a/ etc. to closed syllables. Clearly, the property of being confined to closed syllables, and the converse property of being allowed in open syllables, are such important

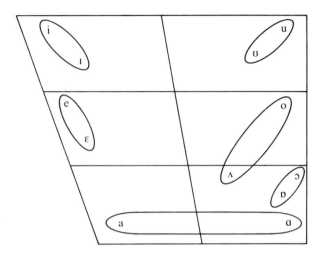

Figure 4.1    The basic English vowel system

ones that we want to define unified classes of phonemes, in terms of features, that reflect this behaviour.

Another benefit of having such a feature would be that it would greatly simplify our account of the basic vowel system. This account will, later in this chapter, involve the introduction of features referring to height and to the Front–Back dimension in the vowel trapezium, among others. As it stands, such an analysis looks like a rather messy task, given that the vowels in figure 4.1 appear to be characterised by a great number of different degrees of height and front/backness. If, however, the phonetically based feature that we are looking for can account for the slight quality differences between /i/ and /ɪ/, /u/ and /ʊ/ etc. in a different way – that is, without referring to height and front/backness – then this feature would serve to divide table 4.1 into the two subsystems shown in figure 4.2, each of them rather tidy. As we can see without going into the details here, each of the two subsystems in figure 4.2 is rather more manageable, in terms of height and front/backness, than the complete system in figure 4.1 is – provided the quality differences between /i/ and /ɪ/, /u/ and /ʊ/ etc. can be 'factored out' of the height and front/backness differentiation.

Notice also that the quality difference between /i/ and /ɪ/ is in itself rather similar to that between /u/ and /ʊ/: there is, at least in that part of figure 4.1, a rather striking symmetry, although the rest of the exposition is not quite as symmetrical. But let us concentrate, for the time being, on these two pairs of vowels and move on to the other ones later.

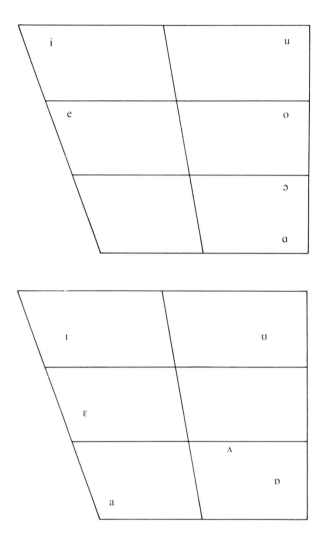

Figure 4.2    The subsystems of vowels

The quality difference between the members of such pairs is usually described as a difference in 'tenseness', such that /i/ and /u/ are **tense vowels** and /ɪ/ and /ʊ/ **lax vowels**. This feature is rather difficult to define; indeed, it has been controversial for many years and is viewed by some phonologists as devoid of phonetic content. Given that both /u/ and /ʊ/ are somewhat high, back and rounded (this expresses their similarity), the feature [+ tense] in /u/ refers to a general tightening-up of the setting of the articulators in comparison with /ʊ/: /u/ is higher, further back and more rounded than /ʊ/ is. (A similar comparison can be drawn for /i/ and /ɪ/, as well as for the other pairs of vowels.) In general, tense vowels are said to have greater force of constriction than their lax counterparts, while the kind and location of such constrictions are the same in both. Also, tense vowels have a tendency in many languages to be longer than lax vowels; we shall return to the question of vowel length in the three reference accents in section 4.2.3. Let us summarise this discussion of the binary feature [Tense] with a definition:

> [Tense]: Tense sounds are produced with a deliberate, ac-
> curate, maximally distinct gesture that involves considerable
> muscular effort; nontense sounds are produced rapidly and
> somewhat indistinctly.

It has to be admitted that this definition (and also the preceding more detailed description) of tenseness is somewhat vague. There seem to be three problems connected with this feature. Firstly, while it is perhaps fairly easy to determine that in a comparison of /i/ and /ɪ/, for example, the former is tense and the latter lax, it is more difficult to tell whether a given sound uttered in isolation is tense or lax. Features like [Sonorant] or [Continuant], in contrast, can be determined in isolated sounds without the necessity of comparison with other sounds. Secondly, while there are reasonably strong phonetic grounds for a tense–lax distinction within the high pairs of vowels (/i/–/ɪ/ for example), such a distinction is not nearly as well motivated, in phonetic terms, among low vowels such as /ɑ/ and /a/. And thirdly, there is, strictly speaking, nothing in this feature that cannot be described in different ways. As we saw, the tenseness of /u/ is manifested by greater rounding, height, backness and sometimes length. It would therefore be possible to express the phonetic properties denoted by this feature through other features instead.

However, weighing up these phonetic problems of the feature [Tense] against its considerable classificatory benefits, we cannot but decide in its favour: as we have already seen, the phonological classification of the English vowel system would without the use of this feature be an extremely difficult task.

We decide, then, to classify /i e u o ɔ ɑ/ as tense vowels and their counterparts /ɪ ɛ ʊ ʌ ɒ a/ as lax. In many cases, the members of vowel pairs are distinct in terms of tenseness alone; in /ɑ/–/a/ and /o/–/ʌ/ there are additional differences, to which we shall return later.

### 4.2.3  *Tenseness and length*

Consider, once again, the difference between /i/ and /ɪ/. Similar differences occur in the other pairs of vowels that are found, to a greater or lesser extent, in the three reference accents, but we shall take /i/–/ɪ/ as being exemplary here. The phonological feature distinguishing /i/ and /ɪ/, we concluded in section 4.2.2, is the feature [Tense], referring to the difference in quality between the two phonemes: /i/ is [+ tense], /ɪ/ [− tense].

In this section we shall try to account for the fact that the quality difference denoted by [Tense] is, in most accents of English, not the only difference between /i/ and /ɪ/: in most accents (though not, as we saw in sect. 3.3.3.2, in SSE) the /i/ in *beat* is also considerably longer than the /ɪ/ in *bit*. Excluding SSE from our discussion for the moment – we shall return to vowel length in this accent shortly – we observe, then, that /i/ and /ɪ/ are distinct in terms of **quality** and **quantity** (length). Very tentatively, let us say that there is a second feature at work, namely the binary feature [**long**]: /i/ is [+ tense, + long] and /ɪ/ is [− tense, − long]. (We shall revise this account further in chapter 6 below, where we shall see that what is expressed by the feature [Long] here lends itself to a more appropriate analysis involving syllable structure. But for the moment, any arguments against the feature [Long] are irrelevant.)

We noted in section 4.1 that we require phonological features to express phonemic contrast as economically as possible. This economy requirement presents us with a problem here: we do not need two binary features to distinguish two phonemes from one another. While on the phonetic level of representation, both [Tense] and [Long] are relevant – simply because in phonetic terms the vowels in *beat* and *bit* differ in quality as well as quantity – one of these two features is redundant on the abstract phonemic level. But which is the phonemically relevant feature and which the redundant one? Is [Tense] phonemically relevant and [Long] redundant, or vice versa? And is this an entirely arbitrary choice, or does one of the two options have advantages over the other?

We have – implicitly so far – chosen the former option, treating the quality (tenseness) feature as the 'more basic' and phonemically relevant one in our three reference accents; this was implied not only in section 4.2.2 but also, perhaps less obviously, in our choice of symbols for the transcription of vowel phonemes. Recall section 3.6, where we opted, in the case of RP and GA, for symbols such as /i/–/ɪ/ rather than /iː/–/i/. Both of these two transcriptions are redundancy-free: in the former, quantity is treated as redundant and in the latter quality. Why have we chosen the former? Why is it preferable to treat the quantity difference as redundant? There are several reasons.

The first reason is that it is at least as difficult to give absolute definitions of 'long' and 'short' as it is to define tenseness in absolute terms. Consider the following words, pronounced in RP or GA:

(3)  /i/  bee  bead  bean  beat
     /ɪ/   –    bid   bin   bit

It is true that, compared in the vertical dimension in (3) – that is, in identical contexts – /i/ is always realised longer than /ɪ/ is. Thus, the vowel in *bead* is longer than the one in *bid*, the one in *bean* longer than the one in *bin* and so forth. However, in each of the two horizontal series, length decreases from left to right: the vowel in *bee* is longer than the one in *bead*, which is in turn longer than the one in *bean* and so forth. Similarly, the vowel in *bid* is longer than the one in *bin*, and the one in *bit* is the shortest. The problem is that the shortest realisation of the 'long' phoneme /i/ (in *beat*) is in fact shorter than the longest realisation of the 'short' phoneme /ɪ/ (in *bid*). We shall not dwell on such problems at this point, but what we can safely conclude is that, in view of such phonetic facts, it would be extremely awkward to distinguish the members of this pair of phonemes (and others) primarily on the basis of quantity: the feature [Long] is at least as difficult to define as the feature [Tense] is.

A second argument against treating the quantity difference as the basic phonemic one in RP/GA/SSE is that it does not, in fact, seem to be the one that listeners use to distinguish the two phonemes. If an RP or GA speaker utters *beat*, for example, with a vowel that has the quality of /i/ but is as short as the /ɪ/ in *bit* would be, then a listener will still interpret this word as *beat* and not as *bit*, relying in his or her interpretation entirely on the quality of the perceived vowel rather than the quantity. This little experiment, which can be reversed with the same effect (*bit*, with the /ɪ/ uttered long as [ɪː]), shows quite conclusively that the quality difference among pairs of vowels is more basic than the quantity difference is. And note that for SSE speakers, this is not even an experiment involving 'unnatural' pronunciations at all: in SSE, the /i/ in *beat* is pronounced as short as the /ɪ/ in *bit* anyway.

This is the third argument against treating the length distinctions among pairs of vowels as phonemically relevant in the three reference accents: not every one of these accents has such a distinction – certainly, SSE does not. Let us review briefly what was said about vowel length in SSE in section 3.3.3.2 above. Unlike in RP and GA, the vowels in pairs like *beat* – *bit*, *bead* –

*bid* etc. do not differ in quantity but only in quality. On the phonemic level, all SSE vowels can be taken to be equally short. On the phonetic level, the Scottish Vowel-Length Rule makes certain vowels long before voiced fricatives, /r/ and at the ends of words but not in any other contexts. Thus, the vowel in *breathe* is realised long and the one in *Keith* short, in *sneeze* long and in *lease* short, and so forth. There are no minimal pairs involving length alone, simply because the contexts in which vowels are long do not permit short ones, and vice versa. Hence length cannot be a phonemically relevant feature in SSE.

If we decided, then, to use [Long] as a phonemically relevant feature in RP and GA (ignoring the arguments against this option that were put forward earlier), then we would have to use an entirely different approach for SSE: /iː/ and /i/ in RP and GA, distinguished through the feature [Long], would correspond to /i/ and /ɪ/ in SSE (distinguished through [Tense]). This would complicate our cross-dialectal study of these three English vowel systems considerably and would make the SSE system appear more different from the two others than it actually is. Given that SSE pairs must and RP and GA pairs should, for independent reasons, be analysed phonemically by referring to tenseness rather than length it would clearly be misguided not to analyse them all in terms of tenseness.

The length of vowels is, then, predictable (and hence phonemically redundant) in all three reference accents, if in a way that sets SSE apart from RP and GA. If we ignore the subtle length differences noted in (3) above, then all GA and RP vowels that are phonemically [+ tense] are, on the phonetic level, also [+ long]. Conversely [− tense] vowels are [− long].

Let us call a rule that predicts a redundant phonological feature from other, nonredundant ones a **redundancy rule**. For RP and GA we may then simply state the following two rules, where the arrow reads 'is also':

(4)   a.  [+ tense] → [+ long]

       b.  [− tense] → [− long]

By applying these two rules to the phonemic representations of vowels, we enrich those with the redundant feature [Long]; on the concrete phonetic level, vowels will then be specified for both [Tense] and [Long].

In SSE, things are different in that length is not an automatic consequence of tenseness but governed by the Scottish Vowel-Length Rule. But we shall see in chapter 8 below that here, too, tenseness plays an important part in defining the vowels that undergo this rule: it is only the tense vowels that are realised long before voiced fricatives, /r/ and word boundaries and short elsewhere; the lax vowels /ɪ ɛ ʌ/ are short in all contexts. SSE, then, has the following rule (5), here stated in provisional form, where RP and GA have rule (4a).

(5)  [+ tense] → $\begin{cases} [+ \text{ long}] \text{ in certain contexts} \\ [- \text{ long}] \text{ elsewhere} \end{cases}$

For the lax vowels, SSE shares rule (4b) with RP and GA. Unlike the redundancy rules in (4), rule (5) is context-sensitive: an allophonic rule, so-called because it predicts the occurrence of different allophones (here, long and short ones) of the same phoneme in different contexts. We shall return to allophonic rules in chapter 8; matters of vowel length, in particular the Scottish Vowel-Length Rule and its problems, will be discussed in section 8.4.

### 4.2.4  *Tongue-body features: [Back], [High] and [Low]*

By introducing the phonological feature [tense] (in sect. 4.2.2), we have divided the rather complex and messy basic vowel system into two rather more manageable subsystems. These are repeated in figure 4.3 – recall that certain accents lack some of the phonemes given in the figure. What we are aiming for, remember, in this and the next chapter is a set of binary features that enables us to express all the phonemic contrasts of English. We want to specify each phoneme of English in terms of a set of features in such a way that it has a 'plus' or a 'minus' for each feature and no two phonemes are specified alike. Concentrating in this chapter on vowel phonemes, we now have to devise some features that distinguish, as economically as possible, the members of each subsystem from one another.

It is quite obvious that such features should refer to the dimensions of the vowel trapezium, that is to the position of the body of the tongue in the oral cavity. In brief, the Front–Back dimension refers to the location of the highest point of the tongue body, whether it is in the front or in the back of the mouth. Or, to put it slightly differently, front/backness describes whether the front or the back part of the tongue body is raised. The High–Low dimension of the trapezium refers to the degree of such raising. (The reader is referred back to section 1.2 for more details of the vowel trapezium.) Let us deal with the Front–Back dimension first.

#### 4.2.4.1  *The feature [Back]*

A glance at the displays in figure 4.3 shows that the basic vowel system can be divided up into front and back vowels. This was done in section 1.2.2 with regard to the idealised cardinal vowels; it is equally useful in the analysis of a 'real-life' vowel system such as the English one in terms

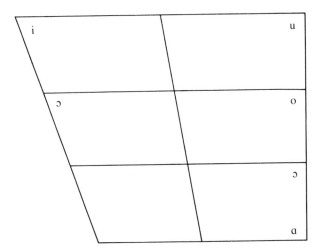

Figure 4.3a  [+tense] vowel phonemes

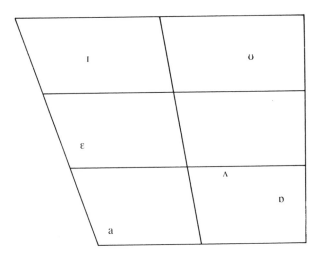

Figure 4.3b  [−tense] vowel phonemes

of features. There are, of course, subtle differences in the degree of
frontness and backness in this vowel system, but note that on each
horizontal level there are at most two vowels, never three. It is for our
purposes immaterial that /ʌ/ is not as far back as /ɒ/, for example, because
there is no vowel further back than /ʌ/ that is of the same height. For the
purpose of expressing contrast, we only require the rather crude distinction

front–back; more subtle differences in this dimension are not phonologically relevant.

For the front–back distinction we only need one binary feature; let us call it [Back]. Back vowels are, of course, [+ back] and front vowels [− back]. Here is a definition of this feature:

> [Back]: Back sounds are produced by retracting the body of the tongue from the neutral position; nonback sounds are produced without such a retraction from the neutral position.

Example (6) demonstrates the classification of English vowels in terms of the feature [Back], together with the previously introduced feature [Tense]:

| (6) | [−back] | [+back] |
|-----|---------|---------|
| [+ tense] | i e | u o ɔ ɑ |
| [− tense] | ɪ ɛ a | ʊ ʌ ɒ |

Both /i/ and /e/ are [+ tense, − back], /u o ɔ ɑ/ are [+ tense, + back], and so forth. Note that each of the four categories contains more than one phoneme. This means that the two features, as we would expect, are not sufficient to express the contrasts of the basic vowel system. We need some more features.

### 4.2.4.2   *The features [High] and [Low]*

That phonological features have to refer somehow to vowel height is as obvious as is the need to make the front–back distinction. But the question is, again, how many heights do we need to recognise as phonemically relevant in English? While in phonetic terms the vowels plotted in figure 4.3 occupy a variety of different heights, we note that, except for the [+ tense, + back] vowels, there are never more than three vowels in one height column. Of the tense vowels in figure 4.3a, two vowels are [− back] and four [+ back]; and of the nontense vowels in figure 4.3b, three are [+ back] and three [− back]. Of the four [+ tense, + back] vowels, /ɑ/ and /ɔ/ are also distinct in terms of lip rounding. If we introduce a feature [Round] – we shall do this in section 4.2.5 below – then we can reduce the four-way height distinction in this set of vowels to three, accounting for the /ɑ/–/ɔ/ contrast by referring to the difference in lip rounding and, consequently, assuming the height difference between /ɑ/ and /ɔ/ to be of no phonological relevance. Overall, then, we need three degrees of height in our phonological analysis, along with the feature [Tense], [Back] and – to be discussed below – [Round].

One binary feature – say, the feature [High] – is obviously not enough for a three-way distinction. But rather than introducing a ternary feature here (that is, a feature with three possible values), let us continue to conform with the principle of binarity and have two binary features: [High] and [Low]. These are defined like this:

> [High]:   High sounds are produced by raising the body of the tongue above the level that it occupies in the neutral position; nonhigh sounds are produced without such a raising of the tongue body.
>
> [Low]:   Low sounds are produced by lowering the body of the tongue below the level that it occupies in the neutral position; nonlow sounds are produced without such a lowering of the tongue body.

Two binary features permit four possible combinations, namely (in the case of [High] and [Low]) these:

$$(7) \quad \begin{bmatrix} + \text{ high} \\ - \text{ low} \end{bmatrix} \quad \begin{bmatrix} - \text{ high} \\ - \text{ low} \end{bmatrix} \quad \begin{bmatrix} - \text{ high} \\ + \text{ low} \end{bmatrix} \quad \begin{bmatrix} + \text{ high} \\ + \text{ low} \end{bmatrix}$$

Of these, the fourth one is impossible; it is, in fact, ruled out by the definition of the two features. No sound can be produced by simultaneously raising and lowering the body of the tongue. More formally speaking, we may say that there is again a redundancy rule at work, such that [+ high] is automatically [- low] and [+ low] automatically [- high]. This redundancy rule, stated below, is universally valid and not, like those discussed in the preceding section, restricted to (some accent of) English.

$$(8) \quad [+ \text{ high}] \rightarrow [- \text{ low}]$$
$$[+ \text{ low}] \rightarrow [- \text{ high}]$$

This leaves us with the required three heights: high vowels are [+ high], redundantly also [- low]; low vowels are [+ low], redundantly [- high]; and vowels of medium height are neither high nor low: [- high, - low].

Together with the features [Tense] and [Back], the two new features can be used to express the contrasts of the basic vowel system as in (9) below. Example (9a) gives the subsystem of tense vowels, which all three reference accents share; the lax subsystem given in (9b) is the richest of the three reference accents, namely that of RP.

(9) a. [+ tense] vowel phonemes: RP, GA, SSE

|  | $\begin{bmatrix} + \text{ tense} \\ - \text{ back} \end{bmatrix}$ | $\begin{bmatrix} + \text{ tense} \\ + \text{ back} \end{bmatrix}$ |
|---|---|---|
| [+ high] | i | u |
| $\begin{bmatrix} - \text{ high} \\ - \text{ low} \end{bmatrix}$ | e | o |
| [+ low] | — | ɔ ɑ |

b. [− tense] vowel phonemes: RP

|  | $\begin{bmatrix} + \text{ tense} \\ - \text{ back} \end{bmatrix}$ | $\begin{bmatrix} + \text{ tense} \\ + \text{ back} \end{bmatrix}$ |
|---|---|---|
| [+ high] | ɪ | ʊ |
| $\begin{bmatrix} - \text{ high} \\ - \text{ low} \end{bmatrix}$ | ɛ | ʌ |
| [+ low] | a | ɒ |

The four features introduced so far express all the phonemic contrasts of the basic vowel system, except one: /ɔ/ and /ɑ/ are both [+ tense, + back, + low]. Of the other phonemes, each one differs from all others in terms of at least one feature. As for /ɔ/ and /ɑ/, the feature [Round], to be discussed in section 4.2.5 below, will express the contrast.

Before that, however, a decision has to be discussed that was made in the feature analysis in example (9b) above: the characterisation of /ʌ/ as [− high, −low]. There is, in fact, little justification for making this specification, except that there happens to be a convenient gap in the system. It will be recalled from section 3.2 that /ʌ/ varies greatly in height from one accent to another: in our three reference accents it tends to be rather low while in the non-Southern accents of England it may be considerably higher or even nondistinct from /ʊ/. This is not really a problem for our feature analysis: notice that /ʌ/ is the only vowel that is [−tense, + back] and nonround (we shall classify /ʊ/ and /ɒ/ in the following section as [+ round]). So, in all accents that actually have /ʌ/, this phoneme will always be distinct from the other nontense back vowels by virtue of its absence of rounding, regardless of its height. /ʌ/, then, has considerable 'freedom of movement' in the vowel system without merging with other phonemes – and it is perhaps not surprising that it is precisely this vowel that has such height variability in the accents of English.

### 4.2.5 *The feature [Round], and more on redundancy*

It was noted earlier that /ɔ/ and /ɑ/ are distinct in terms of lip rounding; according to our display in figure 4.3a, they also differ – if slightly – in height. We have come across this kind of situation before: two phonemes differ in terms of two (or more) phonetic qualities and it is up to the analyst to decide which of them is the phonemically relevant one. In the present case, we decide in favour of rounding for reasons that have already been explained: the English vowel system can then be analysed in terms of three heights, and these are fairly easily expressed by using the two features [High] and [Low]. Relying instead, in the case of the /ɔ/–/ɑ/ distinction, on height would force us to operate with four degrees of height, and these would be more difficult to express in terms of binary features, apart from being rather undesirable in the rest of the system. But as we shall see in a moment, treating lip rounding as phonemically relevant raises new problems: such a feature is only needed in the case of the /ɔ/–/ɑ/ contrast; throughout the remainder of the vowel system it is redundant. Before we turn to this problem, let us define the feature [Round].

> [Round]: Rounded sounds are produced with a narrowing of the lip orifice; nonrounded sounds are produced without such a narrowing.

Using this feature in addition to the others, /ɔ/ and /ɑ/ are now distinct:

$$(10) \quad /ɔ/ = \begin{bmatrix} + \text{ tense} \\ + \text{ back} \\ + \text{ low} \\ + \text{ round} \end{bmatrix} \qquad /ɑ/ = \begin{bmatrix} + \text{ tense} \\ + \text{ back} \\ + \text{ low} \\ - \text{ round} \end{bmatrix}$$

In all other contrasts of the basic vowel system, the feature [Round] is not needed. [Round] is operative on the phonemic level in English, but only to a very limited extent. This feature is, in this respect, different from [Long], which is not needed on the phonemic level at all: it is redundant in all vowel contrasts of English.

On the other hand, both [Long] and [Round] are present in the full specifications of all vowels on the phonetic level: all vowels are phonetically long or short, and like the realisations of /ɔ/, those of /o/ and /u/, for example, are [+ round] while those of /i/ and /e/, for example, are

[− round]. In /ɔ/ and /ɑ/ the rounding specification is present on the phonemic level while in all other vowels it is predictable. For the prediction of rounding in phonemes other than /ɔ/ and /ɑ/, we need more redundancy rules.

There are two ways of looking at the tasks that redundancy rules perform in phonological systems: one way is that they predict all feature specifications that are predictable; the other way is that they account for gaps in the system. For example, the English vowel system is, like many others, characterised by the fact that it has no nonback rounded vowels. Such vowels are perfectly possible in terms of features: the two features [Back] and [Round] can be freely combined. Indeed, some languages do have [−back, + round] vowels; English just does not happen to have them. (In contrast, recall that the combination [+ high, + low] is generally impossible: this redundancy rule is universal.)

Saying that English has no nonback rounded vowels is, of course, the same thing as saying that all English nonback vowels are automatically unrounded. The two different readings of redundancy rules are indeed just two different ways of looking at the same task performed by such rules. We need redundancy rules, then, to characterise the English vowel system by excluding from the set of logically possible feature combinations all those that are universally nonexistent as well as those that this particular vowel system does not happen to have.

Speaking of a single vowel system of English is, of course, inaccurate: we saw in chapter 3 that the three reference accents, chosen somewhat arbitrarily out of a wide range of worldwide accents of English, have different vowel systems, and that these in turn have regional variants. Each such system is characterised by its own set of redundancy rules, which excludes from the system those feature combinations that the accent does not have. Let us state the vowel systems of the three reference accents in terms of features and then, without aiming for completeness, look at some of their redundancy rules.

The system of tense vowels is the same for all three reference accents; it was given in (9) above and amended, to express the /ɔ/–/ɑ/ contrast, in (10). The lax vowel system given there was that of RP; below are the lax vowel systems of GA and SSE.

(11)  [−tense] vowel phonemes

    a.  GA $\begin{bmatrix} - \text{ tense} \\ - \text{ back} \end{bmatrix}$ $\begin{bmatrix} - \text{ tense} \\ + \text{ back} \end{bmatrix}$

[+ high]               ɪ            ʊ

$\begin{bmatrix} - \text{ high} \\ - \text{ low} \end{bmatrix}$      ε            ʌ

[+ low]               a              —

    b.  SSE $\begin{bmatrix} - \text{ tense} \\ - \text{ back} \end{bmatrix}$ $\begin{bmatrix} - \text{ tense} \\ + \text{ back} \end{bmatrix}$

[+ high]               ɪ             —

$\begin{bmatrix} - \text{ high} \\ - \text{ low} \end{bmatrix}$      ε            ʌ

[+ low]              —             —

For reasons that will become evident shortly, we shall not attempt to give a full account of the redundancy rules that hold in the three reference accents; some examples should point the reader in the right direction.

The SSE subsystem of nontense vowels, given in (11b) above, is characterised by the fact that it contains no rounded and no low vowels, as well as neither a high back nor a low back one:

(12)   [− tense] → $\begin{bmatrix} - \text{ low} \\ - \text{ round} \end{bmatrix}$

    $\begin{bmatrix} - \text{ tense} \\ + \text{ back} \end{bmatrix}$ → $\begin{bmatrix} - \text{ high} \\ - \text{ low} \end{bmatrix}$

Some further redundancy rules are valid in all three reference accents. As was noted earlier, for example, none of the three accents have nonback rounded vowels; moreover, among the tense vowels of the three systems, no nonlow one is nonround. The following rules, then, apply to all English vowel systems:

(13)  [− back] → [− round]

    $\begin{bmatrix} + \text{ tense} \\ - \text{ low} \\ + \text{ back} \end{bmatrix}$ → [+ round]

Along these lines, we might now proceed to spell out redundancy rules, some accent-specific and others valid in more than one vowel system, until all the gaps in the three systems are accounted for. We shall not do this; as the principle of how this would work should by now be reasonably clear, there is no need to put it into practice.

Instead, note that there is an alternative but equally legitimate way of stating the pattern of rounding among English vowels: it is also true, for all accents, that if a vowel is rounded then it is also back:

(14)  [+ round] → [+ back]

This rule creates a problem: it does not fit in with what was stated earlier about the contrastive functions of the features [Round] and [Back]. While we have been assuming that [Back] is phonemically relevant throughout the vowel system and [Round] only in the case of the /ɔ/–/ɑ/ contrast, rule (13) makes the converse assumption: it treats [Round] as the underlying specified feature and [Back] as the redundant one.

We have here no way of deciding which of the two possible assumptions about the phonemic relevance of features is the correct one or the more useful one – and more possibilities exist. Given a set of features and a set of phonemes with fairly complex contrasts, there simply is more than one way of expressing the contrasts and supplying the redundant feature specifications by rule. If a choice between the existing possibilities were to be made – and we are here not even making an arbitrary choice – then the economy of the redundancy-free underlying specifications would have to be carefully weighed up against the economy of the attendant redundancy rules. It is quite clear that such a discussion would go beyond the scope of this introductory treatment, especially since we are dealing with three, in principle distinct, vowel systems.

Table 4.2 *A feature analysis of English vowels*

|  | i | ɪ | u | ʊ | e | ɛ | o | ʌ | ɑ | a | ɔ | ɒ |
|---|---|---|---|---|---|---|---|---|---|---|---|---|
| [Consonantal] | − | − | − | − | − | − | − | − | − | − | − | − |
| [Sonorant] | + | + | + | + | + | + | + | + | + | + | + | + |
| [Continuant] | + | + | + | + | + | + | + | + | + | + | + | + |
| [Back] | − | − | + | + | − | − | + | + | + | − | + | + |
| [High] | + | + | + | + | − | − | − | − | − | − | − | − |
| [Low] | − | − | − | − | − | − | − | − | + | + | + | + |
| [Round] | − | − | + | + | − | − | + | − | − | − | + | + |
| [Tense] | + | − | + | − | + | − | + | − | + | − | + | − |

Instead, we summarise the feature analysis of the English vowel system by stating all feature specifications in table 4.2 leaving open the question of what features are phonemic in the case of each phoneme, what the redundant ones in each case are, and what the redundancy rules are that predict them.

**Suggested reading to chapter 4**

The distinctive features presented in this and the following chapter are those proposed by Chomsky and Halle (1968: ch. 7); most of the definitions of the individual features are borrowed from that source. On the development of distinctive-feature theory see Fischer-Jørgensen (1975: chs. 8, 9); also Hyman (1975: ch. 2), Hawkins (1984: ch. 3), Durand (1990: ch. 2). For fairly detailed critical discussions of the Chomsky–Halle system see Ladefoged (1971) and Lass (1984: ch. 5), the former from a phonetic and the latter from a (mainly) phonological point of view.

Section 4.2.2   On tenseness see Jakobson and Halle (1964), Halle (1977), Halle and Clements (1983); critically Lass (1976; appendix to ch. 1), Catford (1977: ch. 10); more positively, regarding the phonetic content of this feature, Wood (1975).

Section 4.2.5   On redundancy see Harms (1968: ch. 8), Stanley (1967).

# 5
# Phonological features, part 2: the consonant system

## 5.1 Why new features?

In this chapter we continue our discussion of the phonological features that are needed in the phonology of English. Features, we noted in section 4.1, have various uses in phonological analysis. On the phonemic level of analysis, they serve to **express phonemic contrast**; and a good set of features would do this economically, that is, involving the smallest possible number of features. On the concrete phonetic level, features are used to **provide phonetic descriptions** of sounds. Moreover, features serve to **define classes of phonemes** required in the expression of phonological generalisations. This third function of features we have done little justice to so far; we shall discuss various kinds of generalisation, and the classes of phonemes they involve, in later chapters.

Having discussed the features that are needed to characterise the members of the basic vowel system in the preceding chapter, we now turn to the consonant phonemes. To remind ourselves of what phonemes are involved and how we have been characterising them, let us consider again table 2.2 of section 2.3.4, repeated here as table 5.1. Recall that the features used in table 5.1 are those that we used, as rather informal labels denoting phonetic properties, in our detailed description of speech sounds in chapter 1. In our exposition of the consonant phonemes of English in chapter 2, we adopted these features without discussing whether they were, in fact, the ones that we ought to be using. Somewhat belatedly, and following a line of enquiry already begun in chapter 4, we must ask ourselves whether this set of features is the best one we can think of. These features do express the contrasts among English consonant phonemes, and they do have a sufficiently precise phonetic basis; but do they constitute an optimally economical set? And do they define classes of phonemes in the way we require them to?

Table 5.1 *English consonant phonemes*

| | Bilabial | Labiodental | Dental | Alveolar | Post-alveolar | Palato-alveolar | Palatal | Velar | Glottal |
|---|---|---|---|---|---|---|---|---|---|
| Nasal (stop) | m | | | n | | | | ŋ | |
| Oral stop | p  b | | | t  d | | | | k  g | |
| Affricate | | | | | | tʃ  dʒ | | | |
| Fricative | (ʍ) | f  v | θ  ð | s  z | | ʃ  ʒ | | x  ʍ  h | |
| Approximant | (w) | | | r | | | j | w | |
| Lateral (approximant) | | | | l | | | | | |

### 5.1.1 *Excess of features*

To answer such questions, let us first consider the option that would be by far the easiest one for us: namely, that of adapting the features used in table 5.1 by simply making them binary, so that we have, for example, the binary features [± nasal stop], [± oral stop], [± bilabial] etc. As for the manner of articulation features (in the vertical dimension), we have already introduced an alternative that expressed the most important manner categories in a more economical way. This alternative was discussed in section 1.2.3 and again in section 4.1. Except for the categories 'affricate' and 'lateral', which will require our separate attention later, manners of articulation can be expressed by the four possible combinations of the two major class features [± sonorant] and [± continuant]. Here is, again, a display of this classification:

(1)          Nasal (stop)   Oral stop   Fricative   Approximant

| | Nasal (stop) | Oral stop | Fricative | Approximant |
|---|---|---|---|---|
| [Sonorant] | + | − | − | + |
| [Continuant] | − | − | + | + |

Recall that in section 4.2.1 we introduced the additional feature [Consonantal], which subdivides the class of sonorants into those with close approximation – the 'liquids' /l/ and /r/ – and those with open approximation – the 'semivowels' /j/ and /w/. The former subclass is [+ consonantal], together with all other consonants, while the latter subclass as well as the vowels is [− consonantal]. For the moment, this feature need not concern us any further; let us concentrate on the features [Sonorant] and [Continuant]. Why is it better to use these two features than it is to use [Nasal stop], [Oral stop] etc. as binary features? There are two reasons.

The first reason is that using two features to define four categories of phonemes is optimally economical. Two binary features can be combined in four different ways – generally, $n$ binary features can occur in $2^n$ different combinations – and in this case we are actually using every one of the possible combinations; none of them fails to occur in the language and has to be forbidden by a redundancy rule. Using [Nasal stop], [Oral stop] etc. as binary features would, on the other hand, produce a great deal of useless feature combinations: to be precise, these four features could be combined with each other in $2^4 = 16$ different ways, and only four of those we would want to allow. The others would have to be excluded by means of redundancy rules such as '[+ nasal stop] → [− oral stop]', '[+ nasal stop] → [− fricative]' and so forth. Obviously, this would be undesirable.

The second reason for preferring the features [Sonorant] and [Continuant] over the four others is that these two features define, in addition to the four manner categories, several additional (and more general) classes of phonemes: nasal stops and oral stops share the feature [− continuant]; nasal stops and approximants are [+ sonorant] and so on. We shall see in later chapters that a number of important phonological generalisations refer to such major classes of phonemes: all phonemes that are members of a certain class behave in a certain way while all nonmembers behave differently. In this respect, the features [Continuant] and [Sonorant] will prove particularly useful, while, on the other hand, features like [Nasal stop] etc. fail in the definition of major classes.

For these reasons, then, we adopt the features [Continuant] and [Sonorant]; but what of the place of articulation features that were used in table 5.1? Again, our easiest option would be to turn the labels 'bilabial', 'labiodental' etc. into binary features. But arguments against doing this are easily found: nine binary features can be combined in $2^9 = 512$ different ways, of which we need only nine. We came across the same problem earlier, in the case of the manner features: like those, the place features of table 5.1 cannot be allowed to be combined with each other; redundancy rules would have to forbid any feature combination that entails more than one 'plus' specification. This means that we would fail to make use of the greatest advantage of binary features: namely, that of economical (that is, feature-saving) cross-classification.

Going still further, we have to ask ourselves whether we need as many as nine different place categories (expressed by individual features or by combinations), given that some of the columns in table 5.1 are rather poorly used. Only one phoneme, for example, is post-alveolar, only one palatal. The question is here, as it was repeatedly in chapter 4 above, whether a given phonetic difference between two sounds is the only difference between them or whether it is accompanied by others, which it would be more economical to use in the expression of contrast. We shall see below that in several cases ways of expressing contrasts can be found that are indeed more economical than those in table 5.1.

### 5.1.2 'Vowel features' and 'consonant features'

The discussion in section 5.1.1 has given us sufficient reason for a radical revision of the features used in the analysis of the English consonant system: the labels given in table 5.1 are in several ways unsuitable for use as binary features. Before we replace them with new features, let us recall a problem that has been inherent in our discussion of vowels and consonants so far, and that in our revision of the features we must try to avoid: the problems of having distinct sets of features for vowels and consonants.

Having two such distinct sets of features is, firstly, rather undesirable where the expression of the phonemic contrasts of a language is concerned. Certainly, the set of features could be economised if the vowel features were allowed to play some part in the analysis of consonants and vice versa. Secondly, such a sharp division into consonant and vowel features makes little sense in phonetic terms and is, thirdly, an obstacle in the expression of phonological generalisations.

That it makes little sense to analyse vowels and consonants by means of different sets of features was shown in section 1.2.4: analysing /i/, for example, as [+ high, − back] and /j/ as palatal only serves to disguise the fact that the two sounds are in phonetic terms strikingly similar. Clearly, we want our set of features to express such similarities, which are by no means restricted to /i/ and /j/, directly.

It is precisely this failure to express similarities between certain vowels and certain consonants that can prove to be an obstacle in the expression of phonological generalisations. To demonstrate this, let us just recall one generalisation that was noted in section 2.1, namely that in *Kay* and *key* the /k/ is realised further in the front of the mouth than it is in *coo* and *cold*. In terms of the features used in chapters 2 and 3, we would have to say that /k/ is realised as a palatal before front vowels and as a velar before back vowels. This is, of course, a possible way of stating this generalisation − one of the rules governing allophonic differences in English − but it is unsatisfactory because it fails to explain why this difference among allophones arises. Clearly, what we really want to say is that /k/ automatically assumes the same tongue position as the following vowel: it is [− back] before [− back] vowels and [+ back] before [+ back] vowels. But in order to be able to say this, we must permit the use of features like [Back] in the classification of consonants.

There is nothing in the definitions of the tongue-body features discussed in chapter 4 that forbids us to use them for consonants also, and we have just seen some good reasons for doing so. On the other hand, it is quite clear that these features alone are not enough to express all the place of articulation contrasts in the consonant system: the columns in table 5.1 simply cannot be condensed into [+ back] and [− back], even with the additional help of [High] and [Low]. We shall in the following paragraphs, therefore, define some place of articulation features − no more than are needed for the expression of the consonant contrasts of English with the help of the tongue-body features that we have already introduced. These tongue-body features will be applied to consonants in section 5.3. Towards the end of this chapter, we shall return to the problem of redundancy.

## 5.2 Replacing place features: [Anterior], [Coronal] and [Strident]

What our task consists of is by now clear: of finding a suitable alternative to the place of articulation features used in table 5.1 above. The features used there are, as we saw in section 5.1, in several ways unsuitable for use as binary features. What we are after, then, is a set of features, as small as possible, to replace those.

Instead of using [Bilabial], [Labiodental] etc. as binary features, let us have two new ones: [Anterior] and [Coronal]. We define these as follows.

> [Anterior]: Anterior sounds are produced with an obstruction that is located in front of the palato-alveolar region of the mouth; nonanterior sounds are produced without such an obstruction.

In terms of our phonetic description of consonants, [+ anterior] is a cover term for bilabial, labiodental, dental and alveolar places of articulation; we classify the 'post-alveolar' category (with /r/ as the only member) as [− anterior], together with palato-alveolar, palatal, velar and glottal sounds. A display of this classification is given in table 5.2.

> [Coronal]: Coronal sounds are produced with the blade of the tongue raised above its neutral position; noncoronal sounds are produced with the blade of the tongue in the neutral position.

Table 5.2 *Consonantal features: cross-classification*

| | [+ anterior] | | [− anterior] | | |
|---|---|---|---|---|---|
| [− continuant] | m | n | | ŋ | [+ sonorant] |
| | p | t | | k | [− sonorant] |
| [+ continuant] | f | θ s | ʃ | x h ʌ | |
| | l | r | | j w | [+ sonorant] |
| | [− coronal] | [+ coronal] | | [− coronal] | |

Recall here from section 1.1.4 what the term 'blade of the tongue' refers to. This is the part of the tongue that is, rather illogically, further forward than the 'front' of the tongue. Roughly speaking, it is the part of the tongue that is raised in [n] but not in [j]. [j] is a [− back] sound like [n], but, unlike [n], it is [− coronal].

The two features [Anterior] and [Coronal] are, admittedly, somewhat non-mnemonic. However, in terms of their classificatory possibilities they have great advantages over the place labels employed in table 5.1: as we shall see, their four possibilities of combination are put to full use in the consonant system. Table 5.2 lists the consonant phonemes of English in such a way that the different rows represent the four combinatory possibilities of [Continuant] and [Sonorant], and the four columns the combinatory possibilities of [Anterior] and [Coronal]. Affricates are omitted, as are the 'voiced' obstruents /b d g v z/ etc. – these would in this display coincide with /p t k f s/ etc. Contrasts like /p/–/b/ will be discussed in section 5.4 below. /w/ is treated as velar, disregarding for the moment the fact that it is also listed in the bilabial category in table 5.1 above. Again, this is a problem that we shall return to.

Four binary features have $2^4 = 16$ combinatory possibilities; each of these is represented by a separate 'box' in table 5.2. /m/, for example, is [− continuant, + sonorant, + anterior, − coronal]. Note that the combinatory possibilities of [Anterior] and [Coronal] are fully used, as the four combinatory possibilities of [Continuant] and [Sonorant] are: while table 5.2 contains some empty 'boxes' it has no rows or columns that are entirely empty. Like the major class features, then, [Anterior] and [Coronal] are rather efficient in their classificatory function.

There are, consequently, few cases where two or more phonemes are in the same box; such phonemes share the same specifications for the four features and are, therefore, not yet distinguished by the features so far introduced. The following contrasts are not expressed by the four features:

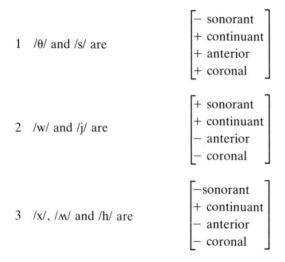

1 /θ/ and /s/ are

$$\begin{bmatrix} - \text{ sonorant} \\ + \text{ continuant} \\ + \text{ anterior} \\ + \text{ coronal} \end{bmatrix}$$

2 /w/ and /j/ are

$$\begin{bmatrix} + \text{ sonorant} \\ + \text{ continuant} \\ - \text{ anterior} \\ - \text{ coronal} \end{bmatrix}$$

3 /x/, /ʍ/ and /h/ are

$$\begin{bmatrix} - \text{sonorant} \\ + \text{ continuant} \\ - \text{ anterior} \\ - \text{ coronal} \end{bmatrix}$$

In addition, there are, of course, the /p/–/b/, /s/–/z/ etc. contrasts. In the rest of this chapter we shall be concerned with finding features that express these remaining phoneme distinctions. We begin with the /s/–/θ/ contrast.

To express this contrast, it would be possible to introduce a more subtle place of articulation distinction – this, remember, was the approach taken in chapter 1 and in table 5.1. Alternatively, the /s/–/θ/ contrast could be expressed by referring to a difference between the two that is not one of place of articulation.

Arguments either way are hard to find. Introducing another place feature would disrupt the neat cross-classification achieved by [Anterior] and [Coronal] and result in a number of unwanted redundancies, some of which would be universal rather than language-specific – recall our discussion of the problems that the excess of place features causes (sect. 5.1.1 above). On the other hand, any feature that we now invoke will cause redundancies (at least, English-specific ones) simply because we have already accounted for most of the contrasts.

With little justification coming from the English consonant system (but with some support in terms of universal feature theory), we choose the second option and invoke a feature that does not further differentiate places of articulation but refers to an acoustic difference between /s/ and /θ/ instead. The feature is called [Strident] and refers to the difference in the amount of noise caused by different fricative articulations.

> [Strident]: Strident sounds are marked acoustically by greater noisiness than their nonstrident counterparts are.

Table 5.3 *Consonant phonemes and features (partial analysis)*

|  | m | n | ŋ | p | t | k | f | θ | s | ʃ | x | h | ʍ | w | j | r | l |
|---|---|---|---|---|---|---|---|---|---|---|---|---|---|---|---|---|---|
| [Consonantal] | + | + | + | + | + | + | + | + | + | + | + | + | + | − | − | + | + |
| [Sonorant] | + | + | + | − | − | − | − | − | − | − | − | − | − | + | + | + | + |
| [Continuant] | − | − | − | − | − | − | + | + | + | + | + | + | + | + | + | + | + |
| [Anterior] | + | + | − | + | + | − | + | + | + | − | − | − | − | − | − | − | + |
| [Coronal] | − | + | − | − | + | − | − | + | + | + | − | − | − | − | − | − | + |
| [Strident] | − | − | − | − | − | − | + | − | + | + | − | − | − | − | − | − | − |

Since there is a noticeable different in noisiness between /ʃ s f/ on the one hand and /θ x ʍ h/ on the other, the cut-off point for [+ strident] can be conveniently (if somewhat arbitrarily) placed between /s/ and /θ/. /s ʃ f ʒ z v/ will then be [+ strident] and all other phonemes, notably the other fricatives /θ ð x ʍ h/, are [− strident]. In English, this feature is contrastive only in the case of /s/ and /θ/; it is redundant in all other phonemes. (Other languages make more contrastive use of this feature.)

Let us summarise our findings by specifying the consonant phonemes of English in terms of the features that have been defined so far (table 5.3). /v ð z ʒ/ and the affricates are again omitted. The contrasts that are not expressed by the set of features as it stands are in bold type.

### 5.3 [Round], [High], [Low] and [Back] revisited

The primary use of [Round] and the tongue-body features is, of course, in the vowel system, where they express phonemic contrasts as well as serving in the phonetic specifications on the concrete level. But we saw in section 5.1.2 that it is desirable to use these features in the analysis of consonants, too: at the very least, they play a part in the phonetic descriptions of consonants and in some allophonic rules; and possibly they can also be employed to express phonemic contrast among consonants. Indeed, we still have to come to grips with a few consonant contrasts – the phonemes not so far distinguished are in bold type in table 5.3. Let us deal with the feature [Round] first and see what use we can put it to in the consonant system.

Recall the place of articulation category 'bilabial' in table 5.1 above, containing /m p b ʍ w/. It is true, all these phonemes are characterised by some involvement of both lips in their articulation. But the posture of the lips is not the same in all of them: while /w/ and /ʍ/ have lip rounding (similar to the rounding found in many vowels), /p/, /b/ and /m/ have bilabial closure without any rounding of the lips. The category 'bilabial', then, is in phonetic terms not quite precise. In /w/ and /ʍ/, lip rounding goes together with a velar constriction (approximation in the former – hence [+ sonorant, + continuant] – and friction in the latter: [− sonorant, + continuant]). The velar articulation, characterised as [− anterior, − coronal], they have in common with several other consonants, but the lip rounding is distinctive. And since we have already been using the feature [Round] in the vowel system – recall its definition in section 4.2.5 – we can easily distinguish /w/ from /j/, and /ʍ/ from /x/ and /h/, without having to invoke a new feature. /w/ and /ʍ/ are [+ round], all other consonants [− round]. The full specifications of English consonant phonemes can be found in table 5.4 in section 5.6 below.

The tongue-body features [High], [Low] and [Back] are in the consonant system largely – but as we shall see not entirely – redundant. This is hardly surprising: given that the features introduced so far provide a fairly detailed place/manner classification, we do not really expect consonants to be distinct in terms of additional features that refer to the position of some part of the tongue – except perhaps where a tongue-body feature, already in use in the phonemic contrasts of English, may save the introduction of a new place or manner feature. We have employed the strategy of preferring already-introduced features over new ones before. Indeed, the /h/–/x/ distinction – the only one, remember, that we have not so far made – is a case in point. The place features [Anterior] and [Coronal] make no distinctions among velars and sounds that are articulated behind the velum (see table 5.1 above); yet, /x/ is a velar and /h/ a glottal or perhaps pharyngeal fricative. But the two sounds are also distinct in terms of tongue height: in /x/, the body of the tongue is raised and in /h/ lowered (and possibly retracted). We therefore need not make the additional place distinction but can refer to the height features instead. /x/ is then [+ high] (and redundantly [− low]) while /h/ is [− high, + low].

Among all other consonant phonemes of English, the height specification is redundant: it is, for each consonant, 'plus' or 'minus' on the phonetic level, but in each case this specification is derivable from the other feature specifications. There is no need to discuss these redundant specifications here; they are usually self-evident and can, in any case, be read off table 5.4 in section 5.6 below.

The features [Low] and [Back] can be treated as entirely redundant for English consonant phonemes. While they do not figure in phonemic representations of English consonants, they only play a part in certain allophonic rules. One such rule we came across in section 5.1.2: it is necessary to use the feature [Back] to account for the noncontrastive place difference of the /k/ realisation in *key* and that in *coo*. Once again, we do not discuss the details of the redundant [Back] and [Low] specifications for each consonant; the reader is instead referred to table 5.4 in section 5.6 below, which contains these specifications.

## 5.4   Pairs of obstruents: [Voice] and [Tense]

The English consonant system contains a further series of phonemic contrasts that has so far been excluded from the discussion. This series comprises the following phonemes:

$$
\begin{array}{lll}
(2) \quad \text{a.} & \begin{bmatrix} - \text{ sonorant} \\ - \text{ continuant} \end{bmatrix} & \left\{ \begin{array}{l} /p/-/b/ \\ /t/-/d/ \\ /k/-/g/ \end{array} \right. \\[2em]
\text{b.} & \begin{bmatrix} - \text{ sonorant} \\ + \text{ continuant} \end{bmatrix} & \left\{ \begin{array}{l} /f/-/v/ \\ /\theta/-/\eth/ \\ /s/-/z/ \\ /\int/-/\math_3/ \end{array} \right. \\[2.5em]
\text{c.} & \begin{bmatrix} - \text{ sonorant} \\ + \text{ continuant} \\ - \text{ anterior} \\ - \text{ coronal} \end{bmatrix} & \left\{ \begin{array}{l} /x/ \\ /\Lambda/ \\ /h/ \end{array} \right.
\end{array}
$$

The phonemic contrast in question is, of course, one of **voicing**. Voicing contrasts occur only within the class of [− sonorant] ('obstruent') phonemes, such that all oral stops (2a) and some of the fricatives (2b) occur in voiced vs. voiceless pairs. No such contrast is found among sonorants (which are always voiced); moreover, the voiceless fricatives /x ʌ h/ (2c) do not have voiced counterparts.

What complicates the issue is the fact that the voicing contrast among obstruents is not obvious in all contexts: due to allophonic rules which will be discussed in section 8.3, 'voiced' obstruents may be to a greater or lesser extent 'devoiced' in word-initial as well as word-final positions. Full voicing occurs only in fully voiced contexts:

(3)   a.   buy  lob          b.   lobbing
           pie  lop               lopping

While items such as these evidently constitute minimal pairs, establishing the phonemic status of /p/ and /b/ in all three contexts, it is only in (3b) that voicing is directly – and saliently – manifested in the contrast. On the other hand, in cases such as *buy* and *lob*, even where the /b/ appears to be totally devoiced, the setting of the glottis has been shown to be different from that found in *pie* and *lop*: at the very least, the former will display the narrowing of the glottis that may facilitate vocal-fold vibration – even if such vibration, in the case of total devoicing, does not actually take place. Here is the definition of the feature [Voice]:

> [Voice]: A voiced sound is produced with a glottal setting consistent with vocal-fold vibration; a voiceless sound is produced with a glottal setting inconsistent with vocal-fold vibration.

A phoneme specified as [+ voice], then, is **potentially voiced** – it may be fully voiced or to a greater or lesser extent devoiced depending on its context – while a [− voice] phoneme is voiceless in all contexts.

As was noted above, the feature [Voice] is contrastive among the majority of English obstruents; among the sonorants – vowels and sonorant consonants – as well as among the obstruents /x ʍ h/ it is redundant in such a way that the former are invariably voiced while the latter are invariably voiceless. The following redundancy rules govern the distribution of this feature:

(4) a. [+ sonorant] → [+ voice] (= /j w r l m n ŋ/, vowels)

b. $\begin{bmatrix} - \text{sonorant} \\ + \text{continuant} \\ - \text{anterior} \\ - \text{coronal} \end{bmatrix}$ → [− voice] (= /x ʍ h/)

The feature is nonredundant among all phonemes not specified in (4) – more particularly, among obstruents other than those in (4b). Context-specific devoicing of voiced obstruents is governed by allophonic rules, which will be discussed in section 8.3 below.

In response to the problems concerning the actual voicing behaviour of phonemes classified as 'voiced', it has been suggested that the relevant contrast should be described as one of 'lenis' vs. 'fortis' phonemes rather than 'voiced' versus 'voiceless'. Thus, /b d g v ð/ etc. are referred to as **lenis** consonants and their counterparts /p t k f θ/ etc. as **fortis**. It is tempting to equate this binary distinction with that made by the feature [Tense], discussed in relation to vowels in section 4.2.2 above. Instead of classifying /b d g/ etc. as [+ voice] and /p t k/ etc. as [− voice], these would then be underlyingly characterised as [− tense] and [+ tense] respectively; and their actual voicing behaviour would be described by a phonemically redundant, gradient feature [Voice] which might then describe actual rather than potential voicing):

(5)  a.  $\begin{bmatrix} - \text{ sonorant} \\ + \text{ tense} \end{bmatrix}$  →   [− voice]

b.  $\begin{bmatrix} - \text{ sonorant} \\ - \text{ tense} \end{bmatrix}$  →  $\begin{cases} \text{[fully voiced] in certain contexts} \\ \text{[partially voiced] in other contexts} \end{cases}$

In terms of the overall classification of the English phoneme system, this proposal has considerable attractions: given that we have already seen that among sonorants voicing is redundant, while, on the other hand, the feature [Tense] does play a part elsewhere in the system (namely, among vowel phonemes), using [Tense] instead of [Voice] in the obstruent system would mean that we could banish the latter from the phonemic level altogether while putting the former to full use. No English phoneme would then have to be specified underlyingly for [Voice].

But there are certain problems with this approach, and perhaps unsurprisingly these relate, once again, to the phonetic content of the feature [Tense]. We noted in section 4.2.2 the difficulties of giving a unique definition of this feature in relation to vowels; among obstruents, these difficulties are compounded. [+ tense] ('fortis') obstruents may be distinct from their [− tense] ('lenis') counterparts in terms of a variety of phonetic properties, among which are voicing (as we saw above) as well as other – but equally context-specific – phenomena. We need not go into the details here – these will be discussed at length in section 8.3 below. Suffice it to say that the feature [Tense] among obstruents would denote a syndrome of properties that are hard to relate to each other, rather than a single property that might serve in the feature's definition.

Moreover, this proposed elimination of the feature [Voice] from the phonemic level is only achievable if the obstruents /x ʍ h/ are underlyingly characterised as [+ tense]: only then can [− voice] be supplied by redundancy rule (5a) above. And it appears that at least for /h/ (and probably for /ʍ x/ also), the feature specification [+ tense] is in phonetic terms untenable.

These problems of defining [Tense] are not, of course, radically different from those that we encountered in connection with tenseness for vowels. Rather tentatively, however, we decide for the remainder of this book in favour of [Voice] (rather than [Tense]) as the phonemically relevant feature in the obstruent system: we shall refer to /p t k f θ/ etc. as 'voiceless' rather than 'fortis' and to /b d g v ð/ etc. as 'voiced' rather than 'lenis'. But it should be borne in mind that the alternative analysis involving 'fortis/lenis' ([± tense]) is favoured by other phonologists. To do justice to this alternative, consonants will be specified for tenseness as well as voicing in table 5.4 below.

### 5.5 [Nasal] and [Lateral]

The set of features established in this chapter and the preceding one accounts for all phonemic contrasts found in English. Surprisingly, perhaps, it does so without referring to the manner of articulation categories 'nasal' and 'lateral'. While 'nasal' and 'lateral' are clearly defined phonetic properties of certain sounds of English, they evidently do not need to be employed in the expression of any of the phonemic contrasts found in the language. We conclude our discussion of phonological features by asking why these two features are not needed on the phonemic level in English and why they are needed on the concrete phonetic level of analysis. Let us first deal with the feature [Nasal].

> [Nasal]: Nasal sounds are produced with a lowered velum, which allows the air stream to escape through the nose; nonnasal sounds are produced with a raised velum, so that the air stream can only escape through the mouth.

It follows from the definitions of the features [Sonorant] and [Continuant] that a sound that is both a sonorant and a noncontinuant must be a nasal. This fact is expressed by the following universal redundancy rule:

$$(6) \quad \begin{bmatrix} + \text{ sonorant} \\ - \text{ continuant} \end{bmatrix} \rightarrow [+ \text{ nasal}]$$

What makes the feature [Nasal] redundant not only in sonorant noncontinuants but in all phonemes of English is the fact that the language has no nasal phonemes other than sonorant noncontinuants; in particular, English does not have the nasal vowel phonemes that are occasionally found in other languages. Since (for universal phonetic reasons) all [+ sonorant, − continuant] phonemes are [+ nasal], and (peculiar to English) only those, the feature [Nasal] is noncontrastive in English.

On the phonetic level, however, the feature is needed. One reason for this is self-evident: nasality is a distinct phonetic property that simply must form part of a detailed phonetic description. Moreover, the feature is necessary for the expression of certain phonological generalisations.

While not phonemic in English, nasal vowels can occur as allophones of vowels in certain contexts. Thus, the vowels in *ham, hand* and *hang* are usually nasalised – obviously due to the following nasal. Below are two attempts to state the allophonic rule (which will be discussed in detail in sect. 8.2.2 below):

(7)  a.  $V \rightarrow \begin{bmatrix} + \text{ sonorant} \\ - \text{ continuant} \end{bmatrix}$  before  $\begin{bmatrix} + \text{ sonorant} \\ - \text{ continuant} \end{bmatrix}$

b.  $V \rightarrow [+ \text{ nasal}]$  before  $[+ \text{ nasal}]$

Rule (7a) is wrong. The vowel is already a sonorant and it certainly does not in this context turn into a noncontinuant. Rather than changing into /m/, /n/ or /ŋ/ (as rule (7a) would predict), the vowel acquires the phonetic quality of nasality that sonorant noncontinuants redundantly have; in other words, the vowel retains the feature specifications [+ sonorant, + continuant] and acquires additionally the feature [+ nasal]. This is quite a different matter, for whose expression the feature [Nasal] is clearly needed. Rule (7b) is, then, the correct way of stating this allophonic rule. We shall return to the redundancy of the feature [Nasal] shortly, but let us first discuss [Lateral].

This feature is defined as follows:

> [Lateral]: Lateral sounds are produced by lowering the mid section of the tongue at one or both sides, thereby allowing the air to flow out of the mouth in the vicinity of the molar teeth; in nonlateral sounds no such side passage is open.

The feature [Lateral] is, like [Nasal], redundant on the phonemic level in English, although perhaps not in quite such an obvious way as [Nasal] is. Here is the redundancy rule:

(8)  $\begin{bmatrix} + \text{ sonorant} \\ + \text{ continuant} \\ + \text{ anterior} \\ + \text{ coronal} \end{bmatrix} \rightarrow [+ \text{ lateral}]$

English only has one lateral phoneme (namely /l/); and that happens to have the feature specification given on the left in rule (8). Since these features alone suffice to distinguish /l/ from all other English phonemes, and since the language has no other phonemes that are [+ lateral], the feature has no contrastive function in English. Not even /l/ needs to be specified for [Lateral] on the phonemic level.

Note, however, that rule (8) is by no means universal: that /l/ is lateral does not follow automatically from its other feature specifications in the way nasality follows automatically from noncontinuant sonorancy in rule (6) above. Rather, the only English lateral happens to be also [+ sonorant, + continuant, + anterior, + coronal], and there happens to be no other nonlateral phoneme that has the same specification. Such a nonlateral phoneme is perfectly conceivable, and it is only because the only English lateral happens to fill this accidental gap in the consonant system that the feature [Lateral] is actually redundant in English.

For this reason alone, the feature [Lateral] is needed on the phonetic level. Since the laterality of /l/ realisations is by no means automatically predicted by other features, the specification of [+ lateral] is an essential part of the full phonetic characterisation of the realisations of /l/. How this specification is achieved is clear: through the redundancy rule given in (8) above. But what is important to note is this: the feature [Lateral] expresses a difference between the realisations of /l/ and those of all other phonemes that is, in phonetic terms, an important one; that the feature is nevertheless redundant is due only to the existence of an accidental gap, in a convenient place, in the English consonant system.

### 5.6   A final note on redundancy

Consider the following redundancy rules:

(9)
a.  $[+ \text{nasal}] \rightarrow \begin{bmatrix} + \text{sonorant} \\ - \text{continuant} \end{bmatrix}$

b.  $[+ \text{lateral}] \rightarrow \begin{bmatrix} + \text{sonorant} \\ + \text{continuant} \\ + \text{anterior} \\ + \text{coronal} \end{bmatrix}$

These two rules reverse the statements of redundancy made by rules (6) and (8) above. They are just as true for English as those are: the only three nasal phonemes of English are also [+ sonorant, – continuant]; and the only English [+ lateral] phoneme also has the feature specification given on the right of (9b).

The problem is that if we assume (as we do) that phonemic representations are only specified in terms of nonredundant features, then only one version of these two statements can be made; either (6)/(8) or (9a, b), but not both. Rule (6) presupposes that the [+ sonorant, – continuant] specification is present in the underlying representation of /m n ŋ/ and the feature [+ nasal] redundant, while (9a) assumes [+ nasal] to be present underlyingly and [+ sonorant, – continuant] to be supplied by redundancy rule. Similarly, (8) assumes an underlying analysis of /l/ as [+ sonorant, + continuant etc.] on the phonemic level, with [+ lateral] redundant, while in (9b), /l/ is underlyingly specified as [+ lateral] only. Being the only English lateral phoneme, /l/ is distinct from all other English phonemes by virtue of this feature alone; all other features can therefore be treated as redundant. We came across the same kind of situation in section 4.2.5 above, where we saw that either the rounding of vowels can be predicted by their backness or, alternatively, backness by rounding.

To be able to decide, then, whether (6)/(8) or (9a, b) are to be part of our phonology of English, we have to decide first which features are used for the expression of contrast on the phonemic level; all other features will then be redundant. As was noted in section 4.2.5 above, and as we see again here, given a set of phonemes and a set of features, it is not uncommon that several possibilities should exist for the expression of the phonemic contrasts of the language.

The problem that we are here encountering is really this. Given that we require phonemic representations to express contrast as economically as possible, the notion of economy itself is ambiguous and gives rise to two alternative interpretations. Do we mean by this that each phoneme is to be represented by the smallest possible number of features? In this case, it is preferable to represent nasals underlyingly as [+ nasal] rather than as [+ sonorant, − continuant]. Or do we mean that we want to employ the smallest possible number of features in the whole of the phonemic level of the language? In this case, we would wish to avoid the use of the feature [Nasal] on the phonemic level altogether and prefer to use [Sonorant] and [Continuant] instead: clearly, these two features are needed elsewhere on the phonemic level and have a far greater contrastive function than the feature [Nasal] has.

Any choice between the two possible interpretations of the notion of economy would have to be an arbitrary one here. It suffices to make the reader aware of the problem; we neither can nor need to solve it in a principled way. As was noted earlier, a detailed discussion of the various analytical possibilities that exist, under the two different interpretations of the economy requirement, would be too lengthy for an introductory treatment of features – and it would not even be particularly desirable to end up rejecting either (6)/(8) or (9a, b): both versions of these redundancy rules are interesting in their own right and helpful for the understanding of the English consonant system.

Indeed, our future use of feature specifications in this book does not even make it necessary for us to arrive at a definitive statement of redundancy-

Table 5.4 *Feature specifications of English consonant phonemes*

|  | m | n | ŋ | p | t | k | b | d | g | f | θ | s | ʃ | x | M | h | v | ð | z | ʒ | l | r | w | j |
|---|---|---|---|---|---|---|---|---|---|---|---|---|---|---|---|---|---|---|---|---|---|---|---|---|
| [Consonantal] | + | + | + | + | + | + | + | + | + | + | + | + | + | + | + | + | + | + | + | + | + | + | − | − |
| [Sonorant] | + | + | + | − | − | − | − | − | − | − | − | − | − | − | − | − | − | − | − | − | + | + | + | + |
| [Continuant] | − | − | − | − | − | − | − | − | − | + | + | + | + | + | + | + | + | + | + | + | + | + | + | + |
| [Anterior] | + | + | − | + | + | − | + | + | − | + | + | + | − | − | − | − | + | + | + | − | + | − | − | − |
| [Coronal] | − | + | − | − | + | − | − | + | − | − | + | + | + | − | − | − | − | + | + | + | + | + | − | − |
| [Strident] | − | − | − | − | − | − | − | − | − | + | − | + | + | − | − | − | + | − | + | + | − | − | − | − |
| [Round] | − | − | − | − | − | − | − | − | − | − | − | − | − | − | + | − | − | − | − | − | − | − | + | − |
| [High] | − | − | + | − | − | + | − | − | + | − | − | − | + | + | + | − | − | − | − | + | − | − | + | + |
| [Low] | − | − | − | − | − | − | − | − | − | − | − | − | − | − | − | + | − | − | − | − | − | − | − | − |
| [Back] | − | − | + | − | − | + | − | − | + | − | − | − | − | − | + | − | − | − | − | − | − | − | + | − |
| [Tense] | − | − | − | + | + | + | − | − | − | + | + | + | + | − | − | − | − | − | − | − | − | − | − | − |
| [Voice] | + | + | + | − | − | − | + | + | + | − | − | − | − | − | − | − | + | + | + | + | + | + | + | + |
| [Nasal] | + | + | + | − | − | − | − | − | − | − | − | − | − | − | − | − | − | − | − | − | − | − | − | − |
| [Lateral] | − | − | − | − | − | − | − | − | − | − | − | − | − | − | − | − | − | − | − | − | + | − | − | − |

free phonemic representations at this point. When we discuss the regularities of the concrete phonetic level of representations (in chapter 8 below), we shall no longer need to distinguish between redundant and nonredundant features simply because all features will be specified on that level; in particular, the redundant ones will by then have been supplied by redundancy rules. We do not discuss the complete set of redundancy rules but simply assume that by the time the phonetic level of the derivation is reached, they have all operated.

Consequently, it will be possible for the rules of the phonetic level (the allophonic rules) to make reference to nonredundant and redundant features alike. To return to an example of such a rule, the nasalisation of the vowels in *ham*, *hand*, *hang* etc. can then be stated in terms of rule (7b) above, regardless of whether the feature [Nasal] is on the phonemic level redundant or not. On the phonetic level, it is specified in either case.

We conclude our discussion of phonological features with a list of the complete feature specifications of the English consonant system. For reasons that are by now clear, no distinction is made between redundant and nonredundant features. Table 5.4 does not tell us which features are, for any given phoneme, present on the underlying level and which are not. Nor do we attempt to spell out a full set of redundancy rules.

Compare, finally, this table with the one that analyses the English vowel system at the end of chapter 4 (table 4.2). Why is it that table 5.4 contains more features than table 4.2 does, when we have been assuming that a single set of features characterises vowels and consonants alike? The answer is clear: the features that are missing in table 4.2 – these are the ones introduced in this chapter – are not needed for the specification of vowels; they are, without exception, redundant in the vowel system. This is not to say, of course, that they cannot be specified in the case of vowels. On the contrary: in principle, a full specification of a given vowel should contain 'plus' and 'minus' values for all features, including [Anterior], [Coronal], [Nasal] and such like. But since these features are redundant for vowels, and since we shall not even need to refer to them on the phonetic level, we need not now return to chapter 4 and re-open the discussion of English vowels in terms of new features.

### Suggested reading to chapter 5

See the reading to chapter 4 – the literature referred to at that point also covers the features introduced in this chapter. In addition:

Section 5.4   On voicing and the feature [Voice] see Ladefoged (1971: ch. 2), Catford (1977: ch. 6), Catford (1988: ch. 3). On tenseness and the 'fortis/lenis' distinction in consonants see Jakobson and Halle (1964), Catford (1977: ch. 10). 'Fortis' vs. 'lenis' (instead of 'voiceless' vs. 'voiced') is used in the analysis of the (RP) English consonant system by Gimson (1989), for example.

# 6
# Syllables

## 6.1 Phonetic and phonological units

So far, our study of the phonology of English has been concerned exclusively with phonological **segments**. To be precise, we have dealt with the **phonemes** of English, which make up the underlying phonological representation of every word of the language, as well as with the **phonological features** in terms of which these phonemes can be analysed. Phonemes, it was said in chapter 2, are the smallest successive units in phonology (and features are their simultaneously occurring components) – but we have as yet encountered no units larger than phonemes. In this chapter, we shall see that there are indeed phonological units that are larger than individual phonemes and that these units play an important part in phonological analysis.

Consider a simple example – the phonological analysis of the phrase *little tent*:

(1)  a.  Phonemic representation  /lɪtltɛnt/
      b.  Phonetic representation [ˈlɪʔtɫ'tʰɛ̃nʔt]

As we saw in chapter 2, phonemic representations such as the one in (1a) contain nonredundant (and therefore phonemic) information only; phonetic representations like (1b) contain additional phonetic details of the real-life utterance – ideally, all such details, but as we shall see in chapter 8, this ideal is really unattainable. Whenever such details are not part of the phonemic representation they are redundant, predictable through rules that we have yet to devise.

*Little tent*, for example, contains two different kinds of [l] sounds for many speakers: a 'clear' [l] and a 'dark' and 'syllabic' [ɫ]. The first realisation of /t/ in *tent* is 'aspirated' [tʰ], the second one as well as that in *little* 'glottalised' [ʔt], for most speakers. The vowel in *tent* is nasalised [ɛ̃]. And perhaps most noticeably, *little tent* consists of three syllables, the first and third of which are stressed. (A stressed syllable is marked in (1b) by a preceding '".) Details such as these still need to be considered systematically; the task that we now face is that of fleshing out the skeleton of phonemic information by accounting for the redundant phonetic facts of speech.

We begin this task by studying one particular kind of phonetic detail: namely, the fact that speech sounds are grouped into **syllables** and those in turn into higher-order rhythmic units that we may call 'stress feet' or simply **feet**: these are the phonological units larger than the segment that were mentioned earlier. Since syllables and feet seem to be indisputable facts of phonetic representations, we obviously have to concern ourselves with their nature and with the principles that govern them. But there is more to these larger-than-segment phonetic units than just that. Not only do they need to be accounted for in the interests of the completeness of our phonetic description; they in turn will prove instrumental in accounting for other things. Certain facts of the phonetic representation cannot be explained without reference to syllables and feet. The different realisations of /l/ and those of /t/, for example, in *little tent* are due to their different positions within the syllable and within the foot.

To put it more formally: segments, syllables and feet are not only **phonetic units** but also **phonological units**. They form (part of) the **phonological structure** of the language, which as a whole serves as a framework for the expression of phonological generalisations. To complete our picture of the phonology of English, we have to find out what the phonetic evidence for such units is, what phonological regularities they are governed by, and in what ways they figure in the analysis of further regularities. Let us begin, in this chapter, with the syllable.

### 6.2   What is a syllable?

Intuitively, syllables seem to be fairly straightforward objects. Speakers will normally have little difficulty in deciding how many syllables a given word of their language contains. *Tent* and *the* are single syllables; *little*, *pity* and *Peter* contain two syllables each, *syllable* and *determine* three, *phonology* four, *phonological* five, and so on. There are a few English words that may have variable pronunciations with different numbers of syllables – *bottling* may be pronounced with two or three syllables, *realistic* with three or four etc. – and in some such cases the difference in the number of syllables may be a matter of what the listener perceives rather than one of the actual pronunciation. On the whole, it would seem that such problematic cases constitute a small minority only. But that does not mean that it is easy to say what a syllable actually is, in phonetic and phonological terms.

131

Let us begin with the phonetics of the syllable. This is a rather complex subject, and the 'sonority theory' presented in this section is far from being universally accepted. It is adopted here because it lends itself, as we shall see later, particularly well to the statement of certain phonological generalisations in English.

When we discussed the initiation process (in sect. 1.1.1 above) we noted that the pulmonic air stream required for the production of speech does not flow at a constant rate; rather, it occurs in a series of pulses. To some extent, this pulsation is caused by bursts of activity on the part of the chest muscles, giving rise to variation in the flow rate of air. These major pulses will become especially relevant in chapter 7 below where feet and stress will be discussed. In addition to these, there are minor retardations in the air flow, caused either, again, by chest-muscle activity or by constrictions in the articulatory tract, or indeed by both.

Consider the pronunciation of a series of letters of the alphabet, say P-T-K [pitike]: note how the closures of [t] and [k] interrupt the air flow and how the string consists of three successive bursts of air, coinciding with three syllables. In E-F [iɛf], on the other hand, no such articulatory closure can be held responsible for syllable division – nevertheless, the transition from [i] to [ɛf] is marked by a syllable boundary. Here, the retardation of the air flow is of the former of the two kinds noted above: it is caused at the source of the air stream – the chest muscles – rather than by any narrowing or closure of the articulators.

According to such a 'pulse theory' of the syllable, then, each syllable corresponds to a peak in the flow rate of pulmonic air. The intervening troughs may have different causes and are not necessarily connected with chest-muscle activity. The problem with this pulse theory of the syllable is that, left as it stands, it explains very little. The air stream is inaudible, of course – how, then, can a word like *poetical* be perceived as having four syllables? The answer lies in the fact that the (kinetic) energy of the air-stream pulses is in speech translated into acoustic energy, one manifestation of which is **sonority**. The pulses of the air stream correspond to peaks in sonority. But now the notion of sonority has to be defined.

*The sonority of a sound is its relative loudness compared to other sounds*, everything else (pitch etc.) being equal. Speech sounds can be ranked in terms of their relative sonority: voiceless oral stops are of minimal sonority while low vowels have the highest degree of sonority of all speech sounds. All other sounds are ranked in between these two extreme points of the **sonority scale**, which is given in table 6.1 in a form sufficiently detailed for our purposes. With the help of this sonority scale, our theory that syllables

Table 6.1 *Sonority scale*

| Oral stops | | Fricatives | | Nasals | Liquids | Semivowels | Vowels | |
| Voiceless | Voiced | Voiceless | Voiced | | | | High | Low |
|---|---|---|---|---|---|---|---|---|
| p | b | f | v | m | | | | |
| t | d | θ | ð | n | | j | i | a |
| k | g | s | z | ŋ | l   r | w | u | ɑ |

s o n o r i t y ⟶

are associated with peaks of sonority is able to predict the right number of syllables for a great majority of English words, leaving unexplained only a small number of cases, to which we shall turn in the next section. Let us first apply our theory to some examples.

Consider first a monosyllabic word such as *clamp*. What we have is the phonemic representation /klamp/ – but why is it monosyllabic? According to the sonority scale (table 6.1), /k/ is less sonorous than /l/, which is less sonorous than /a/. This is more sonorous than /m/, which in turn is more sonorous than the final /p/. In a rather impressionistic graphic representation, the sonority profile of *clamp* is as in (2) below, clearly showing a single sonority peak:

(2)  sonority

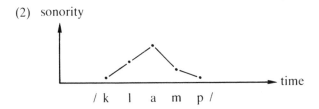

/ k   l   ɑ   m   p /

In comparison, let us represent a bisyllabic word such as **Andrew** in the same graphic form:

(3)  sonority

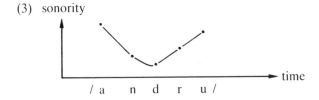

/ a   n   d   r   u /

Again, the two peaks in the diagram reflect the fact that the word has two syllables.

133

There are, finally, some rather striking examples where the members of a pair of words contain the same phonemes but in different order. One member is monosyllabic, the other bisyllabic. Such cases are *alp – apple*, *lilt – little*, *wind* (verb) – *widen*, *pelt – petal*:

(4)  sonority

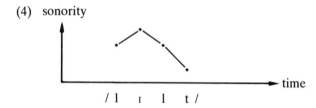

/ l    ɪ    l    t /

sonority

/ l    ɪ    t    l /

So much for the cases where the sonority theory of the syllable makes the right predictions: in each case, the perceived number of syllables corresponds to the number of peaks in a sonority profile, assuming the sonority scale (table 6.1). Some problems and questions, however, remain.

### 6.3   Some unanswered questions

The sonority theory, outlined in the preceding section, gives us a general understanding of what syllables are: they are associated with peaks in sonority in such a way that in a given string of phonemes, every syllable corresponds to a single sonority peak. While this phonetic definition is probably universal – the syllables of all languages can be described in this way – it leaves a number of questions unresolved and facts unexplained, some of which are also universal while others relate specifically to English. Let us identify these problems now; in the remainder of this chapter we shall try to answer them.

First, consider the two phrases *hidden aims* and *hid names*, both of which may, in terms of phonemes, be identically represented as /hɪdnemz/. The problem is that despite this segmental identity, *hidden aims* has three syllables and *hid names* two. The reason for this discrepancy is quite obvious (but not provided by the sonority theory): *hidden aims* has three syllables because *hidden* has two and *aims* one; *hid names* is bisyllabic because it consists of two monosyllabic words:

(5)   *hidden aims*

(5)   sonority

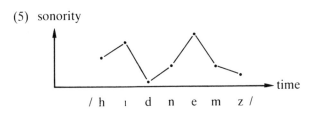

*hid names*

sonority

This example demonstrates a general property of the rules that govern the way in which strings are divided into syllables: these rules (which we shall henceforth call rules of **syllabification**) take into account the boundaries between words. More precisely: the domain of syllabification is the single word. Words are syllabified individually and then put together into phrases and sentences. We are justified, therefore, in discussing the syllabification of words in this chapter without reference to larger domains such as the phrase. Connected speech is, however, subject to a few adjustments in syllabification, to which we shall return in chapter 9.

The second question that the sonority theory does not answer concerns the positions of syllable boundaries within words. Consider, for example, some longer words such as *aroma* and *phonology*:

(6)   sonority

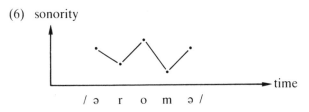

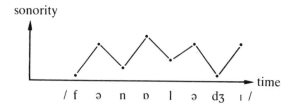

It is clear (and this much the sonority theory does predict) that *aroma* has three syllables and *phonology* four. But where do the syllable boundaries fall? Most speakers would agree on the following syllabification (where syllable boundaries are marked by dots): *a.ro.ma, pho.no.lo.gy* – but while the sonority theory identifies the troughs between the syllable peaks, it does not predict what appears to be quite a simple regularity: the consonant that constitutes such a trough is in each case part of the following rather than the preceding syllable. Typically, speakers do not syllabify *phonology* as *\*phon.ol.og.y*.

The third question: how many phonemes can a syllable contain and what phonemes can occur next to each other in a syllable? Let us start here with a rather absurd example: why is *\*/pljaʊlmp/* an impossible syllable in English? Clearly, not because of any conflict with the sonority theory: the string has one sonority peak only:

(7)   sonority

The reason is clearly that no English syllable can contain that many phonemes; it would appear that a word like *clamp* just about exhausts the potential of a single syllable.

But here again we run into a new problem: if /klamp/ is permissible in English then why is *\*/knamp/* not? Once again, the sonority theory has to be amended by further constraints on possible English syllables: the single-peak criterion alone is not enough. We additionally have to spell out the rules for the permissible number of phonemes in a syllable and for the ways in which phonemes can cluster. *\*/kn/* is forbidden in English even though it does constitute the upward sonority slope that the beginning of a syllable requires.

Finally, consider the monosyllabic word *sticks*:

(8)  sonority

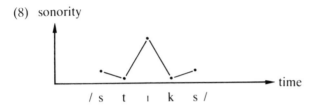

Why does this word constitute a single syllable in English when it evidently contains three sonority peaks? This problem is in a sense the most serious one of the four identified here: in the ones raised previously – the syllabification of *hidden aims* etc., of *aroma* etc., and the */pljaʊlmp/ and */knamp/ problems – we realised that English has syllabification rules in addition to the single-peak criterion provided by the sonority theory. None of these rules is in contradiction to the sonority theory; rather, they are amendments to this rather loose theory of the syllable. In the case of *sticks*, on the other hand, we are faced with a syllabification rule of English that contradicts the single-peak principle of the sonority theory by allowing three peaks to make a single syllable.

In the paragraphs that follow, we shall deal with the problems just raised in this order: first, we shall discuss in some detail the structure of monosyllabic words, thereby dealing with the */pljaʊlmp/, */knamp/ and /stɪks/ problems. Then we shall turn to polysyllabic words and discuss *aroma* etc., comparing the syllable structure of monosyllables with that found in words containing more than one syllable.

### 6.4   The structure of monosyllabic words

One of the questions raised in section 6.3 above was that of the maximum number of segments in a syllable. We pursue this question here by studying the segmental composition of monosyllabic words: clearly, whatever is a well-formed monosyllabic word is also a well-formed syllable. This strategy simplifies matters by enabling us, for the moment, to side-step the difficult problem of locating the boundaries between two syllables in polysyllabic words like, say, *pity* or *phonology*. Moreover, monosyllabic words will give us some evidence for intermediate phonological units within the syllable: units that comprise more than one segment but are smaller than a whole syllable. Thus, we shall see that a syllable like *clamp* is best analysed in terms of the structure (9b) rather than (9a):

(9) a.  Syllable          b.  Syllable

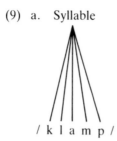 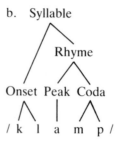

We shall refer to the **syllabic** segment, the peak of the sonority curve, simply as the **peak** of the syllable. The peak may be preceded by one or more consonants; we shall call this part of the syllable the **onset**. Following the peak may be more consonants, referred to as the **coda**. And perhaps most importantly, we shall group the peak and the coda together and call the resulting unit the **rhyme** of the syllable. The reasons for recognising such a phonological unit (and not, for example, one that contains the onset and the peak) will become clear shortly. The reason for its name is obvious: it is precisely this part of the syllable that plays an important role in the rhyming conventions of poetry – for example in *lie – die, man – ran, milk – silk* etc.

### 6.4.1  *The onset*

Consider the following examples:

(10) a. eye      b. pie      c. pry      d. *pfry      e. spy
     eat         seat        sleeve      *tsleeve      street
     ink         wink        swing       *kswing       spring

We note, firstly, that syllables need not have onsets: in (10a), *eye, eat* and *ink* begin with the syllabic element (the peak). Next, if there is an onset then it may contain either one consonant position (10b) or two (10c). Example (10d) gives some ill-formed syllables, all of which contain three consonant positions in the onset. Let us venture the generalisation – despite some apparent counter-examples in (10e)! – that the two-position onset constitutes some kind of upper limit on the complexity of this phonological unit.

But what about (10e)? Clearly, *street* and *spring* contain three onset consonants and are nevertheless well formed. However, the reason why we nevertheless maintain the generalisation, for the moment, that the onset proper consists of maximally two consonant positions is that the /s/ in /str/, /spr/, /st/ etc. behaves oddly in another respect too: it violates the sonority-based definition of the syllable. Both (10b) and (10c) conform with this definition: a single consonant as in (10b) will always be less sonorous than the peak following it, and if there are two onset consonants, as there are in (10c), then the first must be less sonorous than the second (which in turn will be less sonorous than the peak): /pl/, /sl/, /sw/ (and many more) are possible onsets while their mirror images /lp/, /ls/, /ws/ never are. The /s/ in the examples of (10e), then, has a special status: it can occupy an otherwise inadmissible consonant position in the onset and it violates the generalisation that onset sequences increase in sonority. We shall return to this problem in section 6.4.5 below; ignoring it here, we represent our (as yet incomplete) findings as follows:

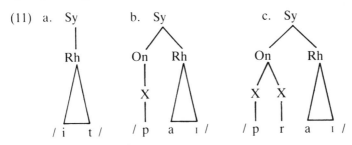

(11) a. Sy  b. Sy  c. Sy

Briefly, a note on the notation used in (11). The triangle simply covers unanalysed material: we have as yet said nothing about the structure of the rhyme. Each 'X' in the onset stands for a position occupied by a single consonant phoneme. For the moment, these X-positions are just a shorthand notation for single phonemes; they will turn into rather more complex entities later.

### 6.4.2 The coda

The coda of the syllable is the consonant or sequence of consonants that follows the peak. It is a phonological unit that is in several respects similar to the onset, except that it is the mirror-image of the onset, of course: while onset and peak constitute an upward slope in sonority, peak and coda make a downward slope. Consider the following examples:

(12)  a. pie   b. seat   c. clamp   d. *filmp   e. clamps
        free     feel       film       *firlm       adze
        fill       clasp     *clamsp      act

Like onsets, codas are optional: (12a) exemplifies well-formed syllables that have no codas. Also like an onset, a coda can contain one consonant position (12b) or two (12c). And again, two such consonant positions seem to constitute the upper limit: the syllables in (12d), containing three coda consonants, are ill formed. But once more we are faced with a problem:

consider the examples in (12e). *Clamps* contains three coda consonants and seems, therefore, to violate the rule that we have just established. Note, however, that the final consonant in *clamps* not only gives the coda more than two consonant positions; it also fails to participate in the downward sonority slope that otherwise characterises that part of the syllable: /s/ is more sonorous than the preceding /p/ and therefore constitutes a new peak. Similarly, the /z/ in *adze* and the /t/ in *act* are not less sonorous than their left neighbours. We conclude, tentatively for the moment, that the coda proper is limited to two consonant positions but that it can be followed by certain consonant phonemes – /s/, /z/ and /t/, for example – that may also violate the sonority generalisation. Such phonemes, then, have special status. We shall return to this problem, which is strikingly similar to the one encountered in onsets containing /spr/ etc., in section 6.4.5 below. For the moment, we represent our findings regarding the coda schematically like this:

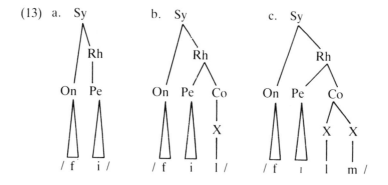

### 6.4.3 *The peak*

The peak of the syllable contains the 'syllabic' element: the segment that is more sonorous than both its neighbours. Here is the example of *clamp* again, which we can now fully analyse:

(14)

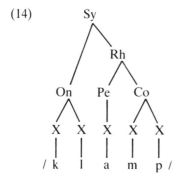

It is at this point that we turn our attention to the X-positions marked in our syllable diagrams. So far, this notational device has been rather inconsequential: X-positions and consonant phonemes have been simply corresponding one-to-one. If we extend the scope of what X-positions can denote, then we can make some rather interesting generalisations.

Recall the fact, discussed at some length in section 4.2.3, that lax vowels in RP and GA are short and tense vowels as well as diphthongs long – remember examples such as *bit* vs. *beat*, *bite*. It was argued at the time that in pairs of phonemes like /i/–/ɪ/, the tense–lax distinction is the phonemically relevant one while the accompanying long–short distinction is redundant: predicted, by rules that we still have to spell out, from the underlying tense–lax distinction.

Now it would, of course, be possible simply to express vowel length by means of a binary feature [Long] – this was the way in which we expressed vowel-length differences, provisionally, in section 4.2.3. However, we noted there that such a feature [Long] has a somewhat unreliable phonetic content: the [+ long] vowel in *beat* is rather shorter than the one in *bead*; the [− long] one in *bit* shorter than the one in *bid*. We can avoid the use of the segmental feature [Long], poorly defined as it is, by treating vowel length instead as a property related to syllable structure. As we shall see, expressing length in terms of X-positions has several advantages, with respect to the generalisations that follow from it, over the segmental feature [Long].

Let us simply analyse a lax vowel (like the one in *clamp*, (14) above) as being associated with a single X-position. Let us also say that diphthongs, like the ones in *pie*, *cow*, *boy*, are associated with two X-positions, like this:

(15)

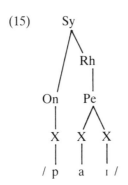

In this way we express the fact that diphthongs in RP and GA are longer than lax monophthongs are: X-positions can simply be counted as timing units. And then we can express the length of tense vowels by associating each such vowel with two X-positions. Here are, for example, the syllable analyses of *fill* (lax vowel) and *feel* (tense vowel):

(16)

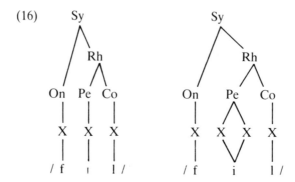

Let us formulate the rules that specify the association of vowels with X-positions as follows:

(17)   *Vowel-Length Rule (RP, GA)*

    a.   Associate a [− tense] vowel with one X-position.
    b.   Associate each element of a diphthong with one X-position.
    c.   Associate a [+ tense] vowel with two X-positions.

It will be remembered that in SSE, matters regarding vowel length are rather less straightforward than they are in RP and GA. We noted in section 4.2.3 that SSE tense vowels are long in certain contexts only (namely, before voiced fricatives, /r/ and word boundaries) and short elsewhere, while lax vowels are always short. While a treatment of these facts in terms of X-positions is not hard to imagine, its detailed discussion will be postponed for the moment. We shall return to this question in chapter 8.

So far so good: differences in vowel length can be expressed in terms of X-positions. But why is this notation better than the one using the segmental feature [Long]? Surely, any charge of phonetic unreliability levelled against the feature [Long] must also hold with respect to the 'X' vs. 'XX' distinction? This is true. The problem of length differences among the realisations of each vowel phoneme has not simply gone away and is not solved by the X-notation. But the use of X-positions for the notation of length has other advantages. These will show up in the analysis of the rhyme.

### 6.4.4 *The rhyme*

The rhyme of a syllable, as was noted before, is a unit that consists of the peak and the coda. It would seem, then, that this unit presents no further problems, given that peak and coda have already been discussed. But one question arises here: why do we need to recognise the rhyme as a phonological unit in addition to the ones that we have already established? Why do we not simply analyse a syllable (such as, again, *clamp*) as in (18a) and propose instead the rather more complex analysis (18b)?

(18)   a.  *Sy          b.  Sy

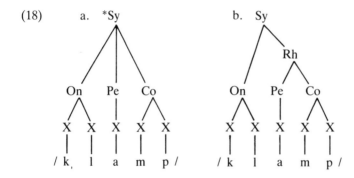

The reason for having the rhyme as a unit is that peak and coda 'function together' rather than separately in a number of ways. In the case of monosyllabic words, it can be shown that it is the number of X-positions in the rhyme (rather than the number of X-positions in peak and coda counted separately) that determines whether or not a syllable is well formed. Consider the following examples:

(19)   a. eye   b. sit   c. seal   d. clamp   e. */klaɪmp/   f. finds
          free      fill      pine      elm           */sɪlm/        seals

Ignoring once again the examples in (19f), we find that (19a–d) are well-formed syllables while those in (19e) are not. Here are their full analyses in terms of the notation developed above:

(20)

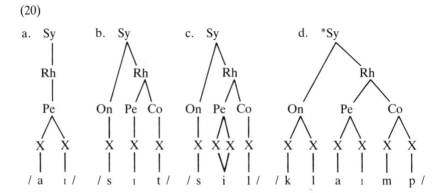

Provided we can account for *finds* and *seals* by different means – and this problem is by now nothing new: recall section 6.4.2 – we can make the generalisation that well-formed syllables contain no more than three X-positions in the rhyme. This statement will have to be amended below in order to accommodate (19f); for the moment it will suffice. Notice how peak and coda interact in this calculation of maximal syllables: it makes no difference to the wellformedness of a syllable whether the peak contains two X-positions and the coda one, or vice versa. It is the sum of X-positions in peak plus coda that counts, not the way in which these X-positions are distributed. This is the reason, promised earlier, for introducing the rhyme into our model of syllable structure: without the rhyme, it would be rather difficult to make generalisations about maximal syllables.

This generalisation is also the reason why, when faced with the choice of representing vowel length either by the segmental feature [Long] or by the distinction of 'X' vs. 'XX', we opted for the latter. Using [− long] vs. [+ long] instead, we would have to describe the maximal rhyme as 'either a [+ long] monophthong or a diphthong plus X, or a [− long] monophthong plus XX'. Evidently, this generalisation is inferior to the one that the X-notation for vowel length enables us to make.

Note, incidentally, that there is no evidence for onset and peak being tied up together in a single unit in the way peak and coda are in the rhyme. The possible complexity of the onset (ranging, as we saw in sect. 6.4.1, from zero to (for the moment) two X-positions) is a variable in syllable structure that is quite unrelated to the rest of the syllable. The peak of the syllable functions together with the coda but not with the onset. Our model of syllable structure predicts this close relationship, and the absence of a similar relationship between onset and peak, correctly.

Finally, having established the maximum number of X-positions in the rhyme, we face the question, what is the minimum number? Is a two-X rhyme, as in *free* or *sit*, the minimum or are single-X rhymes also possible? Consider (21):

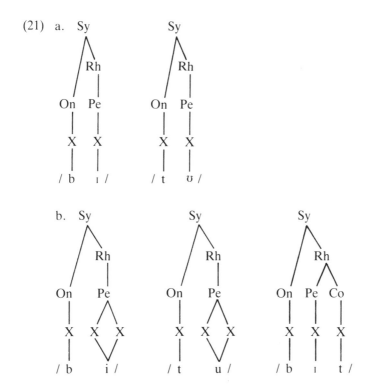

(21) a.

/ b ɪ /

/ t ʊ /

b.

/ b i /

/ t u /

/ b ɪ t /

Clearly, the examples in (21a) are impossible English nouns, verbs or adjectives: such words, referred to as 'lexical' words, minimally have the structure exemplified in (21b). Indeed, we can relate back now to a point that was made in section 3.3 above, where tenseness as a distinctive feature was discussed: it was said there that lax vowels can occur only in such syllables as are closed by a consonant (such as *bit*) while tense vowels can occur in open and closed syllables (*bee* and *beat* respectively). Expressed in terms of syllable structure, the generalisation would be that a syllable has minimally two X-positions in the rhyme.

But is this generalisation true? Some apparent counter-examples come to mind, such as the articles *the* /ðə/, *a* /ə/, the preposition *to* (/tʊ/ or /tə/) and a few more. To accommodate these, we have to qualify the generalisation just

made and say that *stressed syllables have a minimally two-X rhyme*, while
unstressed syllables may have a rhyme with a single X-position. Stress is a
phonological variable that will be discussed in some detail in chapter 7
below; here, we only give a brief outline of the way stress and syllable
structure are related.

Let us call a syllable that has a two-X rhyme a **heavy syllable** and one with
a single-X rhyme a **light syllable**:

(22)  Heavy syllable          Light syllable

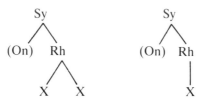

The crucial regularity is that *stressed syllables are heavy*. And since it is the
case that all lexical words (i.e. nouns, verbs, adjectives) have at least one
stressed syllable, monosyllabic lexical words therefore always being
stressed, it follows that such monosyllables must be heavy. /bɪ/, /tʊ/ and /ə/
are therefore impossible nouns, verbs or adjectives.

Single-X rhymes are not, however, impossible in 'function words' such as
articles, prepositions etc. These are (usually) unstressed and do not
therefore need to be heavy syllables. Note that such words often do have
stressed variants: in an utterance like *not 'a book but 'the book*, many
speakers will pronounce articles under stress as /e/ and /ði/ – and in these
cases the articles have heavy syllables on account of their vowels being
tense. Moreover, light syllables are also possible in the unstressed positions
of polysyllabic words: the first and third syllables in *aroma*, for example, are
light.

Let us take stock at this point and summarise the results of our discussion.
In accordance with the sonority theory developed in section 6.2, a syllable is
associated with a single peak in sonority. Every syllable has a 'syllabic'
segment (the peak). This segment is more sonorous, in terms of the sonority
scale (table 6.1), than both its right and its left neighbour. Segments
preceding the peak form a phonological unit called the onset. Sonority
increases in the onset from left to right and the maximum number of
X-positions in the onset is two. Segments following the peak form a
phonological unit called the coda; sonority decreases in the coda from left to

right. Peak and coda form a phonological unit called the rhyme. The minimum number of X-positions in the rhyme is one for unstressed syllables and two for stressed syllables: the maximum number is three. Let us call a syllable that conforms with this description a **core syllable**.

### 6.4.5  *Appendices*

It has been apparent throughout the preceding discussion that monosyllabic words can violate the core-syllable pattern summarised above: recall, for example, the problems posed by the initial /s/ in *spring* and by the final /s/ in *clamps*. In this section, we shall first discuss such violations found in the rhyme and then those in the onset.

As regards the rhyme, we have found that both of the two constraints on the form of this phonological unit can be violated: there may be more than three X-positions, and there may be violations of our generalisation that sonority decreases from left to right. Both these pattern violations are exemplified by the final consonant in *clamps*. But, as we shall see, these violations of our pattern form a pattern in themselves and do not, therefore, force us to abandon any of the generalisations that we have made.

Table 6.2 gives examples of the former and the latter type of pattern violation. Note that it is common for segments at the end of the rhyme to violate both constraints: they may exceed the limit of three X-positions and violate the sonority generalisation. Note also that in some cases, offending segments are inflexional endings (for plural or past tense) while in others they are not. This is worth noting but not crucial to the argument.

Table 6.2 *Syllable-final appendices*

| Three-X exceeded | Sonority violated | Both | Offending segment |
|---|---|---|---|
| mind | begged | lobed | |
| filed | robbed | | /d/ |
| | | | |
| paint | dropped | peaked | |
| hoofed | looked | text | /t/ |
| | | | |
| Giles | adze | minds | |
| beans | lads | globes | /z/ |
| | | | |
| bounce | fox | coax | |
| flounce | text | drinks | /s/ |
| | | | |
| | width | length | /θ/ |
| | | | |
| lounge | | | |
| strange | | | /dʒ/ |

The examples in table 6.2 show clearly that we have to allow for certain consonants to occur after the final consonant of an otherwise well-formed core syllable. This core syllable may or may not already have the maximum number of three X-positions in the rhyme; and the additional consonant may or may not conform with the sonority generalisation. Consider, for example, *mind* and *fox*. In (23) below, the core syllables contained in these words are fully analysed and the final consonants, which in each case cannot be part of the core syllable, are simply appended to the preceding structure. In *mind*, the /d/ cannot be part of the core syllable because it constitutes a fourth X-position; in *fox*, the /s/ violates the sonority generalisation.

(23)

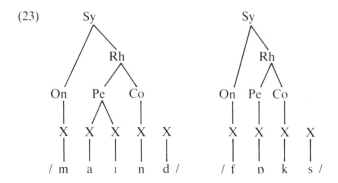

All the examples listed in table 6.2 contain one or more consonants that cannot be part of the core syllable. Here are two examples that contain more than one such consonant: *minds* and *texts*.

(24)

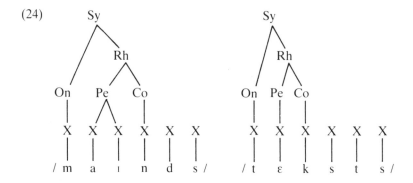

In *minds*, the /n/ must be the final segment of the core syllable because it is the third X in the rhyme, while in *texts*, the /k/ is the final segment of the core syllable because the following /s/ fails to conform with the sonority generalisation.

It would seem at first sight, then, that the constraints on the structure of the rhyme that we formulated in section 6.4.4 are invalid: the examples listed in table 6.2 by no means have the status of rare exceptions to an otherwise general rule. However, what makes our previous generalisations still valid is the fact that the segments that can be appended to the core syllable fall into a very clearly defined class. If any random consonant phoneme could follow the core syllable then the notion of the core syllable itself would be invalid; but the facts are that these appended segments can only be the ones listed in table 6.2. Any other consonant, if appended to a core syllable, produces an ill-formed result: /maɪnd/ is possible but */maɪmp/ is not; /wɪdθ/ is possible but */wɪdf/ is not.

The class of consonants that can follow the core syllable can be defined in terms of distinctive features: such consonants must have the feature composition [− sonorant, + coronal]. It is clear that this restriction is radically different from the constraints that hold within the core syllable: there, we have the sonority constraint, while here we are dealing with a constraint that only allows a certain place of articulation. We are justified, therefore, in maintaining our constraints regarding the core syllable. To accommodate the cases listed in table 6.2, we allow a rhyme to contain *a core rhyme plus further X-positions, which must contain coronal obstruents*, and which we shall refer to as the **appendix**.

Along similar lines, we can account for the problems encountered in the onset of the syllable: here, too, an appendix can occur – although, as we shall see, onset appendices are not as complex as rhyme appendices are. Consider some examples:

(25)  a. spill       b. spring      split      spew
         still          string                   stew
         skill          scream                   skew

Like the cases listed in table 6.2, those in (25) cannot be accounted for in terms of our sonority theory of the syllable: the /s/ in *spill*, *spring* etc. constitutes an additional sonority peak and all the words in (25) are therefore wrongly predicted to be bisyllabic. Moreover, the occurrences of /s/ in (25b) constitute a third X-position in the onset; in this respect, too, these examples fail to conform with the core-syllable pattern developed in the preceding sections.

Once more, however, these pattern violations form a pattern in themselves. It is only /s/ that can violate the sonority generalisation of the onset, and whenever an onset contains three X-positions then the first one of these will be an /s/ that also violates the sonority generalisation. We can maintain our generalisation that core onsets contain two X-positions of increasing sonority by simply treating the occurrences of /s/ in cases such as the ones listed in (25) as appendices: *a core onset may be preceded by an appendix /s/*.

Note that /s/ is once more a coronal obstruent; but unlike the appendix segments found in the right margin of the syllable, onset appendices can only be /s/ – no other coronal obstruent is possible in this position (except the /ʃ/ in Yiddish loan words found in some varieties of English: *shtick*, *shtumm* etc.). Moreover, onset appendices can only contain one segment, while rhyme appendices can contain more than one: recall *texts*. And finally, onset appendices can only occur before /p t k/: onsets such as */sf/, */sfl/ etc. are not possible (except, again, in certain loan words: *sphere*, *sphinx* etc.). We shall discuss such niceties of the co-occurrence restrictions of phonemes in section 6.5; up until now our main concern has been the establishment of an overall picture of what is a possible syllable in English. This overall picture can now be summarised in terms of the syllable template for English monosyllabic words in Figure 6.1.

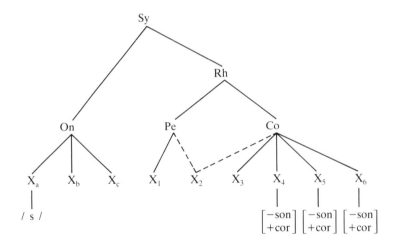

Conditions: (1) $X_{1-2}$ are obligatory.
(2) $X_b–X_3$ are associated with a single sonority peak, the maximum being $X_1$
(3) $X_2$ is associated with either peak or coda.

Figure 6.1    Syllable template

## 6.5 The syllable template and phonotactics

It is part of the phonological study of a language to address the question of how the phonemes of that language can be put together to make well-formed syllables and words: what consonant clusters are permissible; what sequences of vowels and consonants; and in what positions within words and syllables are these clusters and sequences allowed? This aspect of phonology, called **phonotactics**, is our concern in this section.

We assume, for the moment without arguments, that the domain of phonotactics is the syllable: any constraints on possible clusters and sequences hold within the syllable rather than the word. For the monosyllabic words that we are dealing with at the moment, this assumption is somewhat trivial: obviously, if a given sequence of phonemes cannot be a syllable then it also cannot be a monosyllabic word. But we shall have to consider this issue in some detail when we deal with polysyllabic words in section 6.6 below.

Some of the phonotactic constraints of English have been dealt with already (without being called by that name): the constraints that rule out, for example, */pljaʊlmp/ as a possible syllable and */lp/ as a possible onset. As we have seen, the constraints responsible are, in the former case, the limited number of permissible X-positions in onset and rhyme, and in the latter case the generalisation concerning sonority in onset clusters: /lp/ is a possible coda but not a possible onset.

It is the latter kind of constraint, and its particular consequences for English, that we concentrate on in this section. Assuming the validity of the template (figure 6.1), we shall now investigate in detail what sequences of phonemes satisfy the sonority generalisation in the various possible positions within the syllable. Moreover, we shall find that there are some questions that cannot be answered with reference to sonority alone: why, for example, are there no monosyllabic words beginning with */ml/ and none with */kn/ when such onsets should, in terms of sonority alone, be allowed? Before we go into these details, let us take another, less informal, look at the sonority scale, repeated as table 6.3.

The reader will have noticed already that the use of classificatory terms such as 'fricative', 'nasal stop' etc. is, strictly speaking, no longer legitimate for us: in chapters 4 and 5 we have replaced these with binary features and their combinations. And since the use of such features will prove particularly advantageous in what follows, let it be our first task to express the sonority scale in terms of the phonological features introduced in earlier chapters (see figure 6.2).

Table 6.3 *Sonority scale (old version)*

| Oral stops | | Fricatives | | Nasals | Liquids | Semivowels | Vowels | |
| voiceless | voiced | voiceless | voiced | | | | high | low |
| p | b | f | v | m | | | | |
| t | d | θ | ð | n | | j | i | a |
| k | g | s | z | ŋ | l    r | w | u | ɑ |

s o n o r i t y →

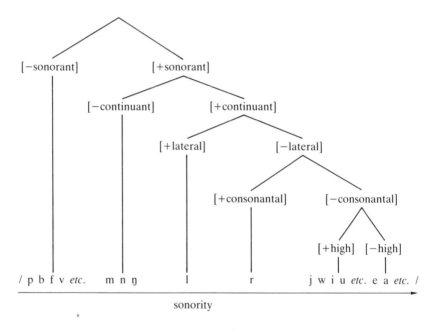

Figure 6.2    Sonority scale (feature-based version)

Figure 6.2 may be read as follows: [−sonorant] is less sonorous than [+sonorant]. Among the latter, [+sonorant, −continuant] is less sonorous than [+sonorant, +continuant] is. Again among the latter of those, [+sonorant, +continuant, +lateral] is less sonorous than [+sonorant, +continuant, −lateral] is, and so forth. Note that this new version of the sonority scale is less detailed than the old one was: there, the [−sonorant] class was divided into several subclasses and sonority differences were said to exist between those. The new version (figure 6.2) is tailored to the needs of the phonotactics of English: although in universal phonetic terms the various subclasses of nonsonorants are said to differ in sonority, the phonology of English does not, as we shall see presently, utilise those in the constraints that govern possible syllables.

### 6.5.1  *Onset phonotactics*

As we saw in section 6.4.1, onsets are not obligatory in English syllables. Where a syllable does have an onset, it can have one or two X-positions, possibly preceded by an appendix /s/.

(26)  Onset template

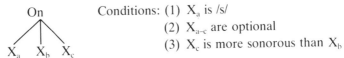

Conditions: (1) $X_a$ is /s/
          (2) $X_{a-c}$ are optional
          (3) $X_c$ is more sonorous than $X_b$

Referring back to the inventory of English consonant phonemes given in chapter 2 (table 2.1) we note that the only consonants that cannot occur in onsets containing a single X-position are /ŋ/ and /ʒ/. Of these, /ʒ/ is a marginal phoneme in English and its absence from onsets may well be due to an accidental gap in the vocabulary. /ŋ/ is a different problem: it is not only disallowed in onsets altogether but also, as we shall see, severely restricted within the rhyme.

Let us now turn to onsets containing two X-positions, more precisely, onsets containing $X_b$ and $X_c$ but no appendix ($X_a$). As we already know, in such clusters $X_c$ has to be more sonorous than $X_b$; but the constraint is actually stricter than that: the first consonant must be [−sonorant] and the second [+sonorant]. Among the set of conceivable onset clusters with increasing sonority, */pf/, /ml/, /lr/ etc. are ruled out. All English onsets have the form:

(27)  Onset template (final version)

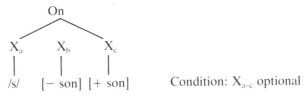

Condition: $X_{a-c}$ optional

Note that the sonority generalisation is now expressed in the feature specifications for $X_b$ and $X_c$ and no longer in the form of a separate condition.

Even (27) does not fully describe the facts: it is not true to say that any [− sonorant] consonant can combine with any [+ sonorant] to form a two-X onset. In table 6.4, [−sonorant] phonemes are listed in the left-hand column and [+ sonorant] consonants in the top line (where /j/ is for the moment excluded). Possible combinations are marked '+'. As the table shows, the template (27) is far too permissive: the majority of clusters permitted by (27) do not occur in English. One way of dealing with this problem would be to specify possible onsets as 'all those permitted by (27) except */pm/, /pn/, /pŋ/, /pw/, ...', thus listing all those clusters individually that are not marked '+' in table 6.4. However, matters can be simplified: the gaps in table 6.4 obey certain regularities and can therefore, at least partially, be stated in more general terms.

Note, for example, that /v ð z ʒ/ do not occur in onset clusters at all. Since these phonemes all share the feature specification [−sonorant, +continuant, +voice], we can simply rule out any onset of the form:

(28)

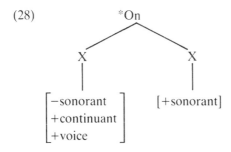

Next, only /s/ can occur with /m/ or /n/. Given that /s/ is [+ strident], it is true to say that no nonstrident phonemes can occur with /m n/:

(29)

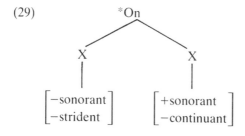

(Notice that (29) does not account for the fact that /f/, which is also strident, cannot occur with /m n/!) Moreover, / t d θ/ (but not /s/) are forbidden to occur with /l/:

Table 6.4 *Possible consonant clusters in onsets*

| | m | n | ŋ | l | r | w | Examples |
|---|---|---|---|---|---|---|---|
| p | | | | + | + | | play, prey |
| b | | | | + | + | | blue, brew |
| f | | | | + | + | | fly, fry |
| v | | | | | | | |
| t | | | | | + | + | try, twig |
| d | | | | | + | + | dry, dwell |
| θ | | | | | + | + | throw, thwart |
| ð | | | | | | | |
| s | + | + | | + | | + | smear, sneer, slow, swing |
| z | | | | | | | |
| ʃ | ? | ? | | ? | + | ? | ?shmuck, ?schnapps, ?shlep, shrew, ?Schweppes |
| ʒ | | | | | | | |
| tʃ | | | | | | | |
| dʒ | | | | | | | |
| k | | | | + | + | + | clue, crew, queen |
| g | | | | + | + | + | glue, grey, Gwen |
| x | | | | | | | |
| h | | | | | | | |

(30)

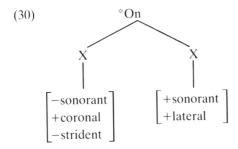

And similarly, /p b f/ (and /v/, but we have already accounted for this) cannot occur with /w/:

(31)

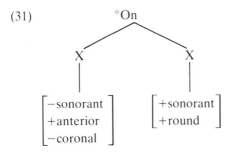

It is quite clear that we would have to formulate quite a few more of these **negative onset conditions**, or **filters**, if we were to account completely for the gaps in table 6.4. We need not embark on this venture here; the principle is clear: the gaps are not entirely random – at the very least we can conclude that a complete list of filters of the kind exemplified in (28)–(31) would be significantly shorter than a list of all the individual ill-formed onset clusters. A statement of the possible syllable onsets of a language (and, as we shall see, a statement of possible rhymes), then, consists of a (positive) template amended by a set of (negative) filters.

Let us apply the same strategy – template plus filters – to onsets containing appendix-/s/. Recall the examples given in section 6.4.5 above; possible onset clusters with appendix-/s/ are listed below, again excluding clusters containing /j/:

(32)  a.  /sp/          b.  /spl/     */stl/    ?/skl/
          /st/              /spr/     /str/     /skr/
          /sk/              */spw/    */stw/    /skw/
          */sf/ etc.        */spm/    */stm/    */skm/
                            */spn/    */stn/    */skn/
                            */spŋ/    */stŋ/    */skŋ/

/s/ cannot occur freely before every one of the well-formed onsets listed in table 6.4; rather, it occurs only before /p t k/ and is absent before /b d g/ and, with a few exceptions such as *sphere*, before fricatives. We express these facts in terms of the following filters:

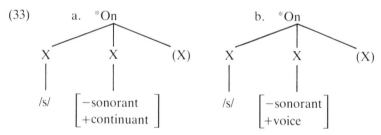

(33)      a.  *On                          b.  *On

(Where the bracketed X-position stands for the optional sonorant that may follow.)

Having so restricted the nonsonorant immediately following an appendix-/s/, we have no further problems with the sonorant that may fill the bracketed X-position. Rather strikingly, the sonorants that may follow single /p t k/ can also follow /sp/, /st/ and sk/, with one exception (or perhaps two): */tw/ is possible (*twig*) but */stw/ is not; and while /kl/ is common, we have to resort to *sclerosis* to attest /skl/. This can easily be accounted for by one or two appropriate filters; what is more important is that none of the filters that holds in two-X clusters without appendixes is violated in /s/-plus-two-X clusters: any cluster that is forbidden without a preceding /s/ is also forbidden with a preceding /s/.

We conclude this section by considering in some detail the behaviour of /j/ in onsets: although this phoneme occurs in single-X onsets as well as clusters as permitted by the template (26), it obeys regularities quite different from those studied so far and poses some problems for our analysis.

In single-X onsets, no problems arise: /j/ is free to occur as it does in *yield*, *you*, *yell*, *yarn* etc. It is, rather, its behaviour in onset clusters that causes problems. Firstly, it clusters with nonsonorants far more freely than any other sonorant does; in some cases, it can occur after nonsonorants that otherwise do not occur in clusters at all, thus contravening filters stated above:

(34)  a.  /pj/  pew       /kj/  queue     b.  /tj/  tune
          /bj/  beauty    /gj/  gules         /dj/  duke
          /fj/  few       /hj/  huge          /sj/  suit
          /vj/  view                          /zj/  Zeus

(Note: the clusters in (34b) do not occur in GA, where *tune*, *duke* etc. are /tun/, /duk/.)

Secondly, and rather disturbingly as regards our general assumption regarding onset structure, /j/ can occur in onsets after sonorants:

(35)  /mj/  mule    /nj/  new    /lj/  lewd    (/nj/, /lj/ not GA)

And thirdly, while single /j/ can occur before any vowel (*yield*, *you*, *yarn* etc.) cluster-/j/ can only occur in such syllables where the peak is /u/: all the examples given above had /u/ and no consonant-plus-/j/ clusters are possible before vowels other than /u/.

Now it will be recalled that our basic division of syllables into onset and rhyme embodies the claim that peak and coda form a phonological unit whereas onset and peak do not. Given that cluster-/j/ and peak have a particularly close relationship (in that such /j/ only occurs before /u/), it is quite evident that in /pju/ etc., /j/ and /u/ do form a phonological unit of some significance. We have to conclude from the /u/ problem, then, that in a cluster of the form 'consonant plus /j/', the /j/ must be part of the peak.

This conclusion is, in fact, consistent with the clustering behaviour of /j/ that we have observed above: if /j/ is part of the peak then we cannot expect it to be constrained by conditions that hold within onsets, such as the template (27) and the filters that we have formulated. We now have an explanation for the fact that /j/, itself [+ sonorant], can occur after [+ sonorant] phonemes as well as after [− sonorant] phonemes that otherwise fail to cluster altogether, such as /z v/ etc. We can express the special status of /j/ in clusters by analysing it in terms of syllable structure as follows:

(36)

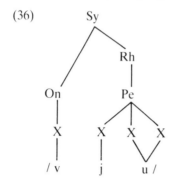

However, there is another side to this problem: cluster-/j/ is demonstrably also part of the onset. If such /j/ were not part of the onset then we would expect to encounter full onsets occurring before /ju/, such as */flju/, /splju/ etc. But the facts are different: whenever cluster-/j/ occurs it occupies one of the X-positions provided by the onset template (27), such that it can only appear after a single consonant or after appendix-/s/ plus one consonant: /fju/, /spju/ etc. Clearly, then, cluster-/j/ must belong to the onset as well as to the peak. In terms of the familiar syllable diagrams, the X-position held by such a /j/ must be associated with both the onset and the peak:

(37)

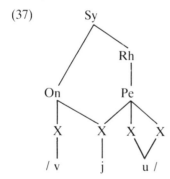

There is another piece of evidence which suggests that cluster-/j/ is not exclusively part of the peak: while all the onset filters discussed above are inoperative where /j/ is involved, there is at least one that is peculiar to onset clusters of the form 'consonant plus /j/'. This filter is of particular importance because it constitutes the one major phonotactic difference between GA and most British varieties of English: in GA, /j/ does not occur after coronal consonants – clusters of the form /tj, dj, nj, lj, sj, zj/ occur in RP and SSE but not in GA (recall (34) and (35) above).

(38)  (GA only)   *Sy

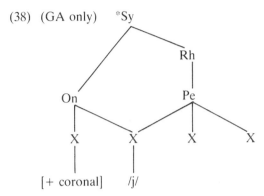

The special status of /j/ is reflected in the statement of this filter. Since /j/ is the only English onset consonant that is associated with onset and peak, we have a simple way of distinguishing between constraints that hold for /j/ and those that hold for consonants other than /j/: any constraint on onsets in which the second element is not also associated with the peak does not hold where this second element is /j/. This is the case for the template (27) and the filters (28–31). Filter (38) is the only constraint in our account of onsets that holds for /j/.

### 6.5.2  *Rhyme phonotactics*

Recall from section 6.4 that the rhyme of a (stressed) monosyllabic word has the structure given in the template below:

(39)       Rh

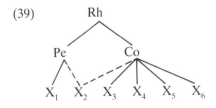

Conditions: (1)  $X_2$ is associated with either peak or coda.
     (2)  $X_{3-6}$ are optional.
     (3)  $X_{4-6}$ are [−sonorant, +coronal].
     (4)  $X_{1-3}$ decrease in sonority left-to-right.

As we did in section 6.5.1 (with regard to onsets), we shall here investigate the consequences of the sonority generalisation for the segmental composition of the rhyme. What features must segments in the positions $X_1$–$X_3$ of the rhyme have in order to satisfy the sonority generalisation? And does English impose further constraints on neighbouring segments within this phonological unit, perhaps in the form of filters such as the one we encountered in our study of onsets?

The validity of the sonority generalisation is shown in (40) below, where rhymes are schematically represented. There, 'V' stands for 'vowel', 'R' for /r/, 'L' for /l/, 'N' for 'any nasal', 'F' for 'any fricative' and 'P' for 'any oral stop'. Note that 'VR' is only possible in rhotic varieties of English and not, therefore, in RP.

(40)

| a. $X_1X_2X_3$ | b. $X_1X_2X_3$ | c. $X_1X_2X_3$ | d. $X_1X_2X_3$ | e. $X_1X_2X_3$ | f. $X_1X_2X_3$ |
|---|---|---|---|---|---|
| V R | *V R R | *V L R | *V N R | *V F R | *V P R |
| V L | V R L | *V L L | *V N L | *V F L | *V P L |
| V N | V R N | V L N | *V N N | *V F N | *V P N |
| V F | V R F | V L F | V N F | *V F F | *V P F |
| V P | V R P | V L P | V N P | *V F P | *V P P |

Examples:

| pier | | | |
|---|---|---|---|
| peel | earl | | |
| bean | earn | kiln | |
| beef | turf | elf | bumf |
| keep | carp | help | bump |

On closer inspection, (40) demonstrates a number of facts concerning English rhymes. The phonotactic constraints of English do not tolerate rhymes in which $X_3$ is more sonorous than $X_2$; this is, of course, entirely consistent with what we already know about the sonority generalisation within syllables. Compare here such pairs as *kiln* /kıln/ – *kennel* /kɛnl/, where the /nl/ cluster in the latter cannot be a rhyme and must therefore constitute a second syllable. Moreover, not even segments of equal sonority can occupy $X_2$ and $X_3$: monosyllabic words ending in /mn/, /sf/, /tp/, for example, are impossible in English.

There are some apparent counter-examples to this generalisation: in words such as *coughs* /fs/, *loves* /vz/, *apt* /pt/ and *nagged* /gd/, segments of equal sonority do occur next to each other. However, in such clusters the second member is always a coronal nonsonorant; and as we already know, our template can accommodate those: they are appendix segments and therefore associated with $X_4$ rather than $X_3$. Cases like *coughs*, then, do not invalidate the generalisation that $X_1$–$X_3$ cannot contain segments of equal sonority.

Note now that VFP sequences also do not occur in rhymes (except, again, where the 'P' element can be analysed as an appendix: *lift*, *list*): there are no words like *\*lifk* etc. This generalisation (which, as we shall see, is not entirely free of exceptions) is explained if we assume that in rhymes, English phonotactics does not utilise the phonetic sonority difference between fricatives and oral stops. Just as they are in onsets, they are here treated as equal in sonority and are thereby banned from occurring next to each other. The sonority distinctions relevant to rhyme phonotactics are (as in the case of onsets) those made by our formal version of the sonority scale (figure 6.2), repeated in slightly modified presentation in figure 6.3. The downward

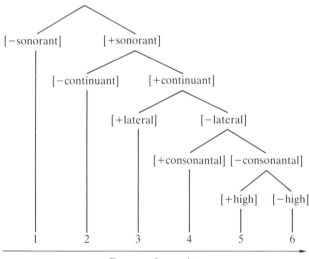

Degree of sonority

Degree 1: /p b f v/ etc.
2: /m n ŋ/
3: /l/
4: /r/
5: /j w i u/ etc.
6: /e o a ɑ/ etc.

Figure 6.3    Sonority scale

slope in sonority that characterises rhymes is adequately expressed in terms of degrees of sonority as defined by figure 6.3. We cannot be more precise about this issue at the moment since we have not yet dealt with the peak itself: it being the starting point of the downward slope, we have to specify it separately. This will be done in section 6.5.3; only then will we be able to characterise individual X-positions in terms of specific degrees of sonority.

A sonority generalisation based on figure 6.3 fails to account for one class of possible English rhymes: those with /sp/ and /sk/ clusters (*lisp*, *clasp*, *disc*). To account for these, we would have to revise figure 6.3 by adding further detail in the place of 'degree 1' sonority. However, we choose to treat the relevant words as exceptions to our model: such a revision would still have to exclude all fricatives other than /s/ – since only /s/ can occur before voiceless stops in rhymes – and the number of attested examples is, after all, rather small. It is worth noting, however, that these exceptions once again involve the coronal obstruent /s/.

We conclude this section by looking briefly at some further constraints on possible rhymes; more precisely, constraints on single consonants and clusters in the coda. These constraints have the form of (negative) filters, amending the (positive) template similarly to the way in which the onset template had to be further constrained by filters.

Firstly, note that the following restrictions on individual consonants are operative in the rhyme:

1　In nonrhotic accents, /r/ does not occur in the rhyme. (For the consequences of this constraint with regard to the vowel system, see section 3.4 above.)
2　/h/ does not occur in the rhyme.
3　/ŋ/ only occurs after lax (single-X) vowels, that is, in the $X_2$ position of the template (39). *Hang, bunk* are well formed but */baɪŋ/, */biŋk/ are not. Recall that /ŋ/ also cannot occur in onsets – $X_2$ is the only position where it can be.
4　Provisionally, /j/ and /w/ do not occur in the rhyme. (But this statement will be considered further in section 6.5.3 below.)

The following configurations, then, are ill formed:

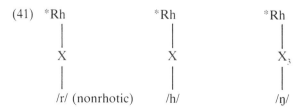

(41)　*Rh　　　　　*Rh　　　　　*Rh

　　　　X　　　　　　X　　　　　　$X_3$

　　　/r/ (nonrhotic)　/h/　　　　/ŋ/

As regards constraints on coda clusters, we do not attempt here to give a complete picture, concentrating instead on clusters involving nasal plus oral stop. Consider the following examples:

(42)  /nt/  lent    /mt/  dreamt  */ŋt/
      /nd/  land    /md/  hummed  /ŋd/  hanged
      */np/         */mp/         */ŋp/
      */nb/         */mb/         */ŋb/
      */nk/         */mk/         /ŋk/  bank
      */ng/         */mg/         */ŋg/

Firstly, note that /b/ and /g/ do not occur after nasals while /d/ does. Since /d/ can, unlike the other two, occupy the appendix position $X_4$, we can generalise that clusters of the form 'nasal plus voiced oral stop' cannot occupy the positions $X_2$–$X_3$:

(43)

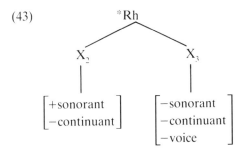

([ŋg] does occur in the English Midlands and North, the [ŋ] in such instances being a realisation of /n/. We do not go into this phenomenon, which was discussed in section 2.3.2 above, at this point.)

A further constraint on nasal-plus-stop clusters concerns the place of articulation of the nasal. As (42) shows, the nasal cannot have a place of articulation different from that of the following oral stop: /mp/, /ŋk/ and /nt/ are permitted while */mk/, /ŋp/ are not. Again, /md/, /mt/ and /ŋd/ are exempt from this constraint by virtue of containing appendix segments. Below, 'Place X' and 'Place Y' are short for 'different places of articulation'.

(44)

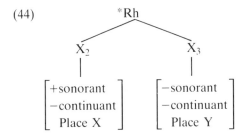

The filters (41), (43) and (44) do not exhaust the constraints that have to be added to the rhyme template (39): this list of constraints still allows some coda clusters that do not, in fact, turn up, such as */lg/, /b/ and a few more. Nor have we considered constraints that hold between the peak and the coda, such as the one that rules out */aʊm/. These are left to the reader to investigate.

### 6.5.3   *The peak: vowels and consonants revisited*

In stressed monosyllables, the only segments that can occur in the peak are vowels. The peak configurations that we identified in section 6.4.3 above are repeated below, where /ɪ/ exemplifies a lax vowel, /aɪ/ a diphthong, and /i/ a tense vowel, whose length (in RP and GA) is expressed by its attachment to two X-positions.

(45)

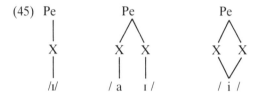

Since no segments other than vowels can occur as peaks in stressed (mono)syllables, and since all vowels are [−consonantal], we can posit the constraint on such syllables that peaks must be [− consonantal]. This, however, raises a few questions. Are there any [−consonantal] phonemes that do not occur in peaks? And are there any [−consonantal] phonemes that occur in other parts of the syllable? And further below we shall have to look at syllables other than stressed monosyllabic words: are these syllables also constrained in such a way that their peaks must be [− consonantal]?

The first two questions are of particular importance here. Recall from chapter 4 above that our (so far entirely informal and largely intuitive) distinction between vowels and consonants does not coincide with the distinction between [− consonantal] and [+ consonantal] phonemes: it is true, all vowels are [− consonantal], but some segments that we have been treating as consonants are also [− consonantal], namely /j/ and /w/. In fact, in terms of the feature analysis carried out in chapters 4 and 5 they are nondistinct from /ɪ/ and /ʊ/ respectively. In our system of English phonemes (unless we revise it), [ɪ] and [j] are treated as realisations of the same phoneme, as are [ʊ] and [w].

Without committing ourselves to any phonemic status for these segments, let us consider their distribution. [j] and [w] are always associated with onsets of syllables (*yell, well, quick*); as we saw, /j/ can be additionally (but never exclusively) associated with the peak: *few*. [ɪ] and [ʊ] occur in peaks but never in onsets (*bit, foot*). In codas, neither pair can occur. Their distribution is therefore complementary: where [j] and [w] can occur, [ɪ] and [ʊ] cannot, and vice versa. [j] and [ɪ], [w] and [ʊ] can never figure in minimal pairs: no pair of words can be distinct only in terms of the difference between [j] and [ɪ], or [w] and [ʊ]. It was not a mistake or shortcoming of our analysis, therefore, to analyse them as featurally nondistinct; the mistake was to treat them as separate phonemes in chapters 2 and 3. What we are dealing with, rather, is a single phoneme with the realisations [ɪ] and [j], and another phoneme with the realisations [ʊ] and [w].

In the light of these findings, let us now reconsider the phonotactic constraint, stated informally in section 6.5.2, that excludes /j/ and /w/ – or rather, [j] and [w]! – from the rhyme. Given the nondistinctness of [j] and [w] from [ɪ] and [ʊ] respectively, this constraint is not quite correct: the phonemes in question can occur in the peak, in the form of the lax monophthongs [ɪ] and [ʊ] or as second elements of diphthongs (as in /aɪ/, /aʊ/ etc.). It is, rather, the coda position where they cannot turn up. If such a segment occupies the $X_2$ position of the syllable template then this position will be associated with the peak rather than the coda. In general terms, if the $X_2$ position is [+ consonantal] then it is a coda consonant and if it is [− consonantal] then it is a vowel, part of the peak:

(46)

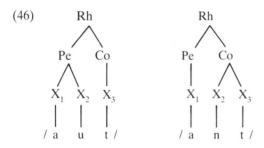

The constraint that bars [j] and [w] from the coda can be stated quite generally like this: no [− consonantal] segment can occur in $X_3$ (or, thanks to the sonority generalisation, on the right of $X_2$):

(47)

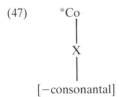

A brief note on our use of the symbols /j/, /w/, /ɪ/ and /ʊ/. It would, of course, be possible now, or even desirable, to ban the former two, or the latter two, from our phonemic alphabet of English: given the phonemic nondistinctness of /j/–/ɪ/ etc., we can no longer speak of different phonemes. Indeed, in the American tradition of phonemic transcription one finds representations of diphthongs as /aj/ (or somewhat misleadingly /ay/), and tense (long) monophthongs may be represented as /ij/ (/iy/) etc. While the possible theoretical merits of the former should have become clear by now – the implications of the latter are not at issue here – we shall continue as before, distinguishing the symbols 'j' and 'ɪ' (and 'w' and 'ʊ') in our transcriptions even on the phonemic level. At the cost of some redundancy, this makes for a more transparent transcription and, not least, does not force us to break what has by now become a habit in this book.

Our observations give us, at last, a clearer understanding of what is meant by 'vowel' and 'consonant': these terms are defined partly in terms of the phonetic content of a segment and partly in terms of its phonological function, that is, of the role it plays in a syllable. [+ consonantal] segments – that is, segments with a greater degree of constriction than [i] and [u] – are always consonants. [− consonantal] segments are consonants if they occur in the onset ([j] and [w]), and vowels if they occur elsewhere (i.e. in the peak).

Let us summarise this discussion by stating in figure 6.4 the final and full version of the template for stressed (mono)syllables. It should be borne in mind that special provision has to be made for two sets of cases: those involving 'consonant-plus /j/' onsets (recall here sect. 6.5.1), and those exemplified by *clasp*. The latter are exceptional in that they have /s/ in the $X_2$ position (rather than a [+ sonorant] segment) and $X_3$ must be [+ consonantal, −continuant, −voice].

Finally, let us return briefly to the constraints on possible peaks. It is true for stressed syllables that they must contain [−consonantal] peaks, but for unstressed syllables this constraint, as well as condition 1 in figure 6.4, has to be relaxed.

As we saw in section 6.4.3, unstressed syllables may be light: they only need to contain one X-position in the rhyme, which is automatically the peak of such syllables. Moreover, this X need not be [− consonantal]: the second syllables in *button* /bʌtn/, *rhythm* /rɪðm/, *little* /lɪtl/ and (rhotic) *butter* /bʌtr/ may contain peaks that are [+ consonantal, + sonorant]. But no other [+ consonantal] phonemes may occur in such peaks: fricatives and oral stops cannot be syllabic. Unstressed syllables can have peaks that are slightly lower on the sonority scale (figure 6.3). Since all [− consonantal]

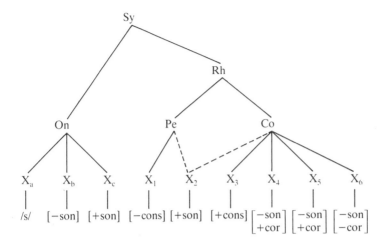

Conditions: (1) $X_1$ plus one $X_{>1}$ are obligatory.
(2) $X_2$ is associated with the peak if [−cons], otherwise with the coda.
(3) Further features of $X_{1-3}$ are such that $X_{1-3}$ decrease in sonority from left to right, in accordance with the sonority scale (figure 6.3).

Figure 6.4    Syllable template

segments are redundantly [+ sonorant] – the combination of [− consonantal, − sonorant] is impossible – we can generalise that in unstressed syllables, the peak may be occupied by any [+ sonorant] phoneme, whether [− consonantal] (and therefore a vowel) or [+ consonantal] (and therefore a sonorant consonant). Note that the /n/ in *button* is still a consonant: although a syllable peak, it does not meet the phonetic requirements by not being [− consonantal].

For unstressed syllables, then, we relax the constraints expressed in figure 6.4 as follows:

(48)    *Amendment to (figure 6.4): unstressed syllables*
a.    $X_1$ may be occupied by any [+sonorant].
b.    Only $X_1$ is obligatory.

### 6.6    The syllabification of polysyllabic words

Finally, we extend our investigation of English syllabification to polysyllabic words. After our rather detailed study of syllable structure and phonotactics in the preceding sections, we still have one claim to substantiate and one important question to answer. The claim, made in section 6.5, is that it is the syllable where the phonotactic constraints of English operate and not the word. So far, in monosyllabic words, this claim was not a very interesting or important one; here, in polysyllabic words, it becomes relevant. It amounts to saying that any well-formed polysyllabic word is a sequence of well-formed syllables; or there can be no polysyllabic word in English that cannot be broken up into well-formed syllables. And what a well-formed syllable is, we know already: a syllable that can stand alone, as a monosyllabic word. The importance – and the correctness – of this claim will become clear in the course of this section.

The question that we have to answer is this: what are the regularities that govern the placement of syllable boundaries in polysyllabic words? As we saw in section 6.3, our sonority-based phonetic theory identifies peaks, slopes and troughs in the sonority profiles of words, thereby predicting the overall number of syllables for a given word as well as the analysis of these syllables into onsets, peaks and codas. It also predicts that syllable boundaries occur in the close vicinity of sonority troughs – consider again the sonority profile of *aroma*:

(49)   sonority

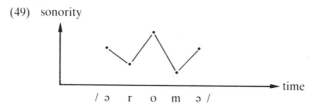

But, as we also noted in section 6.3, this is all that our phonetic syllable theory is able to predict. It does not tell us where, precisely, a syllable boundary is located: is the /r/ in *aroma* the coda of the first syllable or onset of the second? Similarly, does the /m/ belong to the second syllable or the third? As the sonority theory, and what we have made of it in phonological terms so far, leaves both options open in each such case, we have to amend our theory by a rule for the placement of syllable boundaries. But let us first find out what the facts are.

(50)   a. ma.ri.na       b. al.ti.tude       c. a.pri.cot
         a.ro.ma           nigh.tin.gale       al.ge.bra
         pho.ne.mic        a.gen.da            Hum.phrey
         co.di.fy          stan.dard           ma.tron

Syllable boundaries are marked here – and henceforth – with dots. First, an important question: how do we know that these dots are in the right places?

There is, of course, the intuition of the speaker of the language: by and large, speakers will agree with the syllabifications carried out in (50); but it would not be altogether surprising if some readers disagreed with some or even all of the judgements expressed there. Syllable boundaries are notoriously difficult to judge by intuition, one reason being that – like all nonphonemic information – they do not constitute a kind of knowledge of the language that speakers ever need to draw on consciously in the construction of utterances. It would be better to have a test that elicits the speaker's subconscious knowledge about syllable boundaries without overtly asking him or her for an opinion. Here is such a test. Pronounce the words in (50) and in doing so, duplicate each syllable. The result will be *ma-ma-ri-ri-na-na, al-al-ti-ti-tude-tude* etc. The result of this word game will confirm, with a high degree of reliability, the syllabifications carried out in (50).

Let us accept the dots in (50) as facts, then, and attempt to establish a general rule for the placement of syllable boundaries in polysyllabic words. In (50a), we have simple consonant–vowel sequences: (C)VCV(C), where each C constitutes a trough in sonority and each V a peak. The generalisation is a simple one: a single consonant between vowels is a syllable onset rather than the coda of the preceding syllable. Every time, syllabification produces (C)V.CV.CV(C) rather than *(C)VC.VC.V(C). This generalisation of CV being favoured over VC syllables is not only true for English; it is (probably) a universal fact about the languages of the world.

In (50b), we have examples of ...VCCV... sequences, where the first C is more sonorous than the second: in /lt/ (*altitude*), /l/ is more sonorous than /t/; in /ŋg/ (*nightingale*), the /g/ similarly constitutes the sonority trough and so forth. Here, again, the generalisation is pervasive: in a CC cluster between vowels, the consonant that is a sonority trough becomes an onset. The picture here is the same as that found in our discussion of (50a).

Finally, in (50c) we have again ...VCCV... sequences, but this time it is the first C in a CC cluster that is the sonority trough. And again this trough is always part of the onset rather than being the coda of the preceding syllable. As a result, the second syllable in *matron* has a two-X onset: /tr/. Note that in *Humphrey*, the three-consonant cluster /mfr/ has a syllable boundary before the /f/ – again before the consonant that is less sonorous than both its neighbours.

Drawing together our findings regarding (50), we can conclude that syllable boundaries occur immediately before the consonant that constitutes a sonority trough. In other words: syllable boundaries are placed in such a way that each onset contains as many consonants as possible and that each coda contains as few consonants as possible. But before we state this rule in its final form, let us consider a few more examples:

(51)   e.nig.ma    /gm/      at. las      /tl/
        Ag.nes     /gn/      hem.lock  /ml/
        Ed.na      /dn/      de.cath.lon  /θl/

Just like those in (50c), the examples in (51) contain consonant clusters in which the leftmost consonant is less sonorous than the right one: this, the /tr/ in *matron* and the /gm/ in *enigma* have in common. However, while in the former set the syllable boundary regularly precedes the cluster (*ma.tron* etc.), the clusters in (51) are divided by such boundaries: *e.nig.ma* etc. Nevertheless, the examples in (51) are not haphazard counter-examples to the generalisation expressed earlier: they can be explained in terms of what we already know about English syllables. None of the clusters listed in (51) are possible English syllable onsets: they are all ruled out by the onset template and supplementary filters formulated in section 6.5.1 above. Speakers syllabify *enigma* as *e.nig.ma* simply because /gm/ cannot be a syllable onset. The /tr/ in *ma.tron*, on the other hand, is a possible syllable onset.

Accounting for all the facts discussed so far, the rule for the placement of syllable boundaries can be formulated like this:

(52)   *Syllable-Boundary Rule*

Within words, syllable boundaries are placed in such a way that onsets are maximal (in accordance with the phonotactic constraints of the language).

Here are some complete analyses of the syllabification of polysyllabic words, for clarification broken up into two separate steps: syllable boundary placement (53b) and the building of syllable structure (53c):

(53)   a.  Phonemic representation: / m e t r ə n /    / a t l ə s /
        b.  Syllable boundaries:      [ m e . t r ə n ] [ a t . l ə s ]
        c.  Syllable structures:

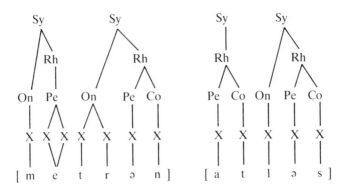

In all the cases discussed so far, the application of the Syllable-Boundary Rule (52) has resulted in a division of words into well-formed syllables; indeed, this was a condition that resulted in different boundary placement in *apricot* and *enigma*. We take this to be a first indication of the truth of our claim that the syllable is the domain of phonotactics: all the words we have discussed so far consist of strings of well-formed syllables. But before we look into this issue more systematically, let us consider some more examples:

(54)  'apple        'pedestal       ma'donna
      'petrol       'camera         ru'bella
      'epic         'labrador       con'fetti
      'metric       'Africa         in'tegrity

The application of rule (52) yields the following results:

(55)  ['a.pl̩]        ['pɛ.də.stəl]    [mə'dɒ.nə]
      ['pɛ.trəl]     ['ka.mə.rə]      [rʊ.'bɛ.lə]
      ['ɛ.pɪk]       ['la.brə.dɔ]     [kən'fɛ.tɪ]
      ['mɛ.trɪk]     ['a.frɪ.kə]      [ɪn'tɛ.grɪ.tɪ]

A problem arises at this point: our Syllable-Boundary Rule (52) is in conflict with the template for well-formed syllables (figure 6.4), which forbids stressed syllables to be light. [a] (in *apple*) cannot be a stressed syllable because it does not have a branching rhyme, nor can [pɛ] in *petrol* and *pedestal*, [dɒ] in *madonna* and so on. In order to comply with the syllable template, the stressed syllable in *apple* must be [ap], that in *petrol* [pɛt] and so forth. The problem is, then, that the /p/ in *apple* must belong to the first syllable due to the branching-rhyme requirement and to the second syllable due to rule (52); the same conflict occurs in all the examples given in (54).

However, what appears to be a problem for our analysis is, rather, quite consistent with the facts of syllabification: there are good reasons to believe that the consonants in question do indeed belong to both the preceding and the following syllable. They are syllabified ambiguously (with both syllables); in short, they are **ambisyllabic**.

To demonstrate this ambisyllabicity, let us conduct the little test that we used earlier to elicit syllable boundaries from speakers. Pronouncing the words listed in (54) with each syllable said twice, we get *ap-ap-ple-ple*, *pet-pet-trol-trol*, etc. Note how the problematic consonant is in each case repeated with both syllables, clearly therefore belonging to both the preceding and the following syllable. We will confirm the result in chapter 8 below: in our study of the concrete phonetic level of representation, we shall find that the /t/ in *petrol* clearly shows the behaviour of both syllable-final and syllable-initial /t/, while that in, say, *matron* ((50) above) is realised like a typical non-syllable-final /t/. In this way, the syllable structures produced in this chapter will facilitate further generalisations, some of which depend crucially on ambisyllabicity in certain contexts.

In what contexts, then, are consonants ambisyllabic? They are ambisyllabic only where the principles of syllabification require them to belong both to the preceding and the following syllable. This is the case where the Syllable-Boundary Rule (52) requires them to be part of an onset and the preceding syllable is stressed and would, without such a consonant, have a single-X rhyme. In brief:

(56)  A consonant is ambisyllabic if it is (part of) a permissible onset (cluster) and if it immediately follows a stressed lax vowel.

Here are some fully analysed examples:

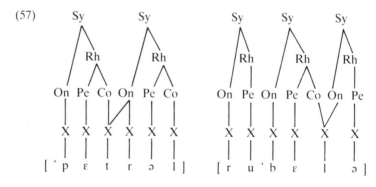

We return finally to the claim that the syllable is the domain of phonotactic constraints; or that all English words consist of strings of well-formed

172

syllables and that no other words can exist. To see how this statement draws a dividing line between possible and impossible words of the language, let us consider some examples of impossible words. Why, for example, are *\*'umbna* and *\*'atctic* impossible (as the reader will no doubt agree)? They are impossible because they cannot be syllabified by means of the mechanisms that we have deployed in this chapter. \*/ʌmb/ is an impossible syllable and so is \*/bnə/, leaving the /b/ stranded between two syllables, unable to go with either. In the latter case, \*/atk/ and \*/ktɪk/ are impossible syllables, so that, again, the /k/ cannot be associated with either the first or the second syllable:

(58)

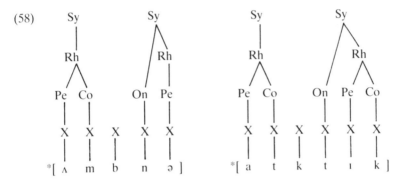

Note that /ʌmbrə/ would be a possible English word (compare *umbrage*): unlike in \*/ʌmbnə/, the /b/ can here be part of the onset: \*/bn/ is an impossible onset while /br/ is possible. Similarly, a change from *atctic* to *arctic* produces a possible word, simply because the problematic /k/ can now be part of the first rhyme: /rk/ is a possible coda (in rhotic accents) while \*/tk/ is not.

(59)

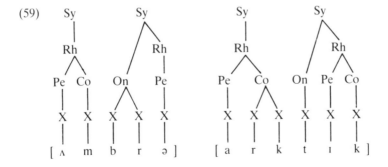

The following, then, is a condition on the structure of well-formed English words:

(60)   Words must be exhaustively syllabifiable.

*Bring* is a well-formed word because /br/ is a well-formed syllable onset and /ɪŋ/ a well-formed rhyme. *\*Bning* is impossible because \*/bn/ cannot be a syllable onset. In polysyllabic words, any consonant must be syllabifiable with either the rhyme of the preceding syllable or the onset of the next. And this would appear to be true: there seems to be no English word that cannot be exhaustively syllabified, given our mechanisms of syllabification. Speakers of the language know instantly that words such as those in (58) above do not just happen to be absent from the language; they are impossible. What is implied here is the following three-way distinction:

(61)             Possible words          Impossible words

        Attested         Unattested

        bring        ? bling        \*bning
        arctic       ? alctic       \*atktik
        umbrage      ? ulbrage      \*umbnage

All strings of phonemes that cannot be syllabified belong in the category of 'impossible words'. All possible words of the language can be syllabified, but that does not mean that all these words actually exist in the language: the set of attested English words (as listed in a dictionary) is merely a small subset of all the strings of phonemes that are available, following the phonotactics of English, to be used as words of the language. While *\*bning* is clearly impossible, there is really nothing wrong with *bling*, except that it does not happen to have a meaning attached to it in English. An advertising agent may well recommend *Bling* or *Alctic* as brand names for new household cleaners, but almost certainly would not consider *Bning* or *Atktik*.

### 6.7   Segments, X-positions and syllables

This chapter has witnessed a considerable increase in the number of notational devices that our theory of phonology, in relation to English, uses. More such devices will be introduced in the following chapters; but it will be helpful to pause at this point and to take stock.

In theoretical terms, the major step forward that we have made in this chapter has been the recognition that phonological representations do not merely consist of segments (that is, bundles of features), arranged in sequence like beads on a string, but that such representations are further structured. Strings of feature bundles make up but one **tier** of our representations: on another such tier, we have X-positions (which are again arranged in sequence, and associated with the elements of the feature tier); and on yet another tier we have rather more complex structures in which X-positions (and therefore ultimately feature bundles) are grouped into higher-order units. Such structures have been demonstrated many times in this chapter – recall, for example, (53) and (57) above.

What is important for our understanding of these three tiers is primarily the way in which they are associated with one another. What are the principles governing the association of feature bundles with X-positions, and what are those that control the way in which syllables are erected on top of the X-tier?

The only statement that we have made regarding the association of feature bundles and X-positions has been rule (17) (in sect. 6.4.3), repeated in (62):

(62)   *Vowel-Length Rule (RP, GA)*

   a.   Associate a [− tense] vowel with one X-position.
   b.   Associate each element of a diphthong with one X-position.
   c.   Associate a [+ tense] vowel with two X-positions.

The details do not need to concern us again, nor does the fact that SSE is not covered by this rule. Two things are worth noting here: firstly, the correspondence between feature bundles and X-position is not necessarily one-to-one; and secondly, in the approach chosen here, the number of X-positions associated with any given vowel is entirely determined by the segmental features of the vowel. The X-tier contains no information that is not also present – if encoded in a different way – in the feature tier. This reflects our assumption, made explicit in sections 3.6 and 4.2.3 above, that in the vowel system(s) of our reference accents any differences in length are redundant: predictable from the differences in quality (for example, tenseness) that we treat as phonemic. Phonemic differences among vowels are expressed on the feature tier rather than on the X-tier. This is not to say, of course, that the X-tier *cannot* contain any phonemic information: all we have said is that in the case of these English vowel systems, it does not. Indeed, an alternative approach to English phonology might well suggest that the English vowel system (more precisely, the RP and GA ones) is bifurcated in such a way that the members of one subset are phonemically associated with 'XX' and the members of the other with 'X', and that the tense/lax specification of any given vowel follows from its properties on the X-tier: an 'XX' vowel would then be redundantly [+ tense] and an 'X' vowel

[− tense]. In terms of phonemic transcription, this would imply that pairs of vowels should be transcribed as, for example, /iː/ vs. /i/ (so that the difference in length, here accounted for as 'XX' vs. 'X', is the underlying one). Recall that the main argument advanced against this strategy, and in favour of tenseness as the underlying distinction, was the fact that in SSE we do not get such a one-to-one correspondence between tenseness and length: phonemic vowel contrasts in SSE would then have to be analysed radically differently from those in GA and RP.

Nothing has been said about the association of consonants with X-positions; we have simply assumed that such an association is always one-to-one, as in (63a) below. But again, this need not be so: as is possible in the case of vowels, a consonant might be associated with two X-positions, thereby being 'long'. Such a configuration is given in (63b) below; however, English consonants do not have long–short distinctions and structures such as this one do not occur, although they are, in principle, perfectly possible.

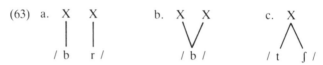

Consider now (63c). Here we see for the first time the association of two elements of the segmental tier with one X. Again, there is no principled objection to such a configuration; indeed, it provides us, at last, with a method of accounting for **affricates**.

Affricates are, in phonetic terms, stop-plus-fricative sequences which share the same voicing specification and the same place of articulation. In phonological terms, however, they function as single units – primarily in phonotactic terms: recall, for example, that the onset template (27) above does not permit sequences of two [− sonorant] segments; yet /tʃ/ and /dʒ/ – the only affricates of English – do occur in onsets: *chin, gin*. Invoking the X-tier, we can resolve this apparent contradiction: affricates consist of two feature bundles associated with a single X-position. We actually anticipated such a solution as early as in chapter 2, without spelling it out, by treating affricates as 'single phonemes' while transcribing them as sequences of two symbols; and our symbols encode only such information as is contained in the feature bundle. In chapter 8 we shall see that affricates are not the only cases where two feature bundles share an X-position in English: while in most varieties of English, all diphthongs are represented as in (64a) below, there is one in SSE (namely /aɪ/) that is associated with a single X in certain contexts, as in (64b):

This discussion has left us with an ambiguity: when we refer to **segments**, do we mean feature bundles or X-positions? If we mean feature bundles, then we are operating, implicitly, with a three-way length distinction among 'segments': any such units may be associated with two X-positions, or with one, or it may share an X-position with another 'segment'. And if by 'segments' we mean X-positions then we have, again implicitly, analysed GA and RP tense vowels as two 'segments' sharing a feature bundle. While the second option is in some ways more in line with our assumptions regarding the nature of the X-tier, we leave this question open and the ambiguity unresolved. But we shall return to this question in chapter 10, where the properties of the 'segment' will be further discussed.

Let us turn now, briefly, to the association of X-positions with syllable structures. Little needs to be said about this association, which is relatively straightforward. The elements of the X-tier constitute the bottom elements of the tree structures that represent syllables: X-positions are grouped into onsets, peaks and codas; and the latter two are in turn grouped into rhymes, which, together with onsets, form syllables. The X-tier, then, simply marks the number of slots that any given 'segment' occupies in a syllable. However, we have come across two separate cases where an X-position was analysed as being part of two higher-order units at the same time. Sample analyses are repeated in (65):

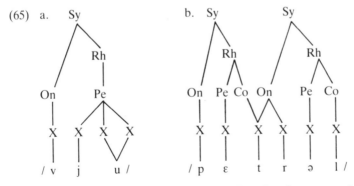

The /j/ in *view* (65a) forms part of both onset and peak – the reasons for this rather complicated analysis were discussed in section 6.5.1 above and need not be repeated here. And in *petrol* (65b), the /t/ belongs to both syllables: it constitutes the coda of the first syllable, thus making this syllable heavy,

177

while at the same time being part of the onset of the second syllable. Note that this analysis does not imply that the /t/ in *petrol* is 'long': it is represented by one X-position only, unlike the (hypothetical) long consonant in (63b) above. For the kind of dual association of X-positions with syllable structures shown in (65b) we used a special term: 'ambisyllabicity'. The conditions under which ambisyllabicity occurs were defined in (56) above. The phenomenon described by this term will crop up again, on various occasions, in the following chapters.

### Suggested reading to chapter 6

Sections 6.1, 6.2   For introductory treatments of the phonetics of the syllable see Couper-Kuhlen (1986: ch. 1), Ladefoged (1982: ch. 10), Catford (1988: sect. 9.2). For phonological introductions to this subject see Hogg and McCully (1987: ch. 2), Lass (1984: sect. 10.3) – both different in a number of details from the account presented here.

Sections 6.4, 6.5   On syllable-internal structure as well as phonotactics see O'Connor and Trim (1953), Fudge (1969), Fudge (1987), Selkirk (1982) and Selkirk (1984). On appendices ('affixes') see Fujimura (1979). Bell and Hooper (1978) contains a number of articles that are relevant to the discussion.

Section 6.6   On the syllabification of polysyllabic words see Selkirk (1982), Kahn (1980), Vennemann (1972); for an alternative view Anderson and Jones (1974), Jones (1976). On experimental evidence for syllable boundaries (and ambisyllabicity) Fallows (1981), Treiman and Danis (1988).

Section 6.7   On 'tiers', especially the X-tier (there incorporating the consonantal–nonconsonantal distinction and hence called 'CV-tier') see Clements and Keyser (1983). On the X-tier, in roughly the form assumed here, see Levin (1983) and Levin (1985). Durand (1990: sects. 6.1.7, 7.3.3) gives an overview of the rather technical debate concerning the form of the tier. On the treatment of (vowel) length in terms of syllable structure rather than segmental features see Ingria (1980) and Leben (1980).

# 7
# Word stress

## 7.1 On the nature of stress

When syllables are uttered in sequence, in polysyllabic words, for example, they are perceived as having different degrees of prominence, or stress. In each of the following words one syllable is stressed, the other(s) unstressed: ˈsequence, phoˈnology, perˈceive. In many words, the prominence of syllables is further differentiated; thus in ˌpolysylˈlabic, ˌkangaˈroo, halˌluciˈnatory the syllables marked ˌ bear secondary stress: stress that is weaker than the main (or 'primary') stress but stronger than that of an unstressed syllable. In longer words, further differentiation of stresses can be found: in ˌantiˌdisesˌtablishmenˈtarianism, the main stress falls on -ta- and the weaker stresses, all marked ˌ, are of different strength. English is said to be a stress language: every (lexical) word – noun, verb, adjective or adverb – has a stressed syllable, and where more than one syllable bears stress (as in some of the examples given above), one of these stresses will be the main stress, and the others subordinated.

In phonetic terms, *stressed syllables in English are produced with a stronger burst in initiatory energy* – a more powerful contraction of the chest muscles – than unstressed syllables are. (Recall here, for comparison, the phonetics of the syllable discussed in sect. 6.2 above.) On the acoustic side, this increased energy input results in greater loudness, increased duration and often – mainly in the case of primary stress – a change of pitch. It is not possible to quantify any of the physical correlates of stress in absolute terms. A syllable's property of being stressed is primarily a relative one: while it is no problem detecting that in a bisyllabic word (such as ˈsequence) one syllable is more prominent than the other, it makes no phonetic sense to say that, in isolation, monosyllables like *Alf, dumb, is* etc. are stressed (or, for that matter, unstressed). On the other hand, it is true to say that in a polysyllabic utterance (*Alf is dumb*), *Alf* and *dumb* are (usually) stressed and *is* unstressed. Similarly, there is no phonetic justification for saying that the first syllable in *lampoon* has secondary stress, distinct from no stress: the phonetic facts only suggest that the first syllable is less stressed than the second. But a comparison with, say, *balloon* reveals that the first syllable in *lampoon* is different: it bears some of the characteristics of stressed syllables that the first syllable of *balloon* does not have. Typically, for example, the reduced vowel schwa [ə] is associated with unstressed syllables (see section 3.5 above) – and it is present in *balloon*, while *lampoon* has a full, unreduced vowel in its first syllable. And, going back to lexical monosyllables like *Alf* and *dumb*, we can observe there, too, that such syllables bear the segmental (and, as we saw in ch. 6, phonotactic) characteristics of stressed syllables: absence of reduced vowels, branching rhymes etc. – despite the fact that the purely phonetic parameter 'stress' is inapplicable in an isolated syllable.

These observations are important in that they show that stress is another of those phenomena whose analysis, in relation to the sound pattern of a given language, cannot be purely phonetically based. Just as our investigation of the syllable in chapter 6 had to go beyond 'pure' phonetics and include phonological reasoning, so does the full discussion of stress in English have to include phonological generalisations, rather than being confined to what is phonetically measurable. We treat *Alf* as stressed because it is usually stressed in connected speech and because it has the same characteristics that a stressed syllable in a polysyllabic word does. The first syllable in *lampoon* has a secondary stress because it does not behave like an unstressed syllable, and so forth. Stress, as we shall see more clearly below, is a phonological phenomenon as well as a phonetic one.

To a limited extent, stress in English is phonemic. There are some pairs of words that are segmentally identical but distinct in terms of stress placement: ʹ*differ* vs. *deʹfer* for many speakers, for example, as well as a number of noun–verb pairs, where the placement of stress signals the syntactic category. Thus ʹ*abstract* is a noun and *abʹstract* a verb, ʹ*pervert* a noun and *perʹvert* a verb – the reader will easily find more such examples. On the whole, however, this phonemic function of stress in English is not very significant – unlike in some other languages. But it is important to note that in the vast majority of English words where stress does not give rise to phonemic distinctions, speakers are not at liberty to stress whichever syllable they like: each word, with a few exceptions that will be discussed below, has a single possible stress pattern, and it remains to be seen whether these stress patterns are predictable from other properties of the word, or whether they are unpredictable (and therefore totally phonemic even if the number of available minimal pairs is small).

Given the small number of minimal pairs, it is quite clear that the main function of stress in English is not one of differentiating words. This main function is quite different: stress is instrumental in the maintenance of rhythm in connected speech. English is said to be a **stress-timed** language: stresses occur at (roughly) equal timing intervals – unlike French, for example, where the syllable is the most important timing unit of connected speech. Consider an utterance such as *'This is the 'house that 'Jack 'built*: the stresses occur rhythmically so that it is possible to tap rhythmic beats coinciding with stressed syllables. Note that this **isochrony** (equality in time) holds regardless of the fact that, in our example, the number of unstressed syllables between stresses varies from none (as in *'Jack 'built*) to two (*'This is the 'house*). Stress isochrony is maintained by variation in the delivery rate of individual syllables. We shall look at speech rhythm in some more detail in chapter 9 below, where we deal with connected speech in more general terms; here, we note the phenomenon of stress-timing only in order to establish, for future discussion, a higher-order phonetic (and, as we shall see, phonological) unit: the **foot**. If we define a foot as *a stretch of phonetic material that begins at the onset of a stressed syllable and ends at the onset of the next stressed syllable*, then we can treat the foot as a phonetic unit characterised by its isochrony. Stress, then, marks the syllable that begins a foot. In this way, we have established a level of organisation above the syllable: the segments of an utterance are organised into syllables, and the syllables into feet:

(1)

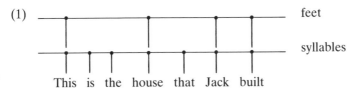

We shall see in later chapters that the foot is not only an important phonetic (timing) unit in English speech but that it also serves in the expression of a variety of phonological generalisations: the realisations of phonemes can, as we shall see, in many cases be predicted by reference to their position in the foot. In this respect, the foot is a unit whose phonological status is similar to that of the syllable: it has a phonetic basis, and it serves in the expression of phonological generalisations. We shall deal with the formal characterisation of the foot as a phonological unit in section 7.4 below; let us meanwhile return to the notion of stress – instrumental in the definition of the foot as well as, of course, worth investigating in its own right.

### 7.2 Stress and syllable structure

We saw in chapter 6 that there is a correlation, in English, between syllable structure and stress: in order to be able to bear stress, a syllable must satisfy certain structural requirements. This correlation will be studied further in this section; in particular, we shall look at some of the ways in which the placement of stress in a polysyllabic word (such as *camera, aroma, magazine*) may be determined by the structure of its syllables. But let us, as a starting-point to this investigation, first recapitulate the relevant points made in chapter 6.

*Point 1.* Stressed syllables must be heavy while unstressed syllables may be light: any stressed syllable, whether it is a monosyllable or part of a polysyllabic word, must have a complex rhyme (that is, a rhyme containing at least two X-positions). It is a consequence of this condition on stressed syllables that there can be no lexical words of the form */bɪ/ in English ((2a) below): being stressed, such words must have more than a single X-position in their rhymes. In (2b) below, some examples of well-formed stressed syllables are given:

(2)

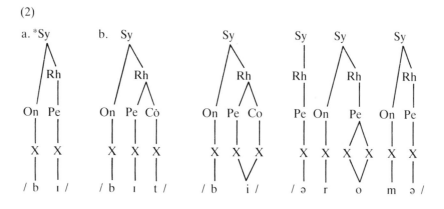

*Point 2.* Ambisyllabicity – the association of a consonant with two syllables at the same time – is connected with stress. In a word such as '*pity*, for example, the medial consonant is ambisyllabic because the Syllable-Boundary Rule ((52) in ch. 6) places a syllable boundary before it, thereby making the /t/ part of the second syllable, while the complex-rhyme condition on stressed syllables ensures that this consonant is also part of the first syllable. Below are, again, some examples:

(3)

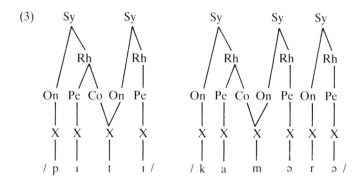

Ambisyllabicity has the effect of making stressed syllables heavy that would otherwise be light. It would appear, then, that any syllable can become heavy provided a consonant is available for ambisyllabicity. But does that mean that in a polysyllabic word any syllable can be stressed? As we have already seen, the answer is no: every word has exactly one correct stress pattern. *Ca'mera, 'aroma are clearly wrong, although the weight condition on stressed syllables could be met, in each case, through making the /r/ ambisyllabic. Stress placement in polysyllabic words is governed by certain regularities that are clearly contravened in these examples. Without attempting to come to grips with these regularities fully, let us look at some of the many stress patterns found in English words, and at the syllable structures that go with them.

### 7.2.1 *Final stress*

The words listed in (4) below have final stress (as marked) for many speakers. Some items may have alternative stress patterns such that the main stress falls on the initial rather than the final syllable: 'bou‚quet, 'comman‚dant. Such variation will be discussed below.

(4)  a. ca'det    b. Ju'ly    c. ba'lloon    d. e'llipse
     ca'nal      de'gree      bri'gade      la'ment
     ga'zette      ca'noe      ra'vine      ri'poste
     du'ress      ‚bam'boo      ‚cham'pagne      ‚au'gust
     ‚ho'tel      ‚mar'quee      ‚lam'poon      ‚Pen'zance
     ‚catama'ran      ‚bou'quet      ‚ar'cade      ‚ar'tiste
     ‚courte'san      ‚frica'ssee      ‚caval'cade      ‚comman'dant
     ‚marzi'pan      ‚bally'hoo      ‚maga'zine      ‚Buca'rest

Our syllable-weight requirement for stressed syllables makes the prediction that there are no final-stressed words in English that end in a light syllable –

just as there are no monosyllabic words consisting of a light syllable. This prediction is correct: no English word with final stress ends in a lax (= single-X) vowel. All the examples in (4) end in heavy syllables: (4a) ends in VC, (4b) in V:, (4c) in V:C and (4d) in VCC. This fact confirms what was said earlier about the correlation between syllable weight and stress. Another observation regarding this correlation can be made here: among the bisyllabic examples in (4), secondary stress occurs on the first syllable only where that syllable is also heavy – compare, for example, ˌbam'boo and ˌar'tiste with Ju'ly and ba'lloon.

What the list in (4) does not reveal is the fact that nouns with final stress are comparatively rare in English; indeed, the length of this list is somewhat misleading. Many of the examples given there are rather uncommon loan words, and it would be difficult to compile such a collection if one were to exclude such rare words, just as it would be to double the list. Verbs and adjectives with final stress, on the other hand, are quite common. Here are just a few examples:

(5)  a. o'bey              b. ob'scene
     a'tone                di'vine
     ˌbap'tise             se'cure
     ˌinter'vene           se'rene
     ˌsuper'sede           ab'surd

Note again that the final syllable in all such cases is heavy; but notice also that, unlike in nouns, heavy initial syllables do not necessarily have secondary stress: ˌar'tiste vs. ob'scure (and not *ˌob'scure).

For the first time, we note here an interesting fact about stress placement in English: the regularities that govern it depend to some extent on **nonphonological information**: here, on syntactic-category information. While verbs and adjectives with final stress are common, nouns with that stress pattern are somewhat exceptional: the list in (4) cannot be extended much further, and some further observations regarding this exceptional character will be made below.

Firstly, the reader may well have disagreed with some of the stress patterns given in (4): for example, in some dialects (or for certain speakers, or in colloquial speech) we find 'commanˌdant, 'marziˌpan, 'arˌcade, 'bou-ˌquet etc. Notice also the variable stress patterns in the following words, not listed in (4):

(6)  finance:  [fɪ'nans]   or   [ˌfaɪ'nans]   or   ['faɪˌnans]
     romance:  [rə'mans]   or   [ˌro'mans]   or   ['roˌmans]

The variation found in these words is of some significance in that *['fɪˌnans] is clearly impossible. In each case, the variant with a light–heavy syllable pattern must have final stress while the variant with two heavy syllables may have the stress pattern secondary–primary or primary–secondary. This is consistent with the observation made earlier that bisyllabic words in (4) have a secondary stress on the first syllable only if this syllable is heavy. And going back now to words with varying stress, like *marzipan* and *arcade*, we note the same regularity: alternative stress patterns to the ones given in (4) are only possible where the first syllable already has some degree of stress. *ˌAr'cade* alternates with *'arˌcade*, *ˌmarzi'pan* with *'marziˌpan*; but *de'gree* cannot turn into *\*'deˌgree*.

Secondly, even those words listed in (4) that do not have variable stress patterns when uttered in isolation may shift their stress from the secondary–primary to the primary–secondary pattern in certain contexts. Thus, *hotel* and *champagne*, said in isolation, have final stress; but for many speakers they shift their stress onto the first syllable when another strongly stressed syllable immediately follows them, as in *'hoˌtel 'management* or *'champagne 'breakfast*. But note again that the stress pattern of, for example, *July* cannot be so reversed: *\*'Juˌly 'weather* is impossible. And the reason for this is by now clear: *July* does not have a secondary stress on the first syllable, and, as we have seen, stress can be shifted away from the final syllable only onto such syllables that already have some stress.

As a result of these stress shifts (speaker-, dialect-, style- or context-specific), then, the class of end-stressed nouns is unstable – small as it is in the first place. Through the stress shifts just discussed, many of these nouns may join the rather more common class of nouns that constantly have a primary–secondary stress pattern, such as these:

(7)  'rabˌbi        'conˌvoy        'camoˌmile
     'inˌcest       'synˌtax        'chromoˌsome
     'kumˌquat      'texˌtile       'nightinˌgale

Our findings regarding final stress may be summarised as follows. Firstly, the condition that stressed syllables must be heavy, first discussed in chapter 6, has been further substantiated: any final stress (primary or secondary) is only possible in such words as have heavy final syllables. And bisyllabic nouns can have a ˌ–'– or '–ˌ– stress pattern only if both syllables are heavy. Secondly, while final stress in verbs and adjectives is quite common, it seems to be more common for nouns not to have final stress: final stress in nouns is comparatively rare and in several ways unstable. And this rather tentative generalisation about stress placement in polysyllabic words can now, finally, be confirmed by an observation that was first made a little while ago: there are a number of noun–verb pairs in English that are distinguished by their stress patterns, the nouns having nonfinal and the corresponding verbs final stress. Here are some examples:

(8)  *Nouns*          *Verbs*
     'di‚gest          di'gest
     'es‚cort          es'cort
     'sur‚vey          sur'vey
     'tor‚ment         tor'ment
     'con‚vict         con'vict

### 7.2.2 *Nonfinal stress*

We now turn to a second subclass of stress patterns: namely, that where the final syllable of a word bears no stress (primary or secondary). Here are some examples:

(9)  a. a'roma       b. u'tensil      c. A'merica
        to'mato         sy'nopsis        'camera
        an'gina         a'malgam         'cinema
        po'tato         e'nigma          'capital
        ho'rizon        de'cathlon       'discipline
        sa'lami         a'genda          'vertebra
        ma'rina         Be'linda         'anagram

Unlike the list of end-stressed nouns in (4) above, this one can easily be extended; this subclass of stress patterns is quite common in English – and note that, again, we are dealing with nouns. Observe first that in the examples given in (9), the final syllable may well be heavy (as in *utensil*, *discipline* etc.) and that nevertheless there is no stress on such syllables. Let us remind ourselves that in the preceding discussion we did not actually conclude that heavy syllables must be stressed, but merely that stressed syllables must be heavy. The existence of unstressed heavy syllables, as just observed, does not endanger this generalisation. We shall not go into the question of why heavy final syllables in (9) do not have stress, unlike the examples discussed in section 7.2.1. Cutting corners slightly, we simply observe this as a fact and assume that the two subclasses – this one with no final stress and the one with (some) final stress – are distinct, and that membership is unpredictable. Let us now look at the regularities within the present class, just as in section 7.2.1 we studied the regularities found within the final-stress class.

The words in (9a, b) have stress one syllable from the end (on the penultimate syllable) and those in (9c) two syllables from the end (on the antepenultimate syllable). This distribution of stress illustrates the central regularity within this subclass; and this regularity is once again governed by syllable weight. The penultimate syllable is stressed if it is heavy; otherwise, stress falls on the antepenultimate syllable.

Let us look at the penultimate syllables of the words in (9) in more detail. Those in (9a) all contain long (= two-X) vowels (diphthongs or tense monophthongs), those in (9b) contain vowel-plus-consonant sequences, while the examples in (9c) have penultimate syllables whose rhymes merely contain lax (= single-X) vowels. Here are some sample analyses:

(10)

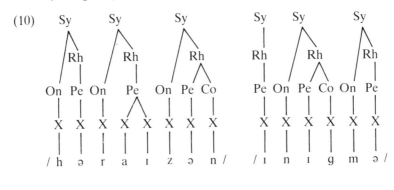

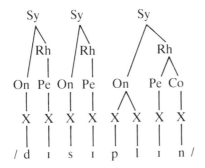

The details of syllable-boundary placement will be familiar from section 6.6 above; but note in particular the difference in syllabification between *e.nig.ma* and *di.sci.pline*: the /gm/ sequence in *enigma* cannot be a syllable onset – no English word begins with /gm/ – and therefore has to be divided between two syllables. The sequence /pl/ in *discipline*, on the other hand, can be a syllable-onset cluster (compare *play*) and is therefore preceded by a syllable boundary. This difference in syllabification makes the penultimate syllable in *enigma* heavy, and hence stressed, and that in *discipline* light so that the stress falls on the antepenult instead. The principles of syllabification developed in chapter 6 are rather strikingly consistent with the stress distribution in this class of words – assuming, of course, the general validity of our stress rule.

We are now in a position where we can be more specific about ambisyllabicity than we have been so far. We have seen that regular stress (in nouns) falls on the penultimate syllable if it is heavy, otherwise on the antepenultimate syllable. Note that words such as *apple* and *metric* have no antepenultimate syllable; stress must therefore fall on the penult. The antepenultimate syllable in a word like *America*, and the penult in *apple*, is the 'last resort' for the stress to go to: it cannot go further back in the word either because the rule does not allow stress to go onto the pre-antepenult (i.e. four syllables from the end), or because the word does not have enough syllables. Now this 'last-resort' syllable may be naturally heavy (as, for example, in *Peter*), in which case we have no problem, or it may be light, as in *America*, *apple* etc. In such a case, where a light syllable must take the stress, this syllable becomes heavy, under stress, through ambisyllabicity. Ambisyllabicity can be viewed, then, as a device for making a light stressed syllable heavy if no heavy syllable is available to take the stress instead. Typically, ambisyllabicity occurs in words such as those listed in (9c) as well as in bisyllabic words.

The picture of stress placement that is emerging here is one of partial regularity. We have established two subclasses of nouns, regarding their stress behaviour, but we have been unable to determine the criteria for membership in either subclass. Moreover, we have seen some unpredictable variation of the form primary–secondary vs. secondary–primary stress in the first subclass (sect. 7.2.1). For the second subclass (the more common one), we have found a rule whereby the penultimate syllable takes stress if it is heavy and the antepenult does if the penult is light. But it would be wrong to assume that any noun that, not having any stress on the final syllable, falls within the second subclass, has entirely predictable stress. Within this second subclass we are again faced with some exceptions, for example these:

(11)  a. 'badminton      b. va'nilla
          'calendar           ma'donna
          'cylinder           con'fetti

The words in (11a) – *badminton* etc. – have heavy penultimate syllables (*-min-* etc.); nevertheless, the stress falls on the antepenult. And the words in (11b) ought to have antepenultimate stress because they have light penultimate syllables; instead, they stress the penult and resort to ambisyllabicity to make that syllable heavy. It is perhaps worth noting that words of this type (*vanilla* etc.) commonly have double consonant spellings, indicating perhaps the ambisyllabicity of the doubled consonant, and thereby the irregular stress behaviour of the word. And one might be tempted to analyse *vanilla* phonemically as /vənɪllə/, assuming that the word has not only a double-*l* spelling but also a geminate (double) /l/ in its underlying phonological (phonemic) representation. This trick would regularise the stress behaviour of the word: [və.nɪl.lə] would have a heavy penultimate syllable. But it is quite clear that such an analysis would indeed be a trick and nothing else: since there is nothing other than the stress behaviour to support the /ll/ analysis, we would be explaining the /ll/ through the stress, and the stress through the /ll/, and nothing would be gained. We have to conclude, then, that the words in (11) have irregular stress, and that the spelling perhaps indicates this irregular stress while not suggesting any peculiarities of the phonemic representation.

It has been the purpose of this section 7.2 both to illustrate in some detail the stress behaviour of English nouns, and to demonstrate some general properties of English word stress. These general properties are, firstly, that stressed syllables are heavy but that not all heavy syllables are stressed; secondly, that stress placement is predictable in some but unpredictable in other respects; and thirdly, that some of the factors relevant in the prediction of stress are phonological (again, syllable weight) while others are nonphonological. Among the nonphonological factors, we have pinpointed lexical-category information: nouns follow patterns that are different from those of verbs and adjectives. More such nonphonological regularities in stress placement will be discussed in the following section.

### 7.3  Stress and nonphonological structure

The phonology of stress is the part of English phonology that is most obviously informed by other parts of the grammar. We can here only briefly take note of the presence of nonphonological information in the regularities that govern stress. A full study would go beyond the aims of this book: it would require us not only to conduct a full investigation into the stress rules of English, but also to get rather deeply involved in the fields of syntax and morphology – for these are the parts of grammar that affect the regularities of English word stress.

The role of **syntax** has already been touched upon and need only be summarised. Firstly, stress is assigned not to any random sequence of syllables in speech but to the syllables of syntactic units called words. Every word has a (relatively) stable stress pattern, which is very little influenced by the context in which the word occurs. This is a fairly obvious fact about stress (and one that stress shares with syllabification); what is perhaps more notable is that stress is only assigned in lexical words – words, that is, that are members of the syntactic categories Noun, Verb, Adjective or Adverb. Function words such as articles, prepositions, pronouns etc. do not bear stress. Secondly, we saw in section 7.2 that there are differences in the stress behaviour of nouns, on the one hand, and verbs (and adjectives), on the other. Verbs frequently have their main stress on the final syllable (*obey, intervene*) while in nouns final stress is rare, and when it does occur it is often unstable. This difference is manifested in the noun–verb pairs listed in (8) above: *'digest – di'gest* etc.

Nothing has been said so far about the interaction of phonology and **morphology**; indeed, morphology has not even been mentioned. Yet the morphological structure of the words – the way, that is, in which words may be made up of **morphemes** (prefixes, roots and suffixes) – plays a major part in the regularities that govern stress placement in English.

We ignore prefixes; but let us look at some words that are morphologically complex in that they consist of roots and suffixes. We shall distinguish between two types of suffixes: **inflexional** and **derivational**. By inflexional suffixes are meant suffixes that produce different forms of the same word: for example, the plural form (*cameras*) of *camera*, the present-participle form (*developing*) of the verb *develop*, the past tense of verbs (*commented*) and so on. Derivational suffixes, in contrast, produce new words; along with compounding (as in *fireplace, snowball*), the derivational morphology forms part of the word-formation devices in the grammar. Thus the suffix *-less* attaches to a noun base and forms adjectives (*penniless, driverless, luckless*); *-ly* attaches to adjectives and forms adverbs (*nicely, carefully*); *-ee* attaches to verbal bases and forms nouns (*employee, payee*) and so forth.

| (12) | Inflexional | | Derivational |
|---|---|---|---|
| | a. tallies | b. penniless | c. atomic |
| | developing | nationhood | solemnity |
| | commented | solemnly | employee |
| | furnishes | interpretable | Newtonian |
| | cameras | openness | divinity |
| | | Stress-neutral | Stress-shifting |

On the phonological side, such suffixes may be divided into two classes – **stress-shifting** and **stess-neutral**; and, as is shown in (12), this division is not congruent with the division, on the morphological side, into inflexional and derivational suffixes.

Let us deal with stress-neutral suffixes first. Such suffixes have two properties that set them apart from the other, stress-shifting class, Firstly, they never make any difference to the stress pattern of their base, that is, of the word to which they are attached. When, for example, the third person singular -*s* is added to the verb *tally* the final syllable becomes heavy (*tallies*); nevertheless, the stress remains on the initial syllable. Similarly, the stress patterns of *developing, penniless* are the same as those of *develop, penny* in isolation. Indeed what is true for the stress patterns of such bases is generally true for their entire phonological forms: the ['sɒləm] in ['sɒləmlɪ] is phonologically identical in every respect with the adjective *solemn*; ['opən] in ['opənnəs] is identical with the adjective *open*. Note that in the latter case a clearly audible **geminate** (double) /n/ results from the attachment of the suffix. Such geminates are only possible in English at the juncture of two morphemes; in this instance the geminate illustrates the phonological integrity of the base word preceding a stress-neutral suffix. The second property of stress-neutral suffixes is that such suffixes are always unstressed – even where they constitute heavy syllables, and even where several such suffixes are stacked together, as in *pennilessness*. Stress-neutral suffixes, then, are simply appended as unstressed material to an entirely unmodified base.

The behaviour of stress-shifting suffixes is different in both respects. Firstly, the stress pattern of their base may differ radically from that of the base word when it occurs without a suffix: compare '*atom* and *a'tom(ic)*, '*Newton* and *New'ton(ian)* etc. Note that there are further differences between the phonological form of the base and that of the corresponding isolated word:

(13)  ['atəm] – [ə'tɒmɪk]
      ['sɒləm] – [sə'lɛmnɪtɪ]
      ['njutən] – [ˌnju'toniən]

Secondly, stress-shifting suffixes differ from stress-neutral ones in that they can bear the main stress of the word. *Employee* in (12c) is such a case; other examples are -*ette* (*usherette, maisonette, launderette*), -*ese* (*Japanese, Cantonese, Chinese*), -*esque* (*picturesque, picaresque, arabesque*) – note that, as expected, such stressed suffixes always constitute heavy syllables.

On the whole, words containing stress-shifting suffixes behave in many ways as if they were morphologically simple words. The phonological form of their base may differ radically from that of the associated unsuffixed word; consonant clusters that are indicative of the presence of morpheme boundaries never occur in words containing stress-shifting suffixes while in words containing stress-neutral suffixes they are common: geminate consonants (the /nn/ in *openness*), also /ldl/ in *mildly* and many others. Indeed, it is sometimes not at all clear whether a word contains a stress-shifting suffix or whether it is morphologically simple – does *picaresque*, for example, contain two morphemes or just one? What about *grotesque*? If *-esque* is a suffix in these words then *picar-* and *grot-* are rather strange bases. Or take the words ending in *-ade*. *Lemonade* is quite plausibly morphologically complex; but what about *cascade*? However, for our purposes this problematic demarcation between simple words and complex words with stress-shifting suffixes is hardly of any consequence because, where stress is concerned, words containing stress-shifting suffixes behave like morphologically simple words in that their stress patterns are always also possible as stress patterns of simple words – compare morphologically simple *A'merica*, *ˌbam'boo*, *va'nilla* with complex *di'vinity*, *ˌChi'nese* and *a'tomic*.

What is more troublesome is the distinction, in many instances, between stress-shifting and stress-neutral suffixes, because a stress-shifting suffix may not in all instances display the diagnostics that were mentioned above. A suffix that shifts stress in some instances does not necessarily do so in all bases that it may attach to: thus, *-ity* shifts the stress of the base in *solemnity* but not in *divinity*. In the latter we still have a diagnostic difference in other aspects of the phonological form of the base; but in *obese – obesity* there is no difference. The suffix *-ity* must be classed as stress-shifting simply because it shifts stress in some instances – that is, in at least one instance.

It follows from our morphological observations that anyone investigating the phonological regularities of English word stress – and word stress in English is still primarily a phonological problem – needs to expect no distortion of the picture caused by the presence of stress-shifting suffixes: the regularities that hold in words containing those are the same as those found in morphologically simple words. Stress-neutral suffixes, on the other hand, do distort the picture: here it is the base alone that will obey any given phonological regularity regarding stress, and the addition of a suffix leaves all stresses in place while it does, of course, alter other aspects of the phonological shape of the word by making final syllables heavy or adding syllables.

## 7.4 Stress and phonological structure: Metrical Phonology

### 7.4.1 *The notation*

We saw in chapter 6 that phonological representations are not strictly linear: they do not merely consist of segments, arranged in sequence like beads on a string. Rather, such representations have a second dimension: a dimension in which segments constitute the bottom level of a hierarchy of phonological units. Chapter 6 was concerned with the syllable as a larger-than-segment phonological unit. Syllables, as well as being phonetically real entities, are also phonological entities: they have recurrent structural characteristics (not all of which follow directly from the phonetic definition of the syllable), and they are the domain of a variety of phonological generalisations. One such generalisation, among many, concerned a segment's property of being syllabic (and our definition of the notion 'vowel' made crucial reference to this property): syllabicity is a relational property, determined by the segment's position in the syllable, rather than a local property of the segment itself that might be expressed in terms of a segmental feature. A segment is syllabic if it is more sonorous than its neighbours and if it therefore constitutes the peak of the syllable.

Stress is similarly a relational property – in this case one that is defined among syllables rather than among the segments within a syllable. Like syllabicity, stress cannot be defined in a local sense: a syllable is stressed if it is more prominent than another syllable. And we have already come across the larger unit within which such prominence relations among syllables may be defined: the foot. Feet are phonetically real in that they are the timing units in English speech. They have recurrent structural characteristics in that they begin with a stressed syllable and end just before the next stressed syllable, and the discovery of stress-placement rules (or foot-assignment rules), in section 7.4.2 below, will add to these structural characteristics. This, then, is the next-higher unit in phonological representations: **syllables** are grouped into **feet**, and the first (or only) syllable of each foot is stressed:

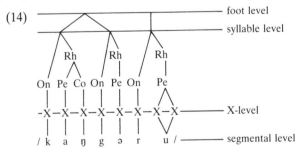

(14)

— foot level
— syllable level

Rh    Rh    Rh
On Pe Co On Pe On   Pe
-X—X—X—X—X—X—X—X ——— X-level
/ k   a   ŋ   g   ə   r    u / ——— segmental level

193

*Kangaroo* has two feet: *kanga-* and *-roo*, two stressed syllables therefore: the first syllable of the first foot and the only syllable of the second foot. But this does not fully describe the stress pattern of the word *kangaroo*: the first syllable has a weaker stress than the third one does; the first foot is subordinate to the second. Clearly, we need yet another level of structure, one on which prominence relations can be defined among the feet of a word. This level of structure is called, for obvious reasons, the **word** level. Below is an example, where *kangaroo* is now represented as a single word-level structure comprising two feet:

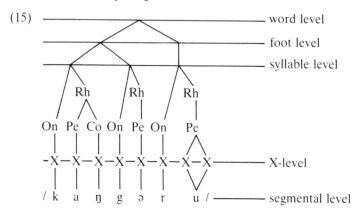

But what is still missing in this representation of *kangaroo* is a statement about the prominence relations that hold within it. Example (15) does not express the fact that it is the first syllable of *kanga-* that bears stress and not the second; nor does it tell us that the second foot is stronger than the first. What we need is a notation that expresses prominence relations within phonological structures.

Say that in a pair of phonological units, one is stronger (more prominent) than the other. We may express such a simple relation as in (16a, b) below:

(16)

The labels *S* and *W* are relationally defined: *S* means 'stronger than *W*' and *W* 'weaker than *S*'. The unit within which this relation holds is represented by a branching structure: both *S* and *W* are part of the same structure, which expresses the fact that they form a unit together. It follows from the strictly relational definition of *S* and *W* that structures such as (16c, d) are ill-formed: an *S* can only be interpreted in the presence of a sister-*W*, and vice versa. Let us say that this constraint on our notation also extends to nonbinary structures such as (16e, f): we rule them out because, again, the strictly relational nature of *S* and *W* permits no interpretation of the sister *S* nodes in (16e) or of the sister *W* nodes in (16f). Units consisting of more than two elements must then be broken up into binary structures, as in (17), where a prominence relationship is defined among any two sister nodes:

(17)  a.                    b.                    c.

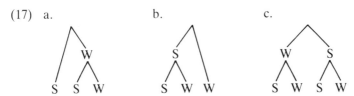

Note that structures of this form make rather subtle prominence distinctions among their bottom elements. In (17a), for example, the second element (*S*) is, of course, stronger than the third (*W*). But the first element is also stronger than the second and third elements on account of being their strong sister, so that (17a) expresses a prominence contour that decreases from left to right. We would be unable to express such contours if we used ternary structures with no node labels other than *S* and *W* – recall (16e), for comparison.

This, in a nutshell, is the basic vocabulary of a rather versatile notational system for all kinds of prominence phenomena in phonology, known in the phonological literature as **Metrical Phonology**. With the levels of structure introduced so far, this notation will enable us to express the facts of English word stress as well as – in section 7.4.2 below – some of the generalisations concerning these facts.

Let us now return to the stress patterns found in English words and see how they are expressed in the notational system just developed. Starting with some simple examples, here are the metrical structures for *camera*, *pity* and *bit* (where phonological structure below the foot level is abbreviated):

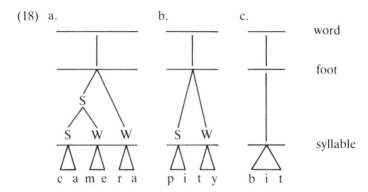

(18) a.　　　　　b.　　　　　c.

camera　pity　bit

Consisting in each case of single feet, these words exemplify the structures found on the foot level. By being represented on the foot level and, as single nodes, on the word level, the fact is expressed that each of these words has (or rather, is) a foot. And where that foot contains more than one syllable the first one is more prominent than the other(s).

Turning now to the representation of secondary stress, compare *'happy*, *'rab‚bi* and *‚bam'boo*:

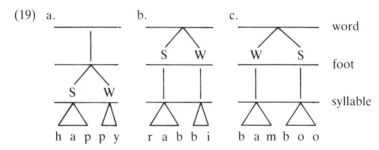

(19) a.　　　　　b.　　　　　c.

happy　rabbi　bamboo

*Happy* has, of course, the same structure as *pity* (18b) does: a single bisyllabic foot. *Rabbi* and *bamboo* are words that have two stressed syllables each, and therefore two feet. Notice how the difference between *happy* and *rabbi* is expressed by branching on the foot level in the former case, and branching on the word level in the latter. And the difference between *rabbi* and *bamboo* is simply a difference in prominence relations on the word level, among the two feet.

From here it only takes another small step to analyse structures such as *‚kanga'roo* (already familiar from (15) above) and *'nightin‚gale*. These have the same distribution of primary and secondary stresses as *bamboo* and *rabbi* (respectively); the only difference is that their initial feet are bisyllabic, and such feet are also familiar:

196

(20) a.   b.

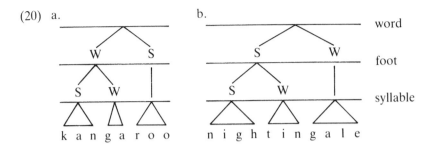

In addition to the three bisyllabic stress patterns analysed in (19) above, there is a fourth possibility, not mentioned so far. This is the pattern found in *Ju'ly*, *Pe'ru*, *ba'lloon* etc., where an unstressed syllable precedes a stressed one – unlike *'bam,boo*, whose first syllable is not unstressed. Such unstressed initial syllables, which are, of course, also found in longer words, such as *a'roma*, *di'vinity* etc., cannot be represented on the foot level (because that would make them stressed); but since they are part of the word they must be dominated by the word-level structure:

(21) a.   b.   c.

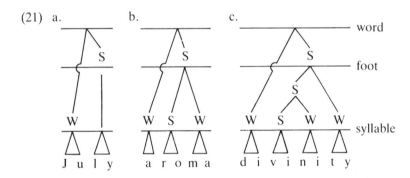

Notice how the word-level structure branches into a syllable and a foot. This is clearly the only way of analysing such word-stress patterns; yet such analyses are somewhat unattractive in that they violate a rather elegant assumption, implied in our discussion so far: the assumption that metrical structures are strictly hierarchical, that no level in the hierarchy can be skipped and that therefore the units on each level must also be represented on the next-lower level. It is obviously our insistence on the integrity of the word as a phonological unit that forces us to abandon this principle – the insistence that all the syllables of a word must come together in a single node on the word level. For the time being, we view cases like

(21) simply as a slight complication of our notational system rather than as a problem; we shall return to this matter in chapter 9 below, as part of a discussion of the metrical phonology of connected speech.

### 7.4.2 *Some generalisations*

In the preceding sections we have on various occasions come across the fact that the stress patterns found in English words, although widely varied, are not random. They are governed by certain regularities, whose underlying principles have already begun to emerge. Such regularities make reference to phonological information (syllable weight) as well as to syntactic and morphological information. We shall not at this point embark on a detailed study of the rules of English word stress – for this, the reader is referred to the relevant literature – but merely outline the shape that such a system of rules might have, and in doing so rely almost entirely on the body of data given in section 7.2 above. In particular, we shall once again deal almost exclusively with nouns.

The rules that determine the form of metrical structures such as those exemplified in section 7.4.1 may be divided into two categories, depending on the level of metrical structure on which they operate: **foot-level rules**, that is, rules that assign feet to syllables and thereby determine what syllables bear (some degree of) stress: and **word-level rules**, rules that assign structure above the foot level and thereby provide the differentiation between primary and secondary stresses. The former make reference, as we have already seen, to syllable weight (as well as to morphological and syntactic information); the latter, too, refer to phonological information, but to the structure of feet rather than to the structure of syllables; and once again they are also sensitive to morphological and syntactic characteristics of the word. Let us deal with the foot-level rules first.

Certain nouns have stress (primary or secondary) on their final syllable. Some examples are given in (22a, b) below, largely taken from section 7.2 but regrouped. (22c) contains words with nonfinal stress.

(22)  a. Ju'ly         b. ca'det        c. 'comic
         ba'lloon          'mo͵ped           'David
         'rab͵bi           e'llipse          'parent
         'tex͵tile         'syn͵tax          'August
         ͵colon'nade       ͵marzi'pan        'discipline
         'nightin͵gale     ͵comman'dant      'cormorant

It is, of course, a condition on final stressed syllables that they are heavy. But not all such heavy syllables are stressed (as was already noted in sect. 7.2): (22b) contains some examples that are, and (22c) some that are not. Note the similarities in the composition of these final syllables: these clearly suggest that stress patterns such as those in (22b) are rather sporadic and unpredictable. Example (22a) presents a different picture: these final syllables are different from those in (22b, c) in that they all contain long vowels; and what is more, nouns that have long vowels in their final syllable have stress on that syllable – primary or secondary – almost without exception. It would appear, then, that the stress in (22a) is predictable on account of the long vowels found in those final syllables, while the stress in (22b) is essentially idiosyncratic. We postpone the precise formulation of the relevant rule until later, and move on to the stress behaviour of penultimate syllables.

Under what conditions do nouns have penultimate stress? Example (23) below shows a range of stress patterns, on which our discussion will be based.

(23)   a. a'roma        b. 'nightin,gale   c. ,bam'boo      d. Ju'ly
          ho'rizon         ,caval'cade        ,cham'pagne      ba'lloon
          de'cathlon       ,chimpan'zee       ,fi'nance         fi'nance

Penultimate syllables in nouns are stressed if they are heavy, as those in (23a) are, and unstressed if they are light (like those in *A'merica* etc.); this much we have already seen in section 7.2.2. This rule, which is widely attested in polysyllabic English nouns, has few exceptions (*'badminton, va'nilla*); but there are further conditions attached to it. Consider first the examples in (23b), which have unstressed heavy penultimate syllables, contrary to the rule as it stands. Heavy penults are evidently not stressed if the final syllable has stress; in other words: a foot aligned with the penultimate syllable has to be bisyllabic, also including the final syllable. It cannot do that if the final syllable is itself a foot. But this is still not enough – consider (23c, d). Monosyllabic feet do occur on heavy penultimate syllables after all, but only where that syllable also happens to be the first one of the word. Again, we postpone the precise formulation of the relevant rules; but before we move on let us pause and see, in a representative sample of nouns, what stresses are accounted for by our, so far informal, rules and what are not.

(24)

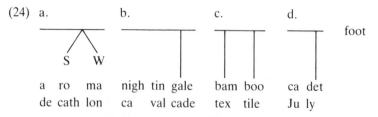

| | | | | foot |
|---|---|---|---|---|
| S W | | | | |
| a  ro  ma | nigh tin gale | bam boo | ca det | |
| de cath lon | ca  val cade | tex tile | Ju ly | |

The only items in this list that still need additional feet are those in (24b), where a bisyllabic foot has to be assigned to the beginning of the word. Notice that there is no syllable-weight requirement in this context. There are some more cases:

(25)   a. 'pity      b. 'camera      c. A'merica      d. 'bit
          'comic        'discipline      di'vinity          'camp

None of these words is affected by the rules that we have come across so far since all these rules assigned stress to heavy syllables only, and in the case of final heavy syllables only to those that contain long vowels. The cases in (25) are, like those in (24b), not constrained by a syllable-weight requirement; typically, these are the contexts in which heaviness is produced as a result of stress, through ambisyllabicity. Nor is stress assignment in monosyllabic nouns so constrained: being lexical words, they always have heavy syllables anyway. All we need to say for these 'default cases' of foot assignment is that strings of syllables not affected by previous rules are grouped, from right to left (*A'merica* etc.), into bi- or trisyllabic feet, and that finally – this is the ultimate default rule – every lexical word must have a foot. Thus we get the following:

(26)

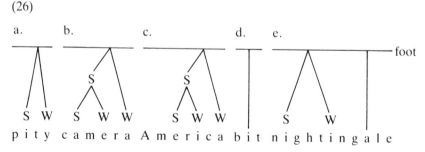

a.    b.    c.    d.   e.

| | | | | | foot |
|---|---|---|---|---|---|
| | S | S | | S | |
| S W | S W W | S W W | | S W | |
| p i t y | c a m e r a | A m e r i c a | b i t | n i g h t i n g a l e | |

The following statement of the relevant rules summarises our findings:

(27)   *Foot Assignment in Nouns*

   a.   Assign a foot to the final syllable if it contains a long vowel, or exceptionally, if it is otherwise heavy.

b. Assign a bisyllabic foot to the penultimate syllable if it is heavy.

c. Assign a foot to the penultimate syllable if it is heavy and initial.

d. Assign a maximal bi- or trisyllabic foot to any remaining string of syllables from right to left, and ensure that the word has at least one foot.

Note that these rules apply from right to left: first the final syllable is checked by rule (27a); then the penult is checked by (27b); and the default rule (27d) also assigns feet from right to left. Here is a final demonstration.

(28) a.

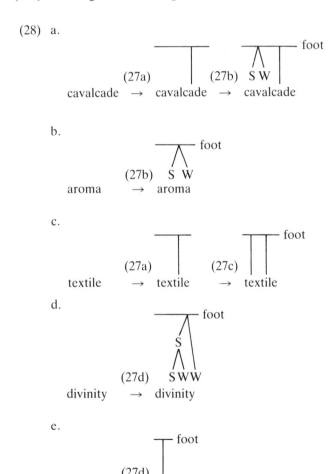

b.

c.

d.

e.

We now turn to the second category of rules, the word-level rules. Such rules build metrical structure on the word level, ensuring that every word is represented by a single node on that level, and assign prominence relations within such structures. Let us take one step at a time and first work out the structures, as we did in section 7.4.1, and then concern ourselves with the prominence relations.

Our task is indicated by the dotted lines in (29):

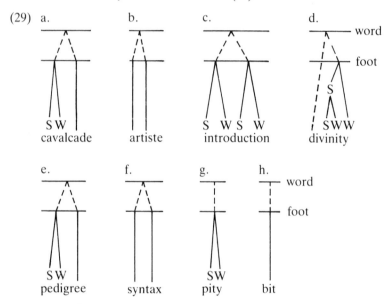

It is clear that, in (29), the principle for the building of word-level structure is:

(30)   *Word Structure Assignment*

Connect all material in a single structure on the word level.

It so happens that in our sample (29) there are never more than two separate units to be connected: either two feet or a syllable and a foot; and in some cases only one (foot) unit has to be taken up to the word level. This does not actually exhaust the possibilities found in English words: there are words that contain more than two feet, such as ˌinexˌplicaˈbility or ˌarchi-ˈmanˌdrite. For these, we would have to determine the exact form of the word-level structure in terms of our binary notation – recall (17) above; but we choose to ignore this question here. Instead, we turn to the prominence relations that hold on the word level.

Consider again some of the words of (29) above, now complete with prominence relations:

(31)

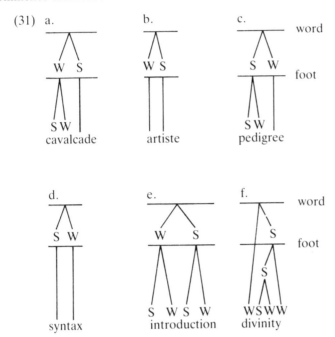

Recall from section 7.2.2 that it is exceptional for nouns to have their primary stress on the final syllable: not only are such nouns comparatively rare and often clearly recognisable as loan words; they are also in many instances unstable (and *cavalcade* is an example of this instability). If there is a stress on the final syllable then this stress is more often than not a secondary one. Thus, such final monosyllabic feet are usually weak on the word level (31b) and only in some exceptional cases strong (31c). On the other hand, it is normal for nouns with two feet to have their main stress on the right if that foot has more than one syllable. *Introduction* is a relevant example; others are *camaraderie*, *serendipity*, *assassination* and many others.

The distribution of *S* and *W* on the word level is easily accounted for, then. The right-hand node of a word-level structure is strong if it branches (that is, if it dominates more than one syllable) as it does in (31c), and in some exceptional cases (31a); otherwise it is weak.

Before we summarise our findings, we briefly turn our attention to the stress patterns of verbs, if only in order to substantiate the earlier claim that the stress behaviour of nouns and verbs is systematically different. Without concerning ourselves with the rules of foot assignment in verbs, which can also be shown to differ from those for nouns (rule 27), let us take a brief look at their word structure. It was said in section 7.2.1 that it is common for verbs to have primary stress on their final syllable; some examples, already noted in (5), are *o'bey, a'tone, ,inter'vene, ,super'sede*. There are verbs which have the opposite pattern (*'exor,cise, 'dele,gate*), and these are subject to separate explanation; but without going into such detail let us simply say that verbs with final main stress are, unlike nouns, by no means exceptional, uncommon or unstable – and this fact ought to be expressed in our rule for word-level prominence relations. We state this rule as follows:

(32)   *Word Prominence Rule*

In a pair of sister nodes $[N_1 \ N_2]_L$, where L is a lexical word, $N_2$ is strong if:
a.   it branches above the syllable level, or
b.   L is an exceptional noun, or
c.   L is a verb

Note that (32a) not only accounts for prominence relations on the word level but also, interestingly, on the foot level. All branching foot structures are left-strong; in other words, on the foot level all right-hand nodes ($N_2$ in (32)) are weak. And this is precisely what (32a) predicts, because no $N_2$ on the foot level ever branches above the syllable level. Rule (32a) holds, then, not only on the word level but actually in the entire word. It is also the most generally applicable of the subrules of (32) – the others are sensitive to additional, nonphonological information – and, as we shall see in chapter 9 below, it also accounts for the prominence relations in certain units that are larger than the single word.

What has been presented in this section is evidently not the whole story of the stress rules of English. (For this, or a bigger part of it, the reader is referred to the specialist literature on Metrical Phonology.) However, the following points have emerged from this discussion: that the phonological variables involved in the rules of stress assignment are syllable count (from the right) and syllable weight; that such rules also make reference to syntactic and morphological information; and – above all – that stress rules have exceptions. In order to minimise the number of unexplained exceptions, or to account for the behaviour of verbs (and adjectives), our system of rules would have had to be even more complex than it already is.

## 7.5   The (non-)predictability of English word stress

The phonological theory that we are developing in this book, step by step, in relation to English makes a crucial distinction between two kinds of phonological properties: phonemic properties, on the one hand, and ones that are predictable, on the other hand. The phonemic properties of a word are unpredictable. Such properties distinguish words from one another; every word of the language is learned in its idiosyncratic phonological form by the speaker as he or she learns the language. Thus the speaker learns words, individually, in their phonemic form: /pɪt/, /pat/, /pɪtɪ/, /kɪtɪ/ etc. Predictable phonological properties of words, on the other hand, are assumed not to be learned individually with every word; instead, the speaker simply acquires the rules that predict them and then assigns these properties to the words, or sounds, as they occur in his or her speech. Syllable structure is, as we saw in chapter 6, such a predictable property: rather than having to learn /pɪt/ and /pat/ in a monosyllabic pronunciation and /pɪtɪ/ in a bisyllabic one, the speaker has at his or her disposal the mechanisms of syllabification and automatically assigns syllable structures to every word that he or she utters. Syllabification rules have no exceptions, and no two words of English are distinct from one another in terms of syllable structure alone.

As regards phonemic properties, we have been making some rather important assumptions. Firstly, we have assumed (without discussion) that all such properties are segmental: the (segmental) phoneme, for us, has been the only possible carrier of unpredictable phonological information in underlying representations. Our study of syllable structure has borne this out: at least this aspect of suprasegmental structure is clearly predictable and therefore not present in underlying phonological representations. Secondly, the domain in which phonemic contrasts are established in the word: minimal pairs, the only proof of phonemic properties, are pairs of words distinct in terms of one sound segment only. It is one of the crucial (if somewhat simplified) assumptions of our phonemic analysis that no other part of the grammar – syntax, morphology – plays a part, or is made reference to, in phonemic analysis. And thirdly, a single minimal pair in a language is enough to establish a given sound segment as a phoneme in this language. If a speaker, for example, has the voiceless velar fricative [x] in the single word *loch* (as a Southern English speaker may well do, having visited Scotland) and nowhere else, then this single occurrence establishes /x/ as a phoneme for that speaker, as the minimal pair *loch – lock* proves (albeit, of course, as a somewhat marginal one). It is not possible to explain away this single occurrence of [x] as an exceptional realisation of some other phoneme, say of /k/. Rules that predict phonological properties have no exceptions. Once a phoneme, always a phoneme.

Seen against this background of assumptions concerning the nature of phonemic and predictable properties, English word stress has a curious status. On the one hand, we have found it possible to devise rules that predict the stress contours of English words; on the other hand, it is also clear that these rules contravene just about every assumption that our phonological theory makes about the nature of phonological rules: they make reference to nonphonological properties – without such reference, the predictability of stress patterns would be drastically reduced. And they have exceptions – recall, for example, *badminton* and *vanilla*.

We know, of course, that true minimal pairs of stress are rare in English; but do the ones that we have found establish stress as a phoneme? The pair *'differ – de'fer* alone clinches the point, in terms of phonemic theory. This pair of words is distinct in terms of stress placement only; we have no choice, therefore, but to mark stress (feet) on the underlying level of representation. Feet are phonemic, and not only in *differ – defer*, but in principle (once a phoneme, always a phoneme!) in every English word. It is only the inclusion of morphological information in our analysis that enables us to reach a different conclusion. Then *differ* and *defer* are not a minimal pair because *differ* is a single morpheme and *defer* two, where the prefix *de-* is also attested in *deploy*, *descend* etc. and the root *-fer* in *refer* and *confer*. If we had paid some attention to the stress behaviour of verbal prefixes in section 7.4.2 then we would no doubt have been able to predict the stress difference between *differ* and *defer*.

The case of the familiar pairs *'digest – di'gest, 'escort – es'cort* is very similar: a single phonological difference (that of stress) corresponds to a difference in meaning in that one member of each pair denotes a thing/ person and the other an activity. But again, the analyst availing himself or herself of nonphonological information – this time of syntactic-category information – will have no trouble predicting these stress patterns even with the limited machinery of rules given in section 7.4.2.

It is clear, then, that in terms of the phonological theory pursued in this book – one in which underlying representations are determined by phonemic contrasts of the kind defined above – sections 7.3 and 7.4.2 have been out of bounds: the mechanisms deployed there, for the prediction of phonological properties, are not permitted by our tightly constrained methodology of phonological (phonemic) analysis. Stress in English is phonemic; the phonemic level of representation therefore contains some suprasegmental information. And the absence of stress patterns such as *,nigh'tingale* in English must be treated as the defective distribution of phonemic properties in words – similar, for example, to the fact that the velar nasal /ŋ/ occurs neither in syllable onsets nor after long vowels in syllable rhymes (a fact which in itself demands an explanation which phonemic analysis cannot provide). It is obviously not possible to reach a conclusion on this issue here, which remains contentious in phonological theory: are stress rules phonological rules or not? All we can say, perhaps, is that no methodology should be sacrosanct. If a theory fails to capture the facts then it should be replaced by a new and more powerful theory. We shall return to such issues of theory in chapter 10.

**Suggested reading to chapter 7**

Section 7.1 On stress in general see Catford (1988: ch. 9), Ladefoged (1982: ch. 10), Couper-Kuhlen (1986: ch. 2), Hyman (1975: sect. 6.2), Hyman (1977). On stress in English words see Fudge (1984), Poldauf (1984).

Section 7.2 The correlation of stress and syllable weight in various languages is discussed in Hyman (1975: sect. 6.2), Hyman (1977).

Section 7.3 On morphology/word formation in general see, for example, Bauer (1983). On the interaction of morphological processes with stress rules in English, see Siegel (1979) – a highly technical dissertation, whose results have been incorporated in most of the subsequent literature on English stress. Less technically, Fudge (1984), Poldauf (1984).

Section 7.4 The first major published work on Metrical Phonology was Liberman and Prince (1977); important later contributions include Selkirk (1980) and Hayes (1982). Introductory reading: Hogg and McCully (1987: ch. 3), Giegerich (1985: ch. 1), Giegerich (1986). The account of English word stress presented here is especially indebted to Selkirk (1980) and Hayes (1982), but differs substantially from both. See Hogg and McCully (1987: ch. 3) for an overview of these individual proposals. For a more recent theory of stress, in a radically revised version of Metrical Phonology, see Halle and Vergnaud (1987).

# 8

# Phonetic representations: the realisations of phonemes

## 8.1 The phonetic level of representation

It will have become clear by now that the phonological analysis pursued in this book recognises two significant levels of representation. On the one hand, there is the abstract **phonemic level**, on which only phonologically relevant properties are represented, where phonological relevance is defined as phonological **contrastiveness**: the representations of two segments differ on this level if this difference serves to distinguish words. Segments that are distinct on this level of representation are called **phonemes**, and minimal pairs (*pit – bit*) constitute proof of the phonemic status of segments (here of /p/ and /b/). Phonemic inventories are not only language-specific; they even differ, as we saw in chapters 2 and 3, from accent to accent. To complete the picture of the phonemic level, we saw in chapter 7 that certain suprasegmental properties may also be phonemic: English word stress is phonemic under a strictly phonemicist methodology – recall minimal pairs such as *'abstract – ab'stract*.

The **phonetic level** of representation, on the other hand, contains not only the phonologically relevant information that is also present on the phonemic level; it contains also all the information that is **redundant** – phonetic features, that is, which are not utilised in the phonemic distinctions of the language. On this level, the representation of an utterance is fleshed out with phonetic details. The question is, how fully fleshed out are such phonetic representations in our theory? Do they give a fully detailed, maximally concrete picture of the phonetic facts of an utterance, or are they merely less abstract than phonemic representations? As we shall be dealing with the elements of the phonetic level of representation in some detail in this chapter, we first need to get a clearer idea of the status and general properties of this level.

As we have seen, phonemic representations are established, on the basis of the phonetic facts, by means of a process of abstraction which isolates the contrastive phonological properties of an utterance from the noncontrastive ones. The phonemic information contained, say, in a word is nonredundant; it is unpredictable in that every word has its own, idiosyncratic phonemic shape, whose building blocks are taken from the phoneme inventory of the language. To do the 'fleshing out' of such representations that produces the phonetic representation, we fill in the predictable (redundant) information; for example, we fill in syllable structure (which is, as we saw in chapter 6, predictable in English and therefore part of the phonetic but not of the phonemic representation). Such predictions are made by phonological rules – like, for example, the rules that determine syllable boundaries, syllable peaks and so forth. Phonological rules are generalisations about the phonological behaviour of a language; together with the inventory of phonemes, they constitute the phonology of the language. A full phonetic representation is achieved after the application of all the rules of the phonology. Clearly, however, even this would not get us 'back' to a level of concreteness that is an exact copy of the phonetic facts, for the following reasons.

Firstly, the present phonological theory is **segment-based**: the minimal consecutive units of this theory are segments on both the phonemic and the phonetic level. And we saw as early as in chapter 1 that the segment itself is a somewhat abstract, idealised representation of the facts: in the reality of the speech continuum, the constant changes in the articulator settings are not so well co-ordinated as to happen in discrete steps.

Secondly, to assume that our phonetic level of representation is an exact copy of the phonetic facts is to claim that all nonphonemic properties of an utterance are predictable, governed by rules. And even the most meticulously worked-out phonology of a language, or of an accent, or of a speaker, cannot uphold this claim: since it is not possible even for the same speaker to give two renderings of an utterance that are phonetically perfectly identical in every respect, it *cannot* be the case that all noncontrastive phonetic facts of an utterance are rule-governed. Even after nonlinguistic (sociological, psychological etc.) variables have been incorporated in phonological rules, there will always be a residue – however small – of random behaviour, of **free variation**. As we shall see, such free variation can to some extent be captured by invoking optional rules – rules that may randomly, for no apparent reason, apply or fail to apply – but it is clear that an attempt to treat all randomness in speech in this way would ultimately make a nonsense of the concept of 'rule' itself.

After these observations, it is clear what the answer to the questions raised above has to be: in our phonological theory, the phonetic level of representation cannot be the exact copy of the phonetic facts that we would perhaps like it to be. In this theory, the phonology of a language (or of an accent or a speaker) consists of an inventory of phonemes that are no smaller than single segments, and of a set of phonological rules. The phonetic level of representation is therefore essentially **segmental** and **systematic** in that it includes only those phonetic facts that are rule-governed. It is not as fully concrete as the phonetic facts themselves that it seeks to describe, but it is, of course, less abstract than the phonemic level.

In this chapter, we shall investigate some of the better-known segmental rules of the phonology of English. They will serve as examples, demonstrating the characteristics of such rules as well as of the phonetic level of representation that they produce, rather than giving a comprehensive picture.

### 8.2 Allophony: the principles

If a phoneme has two or more different realisations then these realisations are called **allophones** of that phoneme. All allophones of a phoneme must be phonetically similar. It follows from this definition, of course, that sounds that have the status of being allophones of the same phoneme do not contrast: if they did then they would be realisations of different phonemes. But let us, before we look at some cases of allophony in detail, remind ourselves of the importance of the phonetic-similarity criterion for allophones.

We saw in chapter 6 that the velar nasal [ŋ] and the voiceless glottal fricative [h] are subject to rather tight phonotactic restrictions: the former is restricted to a particular position in the syllable rhyme, namely the position after a short vowel (*sing, tango, drink*), while the latter can only occur in syllable onsets (*hat, mayhem, comprehend*). These two sounds are therefore in **complementary distribution**: in any given context, only one of the two is permitted to occur (and in several contexts neither); any position in the syllable that permits one does not permit the other. Due to this complementary distribution the two sounds do not contrast: it is impossible for them to occur in minimal pairs, given that a minimal pair proves the ability of two sounds to occur in identical contexts (**parallel distribution**), as /b/ and /h/ do in *bat – hat*. These facts would mean that [ŋ] and [h] are allophones of the same phoneme, unless we impose the condition on allophony that all allophones of the same phoneme must be phonetically similar. It is quite clear that it is desirable to adopt this condition: given that [ŋ] and [h] have virtually no phonetic features in common, the resulting phoneme would be a rather strange entity, incapable of adequate characterisation in terms of features – and every phoneme of a language must, of course, be amenable to such a characterisation. We were undoubtedly correct, in the preceding chapters, to treat /ŋ/ and /h/ as different phonemes. But let us return to allophony, bearing the phonetic-similarity criterion in mind. In particular, we shall now concern ourselves with the two distributional possibilities of sounds – complementary and parallel distribution – and their impact on allophonic rules.

### 8.2.1 *Complementary distribution of allophones: clear and dark /l/*

In many accents of English, for example RP, the lateral phoneme /l/ has two major realisational variants, or allophones: a 'clear' one, transcribed simply as [l], and a 'dark' one – [ɫ]. Both are laterals with alveolar contact; the articulatory difference between the two is that in the former the back of the tongue is lowered while in the latter it is raised towards the velum or retracted towards the uvula (without making contact in either case). Here are some examples for RP:

(1)  a.  'clear' [l]: *l*ull, *l*ip, *l*ow, b*l*ind, sp*l*ice, ye*ll*ow, foo*l*ish
     b.  'dark' [ɫ]: lu*ll*, hi*ll*, poo*l*, he*l*p, so*l*ve, e*l*bow, litt*l*e

The accent that exemplifies the phonetic difference between the two allophones, as well as their distribution, most clearly is RP; in GA the distribution is the same but the phonetic difference is not as strong in that the 'clear' [l], too, is somewhat velarised. In many varieties of SSE all realisations of /l/ are dark; while other accents (for example, Welsh English and Southern Irish English) have clear [l] in all contexts.

What, then, is the distribution of clear and dark /l/ in RP? It is quite clear that there is a rule for this distribution – try to violate it by pronouncing *lull* as *[ɫʌl]! – and that this rule derives the quality of the /l/ realisation from the place that it occupies in the syllable. Recalling the principles of syllabification that were discussed in chapter 6, we note that all the cases of clear [l] in (1a) are sited in syllable onsets while the instances of dark [ɫ] occur in syllable rhymes. In most of the examples this is obvious, but there are some that deserve a full syllable-structure analysis, if only to confirm the point:

(2) a. 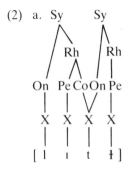    b.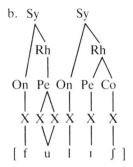

c.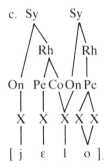

In *little* (2a), the /l/ occupies the syllable peak (which in this case is the only constituent of the rhyme): it is not only dark but also syllabic. In transcription, this syllabicity is marked by a stroke underneath the syllabic sound: [lɪtl̩]. Note that in the alternative pronunciation [lɪtəł], the [ł] occurs in the coda, as it does in all other examples of (1b). In *foolish* (2b), /l/ occupies a syllable onset and is clear as predicted, while in *yellow* (2c) it is ambisyllabic (after a short stressed vowel – recall section 6.6 above). In this case the /l/'s association with the onset is decisive in RP: it is clear rather than dark.

From this analysis of the facts, the complementary distribution of [l] and [ł] is evident: /l/ is realised, in RP, as [l] whenever it occurs in a syllable onset; and it is realised as [ł] elsewhere – to be precise, wherever it is not [l]. Here is a formal statement of the rule:

(3)  '*Clear' and 'dark' /l/ in RP*

$$/l/ \rightarrow \begin{cases} [1]/\underset{\overline{\phantom{xxxx}}}{\overset{\text{On}}{|}} \\ [ł] \quad \text{elsewhere} \end{cases}$$

(Note that it would be wrong to state this rule the other way round, as '/l/ is realised as [ɫ] in rhymes and as [l] elsewhere': this would falsely predict /l/ in ambisyllabic position (*yellow*) to be dark.)

The distribution of clear and dark /l/ in RP constitutes a showpiece of an allophonic rule in several respects. First, the rule is clearly accent-specific, illustrating the point made earlier that accents may differ from each other not only in terms of their phoneme inventories but also in terms of their phonological rules. Second, it provides a good example of complementary distribution and phonetic similarity, which only allows the one conclusion that [l] and [ɫ] must be allophones of the same phoneme. (Recall from our discussion of [ŋ] and [h], above, that complementary distribution alone is not a sufficient criterion for allophony.) Third, the distribution of the two allophones is conditioned by their phonological context: here, by their position in a higher-order phonological unit (namely, the syllable). Fourth, the rule is, for those speakers who have it, obligatory: there are no contexts in which randomly [l] or [ɫ] may occur. And fifth, the rule also has no lexical exceptions: there are no individual words in RP that systematically violate the rule by having [l] instead of [ɫ], or vice versa.

It remains to be seen whether *all* these features of the dark-/l/ rule constitute general characteristics of allophonic rules. Let us look at some other cases of allophony.

### 8.2.2 *Assimilation: optionality versus nonbinarity, and natural classes*

It has already been noted that our apparently elementary notion 'segment' is in itself an abstraction: the phonetic reality is not such that all the phonetic changes that occur in the transition from one speech sound to the next happen suddenly, and simultaneously, at a specific point in time that may be identified as the boundary between two segments; indeed, phonetic evidence for segment boundaries is rather hard to find. Such boundaries are in reality rather fuzzy: a fact that is belied not only by our letter-based transcription system but also by the segment-based phonological theory for which it serves as a notation.

In particular, the way in which the 'place of articulation' characteristics of segments (but by no means only those) are implemented contributes to this fuzziness of segment boundaries: it is extremely common for a segment to anticipate (at least partially) the place of articulation of the following segment. This phenomenon, called (**anticipatory**) **assimilation**, has already been noted in chapter 2 as an important source of allophony – exemplified then by the dental realisation of /n/ before dental fricatives (*tenth*), the fronting of /k/ before front vowels (*key*) etc. – and will here be discussed in some more detail. But before we consider these details, it is worth noting that assimilation in the opposite direction, where features of a speech sound spread over to the following one, is quite unproductive in English, restricted to some 'lexicalised' examples like *it's* [ɪts], from *it is* [ɪtɪz], where the final fricative is voiceless due to the preceding voiceless stop.

Here are some examples of anticipatory assimilation, which will also serve to introduce some diacritic symbols that are common in allophonic transcription:

(4)  a.  /n/ → [n̪] before dental (*tenth, in theory, one thing*), where the subscript 'bridge' indicates dentalisation.

   b.  /k/ → [k̟] before front vowel (*key, keep*). The subscript 'plus' indicates fronting.

   c.  /m/ → [ɱ] before labiodental (*comfort, emphasis, come forward*). [ɱ] denotes a labiodental nasal.

   d.  /a/ → [ã] before nasal (*hand, man*). The superscript 'tilde' denotes nasalisation.

   e.  /k/ → /k̹] before rounded segment (*queer, quack, cool*). The subscript 'ω' denotes labialisation/rounding.

This list could easily be continued; but these examples suffice to make the point that assimilation is a major cause of allophony, and that there is a principle behind it: a given segment acquires a feature (here '[+ F]') from a following segment:

(5)  *Anticipatory assimilation*

$$/X/ → [+ F] / \underline{\quad\quad} [+ F]$$

But given this general principle, the question arises whether all assimilation is rule-governed in the sense in which, say, the /l/ allophony discussed above is: are instances of assimilation *predictable* (for that is what phonological rules do: they predict nonphonemic properties of the phonetic representation), or are they merely random, one-off events in speech that may or may not occur?

In a sense, the answer to both questions is yes; but it has to be qualified in both cases. While it is quite predictable that an assimilation will occur in the speech of an individual whenever its specific context conditions are met, the degree to which this will happen is highly variable, depending on the individual speaker's habits as well as on situational factors: rapid, informal speech displays assimilation to a far greater extent than slow and careful speech does. If one takes a strictly binary view of assimilatory processes (and indeed of allophony in general) by assuming that, for example, dentalisation of /n/ either does or does not occur before /θ/ – a view that is encouraged by the practice of transcription: [n̪] or [n] – then one has to conclude that assimilatory processes are largely optional: there may well be cases where what a speaker says is more like [tɛnθ] than like [tɛn̪θ]. This would then mean that the two realisations of /n/ are not in complementary distribution but rather in parallel distribution: in the context [tɛ__θ], both [n] and [n̪] can occur, and what stops this distinction from being phonemic is that it does not give rise to minimal pairs in English.

This assumption of binarity is simplistic. It may well be the case that it is merely the degree of assimilation that is variable; however subtle, dentalisation of /n/ before /θ/ is, in fact, highly likely to happen in every /nθ/ sequence. Bearing in mind the gradient nature of the phenomenon, which the symbol '-' fails to express, [n] and [n̪] may indeed be in complementary distribution in that [n̪] occurs before /θ/ and nowhere else, while undentalised [n] does not occur in this context. The same is true, of course, for all other assimilation phenomena that were listed in (4) above. It is this gradient nature of many (perhaps all) allophonic processes, as well as their dependence on factors that are hard to formalise – speakers' habits, speech style, tempo etc. – that makes our phonetic level of representation but a poor likeness of the phonetic facts of speech.

Let us turn now to the first question that was raised above: the question of predictability. We have seen that assimilatory phenomena are predictable – although they may be (almost) absent, depending on speaker and speech style – but we have only formulated the general principle (5) that expresses the regular influence of sounds upon their predecessors; the various different assimilation processes observed in (4) follow this general principle (5); yet it is desirable to formulate some individual rules for the various cases of allophony listed in (4) above, and to formulate these as generally as possible. We use as an example the nasalisation of /a/ before /n/, witnessed in *hand*, *man* (4d). The phenomenon of nasalisation is, in fact, far more widespread than these two examples might lead one to believe: we not only get [ã] before the nasal phoneme /n/ but also before the other two nasals /m/ and /ŋ/: *ram* [rãm], *camp* [kãmp], *sang* [sãŋ], *tank* [tãŋk] etc. Moreover, it is not just /a/ that is affected by nasalisation, but also all other vowels: *palm* [pãm], *song* [sõŋ], *lawn* [lɔ̃n] etc. The nasalisation rule may, then, have the following general form, in line with the general principle (5):

(6) *Nasalisation of vowels*

$$/V/ \rightarrow [\tilde{V}] / \_\_\_\_ \begin{cases} /m/ \\ /n/ \\ /\eta/ \end{cases}$$

The generalisation that all nasals have a nasalising influence on preceding vowels is a fairly obvious one – there is no reason to suppose that only the alveolar nasal /n/ is able to spread its nasality to its predecessor, just as there is no reason to suppose that only /a/ should be affected – but it is an important point. Phonemes fall into **natural classes** with respect to their behaviour in the phonological generalisations of the language: if a phoneme is nasal then we expect it to nasalise preceding vowels. As it happens, our formulation of the nasalisation rule (6) is less than perfect in its expression of natural classes, for reasons that will be discussed in section 8.5.2 below; but for the moment it will suffice.

Similar generalisations may now be attempted to make general statements about the other cases of assimilation that were listed in (4), such as the following: if a vowel is front then we expect it to front any preceding segment that is underlyingly back. Thus, the observation made for *key* and *keep* in (4b) may also be expected in *geese, keg, get* etc. Or, if a phoneme is labial it is expected to labialise a preceding, underlyingly nonlabial segment (as in *queer, quack* (4e) but also *twig, swing* etc.). And so forth. It is clear that any rules that we might wish to state formally would be very similar to (6): like the nasal-assimilation rule, they would merely be instantiations of the general assimilation principle (5).

The study of assimilatory phenomena provides us with two interesting observations regarding the general nature of allophonic rules. First, not all allophonic rules are necessarily as neatly binary as the dark-/l/ rule arguably is: many allophonic phenomena are gradient rather than binary. Second, in theoretical terms there are two possible distributions for allophones: complementary and parallel, the latter being allophonic only where it fails to yield minimal pairs in the language. We have so far not come across a convincing case of parallel distribution of allophones (that is, of free variation), noting instead that a simplistic binary view of allophony might suggest the accidental absence of an expected allophonic feature where in reality traces of this feature may well be present. Are there genuinely optional allophonic rules?

### 8.2.3  *Parallel distribution of allophones: unreleased stops*

Segments may be more or less nasalised, labialised or fronted, and we have seen that this gradience of many allophonic features may lead to the oversimplified conclusion that in certain cases the allophonic rule in question optionally fails to apply when in reality, on closer inspection, it may well be implemented to a very slight extent. It makes sense, then, to concentrate our search for a genuinely optional rule on a phonetic feature that is *intrinsically* binary, such as the release characteristics of oral stops. Such stops may be either released (as so far we have always assumed they are) or unreleased. There is no intrinsic gradience in this feature. Here are some examples of unreleased stops, indicated by a superscript 'minus' after the stop:

(7)  a.  captain      [kap⁻tən]          b.  cap     [kap⁻]
         hatpin       [hat⁻pɪn]             hat     [hat⁻]
         blackboard   [blak⁻bɔd]            black   [blak⁻]
         obtain       [əb⁻ten]              cab     [kab⁻]
         good dog     [gʊd⁻dɒg]             good    [gʊd⁻]
         rugby        [rʌg⁻bɪ]              rug     [rʌg⁻]

Unreleased stops occur in two different contexts: before other oral stops – as in (7a) – and at the end of an utterance (7b). The former context can be viewed as another instance of anticipatory assimilation (the [p] in *captain* acquires a secondary alveolar closure in anticipation of the following /t/, which prevents it from being released); and we shall say more about the utterance-final position as a possible context for allophonic phenomena in section 8.3.3 below. What is important here is that in both contexts the release of stops is, in phonological terms, optional: released and unreleased stops in such contexts are in parallel distribution, in **free variation**. Thus [t] and [t⁻] do not contrast, despite their parallel distribution, because they are not utilised in minimal pairs. However, this notion of 'free variation' is only valid when the range of possible variables that may determine allophony is restricted to purely phonological ones, excluding nonlinguistic factors: such stops are most likely to be released in slow, careful speech; they are commonly unreleased in casual or fast speech, and some speakers habitually have more unreleased stops than others. It is by no means certain whether 'absolutely free variation' exists in phonology: variation that remains unaccounted for after *all* possible causes of variation, including nonphonological ones, have been taken into account. If nothing else, this observation once again shows the empirical limitations of the phonetic level of representation in phonological theory.

We conclude this survey of the principles of allophony by revising the tentative list of characteristics of allophonic rules that we drew up in section 8.2.1.

1   All allophones of a phoneme are phonetically similar.

2   Allophonic rules are accent-specific, as we saw in the case of 'dark [l]', and may even vary from one speaker to another.

3   Phonetic features assigned to segments by allophonic rules are not necessarily binary but may be of a gradient nature. This was exemplified above by the various phenomena of anticipatory assimilation.

4   Allophones are conditioned by their phonological context: either by neighbouring segments (as typically in the case of assimilation rules) or by their position in the suprasegmental structure. The latter is again exemplified by the distribution of [l] and [ɫ].

5   Allophonic rules may be optional (e.g. the rule for unreleased stops), but they have no lexical exceptions: no individual words are regularly pronounced in such a way that they violate allophonic rules.

6   Speech sounds may be in complementary or parallel distribution. In the former case they are allophones of the same phoneme if they meet the phonetic-similarity criterion, in the latter if their distribution is governed by an optional rule. (Note that this rule-governedness precludes the existence of minimal pairs, given that such minimal pairs would imply the existence of a lexical exception to an allophonic rule.)

As we shall see in the following paragraphs, not all of these statements about the nature of allophonic rules are without problems.

### 8.3   Allophony in the obstruent system

We embark now on the first of two detailed studies of allophony in major subsystems of the phonemic system of English: the system of obstruents, particularly of oral stops. This study serves several purposes: it will, firstly, introduce some more of the better-known allophony rules of English. Secondly, it will demonstrate how an underlying phonological contrast – here, the voicing opposition – may be obliterated in the surface phonetic representation but maintained by different phonetic features. Thirdly, it will make crucial reference to the principles of syllabification presented in chapter 6, thus providing a kind of supporting evidence for these principles that was not presented at the time.

### 8.3.1 *The allophony of voiceless stops: aspiration and glottalisation*

The English voiceless-stop phonemes are realised in certain contexts in such a way that the voicing of the following segment does not begin immediately, coinciding with the release of the stop, but after a short delay. This phenomenon is called **aspiration**, marked by a superscript 'ʰ'. Thus /p t k/ may be realised as [pʰ tʰ kʰ]. This allophony is present in all accents of English, although it is, of the three reference accents discussed here, weakest in Scottish Standard English.

The context in which aspiration occurs is the syllable-initial position; but (being once again a nonbinary phenomenon) aspiration is strongest in the initial position of stressed syllables. Here are some examples:

| (8) | a. pit | [pʰɪt] | b. spit | [spɪt] | c. bit | [bɪt] |
|---|---|---|---|---|---|---|
| | tie | [tʰaɪ] | sty | [staɪ] | buy | [baɪ] |
| | come | [kʰʌm] | scum | [skʌm] | gum | [gʌm] |

Aspiration does not occur in the examples in (8b), where voiceless stops are preceded in syllable onsets by /s/ – note that /s/ is the only phoneme that can precede a stop in the onset of a syllable. Hence, the /p/ is aspirated in *pit* but not in *spit*, in *tie* but not in *sty*, etc. There is also no aspiration of the voiced stops in (8c) – aspiration is clearly restricted to *voiced* stops.

In syllable onsets where a voiceless stop is followed by a sonorant, the production of the sonorant falls partly or completely within the aspiration period of the stop, and devoicing of the sonorant occurs. Some examples are given in (9):

(9)

| a. pray | [pr̥e] | b. spring | [sprɪŋ] | c. apron | [e.pr̥ən] |
|---|---|---|---|---|---|
| play | [pl̥e] | split | [splɪt] | applaud | [ə.pl̥ɔd] |
| crew | [kr̥u] | screw | [skru] | across | [ə.kr̥ɒs] |
| clue | [kl̥u] | | | proclaim | [pr̥ə.kl̥em] |
| try | [tr̥aɪ] | | | attract | [ə.tr̥akt] |
| twig | [twɪg] | | | matron | [me.tr̥ən] |
| tune | [tjun] | | | | |

| | d. atlas | [at.ləs] | e. brew | [bru] |
|---|---|---|---|---|
| | butler | [bʌt.lə] | blue | [blu] |
| | Watney | [wɒt.nɪ] | drew | [dru] |

Here, the sub- (or super-)script 'ₒ' indicates **devoicing**. Despite the different symbol, which is phonetically more accurate than, for example, [pʰle] would be, we treat these instances of devoicing (but only these) as instances of aspiration. Looking at the examples in detail, we note first that those in (9a, b, e) are unsurprising: the distribution of devoicing here corresponds precisely to that of aspiration in (8a, b, c) – strong support, incidentally, for the claim that this devoicing is to be treated as aspiration. Example (9c) is similarly straightforward: given that all the word-medial clusters exemplified there – /pr/, /pl/, /tr/ etc. – are possible syllable onsets, the voiceless stops are syllable-initial and behave in the predicted fashion. /tl/, however, is not a permissible onset cluster and is therefore divided by a syllable boundary (9d). We discussed such details of syllabification in detail in section 6.6; here, the absence of aspiration – that is, the un-devoiced sonorants – confirms our earlier observations about the placement of syllable boundaries.

Our aspiration rule can now be stated as follows:

(10)   *Aspiration of voiceless stops*

$$\left.\begin{array}{c}/p/\\/t/\\/k/\end{array}\right\} \rightarrow \left\{\begin{array}{c}[p^h]\\{[t^h]}\\{[k^h]}\end{array}\right\} / \ . \ \underline{\phantom{xx}}$$

We turn now to a second type of allophony, which similarly affects voiceless stops but which occurs in syllable-final position only (and again most strongly at the end of stressed syllables), and therefore in complementary distribution with aspiration: **glottalisation**, sometimes called 'glottal reinforcement'. The latter term is perhaps more descriptive of the phenomenon: what happens is that in syllable-final voiceless stops the bilabial, alveolar or velar closure is accompanied – often slightly preceded – by glottal closure, so that a glottal stop [ʔ] is co-articulated with the [p t k] articulation. Examples are given in (11):

(11)   a. cup      [kʰʌʔp]          b. cub      [kʰʌb]
          heap     [hiʔp]               grebe    [grib]
          bit        [bɪʔt]                bid        [bɪd]
          beat      [biʔt]                bead      [bid]
          buck     [bʌʔk]               bug        [bʌg]
          oak       [oʔk]                 vogue     [vog]
          felt       [fɛɬʔt]               felled     [fɛɬd]

This allophony is common in all three reference accents, and like aspiration, it is a gradient phenomenon, depending not only on the usual speaker and speech-style variables but also on its segmental context in the syllable-final position: it is most easily perceived after short vowels (*cup*, *bit*) and probably weakest after consonants (*felt*). Glottalisation occurs in no other context; nor does it occur with any phonemes other than voiceless stops. Notably, it is absent in voiced stops – compare (11a) and (11b). Here, then, is our glottalisation rule:

(12)   *Glottalisation of voiceless stops*

$$\left.\begin{array}{l}/p/\\ /t/\\ /k/\end{array}\right\} \rightarrow \left\{\begin{array}{l}[\text{?}p]\\ [\text{?}t]\\ [\text{?}k]\end{array}\right\} / \underline{\quad\quad}.$$

Let us now look at some more complex examples – cases where clusters involving voiceless stops occur in word-medial position. In some such cases we expect aspiration/devoicing – recall (8c) above – and in others we do not (9d); but what about glottalisation?

(13)

| a. apron | [epɹ̥ən] | b. Cypriot | [sɪʔpɹ̥iəʔt] | c. atlas | [aʔtləs] |
|---|---|---|---|---|---|
| matron | [metɹ̥ən] | petrol | [pʰɛʔtɹ̥əɫ] | Butlin | [bʌʔtlɪn] |
| micro | [maɪkɹ̥o] | macron | [maʔkɹ̥ɒn] | cutlass | [kʌʔtləs] |

What is interesting about these examples, some of which we have seen before in connection with aspiration, is that their medial voiceless stops are syllabified in three different ways, and that these syllabification differences are consistent with their allophonic behaviour. In (13a), the stop is syllable-initial and therefore aspirated – for further examples, recall (9c). The examples in (13c) are also familiar: we noted in (9d) above that /tl/ cannot be a syllable onset and that the absence of aspiration in the /t/ confirms this. Now we can add a further allophonic detail into the transcription: the /t/ is syllable-final and therefore glottalised. The most interesting examples, however, are those in (13b): here the stops are ambisyllabic, associated both with the onset of the second syllable – /pr tr kr/ are well-formed onsets – and with the rhyme of the initial (stressed) syllable, thus making that syllable heavy. (For details of this analysis, the reader is referred back to section 6.6.) This ambisyllabicity of the stops in (13b) is, in fact, borne out by their allophonic behaviour: they are both aspirated and glottalised.

### 8.3.2 *Allophony of voiced obstruents: devoicing*

Unlike their voiceless counterparts, voiced stops are subject to neither aspiration nor glottalisation; instead, they display allophony of a different kind: in certain contexts, they are partially or even completely **devoiced**. Consider the following examples:

(14)

| a. rib | [rɪb̥] | b. buy [b̥aɪ] | c. obtain [əb̥ten] | d. ebbing | [ɛbɪŋ] |
|---|---|---|---|---|---|
| rid | [rɪd̥] | die [d̥aɪ] | bodkin [bɒd̥kɪn] | riding | [raɪdɪŋ] |
| rig | [rɪg̊] | guy [g̊aɪ] | wagtail [wag̊teł] | regal | [rigəł] |

This distribution of devoicing is not restricted to voiced stops: it affects all voiced obstruents (including, therefore, voiced stops as well as voiced fricatives and affricates). Here are some more examples, parallel to the ones given in (14a–d):

(14)

| e. rise | [raɪz̥] | f. zoo [z̥u] | g. whizzkid [wɪz̥kɪd̥] | h. resist | [rɪzɪst] |
|---|---|---|---|---|---|
| drive | [draɪv̥] | veal [v̥ił] | dovetail [dʌv̥teł] | arrival | [əraɪvəł] |
| writhe | [raɪð̥] | they [ðe] | | | writhing [raɪðɪŋ] |

The actual voicing behaviour of /b d g ð z v/ etc. is subject to a generalisation that is, in the light of the examples given in (14), fairly obvious: these phonemically 'voiced' obstruents are realised as fully voiced only in fully voiced environments, as in (14d, h). They are at least partially devoiced in all other contexts: next to voiceless phonemes as in (14c, g), as well as before or after silence – (14 a, e) and (14 b, f) respectively.

A word of clarification is needed regarding 'silence' as a devoicing context: obstruents at the edges of words are devoiced only if these edges constitute the beginning or end of an utterance or if they are adjacent to an utterance-internal pause; the appropriate examples in (14) do *not* indicate that there is a general devoicing rule for English obstruents in word-final position. Thus, the word *rise* ends in a devoiced obstruent if it is uttered in isolation but not in an utterance such as *the rise is...* There, we would expect full voicing of the /z/ (due to its fully voiced context), similar to the full voicing found, for example, in *rising*. This point is important, not only with regard to the facts of devoicing but in more general theoretical terms: in speech, 'silence' (for example, at the end or beginning of an utterance) constitutes a phonetic event but the occurrence of a word boundary does not, given that such boundaries are not usually manifested by a pause within an utterance (or by any other identifiable phonetic phenomenon). Therefore, if a given allophonic rule applies in the context of silence, then this context is a phonological one; but if it is triggered by a word boundary instead, then this context implies a nonphonological trigger for this rule. We have so far assumed that all allophonic rules apply in strictly phonological contexts – and we see here that the devoicing rule is no exception to this assumption. But we shall see later (in sect. 8.4 and especially in ch. 9) that other rules are problematical in this respect: it will turn out that word boundaries do play a part in the formulation of phonological rules.

(15)  *Devoicing of voiced obstruents*

$$/\text{b d ð z}/ \text{ etc. } \rightarrow \begin{cases} \text{[b d ð z] etc. } / \text{ [+voice]} \underline{\quad} \text{ [+voice]} \\ \\ \text{[b̥ d̥ ð̥ z̥] etc.} \quad \text{elsewhere} \end{cases}$$

Like other allophonic rules that we have discussed, (15) poorly expresses the fact that obstruent devoicing is not a binary phenomenon. Firstly, devoicing is often incomplete: it is not usual for an obstruent that is devoiced to be phonetically nondistinct from an underlyingly voiceless obstruent. The distinction between, say, *sip* [sɪʔp] and *zip* [z̥ɪʔp] is preserved. Secondly, the degree of devoicing shows some variation between speakers and between accents. Thirdly, even within a given accent the different devoicing contexts trigger different degrees of devoicing: in any accent, final devoicing is stronger than initial devoicing. Thus, it is probably true for any speaker that in *bib* [bɪb̥] the final /b/ is more strongly devoiced than the initial one. SSE has particularly strong devoicing in final position; in this accent, there is, indeed, some evidence that suggests that devoicing is governed by syllable structure, in that it is triggered in syllable-final positions even in voiced contexts. Many SSE speakers pronounce *obvious* as [ɒb̥vɪəs] – rule (15) predicts no devoicing of the /b/ here; and there is at least one example where SSE final devoicing is complete to the extent that it gives rise to a phonemic difference between RP and SSE: *with* is /wɪð/ in RP (and most of GA) but /wɪθ/ in SSE.

### 8.3.3  *Summary: phonetic correlates of the voicing opposition*

In the preceding discussion we have seen that what is phonemically a voicing contrast – /p/–/b/, /f/–/v/ etc. – is not necessarily manifested in the same terms on the phonetic surface: while some of the underlyingly voiceless obstruents – namely, the voiceless stops – may display additional allophonic features such as aspiration or glottalisation, the voicing distinction itself may be obliterated, at least partly, by the allophonic rule of devoicing that affects the underlyingly 'voiced' obstruents in certain contexts. Voicing, then, is not a feature that can be entirely and exclusively relied upon in the determination of obstruent phonemes. The following chart summarises the obstruent allophony that has emerged in this discussion.

(16)

| | Initial | | Voiced environment | | Final | |
|---|---|---|---|---|---|---|
| /p/ | [pʰ] | pie | [p] | Epping | [ʔp] | cop |
| /b/ | [b̥] | buy | [b] | ebbing | [b̥] | cob |
| /f/ | [f] | fat | [f] | leafing | [f] | duff |
| /v/ | [v̥] | vat | [v] | leaving | [v̥] | dove |

The column headings 'Initial' and 'Final' are, of course, somewhat imprecise: aspiration occurs syllable-initially, glottalisation syllable-finally, and devoicing before and after silence. But since we are here dealing with isolated words as examples, such details do not matter. Moreover, we have seen that medial /p/ may have aspiration and glottalisation, neither of which are indicated here for *Epping*. But what the chart shows quite clearly is that voicing is a reliable clue for the recognition of 'voiced' obstruent phonemes only in voiced environments. Among stops, here exemplified by /p/–/b/, it is not voicing but the presence or absence of aspiration in the initial position, and the presence or absence of glottalisation in the final position, that maintains the contrast. As for fricatives, voicing contrasts such as the one in *fat* and *vat* are at times difficult to determine, given that voiced fricatives are subject to devoicing while their voiceless counterparts never display the secondary clues of aspiration or glottalisation. Especially in the final position (*duff – dove*), voicing constitutes unreliable evidence for /v/ (or any other 'voiced' fricative). But here we do have a secondary clue, one that has not been mentioned before: vowels are longer before voiced fricative phonemes than they are before voiceless ones. Consider the following examples:

(17)  duff – dove  leaf – leave
rice – rise  loose – lose
mouth (n.) – mouth (vb)  loath – loathe

In each pair, the voiced fricative is devoiced – for many speakers fully devoiced. What preserves the distinction is not the presence or absence of fricative voicing but the fact that *leave* has a longer vowel allophone than *leaf* has, *rise* a longer one than *rice* and so forth. This vowel allophony is governed by two different rules: one that is specific to SSE, where the length distinctions exemplified in (16) are strongest; and one that is universal. We shall discuss these in detail in section 8.4.3 below.

### 8.3.4  Glottal stops, taps and some problems

The picture of obstruent allophony presented in the preceding paragraphs – especially that of glottalisation – does not tell the whole story for all accents of English. This picture was a stylised one, in that it paid little attention to the enormous amount of accent- and speaker-specific variation found among allophonic rules: in reality, this variation is so extensive that it is hard to agree on the facts even within a given regional accent. Also, the picture was stylised in that it was excessively tidy: easily accounted for by our phonological theory, and falling into neat patterns of complementary distribution that preserve phonemic contrasts on the phonetic level. A look at some more data, again taken from the obstruent system, will serve to destroy such illusions.

The first set of data deals with the **glottal stop** [ʔ], which in many accents frequently – and contrary to the impression given above – occurs without acting as 'support' for [p t k]. The examples given below come from Cockney; but a similar distribution of [ʔ] is found in many nonstandard British accents (notably nonstandard Scottish English), and although the glottal stop is frowned upon by conservative RP speakers, it is found sporadically – at least in contexts such as (18b) – in casual speech in most varieties of English (including the standard ones).

(18)  a. pit  [pɪʔ]       b. atlas    [aʔləs]      c. pity    [pɪʔɪ]
      belt [bɛɫʔ]       lightning [laɪʔnɪŋ]    bottom [bɒʔəm]

      d. Peter   [piʔə]     e. pill [pʰɪɫ]      f. mat  [maʔ]
      mighty   [maɪʔɪ]     till [tʰɪɫ]          map  [maʔ]
      divinity [dɪvɪnɪʔɪ]   kill [kʰɪɫ]          mack [maʔ]

As long as we ignore (18f), the distribution of [ʔ] shown by these examples is straightforward. [ʔ] is an allophone of /t/ which occurs in all contexts except the onset of a stressed syllable. The problem lies in (18f): in *map* and *mack* the glottal stop is clearly not an allophone of /t/ but of /p/ and /k/ respectively. We have already seen that in this context – syllable-finally before a pause – stops may be unreleased; we now note that they may lack oral closure altogether. This means that [maʔ] may be ambiguous before silence because the voiceless-stop phoneme realised as [ʔ] is unidentifiable:

[ʔ] may here be an allophone of any voiceless stop. In other words, the /p t k/ contrast – which, of course, exists in all varieties of English; see (18e) – is suspended in (18f). For our phonological theory, in its present state of elaboration, this is clearly a major problem: wherever several phonemes have an allophone in common, in a certain context, it is impossible to establish phonemic representations, given that the phonemes that share this allophone do not contrast in that particular position. We leave this theoretical problem unresolved for the moment; but here is another instance of the same phenomenon.

In most varieties of (US) American English as well as in Ulster English, /t/ may be realised as an **alveolar tap**; that is, with merely a very brief alveolar contact of the tip of the tongue. This allophone of /t/, transcribed as [ɾ], occurs in single-consonant onsets of unstressed syllables provided its left neighbour is a vowel or sonorant consonant. It is in complementary distribution with [tʰ], which occurs in onsets of stressed syllables, and with the [ʔt] of syllable-final positions. Some examples of taps are given in (19a); (19b) shows nontap contexts.

(19)

| latter | [laɾɾ] | tip | [tʰɪʔp] |
|--------|--------|-----|---------|
| writing | [raɪɾɪŋ] | wait | [weʔt] |
| waiter | [weɾɾ] | atlas | [aʔtləs] |
| divinity | [dɪvɪnɪɾi] | attain | [ətʰen] |
| startle | [staɾɫ] | matron | [metɾ̩ən] |

What makes this apparently straightforward allophonic rule for [ɾ] problematical is the fact that /t/ once again shares this allophone with another phoneme: /d/ is realised identically in identical contexts; the underlying voicing contrast between /t/ and /d/ is absent in this context so that a similar phonemic ambiguity arises to the one observed in (18f):

(20)

| ladder | [laɾɾ] |
|--------|--------|
| riding | [raɪɾɪŋ] |
| wader | [weɾɾ] |

For many speakers *latter* and *ladder*, *writing* and *riding* etc. are homophones, demonstrating the total suspension of the /t/–/d/ contrast in this particular context; for others, the members of each such pair are distinct, despite the fact that both contain (identical) alveolar flaps. Here, the distinction is maintained in that the stressed vowel in *riding*, for example, is longer than the one in *writing*. This length difference is, of course, not phonemic in itself – English has no phonemic long–short distinctions among diphthongs; rather, it is the effect of an allophonic rule for vowel length that we came across in section 8.3.4 and that will receive more extensive treatment below: vowels are longer before voiced obstruents than before voiceless ones. Despite their identical realisation as [ɾ], then, /t/ and /d/ must for such speakers be somehow distinct underlyingly in that they exert their different influences on preceding vowels. What results is the rather tricky situation where a phonemic opposition is suspended in one segment, while in a neighbouring segment a normally allophonic feature appears to carry the phonemic contrast. As we shall see in section 8.6 below, phonemic analysis has a way of dealing with the context-specific suspension of contrast; but it is unable to handle the 'displacement of contrast' observed in cases like *writing*/*riding*.

## 8.4  Vowel length

### 8.4.1  *Recapitulation*

The second of our detailed studies of allophony in subsystems of the phonemic system of English deals with vowels, in particular with their **length**. As vowel length has already figured in our discussion of the phonemic level of representation, as well as in our study of syllable structure, we begin by briefly summarising these earlier findings.

Example (21) gives the basic vowel systems for RP, GA and SSE, repeated from section 3.2. The unstressed and pre-/r/ subsystems are omitted.

(21)  | a. *RP* | b. *GA* | c. *SSE* |
|---|---|---|
| /i/–/ɪ/ | /i/–/ɪ/ | /i/–/ɪ/ |
| /u/–/ʊ/ | /u/–/ʊ/ | /u/ |
| /e/–/ɛ/ | /e/–/ɛ/ | /e/–/ɛ/ |
| /o/–/ʌ/ | /o/–/ʌ/ | /o/–/ʌ/ |
| /ɔ/–/ɒ/ | /ɔ/ | /ɔ/ |
| /ɑ/–/a/ | /ɑ/–/a/ | /a/ |
| /aɪ/ | /aɪ/ | /aɪ/ |
| /aʊ/ | /aʊ/ | /aʊ/ |
| /ɔɪ/ | /ɔɪ/ | /ɔɪ/ |

To a greater or lesser extent, the members of each system are organised into pairs, for reasons that are both phonological (distributional) and phonetic: firstly, in each pair, the vowel on the left may occur in open and closed stressed syllables (*bee, beat*) while the one on the right can only occur in closed stressed syllables (*bit*). Secondly, the difference in phonetic quality that holds between the members of these pairs is assumed to be recurrent in that the left-hand members are *tense* and the right-hand ones *lax*. Tense vowels (as well as diphthongs) can occur in open syllables while lax vowels only occur in closed syllables. And thirdly, in two of the three reference accents (namely RP and GA) the members of each pair are also distinct in terms of a recurrent quantity difference such that the left-hand (tense) vowel is longer than the right-hand (lax) one is, provided they occur in the same segmental context. This quantity difference in RP and GA was expressed, in chapter 6, in suprasegmental terms in that lax vowels were associated with one X-position in the syllable rhyme and tense vowels with two X-positions, an analysis that not only expresses the dichotomy of 'long' and 'short' vowels and its one-to-one correlation with the tense–lax dichotomy, but also – and this was the decisive argument in favour of such a suprasegmental analysis of length (recall section 6.4) – a number of important phonotactic generalisations involving tense/long and lax/short vowels.

In the present analysis of the RP and GA vowel systems, then, the long–short distinction among vowels is not treated as the basic, phonemically relevant feature that distinguishes vowel phonemes such as /i/ and /ɪ/ from one another. While it would be quite legitimate (if not, as we saw in ch. 3, necessarily advantageous) to say that in these accents there is a phonemic long–short contrast among vowels, this long–short contrast is here treated as a *derived* one rather than a phonemic one: derived from a tense–lax contrast, which is assumed to be phonemic, by means of the following rules:

(22)   *RP/GA Vowel-Length Rule*

      a.   Associate a tense vowel with two X-positions.
      b.   Associate a lax vowel with one X-position.
      c.   Associate each element of a diphthong with an X-position.

These rules are quite different from allophonic rules, in the sense in which those have been characterised in this chapter. While they share with those the characteristic that they derive predictable information (namely, vowel length) from phonemic information (namely, tenseness), they do so in a one-to-one way, without reference to the phonological environment and therefore without producing different **allophones** of tense (or lax) vowels. Given that the information that these rules refer to is binary – the tense–lax distinction – their output too is strictly binary: vowels are either long or short. Such rules, then, are part of the battery of rules that we invoked in chapter 6 to build syllable structures in strings of segments; they are not allophonic rules.

In the varieties of English spoken in Scotland (and to some extent Northern Ireland), the relation between vowel tenseness and length is not as simple as it is in RP and GA: here, tense vowels are not automatically long (i.e. associated with two X-positions in the syllable) but only in certain contexts; in other contexts they are short (single-X) just as lax vowels invariably are. Hence the tense vowel in *breathe* is long while the one in *beat* is short like the lax vowel in *bit*. The details of this rule will be discussed below; but it is clear already that its form will be roughly this (omitting diphthongs for the moment):

(23)   a.   Associate tense vowels with two X-positions in certain contexts and with a single X-position in all other contexts.

        b.   Associate lax vowels with a single X-position.

Is this an allophonic rule? On the one hand, rule (23a) evidently produces realisational variants – allophones? – of tense vowels that are in complementary distribution; on the other hand, it has many characteristics in common with (22), the corresponding rule for RP and GA: its output is strictly binary in that it associates vowels with either one or two X-positions; and it is, like (22), a rule that is rather central among the regularities that govern the erection of syllable structures in strings of segments. In the following paragraphs, the **Scottish Vowel-Length Rule** (**SVLR**) will be discussed in detail; and some facts will come to light that will set it apart from 'proper' allophonic rules. Afterwards we shall return to RP and GA and look at some 'real' allophony of vowel length.

### 8.4.2 *The Scottish Vowel-Length Rule*

The core of this rule has already been stated: tense vowels are either long or short, depending on their context, while lax vowels are invariably short. Consider the following examples:

(24)

| | a. *Long vowel* | *Short vowel* |
|---|---|---|
| /i/ | breathe leave ease ear see | Leith leaf leash leap feel keen |
| /e/ | wave maze bear day | pace waif fake fade fail name |
| /a/ | halve vase par spa | half pass path mad cap calm |
| /u/ | smooth groove sure shoe | youth hoof use loot fool tune |
| /o/ | loathe grove pose shore go | loaf close loath coat foal foam |
| /ɔ/ | pause paw | cough loss bought cot call done |

b.   *Short vowel*

/ɪ/   give fizz pith dish fill lip fin
/ɛ/   rev Des her mess pet tell ten
/ʌ/   love does duff lush pull cup pun

Example (24a) shows the distribution of long and short realisations of the tense-vowel phonemes: they are realised as long before voiced fricatives, /r/ and word boundaries; elsewhere – that is, before voiceless fricatives, oral stops, /l/ and nasals – they are short. The lax vowel phonemes are realised as short in all contexts, including those where tense vowels would be long (*love, live, rev* etc.). As in the allophonic rules discussed earlier in this chapter, some accent- or speaker-specific variability has to be expected in this rule. Reliable measurements are hard to come by; but while all the tense vowels as well as /ɪ/ and /ʌ/ behave according to the rule for practically all speakers of Scottish Standard English, it appears that /ɛ/ is somewhat unstable in its behaviour: it shows no reliable signs of the long–short distinction specific to the context that causes this distinction among the tense vowels – but note the difficulties in finding examples with /ɛ/ before voiced fricatives, and its inability to occur before a word boundary! – and it is invariably short for some speakers and invariably long for others. We treat /ɛ/ as short, in line with the other lax vowels, noting its speaker-specific variability. Interestingly, this vowel will cause problems in other generalisations too, which will be discussed in section 8.6 below.

Of the three diphthongs of SSE, /aɪ aʊ ɔɪ/, the first one somewhat surprisingly is subject to SVLR – surprisingly because in all other varieties of English, diphthongs are systematically classed with the long (two-X) vowels, as indeed the two other SSE diphthongs are. The difference between the 'long' and 'short' realisations of SSE /aɪ/ is one of quality and quantity, the long one perhaps best transcribed as [aˑɪ] (where the half-length marker '·' merely indicates the relative length of the first element compared to the second), and the latter as [ʌɪ]. Here are some examples:

(25)   'long' [aˑɪ]                'short' [ʌɪ]

drive rise writhe shy       life rice light file fine

So far, SVLR has presented few problems for our analysis: the tense vowels constitute a rather neat natural class, which is also manifested in the phonotactic behaviour of these vowels in that they are able to occur in open syllables, unlike the lax vowels. But what is disturbing is the fact that /aɪ/ is the only diphthong that undergoes SVLR: given that it is no more 'tense' than /aʊ/ and /ɔɪ/ are, it does not form a natural class with the monophthongs that lengthen.

Another problem arises from the fact that word boundaries figure in the 'long' context for SVLR: unlike in a previous case (discussed in sect. 8.3.3), 'word boundary' here really means a morphological boundary rather than the position before a pause or at the end of an utterance. In the examples in (26) such a morphological boundary, marked as '#', occurs within a word, where it clearly does not have the phonological correlate of a pause:

(26)  a. *Long vowel*                          b. *Short vowel*

| knee#d brew#ed stay#ed | need brood staid |
| tow#ed gnaw#ed baa#d sigh#ed | toad nod bad side |
| free#ly slow#ness | Healey bonus |

Notice how the context 'before #', clearly a nonphonological context, causes the preceding tense vowel to be long in (26a). As concerns SVLR, examples such as the ones in (26a) suggest that this rule is *not* a 'proper' allophonic rule in that it makes reference to nonphonological information, unlike the allophonic rules discussed earlier in this chapter. Notice also that in terms of our phonemicist theory, *knee#d* [niːd] and *need* [nid], *brew#ed* [bruːd] and *brood* [brud] etc. clearly constitute minimal pairs, given that in this theory no phonological analysis has access to nonphonological information. It is quite clear from these observations that a strictly phonemicist theory, which maintains total autonomy of the phonology in that it does not make use of nonphonological information, can only recognise as permissible phonological rules the 'proper' allophonic rules that we discussed earlier: if SVLR is accepted as a valid rule then nonphonological information is brought into the phonology on a (potentially) large scale, forcing as a next step the conclusion that *kneed* and *need* cannot be a valid minimal pair. It is also clear, however, that SVLR does express an important generalisation about the phonology of SSE, a generalisation that goes uncaptured if we adhere to a totally autonomous phonemicist theory.

What is interesting in the case of SVLR is that it deviates from the hard-line allophonic status in other ways too: unlike all the allophonic rules that were discussed earlier, it is known to have lexical exceptions. Some speakers have long–short contrasts in cases that are in no way warranted by SVLR and can only be accounted for if they are classed as SVLR exceptions. Here are some examples:

(27)  a. *Long vowel*                    b. *Short vowel*

      Leak vain maid joke                leek vane made choke
      phial viper                              file wip#er

Such cases of contrast are sporadic and speaker-specific; but in a strictly phonemicist theory they constitute proof of a phonemic /i:/–/i/, /e:/–/e/ etc. contrast in the phonology of any speaker for whom *leak* and *leek*, *vain* and *vane* etc. are not homophonous. Once a phoneme, always a phoneme; or, a single minimal pair is enough. It should have become clear by now that in the case of SVLR, such methodological purism is unhelpful, in that it misses important generalisations about the phonology of SSE, and that our phonological theory should be revised so as to allow access to morphological information, as well as a limited amount of lexical exceptions. Such a revision of the theory will enable us to accept SVLR as a rule of the phonology of SSE.

The fact remains, however, that SVLR is a rule that is quite different from 'proper' allophonic rules: it is a generalisation of a higher order than allophonic rules are in that it takes morphological structure into account, and is therefore able to treat phenomena as rule-governed that are, in strict phonemicist terms, phonemic (such as the vowel length in *kneed* and *need*). We have come across at least two similar cases of phonological generalisations that make reference to morphological structure before, both involving processes that build suprasegmental structure. The first one concerned the regularities that govern syllabification, discussed in chapter 6: here we found that the difference in the number of syllables in *hidden aims* (three syllables) and *hid names* (two syllables) cannot be derived from the phonemic representation alone, which is identically /hidnemz/ for both, but has to take the position of the word boundary into account: /hidn#emz/ vs. /hid#nemz/. A second, perhaps even more striking example occurred in our discussion of English word stress in chapter 7, where we found that the stress difference in the 'minimal pair' *'differ – de'fer* can be derived by rule if (and only if) the rule takes the morphological boundary in *de#fer* into account; if such morphological information is not made available to phonological analysis then stress has to be treated as phonemic in English. Rules that refer to morphological information, then, are able to treat certain phenomena as rule-governed that are in strictly phonemicist terms underivable: that is, phonemic.

To determine, finally, how we express SVLR, let us briefly return to the rule that expresses vowel length in RP and GA by associating vowels with

X-positions in the syllable – (22) above. Were we justified in treating SVLR as the Scottish counterpart of this rule, as a rule of basically the same form, the only difference being that SVLR is context-sensitive while (22) is not? It would appear that we were, on several counts. The most important of those is that, having restricted rule (22) to RP and GA, we need a rule that establishes the association of vowels with X-positions for SSE; and there is no reason to suppose that rule (22) is applicable in SSE: it would be simply wrong to assume that tense vowels in SSE are associated with two X-positions in all contexts, as in RP and GA. The second reason is that, as we saw in chapter 6, it makes sense to treat at least the binary length distinction among segments as a suprasegmental matter (accounted for in terms of X-positions) – and note that vowel length in SSE is strikingly binary in that tense vowels in 'short contexts' are of the same length as lax vowels are in all contexts. And the third reason is simply that, by treating SVLR as a rule that builds suprasegmental structure, we not only account for the fact that SVLR shares many characteristics with the other rules that build such structure, but also for the fact that for various reasons SVLR cannot be a 'proper' allophonic rule. Here is our final statement of SVLR, followed by some examples:

(28)  *Scottish Vowel-Length Rule*

    a.  Associate tense vowels and /aɪ/ with two X-positions if they occur before voiced fricatives, /r/ or #, and with one X-position in all other contexts.

    b.  Associate all other vowels with one X-position.

(29)

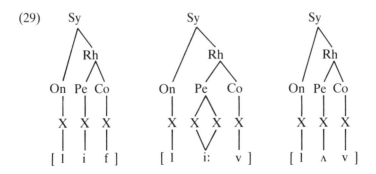

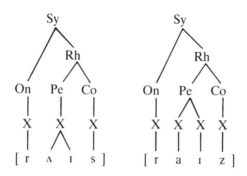

### 8.4.3 *Vowel-length allophony*

As we have seen, the motivation for recognising binary (single-X versus two-X) length distinctions among the vowels of RP and GA derives principally from phonotactic considerations as well as from the fact that on the phonetic level of representation, such length distinctions are clearly observable provided the comparison is made in identical (right-hand) contexts. Thus the RP/GA vowel in *bean* is longer than that in *bin*, the one in *bait* longer than the one in *bet*, *pool* longer than *pull* and so forth. However, every vowel phoneme displays a wide range of durational variation on the phonetic level depending on the nature of the following phoneme. The figures in the chart below give measurements of the average durations of /i/ and /ɪ/ in a typical RP speaker:

(30)

| before: | /v/ | /b/ | pause | /n/ | /f/ | /p/ |
|---|---|---|---|---|---|---|
| /i/ | 36.0 | 28.5 | 28.0 | 19.5 | 13.0 | 12.3 |
| /ɪ/ | 18.6 | 14.7 | – | 11.0 | 8.3 | 7.3 |

Durations are in centiseconds, and the contexts 'before /v/', 'before /b/' etc. are short for 'before voiced fricative', 'before voiced oral stop' etc. Thus, the /i/ in *leave*, *seize* is of an average duration in RP of 36.0 csecs. and the /ɪ/ in *lip*, *bit* of 7.3 csecs. The comparable ratios for other pairs of vowels are similar except that low vowels generally have greater absolute durations than high vowels do; and /a/ has its own durational allophony, which is here not discussed.

Two facts in this chart are worth noting: first, that the long–short contrast of /i/ and /ɪ/ is maintained in every column, that is, in identical right-hand contexts (where /ɪ/, of course, does not occur in final (i.e. pre-pause) position); and second, that the short allophones of the 'long' phoneme /i/ are shorter than the long allophones of the 'short' phoneme /ɪ/. This rather extreme durational variability of the vowel phonemes was noted in section 4.2.3 as a reason for treating the tense–lax contrast of vowels, and not the long–short contrast, as the basic one in RP and GA.

It is obvious that an attempt to formulate an allophonic rule for a gradient phenomenon like allophonic vowel length inevitably comes up against the limitations of the notation used for transcription; but albeit somewhat arbitrarily, we may divide the durational scale into 'relatively long' (transcribed as [iː], [ɪː]), 'half-long' ([iˑ], [ɪˑ]) and 'short' ([i], [ɪ]). Note that these are relative duration values and not absolute ones: 'half-long' [ɪˑ] is shorter than 'short' [i] in absolute terms, and 'long' [iː] is longer than 'half-long' [iˑ]. The allophonic rule that governs this distribution of the durational characteristics of vowels may, then, be stated as follows:

(31)   *Allophonic vowel length*

$$
/V/ \rightarrow
\begin{cases}
[Vː] \: / \underline{\quad\quad} \begin{bmatrix} -\text{sonorant} \\ +\text{voice} \end{bmatrix} \\[2ex]
[Vˑ] \: / \underline{\quad\quad} \begin{cases} [+\text{sonorant}] \\ \text{pause} \end{cases} \\[2ex]
[V] \: / \underline{\quad\quad} \begin{bmatrix} -\text{sonorant} \\ -\text{voice} \end{bmatrix}
\end{cases}
$$

Here, 'V' stands for 'any vowel', so that 'any vowel is long before voiced obstruent, half-long before sonorant or pause, and short before voiceless obstruent'.

A rule that is at least similar to (31) is found in all accents of English; indeed some dependence of vowel durations on the nature of following segments is probably phonetically universal. In SSE, such scalar duration allophony interferes to some extent with the binary outputs of SVLR (in a way that will not be discussed here).

## 8.5   Rules, phonetic representations and binary features

It was argued in chapters 4 and 5 that phonemes, the elements of the underlying level of representation, are amenable to an analysis in terms of binary distinctive features: while phonemes cannot be broken up into shorter contrastive units – the single segment is the minimal consecutive unit in the present phonological theory – they are represented on the phonemic level as bundles of binary features. In consequence, all distinctions between segments on the phonemic level are strictly binary. We saw in our discussion of the distinctive-feature system that the reason for analysing phonemes in terms of features is threefold: an adequate features system, firstly, *expresses phonemic contrasts* in an economical and comprehensive way; secondly, by being phonetically based, the feature system *provides phonetic descriptions* of segments; and thirdly, the feature system serves to *state phonological generalisations*. We dealt with the first task of the feature system in chapters 4 and 5, which were exclusively concerned with the binary expression of phonemic contrast; the second and third points require some more discussion. We shall deal with each in turn.

### 8.5.1 *The nonbinarity of phonetic representations*

One of the conclusions that have emerged in the preceding paragraphs is that *binary* features are inadequate in phonetic representations: the phonetic phenomena that are represented on this level of the phonology are very often of a gradient rather than binary nature. Segments may be nasalised, labialised, fronted and so on to a greater or lesser extent; and such details, which a descriptively adequate phonetic representation must contain, require gradient features. Similarly, vowel length, strictly binary in terms of X-positions in syllables, becomes gradient through the application of the rules of allophonic vowel length (31). This is not to say that *all* the features of the phonemic representation lose their binarity on the phonetic level: some of the 'major class features', for example [Continuant], [Consonantal] and possibly more, perform a merely classificatory function, which is maintained on the phonetic level; moreover, some such features may well be intrinsically binary by virtue of their phonetic definitions; but such exceptions, which need not be discussed in detail, do not alter the fact that phonetic representations are essentially nonbinary.

This must mean that in the derivation of the phonetic from the phonemic level of representation, features lose their binarity and become gradient: of two obstruents that are underlyingly [+ voice], the one that occurs between vowels is phonetically more voiced than the one before a pause. It also means that features that are not present in phonemic representations (because they are noncontrastive) but are added into phonetic representations are typically nonbinary. Aspiration of voiceless stops – rule (10) above – is a case in point. Phonemic representations in English do not make use of the binary feature [Aspirated] simply because this feature does not serve to express phonemic contrasts in the language. It is introduced by the allophonic rule (10) as a gradient feature: as we saw in section 8.3.1, aspiration is stronger in the onsets of stressed syllables than in other onsets.

In a phonology of this form, where underlying representations are binary and surface representations gradient, allophonic rules – rules that determine context-specific realisational variants of phonemes – are not the only rules. There are also rules that determine the typical phonetic implementations of phonemes within a given dialect or for a given speaker, and such rules may well be 'context-free', that is, not restricted to certain contexts. The need for such context-free phonetic-implementation rules is particularly evident in vowels.

As we saw in chapter 4, vowel contrasts are expressed on the phonemic level in terms of the binary features [High], [Low], [Back] and [Round]; none of these requires more than the two values '+' and '−' for the expression of the contrasts found in English. The first three of these can be visually represented as dimensions in the familiar vowel trapezium (figure 8.1), and [Round] is a feature associated with some of the [+ back] vowels in such a way that roundness increases with height. [Round], then, is clearly a gradient feature in phonetic representations; but so are the others: the precise height, lowness or backness of a vowel is not only subject to allophonic variation – for which we might formulate more allophonic rules with typically gradient outputs – but they are also accent- and speaker-specific in a way that is not conditioned by phonological context. For some speakers, the phoneme /i/, classified as [+high, −low, −back, −round], may be typically realised as an extremely high front unrounded vowel while for others it may be not quite as high; and for yet others it may be slightly diphthongised as [ɪi].

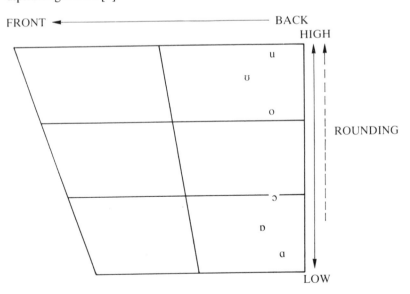

Figure 8.1   Some English monophthongs

Another example: /ɔ/ is underlyingly analysed as [− high, + low, + back, + round]. Yet even within RP, some speakers typically pronounce this phoneme as [ɔ] (close to cardinal vowel no. 5), while for speakers of 'advanced RP' – younger speakers of exclusive social groups – the typical implementation of the same phoneme is much higher, getting close to the [o] point on the trapezium where it would have to be classified as [−high, −low]. Such speakers pronounce *court*, for example, in such a way that the vowel is only slightly (if at all) lower than the one in SSE *coat*. (Note that these speakers maintain the /ɔ–/o/ contrast by typically realising /o/ as [əu]!)

These examples suffice to demonstrate the need for context-free, nonbinary phonetic-implementation rules for phonemes: together with the context-sensitive (and equally nonbinary) allophonic rules that were exemplified in the first part of this chapter, these rules derive the phonetic representation from the underlying phonemic representation.

### 8.5.2 *Rules, features and natural classes*

The form of phonological rules is by now familiar: 'A is realised as B in the context C'. The phrase 'in the context C' is present only in allophonic rules, which are context-sensitive; the phonetic-implementation rules mentioned in the preceding section are context-free and merely state 'A is realised as B'. So far we have dealt with the 'B' element of phonological rules and found that, in the present phonological theory, this element – the output of the rule – is typically nonbinary. We turn now to the 'A' element (the input) and the 'C' element (the context).

It is an obvious aim of the phonology of a language – indeed, of any scientific enquiry – to state rules as generally as possible. Consider the following rules:

(32)   a. /p/ → [pʰ] / . ____
       b. /t/ → [tʰ] / . ____
       c. /k/ → [kʰ] / . ____

What is stated in these three rules is, of course, true, and they contain the valuable generalisation that /p t k/ are aspirated *whenever* a certain condition (namely the syllable-initial position) is met. But another important generalisation is missed in this set of three statements: the three phonemes of English that are subject to aspiration are not random but, rather, constitute a clearly defined **natural class** in that all of them are voiceless stops. English has no other voiceless stops, and no other phonemes of English are subject to aspiration. A fully general statement of the aspiration rule would be that 'all and only voiceless stops are aspirated in syllable-initial position'. Given that it is one of the tasks of a system of distinctive features to express the phonological generalisations of the language, we expect a generalisation such as this one to be statable in terms of our feature system, as indeed it is:

(33)

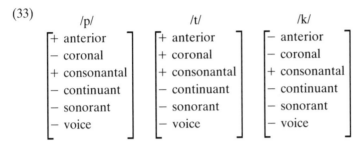

Given that /p t k/ have in common that they are 'plus' for [Consonantal] and 'minus' for [Continuant], [Sonorant] and [Voice], and that no other English phonemes share this specification, /p t k/ are a natural class in terms of our feature system; aspiration is therefore a phenomenon that our feature system can express in optimally general form. Here is the final formulation:

(34)  *Aspiration of voiceless stops*

$$\begin{bmatrix} + \text{ consonantal} \\ - \text{ continuant} \\ - \text{ sonorant} \\ - \text{ voice} \end{bmatrix} \rightarrow [+ \text{ aspirated}] \; / \; . \; \underline{\phantom{xxx}}$$

(Since [Aspirated] is, as we have seen, a gradient feature, the value '+' must here stand for 'greater than zero' rather than indicating a binary '+/−' distinction.)

Consider now a hypothetical allophonic rule – no such rule exists in English – that affects the phonemes /p t g/ (and only those). Here are the feature analyses of these phonemes:

(35)

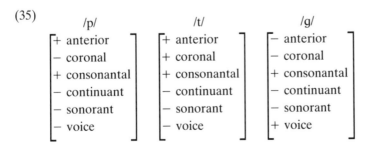

/p t g/ do not form a natural class in terms of our feature system: while they have the specifications for [Consonantal], [Continuant] and [Sonorant] in common (and only those), this specification is not exclusive to /p t g/ but also shared by /b d k/. Thus we would expect there to be rules that affect /p t k b d g/ – that is, all phonemes specified as [− continuant, −sonorant] – but none that affect /p t g/ only. Note that we came across such a rule in section 8.2.3: /p t k b d g/, the 'oral stops', are optionally unreleased in certain positions.

We might now embark on a full review of the allophonic rules stated in the earlier parts of this chapter and restate these rules in terms of features. But such an exercise would produce no surprises: all the allophonic rules stated there affect classes of phonemes that are 'natural' in terms of our feature system. Indeed, we may now add another criterion to our list of characteristics of allophonic rules: *all allophonic rules are natural* in that they affect natural classes of phonemes. However, let us conclude this discussion by returning to two rules that were discussed above: the 'dark' [ɫ] rule (3) and, once again, SVLR (28).

'Dark' [ɫ] first. After our discussion of natural classes it is rather striking that this rule, noted in section 8.2.1 to be 'a showpiece of an allophonic rule', affects only one phoneme of English: /l/. No other phonemes display similar 'clear–dark' allophony. Does that mean that rule (3) is not a natural rule? Clearly not: given that every phoneme in itself represents a natural class of phonetically similar allophones (on the phonetic level), and (in terms of features) a clearly defined natural class of one on the phonemic level, we should not be at all surprised to find allophonic rules affecting single phonemes. The statement of this rule in terms of features would have to be so specific as to exclude *all* other phonemes from the possible inputs to the rule; and this is no problem for our feature system, which, as we saw in chapters 4 and 5, is able to distinguish each phoneme of the language from all others: the statement of phonemic contrasts was the first task of the feature system that we addressed.

SVLR (28), however, presents us with a twofold problem. Firstly, the vowels that are long in the well-known contexts do not constitute a natural class: these vowels are /i e a ɔ o u/ as well as /aɪ/; and while the former set constitutes the natural class of [+ tense] vowels in SSE and conversely /ɪ ɛ ʌ/ the class of [− tense] vowels, not subject to lengthening), /aɪ/ does not fit into this class. Given that SSE has the three diphthongs /aɪ aʊ ɔɪ/, there is no feature combination in our distinctive-feature system that groups /aɪ/ with the tense vowels to the exclusion of /aʊ/, /ɔɪ/ and the lax vowels. The input of SVLR, then, is not a natural class: another respect in which SVLR violates our criteria for allophonic rules. Secondly, as for the context in which SVLR lengthens vowels, this too is not a natural class: vowels are long before voiced fricatives, /r/ and #. The last of these is not a phonological entity anyway; and /r/ is, unlike fricatives (but like /n/, /m/, /ŋ/, /l/ – all of which are not 'lengthening' contexts), specified as [+ sonorant]. It might be suggested here that SSE /r/ is in phonemic terms [– sonorant] – and there might even be some phonetic justification for this, given the 'traditional' trilled /r/ in Scots – but such a suggestion would create severe problems for SSE phonotactics (see chapter 6). It would also merely produce half a solution here: # and the voiced fricatives still would not make a natural class. We conclude, then, that SVLR is simply not a natural rule – a conclusion that in the light of other facts about this rule, which were discussed at length in section 8.4.2, comes as no surprise.

### 8.6 Suspended contrast: the archiphoneme

The relationship between the underlying phonemic and the surface phonetic level is, as we have seen, a bidirectional one. On the one hand, a phonemic representation can be established on the basis of a phonetic representation by means of commutation tests: phonetic differences between sounds are only phonemically relevant if they are contrastive, that is, if they give rise to meaning differences. Through this operation, we establish in any given string the distinction between phonologically relevant and redundant information, crystallising a phonemic representation out of a phonetic one. On the other hand, we have seen that the phonetic representation can be derived from the phonemic representation by means of phonological rules – rules that fill in the redundant phonetic details that are absent from the underlying phonemic level. This derivational aspect has been our main concern in this chapter, where we have studied the nature and scope of phonological rules; we conclude this discussion by returning to the former aspect of the relationship: the establishment of phonemes on the basis of phonetic information. It is clear that the two aspects ought to be exact mirror images of one another: in a derivation by rule, redundant phonetic details are filled in, and in a commutation test, it is exactly those phonetic details that are assumed to be supplied by rule that are abstracted away.

There are, however, certain problems; and these will make it necessary to amend our theoretical apparatus. Consider the case noted in section 8.3.4 above where, in GA and Ulster English, both /t/ and /d/ may be realised as an alveolar tap [ɾ]. Hence we get the following:

(36) writer ['raɪɾɾ] rider ['raɪɾɾ]
petal ['pɛɾł] pedal ['pɛɾł]
bottom ['bɑɾəm] madam ['maɾəm]
party ['pɑɾɾi] pardon ['pɑɾɾn]
repetitive [ɾɪ'pɛɾɪɾɪv] additive ['aɾɪɾɪv]

From the derivational point of view, this presents no problem: both /t/ and /d/ are subject to the same allophonic rule whereby they are both realised as [ɾ] in the same context, that is, between sonorants (vowels or sonorant consonants) where the following syllable is unstressed. Given that /t/ and /d/ form the natural class of coronal oral stops, the rule may be stated like this:

(37)
$$\begin{bmatrix} -\text{cont} \\ -\text{son} \\ +\text{cor} \end{bmatrix} \rightarrow [ɾ] \ / \ [+\text{son}] \ \underset{\text{On}}{\underline{\quad\perp\quad}} \ [+\text{son}] \ \text{(non-foot-initially)}$$

But notice that this rule differs from other allophonic rules affecting natural classes of phonemes in that it predicts identical realisations for all affected phonemes (and not just a single characteristic shared by all of these); in other words, the phonemic contrast between /t/ and /d/ fails to materialise in this context. This is, of course, exactly what the facts demand; but it poses a theoretical problem: it means that in this particular context the phonemic contrast between /t/ and /d/ is suspended. While the accents in question have the /t/–/d/ contrast in *tie* and *die*, and indeed in *write* and *ride*, there is no such contrast in *writer* and *rider*. A phonemic analysis of the latter pair merely yields the result that a coronal oral stop is present (contrast *rhymer, riser, riper* etc.); but it is impossible to determine whether it is the voiceless or the voiced one.

We have to recognise, then, that an unambiguous phonemic analysis is not possible in all contexts; but we also have to recognise that this is not a shortcoming of our theory but a phonologically interesting regularity in itself: recall the fact that the suspended phonemic contrast is not random but within a natural class. It is thus possible to define the entity that does occur in this specific context: a segment specified as in the input to rule (37) above – not a specific phoneme but any member of the natural class of phonemes so specified. Such segments, which are more 'abstract' than phonemes, in that they define natural (phonetically similar) classes of phonemes (just as phonemes are more abstract than allophones, in that they define classes of phonetically similar allophones), are called **archiphonemes**. They are posited in a phonemic analysis in contexts where a phonemic contrast is suspended (or 'neutralised'); and they are denoted by means of capital letters. Hence the (archi)phonemic representation of both *rider* and *writer* (in GA) is denoted as /raɪDr/, where /D/ stands for the archiphoneme realised as [ɾ]. (There is, unfortunately, no universal convention for the choice of the capital letter – /D/ or /T/ – but this does not usually lead to ambiguities as long as a consistent choice is made.)

Suspension of phonemic contrast is a rather widespread phenomenon in the phonology of English, and we shall in the remainder of this section review our phonemic analysis and identify some more cases. This will not only complete this analysis and solve some problems that have been noted before; it will also sharpen our understanding of the concept of the archiphoneme.

The second case of suspended contrast occurs in syllable-initial consonant clusters. Consider the following examples:

(38)  spit      split
      stick     spring
      skill     string
                scrap

The first point to note is that in such clusters, the voicing contrast among oral stops is suspended: /p/–/b/, /t/–/d/ and /k/–/g/ do not contrast after /s/ in syllable onsets. We are therefore unable to determine which member of the respective pairs occurs in such contexts – in terms of contrast, we have no justification for assuming the underlying representation of *spit* to be /spɪt/. We are clearly faced with another instance of an archiphoneme: all we can state is that in this context an oral stop with one of three places of articulation but without a contrasting voicing specification occurs, hence /sPɪt/, /sTɪk/, /sKɪl/. A second interesting point concerns the phonetic realisations of these archiphonemes: they are, of course, phonetically voiceless; but as we saw in section 8.3.1 above, they are also unaspirated in this context – as /b d g/ would be (*bill, dill* etc.) but unlike /p t k/ when they are not preceded by /s/ in onsets: *pill* [pʰɪɫ] etc. The realisation of the archiphoneme therefore has its voicelessness in common with one of the phonemes, and its lack of aspiration with the other phoneme of the suspended contrast. In this case, then, an archiphonemic analysis actually facilitates a generalisation about the phonetic realisation of voiceless stops (as it did, above, in our analysis of alveolar taps): an oral-stop archiphoneme is realised differently from an oral-stop phoneme:

(39)  $\left.\begin{matrix}/P/\\/T/\\/K/\end{matrix}\right\} \rightarrow \left\{\begin{matrix}[p]\\[t]\\[k]\end{matrix}\right\} / /s/ \underline{\quad}$

However, as we shall see presently, not all archiphonemes have such characteristic phonetic realisations. Here is another case: in the syllable coda, a nasal must have the same place of articulation as a following oral stop (provided the latter is not a past-tense morpheme, as in (40b) below). Examples are given in (40a):

(40)  a. lamp [mp]          b. hummed [md]
      lent  [nt]             longed  [ŋd]
      land [nd]
      bank [ŋk]

Given that no nasal other than [m] can occur before /p/, none other than /n/ before /t/ and /d/, and none other than [ŋ] before /k/, nasals simply do not contrast before oral stops in the same morpheme: no minimal pairs are available to determine the precise nature of the nasal phoneme in this context. In a phonemic analysis we have to state *camp* as /kaNp/, *lent* as /lɛNt/, *bank* as /baNk/ etc., where /N/ denotes the archiphoneme 'nasal without place specification'. This is a straightforward case of a suspended contrast; nevertheless, it differs from the cases we have discussed before. Firstly, the contrast that is suspended here is not binary but ternary: /m/–/n/–/ŋ/ (in accents where /ŋ/ is a phoneme: recall sect. 2.3.2). This is not a problem for our analysis, however, since the three phonemes whose contrast is suspended form the natural class of 'all nasals', just as the /t/–/d/ suspension observed earlier affected the natural class of 'all coronal oral stops'. The archiphoneme resulting from our analysis can therefore be uniquely characterised as 'nasal', all other features being unspecified. Secondly, this archiphoneme does not have a single invariable realisation (as the archiphonemes discussed earlier did) but three: it will be realised as [m] before /p/, as [n] before /t d/, and as [ŋ] before /k/. So, in this particular case of suspended contrast the realisations of the archiphoneme are not only variable, they are also phonetically indistinguishable from those of the phonemes /m/, /n/ and /ŋ/ respectively. Here, then, is the rule that governs the realisations of this particular archiphoneme:

(41)

$$/N/ \rightarrow \begin{cases} [n] \ / \underline{\quad} \begin{cases} /d/ \\ /t/ \end{cases} \\ [m] \ / \underline{\quad} \quad /p/ \\ [ŋ] \ / \underline{\quad} \quad /k/ \end{cases}$$

Note that this rule is remarkably similar to the assimilation rules of section 8.2.2 above: a given segment acquires its place of articulation characteristics from the following segments. The difference is, of course, that the assimilation phenomena discussed earlier are allophonic rules – gradient in nature, giving rise to different allophones of a given phoneme – while this one has an archiphoneme as its input, as well as having a nongradient (albeit ternary) output.

We have now established three crucial conditions under which an archiphonemic analysis is possible: firstly, an archiphoneme may be posited in a position where two or more phonemes fail to contrast; secondly, the phonemes that fail to contrast must constitute a natural class; and thirdly, the realisations of an archiphoneme are context-specific. The first of these conditions is obvious: in any position where phonemes do contrast, no archiphonemic analysis is necessary in the first place. The second condition follows from the fact that an archiphoneme must have a feature specification: the archiphoneme will be the 'common denominator' of the phonemes whose contrast is suspended. The third condition, finally, is relevant only where an archiphoneme has more than one realisation, as in the case of the nasals discussed above: here, the realisations are in complementary distribution (that is, context-specific) – a parallel distribution of such realisations would, for obvious reasons, run counter to the concept of the archiphoneme itself in that such a distribution would re-introduce contrast (or free variation) on the phonetic level, while on the phonemic level a suspended contrast is assumed.

Let us test these conditions on archiphonemic analysis against some more data. We return first to consonant clusters in syllable onsets – onset phonotactics is a particularly rewarding testing ground for this analysis. Earlier we dealt with the suspension of voicing contrasts of oral stops in such clusters; now we focus on the only consonant that can precede such oral stops in onsets: [s], exemplified in (37) above. All consonantal contrasts are suspended in this position; we might even say that, given that no vowels can occur in onsets anyway, all segmental contrasts are suspended here. Possibly, this is the most extreme case of contrast suspension one can imagine. In this case, then, we have an archiphoneme that, depending on how far we want to take its 'underspecification', is specified merely as [+ consonantal] or even merely as an empty X-position. Under our criteria, this is a perfectly valid archiphonemic analysis: the suspended contrasts form a natural class ('all consonants' or even 'all segments'). *Spit*, then, has the (archi)phonemic representation /CPɪt/, and the missing details are supplied by rule: /C/ is realised as [s], /P/ as [p]. Notice that it is only with an archiphonemic analysis that we can do justice to the idea that the underlying representation is totally redundancy-free: if we assumed /spɪt/ as the underlying representation (which, of course, we cannot, given the lack of contrast) then we would be tolerating redundancy in this representation in that both the initial /s/ and the following /p/ would be overspecific. Given that the second consonant can only be voiceless, there is no need to specify underlying voicelessness; and more radically, given that the first consonant can only be [s], there is no need to specify it thus underlyingly. A phonemic analysis such as ours, based entirely on contrast, clearly needs the concept of the archiphoneme. But does the concept solve all the problems of distributional restrictions that we have come across in the course of this book? We shall not re-open all these cases here but merely look at two, both relating to vowel contrasts.

Consider first the distribution of vowels in unstressed syllables. Much depends here, as we saw in section 3.5, on what we call 'unstressed'. (Are the final syllables in *motto*, *venue*, *alloy* etc. unstressed, or do they have secondary stresses?) However, even if we assume that secondary stresses occur liberally in final syllables and thereby treat the full vowel contrasts in the words just mentioned as manifestations of the stressed vowel system, there can be little doubt that in fully unstressed syllables two vowels can occur – [ɪ] and [ə] – and that they figure in minimal pairs such as *purist – purest*. There is simply no discernible stress difference between these two words (whereas there arguably is one between *Allan* ['alən] and *alloy* ['a₁lɔɪ]). These facts suggest that vowel contrasts in unstressed syllables are suspended on a large scale – but what archiphoneme(s) can we posit in this context?

We might take the purest view of the archiphoneme and say that *all* vowel contrasts are suspended in unstressed positions and that the resulting single archiphoneme is realised as [ə] or, sporadically, as [ɪ]. The fact that [ə] and [ɪ] are in free variation in many words (*duchess, hamlet, goodness* etc.) would support this view: *purest* and *purist* contrast only in careful speech after all. However, the point is that an analysis that posits a single unstressed archiphoneme cannot account for this contrast – and once a phoneme, always a phoneme!

If we take this purist view of contrast, however, then our analysis runs into trouble. It is not possible to maintain /ɪ/ as a phoneme while [ə] is given the status of the realisation of an archiphoneme that it undoubtedly deserves: 'all vowels except /ɪ/' is not a natural class because there is no feature specification that all vowels except /ɪ/ share. Hence the putative archiphoneme of which [ə] is the realisation cannot be given a unique identification. Our phonological treatment of [ɪ] and [ə] in unstressed syllables must remain unsatisfactory: we are either forced to treat [ɪ] as a free variant of the archiphoneme realisation [ə], ignoring the contrast; or we have to treat the unstressed vowel system as a case of **defective distribution**, where many vowel phonemes unaccountably fail to occur.

For a final set of data we return to vowels before /r/ in rhotic accents, first discussed in section 3.4 above. We noted there that in such contexts (especially where the /r/ shares the syllable rhyme with the vowel rather than being onset to the next syllable) many vowel contrasts fail to materialise. We shall not embark here on a comprehensive archiphonemic analysis of this part of the vowel phonology but merely pick out one of the more conspicuous sets of contrast suspensions.

The three lax vowels of SSE – /ɪ ɛ ʌ/ – pattern before /r/ as follows:

(42)  word    a. [ʌr]    b. ⎫          c. ⎫
      bird       [ɪr]      ⎬  [ʌr]        ⎬  [ɜr]
      heard      [ɛr]      ⎭              ⎭
                           [ɛr]

In the first variety of SSE, demonstrated in (42a), all three lax-vowel phonemes contrast before /r/: *word*, *bird* and *heard* have different vowels. In another variety (42c) all lax-vowel contrasts are suspended in this context: here we have an archiphoneme specified as 'lax vowel', realised invariably as [ɜ]. (The same situation occurs in GA.) What causes a problem for our analysis is the 'intermediate' stage of the step-by-step suspension demonstrated in (42), namely that given in (42b). As it happens, this distribution of lax vowels before /r/ is the one that is most common among SSE speakers. Here, [ʌ] and [ɪ] do not contrast with each other; but the [ʌ] that *word* and *bird* share in this variety does contrast with the third member of the lax-vowel set, namely [ɛ].

The problem is identical to the one we encountered in the unstressed vowel system. It is impossible to define an archiphoneme comprising /ɪ/ and /ʌ/ but excluding /ɛ/:

(43)
|  | /ɪ/ | /ʌ/ | /ɛ/ |
|---|---|---|---|
|  | − consonantal | − consonantal | − consonantal |
|  | − tense | − tense | − tense |
|  | + high | − high | − high |
|  | − low | − low | − low |
|  | − back | + back | − back |

/ɪ/ and /ʌ/ do not form a natural class within this set; therefore, our phonology fails to account for the suspension of the /ɪ/–/ʌ/ contrast. Worse still, the system does allow for the suspension of the /ʌ/–/ɛ/ contrast: these two form a natural class which excludes /ɪ/ in that both of them are nonhigh nonlow lax vowels. But there is no sign that this ever happens in SSE.

Again, there are two possible answers to this problem. Either, we may decide that the distributions shown in (42a) and (42c) are phonologically 'natural' while the one in (42b) is not (despite its popularity among SSE speakers). This would then be another case of an inexplicable defective distribution of phonemes – a highly unsatisfactory solution. Or – and this is perhaps what ought to be done – we might question the feature specifications of the vowels concerned, in particular that of /ɛ/. We have already seen that this phoneme shows signs of unreliable behaviour in another important SSE generalisation, namely SVLR (sect. 8.4.2): while for many speakers /ɛ/ fails to lengthen as do /ɪ/ and /ʌ/, it is for other speakers long in the appropriate lengthening contexts, and for yet others it is long in all contexts. Is /ɛ/, therefore, quite generally in a class of its own for certain speakers? Are the speakers for whom /ɛ/ is a long vowel the same as the ones that have the distribution (42b)? If so, how do we identify this phoneme appropriately in terms of features? We have to leave this problem unresolved. But what has become clear is that both archiphonemic analysis and the feature system on which it is here based have their problems.

### Suggested reading to chapter 8

Sections 8.1, 8.2   For a discussion of allophony, complementary vs. parallel distribution etc. Lass (1984: ch. 2).

Section 8.3   On English obstruent allophony see Gimson (1989: ch. 8), Abramson and Lisker (1970), Lisker and Abramson (1971), Higginbottom (1965), Hoard (1971), Roach (1973).

Section 8.4   On SVLR see Aitken (1981), Abercrombie (1979), McClure (1979), Agutter (1988), McMahon (1991); on allophonic vowel length House (1961), Wiik (1965) - the source of the figure in example (30), Chen (1970).

Section 8.5   On natural classes see Lass (1984: ch. 4).

Section 8.6   On neutralisation see Lass (1984: ch. 3), Trubetzkoy (1939/69), Davidsen-Nielsen (1978).

# 9

# Phrases, sentences and the phonology of connected speech

In the preceding chapter our discussion began to undergo a shift in focus which it is now time to acknowledge, as well as to take further: we have begun to deal with 'real-life' speech events by noting, for example, that the operation of allophonic rules is not in principle confined to single words but typically ignores word boundaries (or any other kinds of nonphonological information). We also noted in passing that the implementation of such rules may depend on tempo and other speech-style variables. Up until then our approach had been essentially word-based in that we used single words, enunciated with optimal clarity and at a fairly slow tempo as 'citation forms', for the establishment of (segmental) phonemic contrasts as well as for the statements of generalisations regarding syllabification and stress.

Attempting to take the realities of speech more seriously than we have done so far, we shall in this chapter widen the scope of our enquiry in two ways: by studying the phonology of linguistic units larger than words, and by acknowledging the fact that citation forms are a form of speech that is, to say the least, somewhat idealised. We shall first look at phonological structures that give rise to phrasal and compound stress patterns such as ‚black 'bird and 'black‚bird respectively; and then we shall study other aspects of the phonology of larger-than-word units, such as the rhythmic patterning found in connected speech. This will lead to further remarks on phonological structure as well as on allophony, taking into account the tempo variable whose existence was merely noted in chapter 8.

But let us first return, briefly, to the rather recalcitrant problem of morphological boundaries in phonological analysis. We have seen that the generalisations that make reference to such morphological boundaries – such as the syllabification and stress rules as well as the Scottish Vowel-Length Rule – constitute an embarrassment for any phonological theory that insists on the autonomy of phonology, thereby denying itself any access to nonphonological information. Our conclusion was that, in order to capture such important generalisations as the stress rules, SVLR etc., the methodological purism that we started off with has to be abandoned. But did not our strict reference to words in the establishment of phonemic contrast already contravene the phonological autonomy principle, in an operation that was arguably the most basic and crucial one of a phonological analysis? The answer is, on closer inspection of the problem, no. It lies in the very nature of the (segmental) phoneme that it fulfils its basic contrastive function in the smallest freely interchangeable meaning units of language, namely single (monomorphemic) words. Moreover, whatever constitutes a minimal pair of citation forms also constitutes a minimal pair within a larger linguistic unit, everything else being equal: the minimal pair *cap – cab* demonstrates the existence of the /p/–/b/ contrast in English; but so does, of course, the pair of sentences *I took a cap – I took a cab*. For segmental contrasts, the size of the linguistic unit in which they show up is simply not crucial, so long as the definition of phonemic contrast is met: 'capable of distinguishing meaning'. In the analysis of suprasegmental phenomena things are different. Consider the pair of linguistic items mentioned above: 'black ˌbird vs. ˌblack 'bird. This is a minimal pair in terms of phonemic analysis, demonstrating that stress contours give rise to a difference in meaning; but note that it crucially involves units larger than single words: what is phonemic here is the relative prominence of two complete word-stress patterns. Phonological contrast in general, then, is not confined to single words: the word as a morphological unit plays no part in phonemic analysis.

But once again it will turn out that by simply treating such stress differences as phonemic in English we miss important generalisations; and, as we did in the analysis of word stress, we shall here formulate rules that do make reference to nonphonological structure. As we shall see, this will not be the only instance where a phonology without word-boundary information runs into problems.

### 9.1 Stress beyond the single word

Wherever a linguistic unit contains more than one stressed syllable, these stresses are perceived as being of different relative prominence. We came across this contouring of stresses in our discussion of word stress in chapter 7, where we saw that polysyllabic words may contain more than one stressed syllable and that in such a case one of the stresses is the strongest ('primary') stress and the other(s) weaker ('secondary' or even 'tertiary'). Recall here examples such as ˌpolysyl'labic, ˌkanga'roo etc. A similar contouring of stresses can be observed wherever several words bearing stress are put together in a larger linguistic unit – a syntactic phrase or a compound word. Thus, both *black* and *bird* bear word stress; but in the noun phrase ˌblack 'bird the second one is more prominent than the first, while in the compound noun 'blackˌbird the first one is stronger than the second.

As regards the phonetic correlates of this stress differentiation, we saw in section 7.1 that 'stress' is in acoustic terms a complex phenomenon: a stressed syllable may have greater duration and loudness than an unstressed syllable has, as well as – in the case of primary stress – being marked in the pitch contour of the string by a change of pitch. In the citation forms of single words discussed in chapter 7, every word bore such a primary stress, marked by a pitch change. In a phrase containing several stresses (which are primary stresses if the word is uttered in isolation), only one of those will bear the phonetic characteristics of a primary stress, namely the pitch change; the others are 'demoted' to roughly the same phonetic status that secondary stresses have in words uttered as citation forms. Thus in 'blackˌbird, the pitch changes in the first (stressed) syllable while in ˌblack 'bird it does in the second.

By noting that the primary stress of a linguistic unit is marked by a pitch change, we have touched upon a different (but closely related) aspect of phonology, namely that of **intonation**. The intonation of an utterance is the pitch contour associated with it. Such pitch contours are determined by a variety of grammatical, semantic, situational and context factors and will not be studied here in any detail. However, compare the phrases *a blackbird* and *a black bird*, each uttered as a statement and as a question: 'What did you see?' (1a): 'A blackbird.' – 'A blackbird?' (1b): 'A black bird.' – 'A black bird?'

(1)

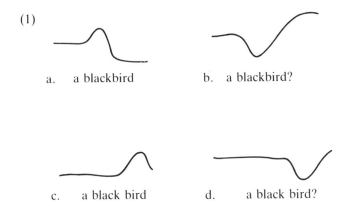

   a.   a blackbird       b.   a blackbird?

   c.   a black bird      d.   a black bird?

Notice how in each case the primary stress is marked by a pitch change, but how in the 'statement' intonation this change is in both cases, *blackbird* (1a) and *black bird* (1c), a downward one, while in the 'question' intonation (1b, d) the pitch rises radically after the primary stress.

No more will be said about intonation in this book; let us return to the stress patterns of phrases and compounds. In the following sections we shall deal with each of these in turn, using the notation of Metrical Phonology already familiar from section 7.4 above: binary branching trees whose branches are labelled *S*(trong) and *W*(eak). For the moment we assume that the stress patterns of single words remain internally unaltered when they are embedded in larger units, ignoring cases where word stresses shift their places if the word occurs in certain contexts (such as ˌcham'pagne vs. 'chamˌpagne 'breakfast*, noted in sect. 7.2 above). In our tree diagrams of higher-level structures, we may therefore omit the metrical structures of single words (except where these are specifically relevant to the discussion).

### 9.1.1 *Phrasal stress*

The basic generalisation concerning the stress contours of phrases is exemplified by ˌblack 'bird*: of two words that constitute a syntactic phrase – in this case a noun phrase – the second (phrase-final) one bears the main stress and the first one a lesser stress. Here are some more examples:

(2)  a. Noun phrases               b. Adjective phrases

good work                     very good
heavy metal                   incredibly heavy
scientific investigations     allegedly scientific

c. Verb phrases               d. Adverb phrases

drinks heavily                rather enthusiastically
knows everything              quite clearly
rested after lunch            very well

e. Sentences

Roger disapproved
cigars stink
Jennifer smokes

The normal, 'unmarked' stress pattern in each of these constructions is one of final stress. Speakers may, of course, deviate from this normal pattern for all sorts of reasons – for contrast or emphasis for example: 'heavy ˌmetal (rather than light metal), *'Roger disap.proved* (but John didn't) etc.

Let us now return to the notation of Metrical Phonology and express these stress patterns, as well as the generalisations that they give rise to, in terms of metrical trees. In the construction of such trees, two questions arise: what is the form of the tree, and what are the prominence relations among its branches? The answer to the former question is here, where we are dealing with constructions containing two constituents, trivial: each branch of the tree dominates one of the two word trees. The metrical tree is here automatically a copy of the (equally binary) syntactic structure. Below are the syntactic structures of some of the examples, analysed in terms of a tree notation in (3).

(3)

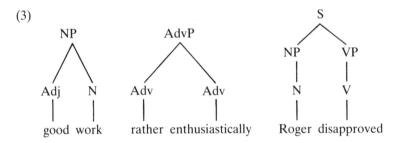

The metrical trees, expressing both structure and prominence relations, then look like this:

(4)

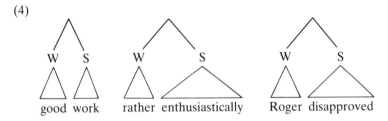

The rule that governs such prominence relations among word trees within phrases has the following form:

(5) *Phrasal Prominence Rule*

In a pair of sister nodes $[N_1 \ N_2]_p$, where P is a phrasal category, $N_2$ is strong.

In more complex constructions, the form of the metrical tree is determined by that of the syntactic tree structure (just as it was, somewhat trivially, in the examples discussed above). Here is a final demonstration:

253

(6)

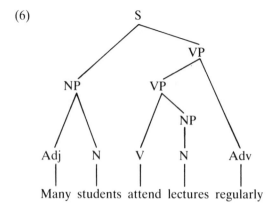

Many students attend lectures regularly

Here, *many* is an adjective modifying *students*; *attend lectures* is a verb phrase, which is modified by *regularly*, with which it forms a higher-order verb phrase. Together with the noun phrase, this verb phrase constitutes the sentence. Below is the corresponding metrical structure, the form of the tree copied from the syntax and the prominence relations assigned by rule (5):

(7)

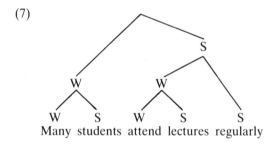

Many students attend lectures regularly

Notice how *students* is more prominent than *many* (although this pattern can easily be reversed for emphasis). In the verb phrase, *lectures* is stronger than *attend*, and *regularly* stronger than *attend lectures*. Finally, the strongest stress in the verb phrase – *regularly* – is more prominent than *students*, the strongest stress in the noun phrase, and is therefore the strongest stress of the whole construction.

### 9.1.2 Compound stress

We have already seen that the distinction between compound words – words made up of two or more single words – and syntactic phrases is marked, in English, by a difference in stress patterns: *black 'bird* is a (noun) phrase and has final stress while *'blackbird* is a compound noun, with stress on the first element. The distinction is not in each case as clear-cut as this; but let us first look at the prominence patterns of such compounds that systematically have nonphrasal stress patterns and then turn to some problem cases. Here are some examples of compounds:

(8)

a. [ ' AB ]

greenhouse
textbook
word-processor
filing cabinet

b. [[ 'AB ] C ]

blackboard eraser
greenhouse effect
word-processing equipment
house-warming party

c. [ A   [ 'BC]]

government working party
office filing cabinet
schools liaison committee
university works department

d. [[ ,AB ] [ 'CD ]]

Labour party finance committee
engine oil filler cap
arts faculty entrance test
car maintenance training course

e. [[ A [ 'BC ]] D ]

home word-processing equipment
schools liaison committee meeting
parish coffee-morning committee
university car-park inspector

The internal structures of these examples are given, for each group, in terms of brackets. Thus, *blackboard eraser* is an [[AB]C] compound in that the term denotes an eraser for blackboards. *Government working party* is [A[BC]] in that it is a working party of the government (rather than something like a party for government working: [[AB]C]). In (8d, e) the internal structures are not in all cases unambiguous: a *car maintenance training course* is most likely to be interpreted as a training course for car maintenance (hence [[AB][CD]]) but might possibly be read as a course on car maintenance training [[AB]C]D]]. Different structures of four-member compounds are possible; and of course five- and six-member compounds with different structures might be constructed.

The prominence patterns displayed in (8) appear at first sight far more complex than those of the phrasal units discussed earlier. But the fact that these patterns fall into groups, clearly determined by internal syntactic structure, suggests the possibility of a generalisation; and as we shall see presently, this generalisation is rather striking. Let us simplify matters by merely looking at (8a–c) in the first instance.

As in the case of phrases (sect. 9.1.1), the form of metrical trees for compounds is determined by the internal (syntactic) structure. One example out of each of (8a–c) is analysed in terms of metrical structure below. Note that in each case the metrical tree is a copy of the internal syntactic structure of the compound, and that the prominence relations in the metrical tree express the stress patterns indicated in (8).

(9)  a.   b.   c.

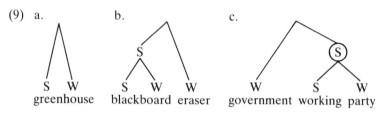

          S  W     S  W  W      W    S   W
greenhouse   blackboard eraser   government working party

This more restricted set of data reveals the generalisation. Looking again particularly at the behaviour of the right-hand node in each pair, we notice that this node is not invariably strong (as it is in phrases: rule (5) above) but only under certain conditions:

(10)  *Compound Prominence Rule*

In a pair of sister nodes $[N_1 \ N_2]_L$, where L is a lexical category, $N_2$ is strong if it branches above the word level.

Hence the circled node in (9c) is strong – this is the only example that does not have stress on the first element – while all other right-hand nodes are weak.

Surprisingly, this relatively simple rule accounts for all the examples given in (8). The remaining structures (8d, e) are analysed below: the Compound Prominence Rule makes the right predictions:

(11)

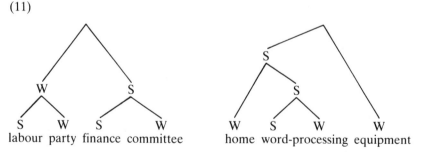

       W         S              S        
S  W  S    W     W  S  W    W
labour party finance committee   home word-processing equipment

Rule (10) ensures that compounds and phrases have distinct prominence patterns in all cases: the Phrasal Prominence Rule (5) invariably makes the phrase-final word the most prominent one, while (10) never assigns an *S* to the final word in a compound. But what makes rule (10) really remarkable is the fact that it is identical with the main rule that governs prominence patterns within morphologically simple words, namely the most general subrule of the Word Prominence Rule ((32 in ch. 7). This rule, which emerged in our discussion of metrical structures within words in chapter 7, makes the right-hand sister node strong if it branches above the *syllable* level. Both rules apply in configurations $[N_1 \ N_2]_L$, where L is a lexical category – compounds bear the lexical category labels Noun, Verb, Adjective or Adverb just as single lexical words do. The only difference between them is that they operate on different levels of the metrical structure: rule (32) of chapter 7 below the prosodic word level, and rule (10) above it. In the notational framework of Metrical Phonology, we can thus make the rather attractive (and wholly unexpected) generalisation that *all* prominence relations in a metrical tree inside a lexical category construction are governed by the same rule. Below is a fully analysed example (syllables are omitted) – witness again the uniform 'strong-if-right-branching' pattern. Note also that we analyse compound structure, like phrasal structure, on the 'phrase' level: there is no need to distinguish the two kinds of structure in terms of separate prosodic levels.

(12)

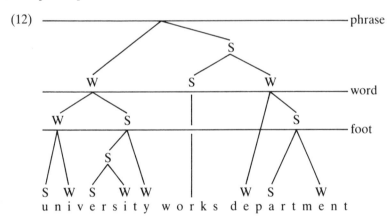

There are, however, compounds in English that do not follow the generalisation expressed in rule (10). Such compounds follow the Phrasal Prominence Rule (5) instead and behave, therefore, in phonological terms as if they were phrases. Here are a few examples:

(13)  pork pie
      school dinner
      home-made

London Road
Christmas pudding

It does not seem possible to determine on principled grounds which compounds are governed by rule (10) and which behave like phrases; and what makes the situation even more complicated is the fact that in purely syntactic terms the distinction between compound and phrase is often hard to draw. But it does seem clear that the prominence pattern alone is *not* in itself an indicator of compound or phrase status (so that every construction with final stress is a phrase and every one with nonfinal stress a compound). If that were so then ‚*London* '*Road* would be a syntactic phrase and '*London* ‚*Street* a compound, ‚*Christmas* '*pudding* a phrase and '*Christmas* ‚*cake* a compound – hardly a categorisation that could be justified on syntactic grounds! We are left with the somewhat unsatisfactory situation, then, that the prominence patterns of compound words idiosyncratically conform with either those of words or those of phrases.

### 9.2 The phonology of rhythm

#### 9.2.1 *Stress-timing in English*

All speech, if it is delivered fluently and without interruption or hesitation, is said to have rhythm: certain identifiable phonetic events recur at roughly **isochronous** intervals (intervals that are roughly equal in time). There are, of course, recurrent 'phonetic events' on various levels of structure, and of various sizes, that might be utilised for such rhythmic organisation. Conceivably, speech might be segment-timed so that segments are isochronous; or it might be **syllable-timed** so that syllables recur at isochronous intervals; or it might be **stress-timed**, the intervals between stressed syllables being isochronous.

As for the first possibility of rhythmic organisation, it is unlikely that the segments of any language might be found to be isochronous. As we have seen, segment durations vary considerably; and in any case such durations would probably be too small, the rate of recurrence too quick, to be perceivable as rhythmic: the psychology of time perception is such that rhythmicity can only be perceived within certain limits; and speech rhythm is a perceptual phenomenon at least as much as it is a feature of speech production. However, the other two possibilities of rhythmic organisation are indeed found in speech, in different languages: it has been claimed that languages are either syllable-timed or stress-timed, where French and

Italian, for example, are said to belong in the former group and English, German and Russian in the latter. Consider again the following utterance:

(14)   'This is the 'house that 'Jack 'built

English being a stress-timed language, the rhythm of this utterance will be such that its four **feet** (the interval stretching from the onset of one stressed syllable to the onset of the next stressed syllable) are isochronous – regardless of the number of syllables that each foot contains. Note that the number of syllables per foot here ranges from three (*'This is the*) to one (*'built*). It is perhaps worth noting that the 'staccato' rhythm of English spoken with a strong French accent is clearly the result of syllable- rather than foot-isochrony (given that French is a syllable-timed language).

But such a strictly dichotomous classification of the languages of the world is misleading in two respects. Firstly, there are languages that show signs of both syllable-timing and stress-timing: in Spanish, for example, both syllables and stresses recur at intervals that appear to be rhythmically structured. The distinction between syllable-timed and stress-timed languages, then, is not dichotomous but scalar. This is not a problem for the present discussion, however, since English is reputedly as stress-timed as any language. Secondly, in the long history of experimental measurements of foot durations in English, it has not been unequivocally shown that foot isochrony 'exists' on the production side of speech: rather, the question remains highly controversial.

But again, at least the following two points make stress-timing, despite the lack of hard evidence in speech production, a phonologically useful concept. Firstly, the observed deviations from strict foot isochrony (which are not entirely random but closely related – as one might expect – to the number of syllables per foot) seem to show that English is at least more stress-timed than it is syllable-timed. Consider again the example given in (14). Uttered with strict stress-timing, all feet would have equal durations. In strict syllable-timing on the other hand, a bisyllabic foot (*'house that*) would have twice, and a trisyllabic one (*'this is the*) three times the duration of a monosyllabic one (*'Jack*). Interestingly, in English this durational relation is not 1:2:3 but more like 3:4:5. If stress-timing vs. syllable-timing is viewed as a scale, then English is clearly closer to the stress-timed end of this scale than to the syllable-timed end. Secondly, such deviations from the isochronous ideal as occur in English are, due to a psychological tendency to regularise perceived recurrent events, to a large extent ironed out in speech perception, so that stress-timing is probably more valid as a perception phenomenon than it is, in precise physical terms, in speech production.

We shall assume, then, that English is a stress-timed language (bearing in mind the problems of verification that such an assumption raises). This gives the foot the status of being the principal unit of timing in English phonetics. But we shall see below that the foot is not only a phonetic unit, significant in speech production and/or perception, but also a unit of **phonological structure**. This has already been tacitly assumed in chapter 7, where the foot was said to be the next-higher unit of phonological structure above the syllable: segments are grouped into syllables, and those in turn into feet. Below we shall substantiate this claim regarding the significance of the foot in the phonology of English: we shall see that, similar to the syllable, the foot is the domain of a variety of phonological generalisations.

### 9.2.2 *Metrical structure and the foot*

#### 9.2.2.1 *A problem: how exhaustive are feet?*

We are now in a position where we can move further towards the completion of our picture of the metrical structure of entire sentences. The building blocks of this picture have emerged in various places before: in chapter 7 we dealt with the metrical structure of single lexical words (nouns, verbs, adjectives and adverbs), where the syllable level, the foot level and the word level of such structures were established, each having maximally binary branching and *S/W* labelling of sister nodes to express prominence relations. Here are some examples:

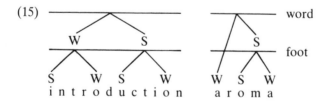

In section 9.1, then, we established the phrase level of metrical structure, on which prominence relations above single words – that is, the stress patterns of syntactic phrases and compound words – are expressed. Another example:

(16)

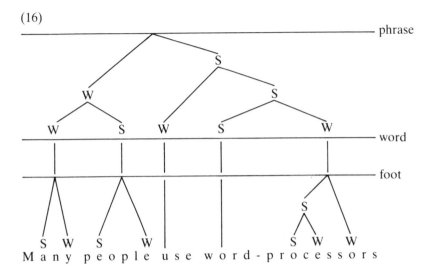

(Here, *word-processors* is a compound noun, *use word-processors* a (verb) phrase, *many people* a (noun) phrase; and the whole construction is, of course, an example of the largest phrasal unit, namely the sentence.)

What remains to be systematically discussed is the foot level: it has become clear by now that our metrical analysis should be such that the syllables of a linguistic unit of any size (word, phrase or sentence) should be exhaustively organised into feet – that is, into phonological units of the form (17):

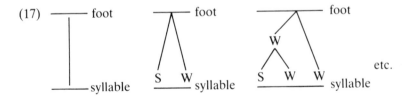

The example given in (16) above presents no problem in this respect: there, all syllables are indeed grouped into feet of the form given in (17). But this is coincidence (or perhaps the result of a careful choice of example). Consider the metrical structure of the sentence *Lots of employers insist on word-processing experience*. Example (18) gives the metrical structures for this sentence up to the word level:

(18)

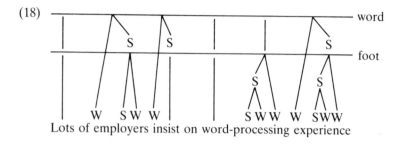

Lots of employers insist on word-processing experience

The problem is immediately apparent. The syllables of this sentence are not exhaustively grouped into feet; and this failure of our analysis to produce appropriate structures on that level is due to two separate features of this analysis. Firstly, unstressed word-initial syllables are not represented on the foot level (if they were then they would have some stress) but are daughters of a word-level node. This has already been noted in section 7.4.1, where we identified such violations of the 'strict layer assumption' as a formal problem of our metrical analysis; now that we pay attention to the foot as a phonetic unit, the problem re-appears with new urgency. And secondly, (18) contains two words – *of* and *on* – that have no metrical structure at all: being unstressed function words (prepositions), these are not subject to the rules devised in chapter 7 and therefore have no word trees (and of course, rightly, no stress). This means that these words are not so far represented on the foot level, and it also means that we cannot erect any phrase-level structure for (18) as long as we have no systematic way of dealing with such words. There are two possible solutions to this problem.

### 9.2.2.2 *Solution 1: syntax overrides phonology*

The first solution runs along the lines pursued in section 9.1.1: we might simply make such function words part of the phrase-level structure as syllables that are represented neither on the foot level nor on the word level. Copying the syntactic structure as we have done elsewhere, we adjoin these syllables to the phrase-level units following them. The Phrasal Prominence Rule (5) will ensure that they are labelled 'W'. A metrical structure of the sentence is given in (19), where structure above the word level is supplied by the syntax and labelled according to the Phrasal Prominence Rule (5):

(19)

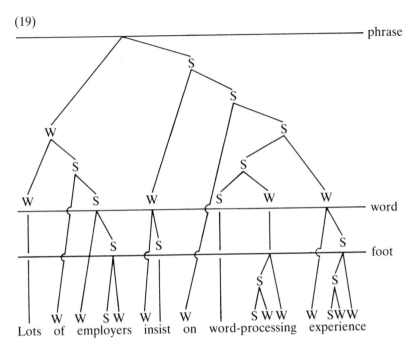

Lots of employers insist on word-processing experience

There is nothing wrong with the tree given in (19) in terms of the prominence relations that it expresses: the real-life stress contour of the sentence follows the predictions made by this metrical analysis. What is problematical about it is its persistent failure to identify feet as phonological units: not only are unstressed word-initial syllables still not part of feet, as we have defined them in (17); we now have even more such 'unfooted' material in our tree (namely, the function words). To adopt such an analysis is to abandon the idea that the foot constitutes a clearly identifiable unit, or level, in metrical structures.

We might, of course, revise our definition of the foot in metrical structure. We could say that any single unlabelled syllable as well as any (linear) sequence of syllables beginning with an unlabelled or strong syllable and ending just before the next unlabelled or strong syllable is a foot. Under such a definition, the foot is not a structural unit (of the form (17)) but simply a sequence of elements (syllables) that may be part of all kinds of different structural configurations. In (19), for example, we would then have the following feet – all differing from one another in structural terms:

(20)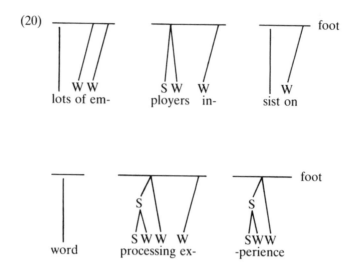

Note that this proliferation of foot structures is brought about by a rather comprehensive copying of syntactic structure in the metrical tree: this metrical tree is an exact replica of the syntactic structure of the sentence.

And there, it seems, lies the problem. Arguably, what we have in (19) is not really a phonological structure – a hierarchy of strictly phonological units – but rather a syntactic structure which happens also to express the stress contour of the sentence. On the one hand, it may well be the case that the different (syntactically inspired) configurations in (20) are overspecific in phonological terms: if they were fully warranted as *phonological* structures then we would expect to associate different phonetic behaviour with each one. On the other hand, a structure like (19) is in phonological terms rather unsatisfactory in that it gives no unique characterisation of the foot: while the facts of English word stress require us to have a 'foot level' in the word tree (recall here *happy* vs. *rabbi*, discussed in sect. 7.4 above), this level is a hindrance rather than a help when it comes to the analysis of larger-than-word units. Let us try an alternative analysis.

### 9.2.2.3 *Solution 2: phonology overrides syntax*

What we want our metrical tree to express is this: syllables are exhaustively grouped into feet in such a way that every unstressed syllable is grouped with the stressed syllable that precedes it. Feet should be units of recurrent form: being phonological units, they should be represented by nodes on the foot level (given that we need this level for the analysis of word stress). These feet should then be subject to higher-level contouring,

governed by the Phrase Prominence Rule (5) and the Compound Prominence Rule (10). Here is a structure that meets these requirements:

(21)

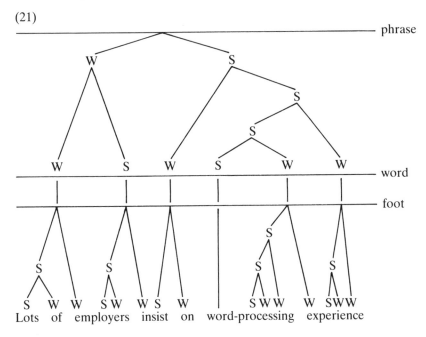

Lots of employers insist on word-processing experience

Structures (19) and (21) are radically different from each other: the former
is, as we have seen, heavily motivated by the syntactic structure of the
sentence, while the latter is, at least in certain parts, decidedly unsyntactic.
The function words in the sentence belong in syntactic terms with the words
that follow them – *of employers, on … experience* are syntactic phrases – but
in phonological terms they form feet with the syllables that precede them,
that is, with members of neighbouring syntactic phrases. And perhaps even
more strikingly, this analysis undoes part of the analysis of word stress
proposed in chapter 7: we have now removed unstressed word-initial
syllables from the word trees that we associated them with (although with
some misgivings) in chapter 7. Such a modification of our analysis should
not be left undiscussed.

In section 7.4 we expressed the stress difference between, say, *͵bam'boo*
and *͵Pe'ru* like this:

(22)

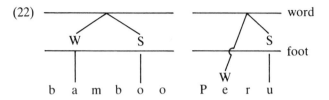

Given that the first syllable in *Peru*, unlike the one in *bamboo*, cannot be represented on the foot level since it is not stressed, and given the tacit assumption that all the syllables of a word are organised into a single tree structure, we had no choice but to analyse *Peru* in such a way that the first syllable is the sister node of a foot, thus violating the strict hierarchy of levels. With the benefit of hindsight we have to admit now that this tacit assumption about the nature of word trees is rather poorly motivated. While it is clear that in morpho-syntactic terms *Pe-* belongs with *-ru*, it is also clear now that in connected speech this syllable forms part of the preceding foot. And since there is no point in simply duplicating in the phonological structure any information that is expressed elsewhere (for example, in the syntactic structure), we may as well *not* insist that the word, as a morpho-syntactic entity, should also necessarily be an entity in the phonological structure. Under this revised analysis, the word trees for *bamboo* and *Peru* will be as follows:

(23)

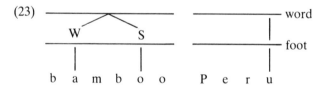

Note that the word level now loses one of its two previous characteristics. While it continues to express the prominence relations among the feet of a word, it no longer identifies the boundaries between words: it is no longer necessarily the case that all the syllables of a word form part of the same word tree. This modification requires only a minor adjustment to be made to the rules for the erection of word trees that we devised in chapter 7: rule (30) of chapter 7, which builds word structure, no longer 'connects all *material* in a single structure on the word level', but merely all *feet*; unfooted initial syllables are, then, not incorporated into the word structure but remain unconnected.

But what about the other generalisations that are behind tree structures such as (21)? Below is an analysis of the sentence giving the word and foot trees (of the revised form) only – how do we get from there to the complete structure of (21) above?

(24)

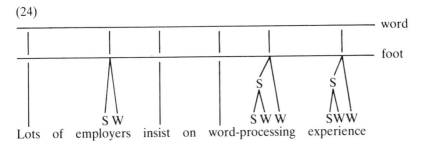

Lots of employers insist on word-processing experience

A single new rule is required to get from (24) to (21), for all we need to do is incorporate unstressed function words and unstressed initial syllables into preceding feet:

   (25)   *Foot formation*

       Adjoin any stray syllable to the foot preceding it.

Below is the complete structure again (= (21)); notice first that the stray syllables are now adjoined (thanks to (25)) so as to form feet.

(26)

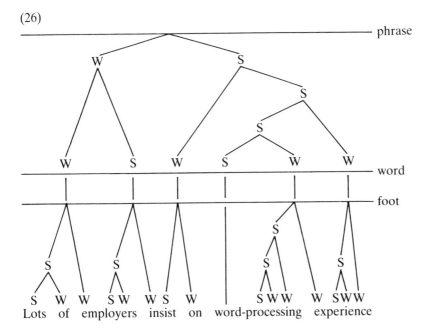

As for the higher-level structure, the existing rules remain in place. The only thing that has changed is the content of the word level. A word-level unit will now always begin with the stressed syllable of a foot – simply because any unstressed material preceding this foot must belong to the preceding foot, and therefore to the preceding word-level unit; for example, in (26) we have a pair of feet covering *lots of em-* and *-ployers in-*. Each of these forms a different word-level unit. On the phrase level, these are connected up into a tree and labelled *W–S*.

We have two possible metrical analyses of sentences, then. The first one expresses a great deal of syntactic information in the metrical tree – quite possibly, too much – at the expense of information about foot structure; and the second one gives us the desired phonological units on the foot level, but at the price of the total absence of syntactic information on the foot level. Our discussion has had an evident bias in favour of the second analysis. But to decide which of the two analyses is the better one, we must assess the evidence for the feet produced in the second analysis (for if there *is* sufficient evidence for such units then we want our analysis to express them); and we must (once again!) address the question of what – if any – syntactic information our phonological analysis requires access to, and how this information can be made accessible.

### 9.2.2.4  *The evidence: the need for syntactic information*

Feet first. There is evidence of various kinds which suggests that the foot is a phonological unit in English comparable in status to the syllable. One kind of evidence was discussed in section 9.2.1: the foot is the principal timing unit in connected speech. To account for the timing behaviour of English, our phonological theory must express the relevant units. A second kind of evidence for the foot is provided by generalisations in the segmental phonology: some such generalisations – for example, a number of allophonic rules – make reference to the segment's position in the foot (just as others make reference to syllable structure). Here is a third kind of evidence: the phenomenon of **enclisis** in English.

The term refers to the phonological attachment of an unstressed syllable – an unstressed function word, for example – to the preceding stressed syllable where in syntactic terms it may well be more closely associated with the next word. The unstressed syllable is then called an **enclitic** (and the word that it attaches to, the **host**). Such enclisis frequently results in the formation of recurrent units where the host and the enclitic are contracted into a single bisyllabic (and sometimes even monosyllabic) unit, which looks and behaves like a single word despite the fact that the enclitic belongs to a different syntactic constituent from the host. This is a case, then, where phonological grouping overrides syntactic grouping; and what makes the phenomenon relevant to our present discussion is the fact that the phonological unit resulting from enclisis is a foot. Here are some examples.

(27)  a.   does not        ⇒   doesn't
          is not          ⇒   isn't
          has not         ⇒   hasn't
          will not        ⇒   won't

      b.   fish and chips       ⇒   fish 'n' chips
          bread and butter ⇒   bread 'n' butter

      c.   cup of (tea)    ⇒   cuppa (...)
          pint of (milk)  ⇒   pinta (...)

      d.   Fred will do it  ⇒   Fred'll ...
          John has done it ⇒   John's ...

      e.   want to (go)    ⇒   wanna ...
          have to (go)    ⇒   hafta ...

Two things may be noted about cases of enclisis such as the ones given in (27). Firstly, the product of enclisis is clearly a single phonological unit: it has the recurrent stress pattern that identifies it as a foot. This is confirmed by the fact that such products meet the phonotactic conditions for being single (one-foot) words – compare *bread'n* and *leaden*, *cuppa* and (nonrhotic) *copper*, *Fred'll* and *peddle*. Secondly, such enclitic units arise even where the underlying syntactic structure is such that host and enclitic belong to different major syntactic constituents. Here is, for example, the syntactic structure of *cup of tea*:

(28)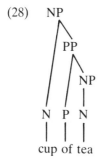

These observations suggest three things in turn: firstly, the domain in which enclisis happens is the foot; secondly, the foot is a phonological unit that overrides (and, at least in the present cases, totally ignores) syntactic structure; and thirdly, the representation of this phonological unit should be the same where it goes across syntactic boundaries as it is within words. The form of the foot *cup of* and *cuppa* should not be different from that of *copper*:

(29)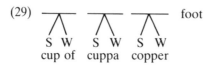

foot

We conclude from these observations that the second version of our metrical analysis of sentences – the one resulting in structures like the one in (26) – is the one that is to be favoured. But there is a problem: the question, namely, whether the relevance of syntactic information to the phonology of connected speech is really as limited as structures such as (26) suggest. Consider the following example:

(30)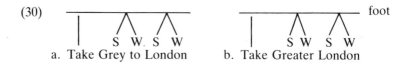

foot

Not only do these two strings have identical foot structures; they also have – in nonrhotic accents – the same phonemic representations. None the less, they are not completely homophonous. The difference lies in the different relative durations of the two syllables in the second foot: in *Grey to*, the first syllable is noticeably longer than the second (with a timing ratio of perhaps 2:1) while *Greater* shows no such clear durational difference between the two syllables, the ratio being more like 1:1.

The basic ingredients of this problem are by now familiar. In a phonology that does not have access to syntactic information, the pair of strings given in (30) constitutes a minimal pair, which would force us to the absurd conclusion that vowel durations in English are phonemic in an extremely complex way. Invoking syntactic information changes the picture: then we can account for the different durational behaviour of the two phrases by formulating rules that make reference to the syntactic difference between them. But what is the precise nature of the syntactic information that such rules refer to? Here are some more pairs of examples which display similar duration differences:

(31)  a.  Make way for biscuits    c.  Make wafer biscuits
          The way to cut it            The waiter cut it
          Show for Ari                chauffeur Ari
    b.  Show Ferrari                chauffeur Ari
          Gnaw Tinelli's pizzas       Naughty Nellie's pizzas

Each example in (31a, b) has a counterpart in (31c) that is – at least in RP – phonemically identical, the latter closely resembling the structure of *Take Greater London*. Examples (31a, b) contain enclitics – but note that the enclitics in (31a) are function words, while those in (31b) are unstressed initial syllables of following polysyllabic words. However, this difference in the precise nature of the enclitic is irrelevant where durational behaviour is concerned: while there is no timing difference between *Show for Ari* (31a) and *Show Ferrari* (31b), they are both distinct from *Chauffeur Ari* (31c). Here are simplified syntactic structures for all three:

(32)

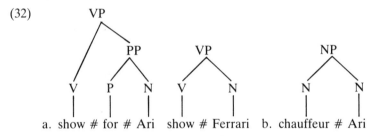

       a. show # for # Ari    show # Ferrari    b. chauffeur # Ari

It is clear that a lot of syntactic structure is simply irrelevant to our discussion; in fact, the only syntactic information that has any bearing on vowel durations is the presence of a word boundary (#) within the foot (*show # for* as well as *show # Fer-*), and the absence of such a boundary in *chauffeur*. Metrical structures, then, have to be amended by word-boundary information but as far as has emerged here by no other syntactic information. In other words, structures such as the following give us all the information we need to predict the performance details of the phrases in question:

(33)  a.                b.                c.

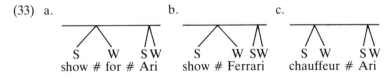

We conclude our evaluation of two alternative models of metrical structure, then, by coming down in favour of the second one. The first one that we discussed provides an excess of syntactic information, while being insufficiently explicit about phonological structure; the second one meets our requirements regarding phonological structure, but it has to be amended with word-boundary information – and word boundaries, as we have seen before, play an important part in a variety of phonological generalisations.

But let us return, once again, to the problem of relative vowel durations within feet: what is the rule that accounts for the duration difference between *show* and *chau-*, and the attendant difference between *for/Fer-* and *-feur?* Recall that in chapter 8 we discussed a rule that governs allophonic vowel length in stressed vowels: rule (31). Our discussion of this rule was inconclusive at the time as regards the precise environment in which it operates: is one of those environments the word boundary – an instance of nonphonological information being relevant to the operation of a phonological rule – or are vowels long simply 'before a pause'? Given that rule (31) of chapter 8 is obviously responsible for the duration differences in the stressed vowels discussed here, we now have an answer to the question of what its environment is: vowels are relatively long before (morphosyntactic) word boundaries.

A final point on this issue. While rule (31) in chapter 8 accounts for the length of the stressed vowel before '#', it does not explain the corresponding shortness of the enclitic. But this is easily explained with reference to the phonetic nature of the foot. If, as forms part of our phonetic definition of this unit, the foot is characterised by its constant timing behaviour, then the lengthening of one syllable within it will automatically result in the compensatory shortening of the rest.

### 9.2.3 *Eurhythmy: the rhythmic adjustment of stress patterns*
The picture has emerged in the preceding discussion that in the production of an utterance, the phonological structures of lexical words are simply put together into a higher-order phonological unit whose form is derived from (although far from identical with) the syntactic structure of the sentence, and that the rhythm of the utterance – the timing and phrasing of connected spech – will then take care of itself regardless of the particular form of the phonological structure. This picture is largely accurate: the speaker's facility to produce (and the listener's facility to perceive) rhythmic patterning in speech is sufficiently flexible to allow the processing of most words, in most sentences, without problems.

But to take this general view is to overlook the fact that in terms of the succession of strong and weak units, there is such a thing as 'perfect rhythm' (or **eurhythmy**): the arrangement of weak and strong units found in some sentences lends itself more readily to rhythmic performance than that found in others. English tends to favour the regular alternation of weak and strong – not only within the foot, where one or two unstressed syllables following a stressed one seem to be the favoured measure – but also above the foot: the alternation of stronger and weaker stresses seems to be favoured over gradually rising or gradually falling stress contours. Poetic metre – of the type found in English, regulating the succession of stressed and unstressed syllables – owes its existence to this 'principle of eurhythmy'; unsurprisingly, the following nursery rhyme (a genre that is perhaps the last survivor of a tradition of oral poetry in the language) illustrates eurhythmy perfectly:

(34)  ˌGeorgie 'Porgie, ˌpudding and 'pie
ˌKissed the 'girls and ˌmade them 'cry.
ˌWhen the 'boys came ˌout to 'play
ˌGeorgie 'Porgie ˌran a'way.

Notice that this passage is eurhythmic on two levels of phonological structure: on the foot level, the number of unstressed syllables per foot is restricted to a maximum of two (and the favoured measure is one). Within this range of variability in the number of unstressed syllables per foot, isochrony is maintained perfectly. Above the foot level, the passage is eurhythmic in that weaker and stronger stresses alternate in each line – in this case, the alternation is brought about by the fact that each line consists of two syntactic phrases (each with a weak–strong prominence pattern). We shall see below that these two levels of eurhythmy are not confined to verse.

Naturally, not all sentences of English conform with this eurhythmic ideal. As was noted above, a speaker is able to process sentences that are less than eurhythmic; but he or she may also take some remedial action. Two strategies are available: the speaker may either move words around in the sentence and produce a more eurhythmic paraphrase of the sentence: or the speaker may keep the sentence as it stands and improve its rhythmic pattern by creating, dropping or moving stresses.

One kind of evidence for eurhythmic constraints in sentence construction comes from co-ordinated constructions ('A *and* B'). This is one of the rare cases in English where the speaker has some scope for changing the word order in a sentence without changing its meaning: 'B *and* A' is usually synonymous with 'A *and* B'. And in such cases, speakers favour the construction that has rhythmic alternation over the alternative one that is less eurhythmic. Consider the following:

(35)    bleak and lonely countryside       sweet and sour
         slim and slender chances           hot and spicy
         hot and bothered                crisp and crunchy
         neat and tidy                    fruit and fibre
         hale and hearty                rum and raisin

The 'A' elements in these examples have no obvious semantic precedence over the 'B' elements. The reason for the preference of *bleak and lonely* over *lonely and bleak*, of *crisp and crunchy* over *crunchy and crisp* etc. is purely rhythmic: one has rhythmic alternation and the other does not.

The other kind of remedial strategy to achieve eurhythmy is, from a phonologist's point of view, more interesting: speakers may change the phonological structure of a sentence by creating or dropping feet, or by changing the prominence relations among feet around in order to achieve the rhythmic alternation of stronger and weaker stresses. The scope of this strategy is quite limited: the rules that may be applied to alter metrical structures are tightly constrained. We shall first deal with two possibilities of creating feet and then with the reversal of stress patterns.

### 9.2.3.1  *Creating stresses*

Consider the sentence *Jennifer must have been in the refectory*. The only lexical words in this sentence are *Jennifer* and *refectory*; the words in between are function words, to which no metrical structures are assigned – they are, in the present model, adjoined to the preceding foot:

(36)

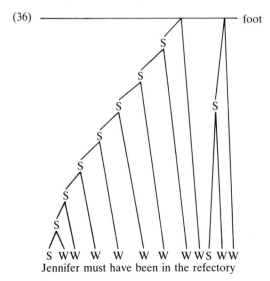

S WW  W   W   W  W   W WS WW
Jennifer must have been in the refectory

It is quite clear that a foot such as the first one, containing no fewer than eight unstressed syllables, constitutes a serious disruption of stress timing in any utterance – contrast the eurythmic pattern of zero to two unstressed syllables per foot found in the passage (34). Speakers are more likely to adopt one of the following scansions:

(37)  a.  'Jennifer ‚must have been in the re'fectory
      b.  'Jennifer must have ‚been in the re'fectory
      c.  'Jennifer ‚must have ‚been in the re'fectory

Note that none of these three versions of the sentence places any particular emphasis on any of the words that have now received additional beats in performance – to give such emphasis, the speaker would have to stress one of them more strongly than the others. Here is the metrical structure of (37c), omitting prosodic levels:

(38)

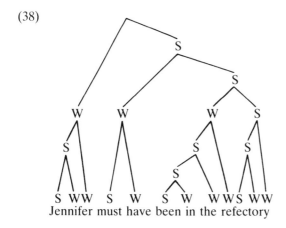

Jennifer must have been in the refectory

Given that the newly assigned feet are part of the verb phrase, the structure above the word level is determined by the Phrasal Prominence Rule (5).

We leave aside the question of what function words are capable of receiving such rhythmically motivated stresses. Clearly, a scansion such as *must ‚have been in ‚the re'fectory* is unlikely; and the reason for this must be that some function words are more amenable to such rhythmic stressing than others. Consider instead the following:

(39)  a.  'Jennifer must ‚be in the re'fectory
      b.  'Jennifer ‚must be in the re'fectory
      c.  *'Jennifer ‚must ‚be in the re'fectory
      d.  'John must ‚be in the re'fectory
      e.  *'John ‚must be in the re'fectory

Note that the starred sentences (39c, e) are only acceptable if they carry some emphasis on the stressed function words; the others have once again no particular emphasis on any of the stressed syllables. This observation reveals a rather interesting principle that governs such rhythmic stressing of function words: to receive such a stress in an utterance, a function word must be surrounded by unstressed syllables on both sides – hence *ˌmust ˌbe cannot both receive a nonemphatic stress while ˌmust have ˌbeen (37c) can; and similarly *'John ˌmust be is possible only under emphasis while 'Jennifer ˌmust be is again unmarked for emphasis. The more general principle behind this is, of course, that of eurhythmy: English favours the regular alternation of stressed and unstressed syllables; and function words can receive stress, in the contexts just discussed, for just that effect.

Another device of creating rhythmic beats in an utterance is that of inserting **silent stresses** – beats that are not filled by syllables but by brief pauses. Consider again the statement of Jennifer's whereabouts, this time uttered like this: 'Jennifer' ˄ must have ˌbeen in the re'fectory. Or perhaps like this: 'Jennifer must have ˌbeen ˄ in the re'fectory (where in each case the '˄' indicates a silent stress). The rhythmic difference between these and the various possibilities listed in (37) above becomes apparent when rhythmic beats are accompanied by taps of the hand during the utterance: in the varieties of the utterance given in (37), such taps coincide with syllables; here they fall between syllables, marking silent stresses. The foot structure of the former utterance including the representation of the silent stress might look like this:

(40)

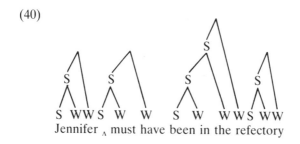

Jennifer ˄ must have been in the refectory

Unlike the distribution of (hesitation) pauses in speech, that of silent stresses in a sentence is not random. The former, like the insertion of hesitation sounds (*er…*), can occur practically anywhere in an utterance and tend to disrupt the rhythmic flow of speech rather than support it; silent stresses, on the other hand, seem to occur principally at major syntactic boundaries – indeed, it is one of the functions of silent stresses to mark such boundaries in speech, and thereby possibly to resolve ambiguities. Consider the phrase *old men and women*: this phrase is ambiguous in that it may either mean 'old men, and women of unspecified age', or 'men and women, all of whom are old'. In speech the ambiguity may be resolved by silent stresses: 'old 'men$_\Lambda$ and 'women has the former meaning and 'old$_\Lambda$ 'men and 'women the latter.


### 9.2.3.2 Reversing stresses

In our brief discussion of the nursery rhyme (34) we noted eurhythmic patterning on two levels: the number of unstressed syllables per foot was restricted to maximally two (and within this range of variability the most common foot was one containing one unstressed syllable); and on a higher level, stronger and weaker stresses (feet) also alternated. We saw in section 9.2.3.1 that in speech, foot size is similarly (if, of course, less tightly) constrained: long stretches of unstressed syllables in a sentence tend to be broken up by supporting stresses on normally unstressed function words, or by silent stresses. Both strategies produce eurhythmic feet; in addition, the latter also serve to mark syntactic structure in speech. We turn now to a strategy that produces alternation among feet.

Consider the stress patterns demonstrated in (41):

(41)  a.  ˌthirˈteen          b.  ˈthirˌteen ˈmen
          ˌHeathˈrow              ˈHeathˌrow ˈAirport
          ˌDunˈdee                ˈDundˌee ˈmarmalade
          ˌchamˈpagne             ˈchamˌpagne ˈbreakfast
          ˌPiccaˈdilly            ˈPiccaˌdilly ˈCircus
          ˌantiˈcommunist         ˈantiˌcommunist ˈviews
          ˌtwenty-ˈfive           ˈtwenty-ˌfive ˈlectures

The words in (41a) all share the same metrical structure in that they consist of two feet (albeit with variable number of syllables), of which the second one is stronger than the first. In (41b) the same words are first members of phrase-level constituents; they are followed therefore in each case by a stronger stress. In such a context, the weak–strong pattern of the word uttered in isolation (as well as in contexts other than those in (41b): *go to* ˌHeathˈrow, *he's over* ˌtwenty-ˈfive) is reversed to strong–weak.

(42)

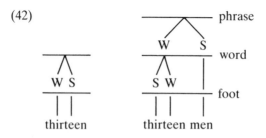

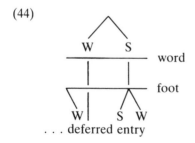

In general terms, we may state this regularity of **stress reversal** in terms of the following rule:

(43)      *Reversal*

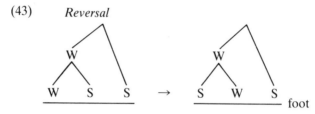

Reversal only happens among nodes in a metrical tree that dominate (at least) entire feet; in other words, a word-initial syllable whose stress is strengthened through (43) must have some stress to start with. There is no reversal in cases like *de ferred 'entry, di ˌvine 'will, a ˌroma 'therapy*, where the initial syllables are unstressed. Note that under the analysis for phrasal structure proposed in section 9.2.2.3 above, such phrases do not have the structure required by (43) as input to the Reversal rule: unstressed initial syllables are not part of the word's structure but extensions of the preceding foot:

(44)

The eurhythmic motivation of this reversal of stress patterns is evident: the Reversal rule (43) changes a pattern of three feet that increase in prominence into one where prominence alternates: weak–stronger–strongest into stronger–weaker–strongest. However, it is worth noting that (43) is the only device available in English to adjust 'un-eurhythmic' sequences of feet; notably, the mirror-image of the input to rule (43) – a pattern of decreasing prominence among feet – cannot be turned into an alternating pattern. Hence the noun 'pro‚duce does not turn into *pro'duce in *farm produce*; similarly in *Lake District*, the falling pattern among the two feet in 'dis‚trict remains unaltered.

As a final demonstration of the Reversal rule, consider the two phrases *one-thirteen George Street* and *John's thirteen lectures*. In the former phrase, the stress pattern of ‚one-thir'teen should be subject to Reversal, and in the latter that of ‚thir'teen: the opposite patterns *'one-‚thirteen and *'John's thir‚teen are clearly wrong. Our Reversal rule (43) predicts precisely this: in (45) only the circled nodes answer the input description of the rule; no other reversal is predicted by rule (43).

(45)

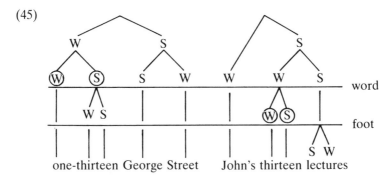

one-thirteen George Street    John's thirteen lectures

### 9.3  Syllables in connected speech

In section 9.1 above we studied in some detail the ways in which phonological structure of the foot level and above relates to syntactic structure; our conclusion was that while phonological structure is clearly informed by the syntax, it overrides syntactic structure at least on the foot level, where unstressed syllables may be adjoined to preceding feet disregarding syntactic constituency. In particular, we saw that the formation of feet in connected speech is insensitive to word boundaries.

This investigation into the formation of phonological units in connected speech will now be continued to the level of the syllable: is connected speech a sequence of syllables precisely of the form that we identified in citation forms (in ch. 6), or are there adjustments? In particular, do syllables, similar to feet, spread across word boundaries in connected speech? As we shall see, they do. The phonological structure of connected speech overrides word boundaries not only when syllables are connected into feet but also when segments are connected into syllables.

### 9.3.1 *Liaison*

Recall, from section 6.6, the following two features that charac-terise the syllabification of polysyllabic words: firstly, syllable boundaries are placed in such a way that onsets are maximised (rule (52) of ch. 6); secondly, in certain contexts it is possible for segments to belong to two syllables at once (to be 'ambisyllabic'). Ambisyllabicity arises to citation-form syllabification wherever rule (52) of chapter 6 makes a consonant part of an onset while at the same time the weight requirement for stressed syllables makes it part of the (preceding) rhyme, as in *ru'bella*. Here, the /l/ is ambisyllabic. In most accents of English, both these phenomena – the maximisation of onsets and the possibility of ambisyllabicity – are genera-lised across word boundaries in connected speech.

Consider the sentence *These are old eggs*. It is, of course, possible to utter this string as a rapid sequence of citation forms, in which case syllable boundaries would coincide with word boundaries, marked by brief periods of silence and possibly even by glottal stops preceding the word-initial vowels: [ðiːz.ʔɑː.ʔoʊld.ʔɛgz]. Note also that *are*, uttered in this fashion, has an /r/-less pronunciation for nonrhotic speakers.

However, this is clearly not an accurate rendering of connected speech for most accents of English (perhaps the only exception being South African English, which does display such a distribution of syllable boundaries – and prevocalic glottal stops – in connected speech). In other accents, for example RP, this syllabification would be found: [ðiː.zaː.roʊl.dɛgz], where word-final consonants form onsets for otherwise onset-less following syll-ables. To be precise, such consonants are probably not totally dissociated from the preceding syllables, as the transcription would suggest, but become ambisyllabic:

(46)

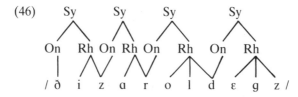

Although this maximisation of syllable onsets in connected speech – often called **liaison** – is most evident in cases such as this one, where onsets that are empty in citation forms are filled by preceding word-final consonants, the phenomenon is not necessarily restricted to such contexts. Similarly, onsets may be maximised in cases like *old wine*, where the /dw/ sequence may form a connected-speech onset (the /d/ being ambisyllabic); and perhaps liaison even takes place in *with luck*, where the /ðl/ or /θl/ sequence would not be a possible syllable onset in a citation form. Evidence for or against liaison in such cases is hard to come by; and what complicates the issue is the fact that speech style and tempo are major variables determining the phonology of connected speech. What is clear, however, is that liaison of the kind exemplified in (46) is a feature of all but the slowest performance of connected speech.

### 9.3.2 *Some effects of liaison*

If, as was demonstrated in the preceding paragraphs, syllabic structure is adjusted in connected speech so that certain segments become (parts of) onsets that in citation forms are (parts of) codas, then such restructuring should have certain effects in the segmental phonology: many of the segmental generalisations that were discussed earlier in this book refer to a segment's position in the syllable. If a phoneme, for example, has an allophone specific to syllable codas and another specific to onsets, then a citation form may display the former allophone while in connected speech the latter may occur. We shall investigate some such cases – not all of them concerned with allophony – in this section.

#### 9.3.2.1 *Linking /r/ in RP*

Perhaps the most striking evidence for liaison is provided by **linking** /r/ in nonrhotic accents such as RP. As was discussed in section 3.4 above, nonrhotic accents have a phonotactic constraint whereby /r/ can occur in syllable onsets but not in rhymes. Such accents have retained some residue of historic rhyme-/r/ in the form of the centring diphthong phonemes /ɪə/, /ɛə/ and /ʊə/, but in other vowels no such traces of historic /r/ are left: *bar* has the same vowel phoneme /ɑ/ as *spa* does. In such accents, then, /r/ occurs only in syllable onsets: it fails to occur in *hear* /hɪə/ but it is present in *hearing* /hɪərɪŋ/. Consider the following examples:

(47)

| a. | | b. | | c. | |
|---|---|---|---|---|---|
| hammer | /hamə/ | hammering | /hamərɪŋ/ | hammer it | /hamərɪt/ |
| bar | /bɑ/ | barring | /bɑrɪŋ/ | bar it | /bɑrɪt/ |
| bore | /bɔ/ | boring | /bɔrɪŋ/ | bore it | /bɔrɪt/ |
| hear | /hɪə/ | hearing | /hɪərɪŋ/ | hear it | /hɪərɪt/ |
| cure | /kjʊə/ | curing | /kjʊərɪŋ/ | cure it | /kjʊərɪt/ |
| tear | /tɛə/ | tearing | /tɛərɪŋ/ | tear it | /tɛərɪt/ |
| fur | /fɜ/ | furry | /fɜrɪ/ | fur is | /fɜrɪz/ |

Example (47a) shows the range of vowel phonemes that are found in contexts of historic /r/ – note that rhotic accents such as GA and SSE have retained /r/ in these contexts: /hamər/, /bɑr/ etc. Example (47b) demonstrates the occurrence of /r/ in RP (and equally, disregarding differences in the vowel phonemes, in rhotic accents) in words that are morphologically related to those in (47a). In these cases /r/ is in the syllable-onset position (*hamme.ring*, *hea.ring* etc.) and is therefore not barred from occurring.

What is of interest here is the list of items in (47c), where /r/, although word-final, does occur in the context of the following word beginning with a vowel. This is the phenomenon of 'linking /r/', common in nonrhotic accents including the most formal variety of RP. Liaison provides us with the means of accounting for such cases. With regard to /r/, liaison has the same effect as the regularities of word-internal syllabification do: just as in *hammering*, the /r/ in *hammer it* occupies a syllable onset in connected speech (due to liaison) and is therefore pronounced in the speech of nonrhotic speakers.

No account of linking /r/ is complete without a discussion of the closely related phenomenon of **intrusive /r/**, the insertion of /r/ in the same contexts as those in which linking /r/ is found, but in words where there is no historic /r/ (and, consequently, no /r/ in rhotic accents). Like linking /r/, intrusive /r/ is common in nonrhotic accents, but unlike the former, it is stigmatised in formal RP. Examples of intrusive /r/ are given in (48b). In contrast, no intrusive /r/ is possible after the vowels exemplified in (48c):

(48)

| a. Brenda | /ə/ | b. Brenda and | /brɛndərənd/ | c. see it | */sɪrɪt/ |
|-----------|-----|---------------|--------------|-----------|----------|
| spa | /ɑ/ | spa is | /spɑrɪz/ | do it | */dʊrɪt/ |
| law | /ɔ/ | law and | /lɔrənd/ | lay it | */leɪrɪt/ |
| idea | /ɪə/ | idea is | /aɪdɪərɪz/ | show it | */ʃɔɪt/ |
| skua | /ʊə/ | skua is | /skjʊərɪz/ | boy is | */bɔɪrɪz/ |
| Eritrea | /ɛə/ | Eritrea is | /ɛrɪtrɛərɪz/ | now is | */naʊrɪz/ |
| ? | /ɜ/ | ? is | /...ɜrɪz/ | why is | */waɪrɪz/ |

This distribution raises two questions. First, why does intrusive /r/ only occur in (48b) but not in (48c)? Second, how do formal RP speakers manage to avoid intrusive /r/ (48b) while permitting linking /r/ (47c), given that the vowel phonemes after which they permit linking /r/ are identical to those after which they shun intrusive /r/? This last observation provides the decisive clue to the former question.

Let us imagine, for the moment, a nonrhotic speaker who is illiterate, as well as having no knowledge of the history of the language or of rhotic accents. This speaker will probably have acquired linking /r/ as in (47c). But given his poor education, he has no way of distinguishing the contexts for linking /r/ from those for intrusive /r/ (48a, b); he will therefore use intrusive /r/ in precisely those phonological contexts in which linking /r/ occurs, that is, after vowel phonemes that *might also be* (but in instances where they are actually not) reflexes of historic /r/. For this speaker, /r/ simply occurs indiscriminately, in the appropriate contexts, after the vowel phonemes in (47a/48a) – but not after the vowel phonemes in (48c). The latter are vowel phonemes that cannot be reflexes of historic /r/. However, the RP speaker does not actually need to know this fact in order to make the distinction: they form a natural class in that all of them are high vowels, or at least surface diphthongs with high second elements, while the vowels that attract /r/ are nonhigh. For this speaker, then, a phonological constraint is available that limits the occurrence of linking/intrusive /r/, but there is no phonological constraint that would enable him to distinguish between the two phenomena of linking and intrusion.

How, then, does the formal RP speaker manage to make the distinction between permissible linking and stigmatised intrusion? The answer is by now obvious: *not* on phonological grounds. He has to draw on knowledge of the history of the language (which he is unlikely to have), or of rhotic accents (which he may have), or of spelling – and formal RP speakers are, as a rule, literate. In whatever way the distinction between linking and intrusion is acquired, it is not one that arises from a phonological generalisation.

### 9.3.2.2 *Allophonic effects*

Similar effects of liaison can be observed in the operation of certain allophonic rules: as we noted above, if a given allophonic rule predicts a particular allophone in syllable onsets, then we would expect the implementation of that rule in connected speech whenever liaison has caused the phoneme in question to become syllable onset. We look here at two such rules, both of which were discussed in detail in chapter 8: the rule for clear and dark /l/ in RP (sect. 8.2.1) and that for voiceless stop aspiration (sect. 8.3.1).

Recall rule (3) of chapter 8 whereby the 'clear' allophone of /l/ – [l] – occurs in syllable onsets while the 'dark' (velarised) allophone [ɫ] occurs elsewhere. Hence we get the following alternation in RP, depending on the position of the phoneme within the syllable:

(49)   a. [ɫ]                  b. [l]                  c. [l]
          feel                    feeling                feel it
          kill                    killer                 kill it
          tell                    telling                tell us

As predicted, liaison (49c) has the same effect on the quality of the /l/ as word-internal syllabification does (49b): in both cases the /l/ is in the onset position and is consequently realised as clear. The distribution of the two allophones is as clear-cut as this only in RP. As was noted in section 8.2.1, SSE has little or no clear–dark allophony, and while GA seems to have essentially the same distribution, its 'clear' [l] is slightly velarised and therefore less distinct from the dark allophone than it is in RP.

The distribution of aspiration among voiceless stops in connected speech follows similar lines; but again it is less clear-cut than that of the /l/ allophones in RP is. There does seem to be some aspiration in *keep it* as there is in *keeping*, in *kick it* as there is in *kicking*, etc. However, the facts are obscured by two factors. Firstly, recall that voiceless stops in syllable-*final* position are subject to glottal reinforcement; this was discussed in detail in section 8.3.1. If we are correct in saying that liaison results in widespread ambisyllabicity (sect. 9.3.1 above) then we would expect the /k/ in *lick it*, for example, to be both aspirated and glottalised. This seems to be the case; and we do not therefore get the aspirated and nonglottalised allophone that we are looking for in syllable-initial position. Secondly, as was also noted in section 8.3.1, aspiration is a gradient phenomenon which is much stronger in the onsets of stressed syllables than it is in unstressed syllables. In *keep it* and *kick it*, *it* is unstressed and we can expect only weak aspiration. And if we choose stressed second syllables (*keep out, kick Eric* etc.) we may well experience the failure of liaison to take place altogether: [ˈkʰɪʔkˈʔɛrɪʔk]. Liaison of syllables seems to be more common within feet than it is across foot boundaries. These are complicated and rather subtle issues; and allophony in connected speech is too much influenced by performance variables such as style and tempo to lend itself to a comprehensive, systematic and formal phonological analysis.

### 9.4   Structure simplification in connected speech

We have already seen that connected speech is not merely a sequence of citation forms: in section 9.1 we saw that units larger than words have distinct phonological shapes; in section 9.2 we studied rhythmic constraints and adjustments that operate within such units; and in section

9.3 we saw the liaison that takes place among syllables in speech, as well as some of its segmental effects. Our interest remains with the segmental phonology in this section: we shall investigate here some aspects of structure simplification – the loss of phonological information – that takes place in connected speech. Depending on their position within the suprasegmental structure (in particular on their position within the foot), as well as once again on tempo and stylistic variables, segments may lose their phonological identity by being 'reduced' or even lost, or by acquiring phonological features from neighbouring segments through assimilation.

### 9.4.1 *Vowel reduction and weak forms*

Recall from chapter 3 that the full range of English vowel contrasts occurs only in stressed syllables; in unstressed syllables, as we saw in sections 3.5 and 8.6, most vowel contrasts are suspended. The only vowel contrast found in unstressed syllables is that between /ɪ/ (as in '*purist*) and the central vowel schwa /ə/ ('*purest*), a vowel that has no specification in either the high–low dimension or the front–back dimension, and that can only occur in unstressed syllables. Words like *gymnast, compost, mayhem* etc., which do have full vowels in their final syllables, have secondary stress on those syllables. Moreover, the /ə/–/ɪ/ contrast is, as we also saw in those earlier discussions, rather unstable: many words show free variation (*bracelet, duchess* etc.); and the contrast is in any case mostly restricted to citation forms, while being suspended in most instances of connected speech. Ignoring, then, some minor analytical details such as the sporadic possibility for /ɪ/ to occur in unstressed syllables, we can state that English has a phonotactic constraint whereby vowels in non-foot-initial positions are schwa – and therefore devoid of any high/low or front/back specifications – whereas in foot-initial positions vowels will have such specifications.

This phonotactic constraint is not restricted to citation forms. In connected speech, schwa can occur in positions in which corresponding citation forms have full vowels; and in such cases the **reduction** of the vowel can be put down to a loss of stress: a syllable that is stressed in a citation form may be unstressed in connected speech. Consider the following examples:

(50)

| | | | |
|---|---|---|---|
| compost | /ˈkɒmˌpɒst/ | compost heap | [ˈkɒmpəstˌhip] |
| veto | /ˈviˌto/ | veto the proposal | [ˌvitəðəprəˈpozəɫ] |
| potato | /pəˈteˌto/ | potato peeler | [pəˈtetəˌpilə] |
| uneven | /ˌʌnˈivən/ | rather uneven | [ˌrɑðərənˈivən] |

285

In cases such as these, citation forms contain syllables with secondary stress (and full vowels), while the same forms may occur without those secondary stresses in connected speech, with attendant reduction of the vowel. In structural terms, such cases exemplify loss of structure on two levels: firstly, the loss of a foot in the suprasegmental structure; and secondly, the loss of distinctive features in the segmental representation of the vowel. Such loss of secondary stress may in turn be determined by rhythmic factors and in particular relate to speech tempo: if feet are isochronous (recall sect. 9.2 above) then an acceleration of speech tempo might lead to the dropping of stresses; and weak (secondary) stresses would be obvious candidates for this. On the other hand, the variability exemplified in (50) is clearly not entirely determined by rhythmic context and related variables: many speakers would have *potato* as /pətetə/ in all contexts, so that citation forms such as /pəteto/ are those of a more formal standard (and even such speakers will tend to have the reduced form in connected speech) and the reduced forms those of a less formal variety of the same accent.

Similar variation between stressed and unstressed forms of the same word can be observed in function words, which are usually cited in their 'strong' (stressed) forms (*of* /ɒv/, *as* /az/ etc.) while in connected speech they frequently occur in unstressed positions, displaying their 'weak' forms /əv/, /əz/ etc. Below are some examples:

(51)  and     /and/        the king and [ənd] I
                            come and [ən] see
                            Fred and [n̩d]~[n̩] I
                            bread and [n̩] butter
      but     /bʌt/        smart but [bət] casual
      than    /ðan/        stronger than [ðən] I
      us      /ʌs/         give us [əz] a break
      them    /ðɛm/        show them [ðəm]
                            give them [əm] a drink
      of      /ɒv/         Head of [əf] Spanish
                            Head of [əv] English
      at      /at/         stay at [ət] home
      as      /az/         good as [əz] gold

Example (51) is a random selection of words that have strong and weak forms. In such cases, the reduction that takes place when such a function word is placed in an unstressed position in speech results in schwa: again, the vowel loses the 'structure' that it has in the citation form. Schwa is the typical and most common vowel found in weak forms, but not the only one:

/ə/ and /ɪ/ tend to contrast in weak forms just as they do in citation forms. Hence *she* /ʃi/ and *he* /hi/ reduce to [ʃɪ] and [hɪ] in connected speech, as in *will she come?* [ˌwɪlʃɪˈkʌm].

We have seen in this section that for various possible reasons a syllable that bears some stress in a citation form may be unstressed in connected speech, and that in such cases the vowel in such a syllable will be reduced to schwa. However, this particular case of the reduction of vowels to schwa does not exhaust the possibilities of reduction that may be found in speech. Vowels may be reduced to the extent of total loss; similarly, consonants may be reduced. The list of weak forms (51) contains several cases of such reduction beyond schwa. We shall look at these in the following paragraphs: the phenomenon of reduction may affect segments, syllables and (as we have already seen) feet.

### 9.4.2 *Reduction, elision, assimilation*

Let us start with *bread and butter* [ˌbrɛdn̩ˈbʌtə], given in (51) above. Similar cases were discussed in section 9.2.2.4 in relation to the structure of feet in connected speech; in the present discussion they provide examples of reduction resulting in the loss (**elision**) of segments: compared to the citation form /and/, all that is left of the word in this context is a syllabic [n̩]. We deal with the elision of the vowel first.

Elision of schwa is common especially before sonorant consonants: given that it is possible for such consonants to be syllabic, they will occupy the peak of the syllable (thereby preserving the syllable) in cases where the vowel is elided. Indeed, we saw as early as in section 3.5 that schwa is optional in many such contexts even in citation forms: *button* may be phonemically analysed as /bʌtən/ or /bʌtn/, *little* as /lɪtəl/ or /lɪtl/, and so forth. However, it would appear that such free variation in citation forms is restricted to unstressed final syllables; unstressed initial or medial syllables have schwa in citation forms – but not necessarily in casual speech. Consider the following:

(52)

| police | a. /pəˈlis/ | b. [pl̩is] | c. [plis] |  |
| canoe | /kəˈnu/ | [kn̩u] | [knu] |  |
| balloon | /bəˈlun/ | [bl̩un] | [blun] |  |
| solicitor | /səˈlɪsɪtə/ | [sl̩ɪsɪtə] | [sl̩ɪṣtə] | [slɪstə] |
| federal | /ˈfɛdərəl/ | [fədr̩l] | [fɛdr̩l] |  |
| catalyst | /ˈkatəlɪst/ | [katl̩ɪst] | [katlɪst] |  |
| botany | /ˈbɒtənɪ/ | [bɒtn̩ɪ] | [bɒtnɪ] |  |

In (52b) schwa is elided before sonorants; the syllable is maintained through syllabicity of the sonorant. But in even faster speech, reduction can go yet further, affecting the syllable itself and also eliding unstressed vowels before obstruents. In (52c) sonorant consonants are no longer syllabic (except for the final one in *federal*); hence *police, canoe* etc. have monosyllabic pronunciations in fast speech. In *solicitor* the penultimate vowel is elided, with or without maintenance of that syllable through syllabicity of the /s/. Notice that in this column, containing hypothetical 'fast-speech' forms (but omitting various other allophonic details), the structures left over from the various elisions are in violation of phonotactic constraints that we established in chapter 6 for citation forms: the [kn] in *canoe* is not a possible syllable onset in citation forms; and syllabic [ş] (*solicitor*) is similarly impossible in such forms.

The examples of weak forms in (51) above also exemplify the elision of consonants. The final /d/ of /and/, for example, is likely to be elided in *come and see* [ˌkʌmən'siː]; similarly, *give them* may be ['gɪvəm]. In both cases, the elision of the consonant results in the simplification of a consonant cluster: the /d/ drops out of the /nds/ sequence in the former case, and the /ð/ out of the /vð/ cluster in the latter. Again, this kind of consonant elision and cluster simplification is not restricted to weak forms of words. Here are some more examples:

(53)  West Germany  /ˌwɛst'dʒɜːmənɪ/  [wɛsdʒɜːmənɪ]
      thousand times  /'θaʊzənd'taɪmz/  [θaʊzn̩taɪmz]
      hold still  /hold'stɪl/  [holstɪl]
      textbook  /'tɛkstˌbʊk/  [tɛksbʊk]

In addition, sequences of identical ('geminate') consonants at word and morpheme boundaries are usually simplified in connected speech:

(54)  keenness  /kinnəs/  [kinəs]
      bus-stop  /'bʌsˌstɒp/  [bʌstɒp]
      weight-training  /'wetˌtrenɪŋ/  [weʔtrenɪŋ]
      call Linda  /ˌkɔl'lɪndə/  [kɔlɪndə]

The final type of structure simplification found in connected speech is **assimilation**, the spread of features of a given segment onto a neighbouring segment. This was discussed in some detail in section 8.2.2, where it was noted that assimilation in English is of the 'anticipatory' kind; that is, segments anticipate features of following segments – the spread of features is 'leftward'. We also noted then that assimilation is a 'true' allophonic phenomenon in that it is insensitive to nonphonological structure (for example, word boundaries). We shall find this confirmed in our present, second examination of the phenomenon, but we shall also see that assimilation in connected speech is a phenomenon more powerful than the allophonies that we discussed in chapter 8: in casual speech, assimilation frequently causes the breakdown of phonemic distinctions that are operative in citation forms. Once again, we can draw our first examples from the list of weak forms in (51), where voicing assimilation occurs in *of* [ɒf] *Spanish* vs. [ɒv] *English*. Similarly, compare the citation form *us* /ʌs/ with the weak form *give us* [ʌz] *a break*. In both cases, the voicing contrast between obstruents is suspended by virtue of the assimilation process. Here are some further examples:

(55)  ten pounds    /tɛnpaʊndz/    [tɛmpaʊndz]
      in Crewe      /ɪnkru/        [ɪŋkru]
      miss you      /mɪsju/        [mɪʃju]
      basket-ball   /bɑskətbɔl/    [bɑskə?pbɔl]

Assimilations such as these are extremely common in casual speech, illustrating once again the simplification – even the breakdown – of the phonological structure found in citation forms. [m] is not an allophone of /n/; but here we have [tɛm] as a realisation of *ten*. The /n/–/m/ contrast is suspended, in casual speech, in this context, as are other consonant contrasts in the other examples.

To gain a final impression of just how much phonological information present in citation forms may be lost in casual speech, consider the examples given below. These are more complex than earlier ones in that they display reduction, elision as well as assimilation at the same time:

(56)  grand piano              /grandpiano/    [grampjanə]
      hand Colin (the money)   /handkɒlɪn/     [haŋkɒlɪn]
      bread and butter         /brɛdandbʌtə/   [brɛbm̩bʌtə]

In *grand piano*, *piano* loses a syllable, in that /i/ turns into nonsyllabic [j] – [pj] becomes syllable onset; /o/ is reduced to [ə]; *grand* loses its final /d/, and the /n/ assimilates to the (now) following /p/. In the second example, the final /d/ of *hand* is elided and the /n/ assimilated to the following /k/ – nevertheless, the context 'the money' makes it unlikely that the phrase is misunderstood as *hang Colin*. And finally, the /and/ in *bread and butter* is reduced, through reduction, elision and assimilation, to [m̩]; and this assimilation spreads further to the left so as to turn *bread* into [brɛb]. How, one wonders, is it possible to understand casual speech? Examples such as these demonstrate quite clearly that the more casual or fast speech is, and the more an utterance deviates from the maximal clarity of citation forms, the greater is the role that the context plays in its comprehension.

### Suggested reading to chapter 9

Section 9.1   On phrasal stress and compound stress see Liberman and Prince (1977), Hogg and McCully (1987: sect. 3.2) and, paying special attention to compounds with 'phrasal stress', Fudge (1984: ch. 5). On intonation the specialist literature should be consulted: for example, Halliday (1970), Ladd (1980), Cruttenden (1986).

Section 9.2.1   On stress-timing in English see Catford (1977: ch. 5), Catford (1988: ch. 9), Classe (1939), Lehiste (1977), Roach (1982), Dauer (1983).

Section 9.2.2   On the foot (phonetically) Catford (1988: ch. 9), in Metrical Phonology Selkirk (1980). On sentence-level metrical structure Liberman and Prince (1977), Giegerich (1985: ch. 4), Hogg and McCully (1987: ch. 6). All these propose analyses based on what is here called 'solution 1'. For a forerunner of 'solution 2' see Giegerich (1986). On enclitics see Abercrombie (1965).

Section 9.2.3   On 'eurhythmy' see Hogg and McCully (1987: chs. 4–6), Giegerich (1985: ch. 4), Hayes (1984), Kager and Visch (1988). Abercrombie (1971) on 'silent stress'.

Sections 9.3, 9.4   On connected speech, liaison etc. see Brown (1990), Gimson (1989: chs. 10, 11), Lass (1984: ch. 12).

# 10
# Representations and derivations

This final chapter will be concerned with **phonological theory**. It has this in common, of course, with the preceding chapters: nothing that has been said about the phonology of English could have been said without reference to a particular theoretical framework. When we talk about the phonemes, allophones, syllables, feet etc. of English we employ theoretical constructs in the analysis of what we perceive to be phonetic facts. The phoneme as such, or any particular phoneme, is not a fact (of English or otherwise) but the result of theoretical reasoning *about* facts. Similarly, the notions of the syllable and the foot are theoretical constructs, albeit ones that are in some respects associated with certain recurrent phenomena in speech that – through no coincidence, of course – bear the same names.

What will distinguish this chapter from the preceding ones is that here we shall more systematically discuss the phonological theory that we have been employing. We shall begin by asking what it is that we expect a phonological theory to do for us, what the typical ingredients of a phonological theory are, and where the one employed in this book stands within the range of possible phonological theories. In the second part of the chapter we shall review some details of our previous analysis that may be identified as shortcomings of the theory; and we shall look into the possibilities of amending or changing the theory accordingly.

## 10.1 On phonological theories

In general terms, a **theory** is a set of devices employed to account for (or perhaps to 'explain') a given range of phenomena. Given that we are here dealing with phonology, the phenomena that we are attempting to account for are phonetic: it is the aim of the phonology of a language to account for the phonetic regularities that occur in the speech events of that language. That phonetic phenomena constitute 'regularities' is an important assumption about the nature of the data; but we noted in chapter 8 above that by restricting our investigation to 'regular' phenomena we exclude other phenomena, namely those that occur in 'free variation'. The phonetic level of representation produced by our theory cannot be a complete likeness of the whole range of the phonetic phenomena that ever occur in all speech events of the language; it is in itself an idealisation and possibly even a theoretical construct. This is a principled limitation that any phonological theory has to live with.

Consider the following example of the theoretical reasoning that has characterised much of the preceding chapters. To explain the fact that speakers of English usually pronounce *pip* as [pʰɪʔp], we first analysed *pip* as a string of phonemes /pɪp/, where the methods of our phonemic analysis produced the interesting generalisation that [pʰ] and [ʔp], despite their phonetic differences, are underlyingly the same: /p/. We then assigned a syllable structure to *pip* – another piece of theoretical reasoning (the syllable is a theoretical construct), followed by yet another one: the [pʰ] in *pip* and, say, the [kʰ] in *kick* have a number of things in common. First of all, both are aspirated. Also, both are voiceless stops. Moreover, both are syllable-initial; both are followed by /ɪ/; the /ɪ/ is in both cases followed by another instance of the initial phoneme; and perhaps so forth. But out of all these similarities between the two strings of sounds we isolated the following ones, finding the others to be irrelevant: [pʰ] and [kʰ] are aspirated; they are voiceless stops; and they are syllable-initial. Similarly, both [ʔp] and [ʔk] are glottalised; both are voiceless stops; both are syllable-final. And then we took the perhaps most important step in our analysis: we formulated the rule that *all* voiceless stops in English are (and will be, in future utterances, until the language changes) aspirated *whenever* they occur syllable-initially and glottalised *whenever* they occur syllable-finally, assuming our definitions of voiceless stops, of aspiration and of the syllable.

Our 'explanation' is based on a series of **generalisations**: the first instance of /p/ in *pip* is aspirated 'because' all voiceless stops behave in that way if they occur in this particular position in the syllable. This is not, of course, a real **explanation**: there is still the question of *why* all voiceless stops are aspirated in that position. But typically, phonological theories content themselves with generalisations, stopping short of true explanations in the hope, perhaps, that the phoneticians will provide a physiological or acoustic reason why it should be exactly the voiceless stops, whenever they occur in exactly this position, that should bear exactly this feature of aspiration. Often this hope on the part of the phonologist is not disappointed (and if it is then his or her generalisations regarding the phenomenon or its occurrence are likely to have been wrong); but the identification of such true causes is, strictly speaking, outside the domain of phonological theory as it is conceived here.

In most phonological theories, the devices employed in accounting for phonetic facts fall into two categories: phonological theories use formally defined **representational** and **derivational devices**. Consider again *pip*. In (1a) below we have the underlying representation, consisting of a linear sequence of phonemes, each phonemic symbol standing for a bundle of features (not given in (1)). In the course of the phonological derivation, phonemes are associated with X-positions; these are grouped into onsets, peaks, codas; the last two into rhymes; onsets and rhymes into syllables; syllables into feet; and so forth. Predictable segmental features (such as aspiration, glottalisation etc.) are supplied by allophonic rules. A complete phonetic representation is given in (1b):

(1)  a.   Phonemic representation:        / p    ɪ    p /

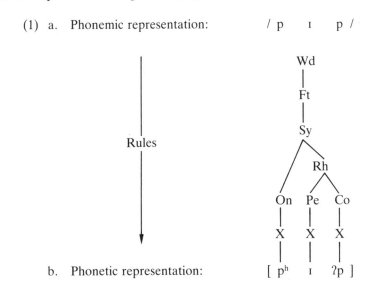

     b.   Phonetic representation:        [ pʰ    ɪ    ʔp ]

On the representational side, then, a phonological theory may employ notions such as 'features', 'segments', 'X-positions', 'onsets', 'rhymes', 'syllables', 'feet' and so forth. Wellformedness conditions – some universal and others language-specific – determine the possible shape of any given phonological unit. There is no principled limit to the number or nature of representational devices a phonological theory may employ, nor is the adoption of any representational device dictated by anything other than the analyst's decision. In chapter 6 we decided, for example, to employ the device of the 'X-position' in phonological representation because it facilitates generalisations that would otherwise be poorly expressed or missed.

The devices used on the derivational side of phonological theory are **rules**. In the course of a phonological derivation, certain phonetic factors are taken to be unpredictable (and therefore part of the **underlying representation** of a given utterance) while others are taken to be predictable (and therefore supplied by rules). Again, the number of derivational devices as well as the scope of the derivation are subject to the analyst's choice. Moreover, the decision about what is predictable and what is not is not always straightforward. We decided, for example, that the single-X association of a lax vowel (such as the /ɪ/ in *pip*) can be derived from the (underlying) laxness of this vowel; but we noted also that the opposite direction of the derivation is possible (if for our purposes less advantageous): we might have assumed all vowel phonemes to be underlyingly associated with either one or two 'X' (thereby making X-positions part of underlying representations), and the tenseness or laxness of vowels might then have been derived by rule from the X-specification.

Most phonological theories (namely, all those that operate with derivations) recognise (at least two) **levels of representation**: an underlying level and a surface (phonetic) level, which is derived from the former. But theories differ in terms of the derivational and representational devices they employ. There is also some dispute over what linguistic regularities fall in the domain of phonology and which belong in other parts of the grammar, for example in the morphology. Consider the following:

(2) 

| divine | – divinity | |
| derive | – derivative | } /aɪ/–/ɪ/ |
| line | – linear | |

| obscene | – obscenity | |
| appeal | – appellative | } /i/–/ɛ/ |
| metre | – metrical | |

| profane | – profanity | |
| compare | – comparative | } /e/–/a/ |
| explain | – explanatory | |

| abound | – abundant | |
| profound | – profundity | } /aʊ/–/ʌ/ |
| denounce | – denunciation | |

Clearly, the examples in (2) display a phenomenon of English which involves vowel alternations (in morphologically related words). But do these alternations constitute *phonological* regularities? Or are they, rather, simply cases of morphemes that have different allomorphs, such that the morpheme {divine} occurs as either /dɪvaɪn/ or /dɪvɪn/, etc.? Those linguists that take the latter option would point out that the alternation pattern suggested by (2) is not actually quite as regular as it looks there: *obese – obesity*, for example, fails to display the /i/–/ɛ/ alternation exemplified by *obscene – obscenity* in (2); moreover, in *confide – confession* we have an /aɪ/–/ɛ/ alternation not listed in (2), in *clear – clarify* we have /i/–/a/, in *domain – dominion* /e/–/ɪ/; and further, if on the whole rather sporadic, examples of different alternations can be found.

The decision about what belongs in the phonology of a language and what belongs in other parts of that language's grammar is not a futile boundary dispute among linguists; it depends on certain assumptions regarding the scope of the phonology. For example, if we tolerate exceptions in phonological rules then we can call what is displayed in (2) a phonological regularity. If, on the other hand, we do not allow phonological rules to have exceptions then whatever is behind the alternations in (2) does not qualify as a phonological rule. Moreover, as we shall see in section 10.2 below, any statement of the rules that account for alternations such as these requires derivational devices that are rather more powerful than the ones permitted in the phonemic theory employed so far in this book. Alternations such as /aɪ/–/ɪ/ are, unlike [pʰ]–[ʔp], outside the scope of phonemic theory because the phoneme constitutes the highest level of abstraction. /aɪ/ and /ɪ/ are phonemes of English; there cannot therefore be a rule that derives one from the other, or both from something else. The theory can, of course, handle allophonic alternations such as [pʰ]–[ʔp]: the entity underlying both is a phoneme.

Compared to other phonological theories currently available, the one adhered to in (most of) this book may be characterised as quite rich and powerful on the representational side, in that it recognises a considerable range of representational devices and phonological units: features, segments, X-positions, syllables, feet and so forth. On the derivational side it has been rather limited. Our highest level of abstraction has been the phoneme; and the range of information available to phonological derivations has not, for example, included nonphonological information such as word boundaries or lexical categories (Noun, Verb etc.). Recall that the instances where such information was invoked were noted, in each case, to be outside the scope of a strictly phonemicist theory. These instances included the analysis of English word stress (chapter 7), the Scottish Vowel-Length Rule (in chapter 8) and the analysis of sentence stress (in chapter 9).

These three areas of investigation demonstrated an interesting (if really quite straightforward) feature of phonological theories, and of theories in general. The richer the devices available to a theory are, the more powerful it will be in terms of the range of phenomena that it is able to account for. The 'high-tech' engine of a Porsche will yield greater performance than the 'low-tech' engine of a lawnmower will. But while both produce kinetic energy by means of the internal combustion of petroleum derivatives, it cannot be said that the 'high-tech' version of this device is simply better than the 'low-tech' one. Fitting lawnmowers with Porsche engines would not necessarily improve them. Sports cars and lawnmowers serve different purposes, and the technological devices they contain are suited to those purposes.

The same can be said about phonological theories. Phonemicist theory is comparatively 'low-tech' (and perhaps even dated); but it has the advantage of being readily testable (minimal pairs establish phonemes once and for all); it is intuitively straightforward and widely used; and it lends itself particularly well to the establishment and comparison of sound systems in different languages and – as has been done here – in different accents of a language. However, there is a price to be paid: its scope for derivation by rule is rather small simply because its derivational devices are severely limited. Phonemicist theory has to treat English word stress as phonemic, as part of each word's underlying representation and not derivable by rule. *'Digest – di'gest* is a minimal pair, which settles the issue. A theory whose derivations may refer to lexical-category information, on the other hand, will be able to predict these two stress patterns by means of rules that take into account the fact that one of the two words is a noun and the other a verb. Similarly, vowel length in SSE can only be treated as rule-governed if word boundaries are referred to in the formulation of the rule: *brood* [brud] and *brewed* [bruːd] are a minimal pair, establishing the phonemic status of vowel length in SSE, unless the fact is taken into account that the latter contains a morphological boundary that is absent in the former.

In the remainder of this chapter we shall look at some theoretical devices – derivational and representational – that may improve the performance of our phonological theory. We are abandoning at this point the derivational constraints of phonemic theory.

## 10.2 Increasing derivational power: Generative Phonology

### 10.2.1 *The velar nasal: phoneme or sequence?*

The velar nasal [ŋ] has posed analytical problems at various points of our discussion of the phonemics and phonotactics of English. Although clearly a phoneme in RP, GA and SSE (as shown by *sung – sun – sum*, (3a) below), it is subject to phonotactic restrictions that set it apart from the other two nasal phonemes /n/ and /m/: unlike those, it cannot occur in syllable onsets (3b); and in rhymes its occurrence is restricted to the position immediately following a lax (single-X) vowel (3c). Moreover, /ŋ/ cannot occur in these accents before word-final /g/ (similar to the way /m/ cannot occur before word-final /b/) – (3d):

(3)  a. sum     b. meat     c. lime     d. limp     *[lɪmb]
       sun        neat        line        lent       [lɛnd]
       sung      *[ŋit]      *[laɪŋ]     sunk        *[sʌŋg]

Also, unlike the other two nasal phonemes, the velar one is not a phoneme in all accents of English: in the English North Midlands, [ŋ] occurs only before /g/ or /k/, so that *sung* is [sʌŋg] (or more likely [sʊŋg]) and *singing* [sɪŋgɪŋg], unlike RP/GA/SSE [sʌŋ] and [sɪŋɪŋ]. In this accent, *sung – sun* and *sung – sum* are not minimal pairs: they differ not only with respect to the quality of the nasal but also through the presence or absence of /g/. [ŋ] consequently does not have phonemic status and has to be treated as an allophone of one of the other nasal phonemes, or, more precisely, as a realisation of the archiphoneme /N/, given that all nasal contrasts are suspended before /g/ and /k/ – recall section 8.6 above.

Clearly, then, [ŋ] has special status. Phonemic theory can express these distributional peculiarities, of course; but it has to do so by means of quite unrelated statements, ruling out onset-/ŋ/ and, after long vowels, rhyme-/ŋ/ by stating two separate phonotactic filters, and by positing a rather radical phonemic difference between North Midlands English and other accents which rather misses the point: the phonological difference exemplified by RP [sʌŋ] and North Midlands [sʌŋg] is more plausibly expressed in terms of the distribution of /g/ rather than in terms of the phonemic status of [ŋ]!

Here is an alternative analysis. Let us say that surface [ŋ] is, in *all* accents of English, underlyingly represented by the sequence /Ng/ or /Nk/, where /N/ is once again the nasal archiphoneme (given that nasals do not contrast with one another before /g/ and /k/). Hence *sung* is underlyingly /sʌNg/ and *sunk* /sʌNk/. Referring to the following /g/ or /k/, the realisation rule for the archiphoneme will derive the velar nasal [ŋ] from underlying /N/; and then the final /g/ (but not /k/) is deleted, in accents other than North Midlands English. Below is a formal statement of this derivation.

(4)  a.  Underlying representations:    / s ʌ N g /    / s ʌ N k /

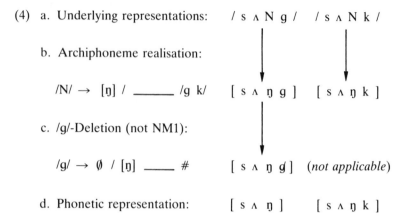

    b.  Archiphoneme realisation:

       /N/ → [ŋ] / _____ /g k/    [ s ʌ ŋ g ]    [ s ʌ ŋ k ]

    c.  /g/-Deletion (not NM1):

       /g/ → ∅ / [ŋ] _____ #    [ s ʌ ŋ g̶ ]    (*not applicable*)

    d.  Phonetic representation:    [ s ʌ ŋ ]    [ s ʌ ŋ k ]

What does this two-step derivation gain us? Perhaps most obviously, it accounts for the difference between the English North Midlands and other accents in a straightforward way: North Midlands speakers do not have the rule of /g/-Deletion (4c). For them, the derivation is completed after (4b) has produced [sʌŋg]. But perhaps more strikingly, the underlying representation /ng/ for [ŋ] makes it possible to account for the phonotactic restrictions of [ŋ] by means of existing constraints on syllable structure: since nasal-plus-stop sequences are impossible in syllable onsets, no [ŋ] can occur in that position in the syllable; and sequences where a long vowel is followed by a nasal plus a stop are only possible as syllable rhymes if the stop is coronal (and therefore an appendix). (Recall here the detailed discussion of the syllable template in chapter 6.) Hence *fiend*, *thing* (5a) below are well formed but a long vowel cannot be followed by /ng/, as it would be in the underlying form of [θiːŋ] (5c):

(5)

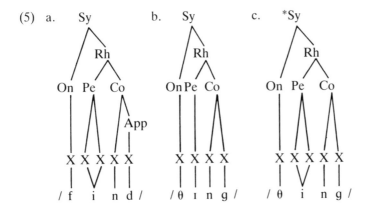

This is a rather striking result: we noted initially that [ŋ] differs from the other nasals of English in three respects, and all three are elegantly accounted for if we assume that [ŋ] is not a phoneme of English but the derivational effect of an underlying /ng/ sequence.

Before we assess the theoretical repercussions of such derivations, let us look a little further into the predictions made by the derivation in (4). According to (4c), any /g/ of an underlying /ng/ sequence is deleted before a morphological boundary. This would imply that the /g/ is preserved in the absence of a morphological boundary, as in the cases in (6a) below; and that it is deleted in the presence of a word-medial morphological boundary (6b). Here, (4c) makes the correct predictions although *English* and *England*, perhaps accent-specifically, have no [g] for some speakers. But more serious problems occur in (6c, d).

(6)

| a. [ŋg] | b. [ŋ] | c. [ŋ] | d. [ŋg] |
|---------|--------|--------|---------|
| anger | sing#er | hangar | long#er |
| tango | sing#ing | dinghy (?) | long#est |
| bingo | hang#er | Bingley | |
| mongrel | hang#ing | Langley | |
| angle | | gingham | |
| English (?) | | | |
| England (?) | | | |

The words listed in (6c) do not contain [g] (with the possible exception of *dinghy*, which is sometimes pronounced [dɪŋgɪ]), although they do not contain the morphological boundary required to trigger the /g/-Deletion rule; and conversely, the examples in (6d) do contain such a boundary but the rule fails to apply. We might now refine the morphological conditioning of the /g/-Deletion rule to account for *longer*, *longest* – unlike the cases in

(6b), these contain adjectives with comparative -*er* and superlative -*est* and therefore, arguably, a different kind of morphological boundary – but cases such as those in (6c) are difficult to reconcile with any formulation of the rule. This rule simply applies sporadically in cases where application is not predicted.

What, then, are the theoretical implications of derivations such as (4)? This derivation is at variance with phonemicist principles in a number of respects. First, such an analysis posits a more **abstract underlying representation** than a phonemic one does, in that it derives [ŋ], a phoneme attested by minimal pairs and therefore underivable in phonemic theory, from an underlying cluster of segments. Second, a **sequence of rules** is required for the derivation – in contrast, phonemic theory invariably produces phonetic representations (allophones) from underlying representations (phonemes) by means of a single rule. There are no intermediate segmental representations in phonemic theory. Third, this analysis crucially involves **rule ordering**: if the order of the two rules is reversed then the place of articulation information that rule (4b) requires is lost before this rule has a chance to apply. Fourth, the second rule is a **deletion rule**, erasing an underlying segment – in phonemic theory, every underlying segment must have a corresponding surface segment. Every phoneme has a realisation; deletion rules are not permitted. Fifth, one of the rules has **lexical exceptions**. And sixth, this rule makes reference to **nonphonological information**: at least to the morphological boundary '#' and, to reduce the number of exceptions, possibly to more detailed morphological information.

It is clear, then, that this account of [ŋ] is only possible if the range of derivational devices of phonological theory is radically increased: such devices must include rule sequences, rule ordering, deletions, exception marking in lexical items, access to nonphonological information, as well as underliers more abstract than the phoneme and therefore not independently testable in terms of minimal pairs as we know them. This is a heavy price to pay, in terms of derivational machinery, for this set of generalisations; and it would hardly be worth paying if the utility of such an enriched derivational theory were confined to a single set of generalisations. This is not the case: a theory as rich as this in derivational terms opens up a wide range of further opportunities for generalisations that phonemic theory does not capture. The account of English word stress presented in chapter 7, for example, made use of rule sequences, rule ordering, exception marking and nonphonological information; and similarly, our statement of the Scottish Vowel-Length Rule (in chapter 8) had exceptions as well as taking into account morphological boundaries. What emerges here is a phonological theory that constitutes a genuine alternative, in derivational terms, to phonemic theory. This is the theory of **Generative Phonology**.

Generative Phonology differs from phonemic theory not merely in technical terms, that is, in the number and nature of derivational devices that it allows itself to use. The main difference between the two theories lies deeper than that. Generative Phonology seeks to establish *a single underlying representation for every morpheme*, from which the speaker will then derive, or 'generate', the appropriate phonetic surface form in any given context. This objective is not shared by phonemic theory. The fact that *long* has the phonemic representation /lɒŋ/ in isolation but /lɒŋg/ in the morphologically complex form *longer* is not a problem for this theory: for a phonemicist, whose primary interest it is to establish the sound system of the language, this is a morphological problem which therefore lies outside his field. For a generativist, on the other hand, complex derivations such as the one deriving [ŋ] from /ng/ are a matter of necessity rather than choice, arising from the overall objective of Generative Phonology. Similarly, vowel alternations such as that in *divine – divinity* ((2) above) fall into the domain of Generative Phonology: here, again, is a morpheme with two different phonetic surface forms which therefore must be derivationally related. For the phonemicist, on the other hand, a pair of words such as this one is without interest except that it instantiates the two phonemes /aɪ/ and /ɪ/. Before we sketch a generative analysis of alternations such as this one, let us return to a topic that we have dealt with before within the phonemic theory – in a way that would be acceptable in a generative framework.

### 10.2.2 /r/ in nonrhotic accents: a partial analysis

A nonrhotic accent is one which, in phonemic terms, does not permit /r/ to occur in syllable rhymes; the phonemic implications of nonrhoticism were discussed in section 3.4. Some words exemplifying nonrhoticism (in RP) are listed in (7a) below; (7b) gives the same words in a rhotic accent (here GA); and (7c) lists those items in contexts where they exemplify **linking** /r/ (again in RP).

| (7) | a. hear | /hɪə/ | b. /hir/ | c. hearing, hear it | /hɪər/ |
| | care | /kɛə/ | /ker/ | caring, care of | /kɛər/ |
| | cure | /kjʊə/ | /kjur/ | curing, cure it | /kjʊər/ |
| | pour | /pɔ/ | /pɔr/ | pouring, pour it | /pɔr/ |
| | tar | /tɑ/ | /tɑr/ | tarring, tar is | /tɑr/ |

As we saw in section 9.3.2.1, the 'linking /r/' of such items occurs in syllable onsets; it is therefore not affected by the ban on rhyme-/r/ that characterises nonrhotic accents and occurs freely in, for example, RP. This list is incomplete in that it does not contain items such as *bird, herd, church, butter*. Our discussion will be confined to those items listed in (7).

As we saw earlier, the fact that in a phonemic analysis an item such as *hear* has the phonemic representation /hɪə/ in isolation but /hɪər/ in linking-/r/ contexts does not constitute a problem for such an analysis; but for a generative analysis it is an unsatisfactory result: given the obvious relatedness of the two forms, it is imperative for a generative phonology to derive both from a common underlier. Here is a possible account in a generative framework.

Let us say that for both RP and GA, the underlying representations of the items listed in (7) are those in (7b); in other words, there is no difference between the rhotic and nonrhotic varieties on the underlying level of representation. In GA, these items surface unchanged: underlying /hir/ corresponds to [hir] on the phonetic surface (provided we disregard some minor phonetic details). In RP, on the other hand, the two surface forms [hɪə] and [hɪər] must be derived from the common underlier /hir/. Using a two-step strategy similar to the one adopted in our earlier treatment of [ŋ], we may say that first the /r/ triggers a change in the vowel, producing, for example, [ɪə] from underlying /i/; and second, the /r/ is deleted in syllable rhymes but not in onsets. Here is a sketch of the derivation, to be fleshed out presently:

| (8) | | hear | hear(ing) |
|---|---|---|---|
| | a. Underlying representation: | / h i r / | / h i r / |
| | b. Vowel change: | [ h ɪ ə r ] | [ h ɪ ə r ] |
| | c. /r/-Deletion: | [ h ɪ ə ɾ̶ ] | (*n/a*) |
| | d. Phonetic representation | [ h ɪ ə ] | [ h ɪ ə r ] |

The rule of /r/-Deletion is straightforward and may simply be stated as in (9) below. Note that in a generative analysis such as this one, it is the presence or absence of this rule, rather than a difference in underlying representations, that accounts for the distinction between rhotic and nonrhotic accents: /r/-Deletion occurs in nonrhotic accents only.

(9) */r/-Deletion (nonrhotic)*

$$/r/ \rightarrow \emptyset \ / \ \underline{\qquad} \overset{\text{Rh}}{\underline{|}}$$

The rule simply dubbed 'vowel change' in (8b) is rather more complex. Firstly, it affects only some of the vowels listed in (7) above: /i/, /e/ and /u/ turn into the centring diphthongs [ɪə], [ɛə] and [ʊə] respectively, while /ɑ/ and /ɔ/ remain unchanged. Secondly, in the affected vowels the rule does two things: it changes them from underlyingly tense vowels into surface-lax [ɪ], [ɛ], [ʊ]; and it inserts [ə] after them. (Note, moreover, that this is where our account will remain incomplete: we do not here consider forms with lax pre-/r/ vowels, such as *bird* etc.)

If we assume that all the vowels given in (7b) represent the class of [+ tense] vowels in English then we may distinguish /ɑ ɔ/ from the rest by characterising them as [+ tense, + low], and the others as [+ tense, − low]. The vowels that turn into centring diphthongs before underlying /r/, then, form a clearly defined natural class: that of the nonlow tense vowels.

Consider now the formation of centring diphthongs itself. Here we shall make use of the representational devices developed earlier in this book, in particular of the syllable template of chapter 6 above. Say we have a rule of 'Centring Diphthongisation', which inserts [ə] between a nonlow tense vowel and /r/:

(10)  *Centring Diphthongisation*

$$\emptyset \rightarrow [\mathrm{ə}] \;/\; \begin{bmatrix} - \text{ consonantal} \\ - \text{ low} \\ + \text{ tense} \end{bmatrix} \underline{\hspace{1.5em}} \;/\mathrm{r}/$$

In terms of syllable structure, such an insertion has an interesting effect: it produces an ill-formed rhyme: namely, one where three X-positions are occupied by vowels – two by the tense vowel plus one by [ə]. If the insertion of [ə] is to take effect, it must in turn prompt a further change: the preceding vowel must be reduced to one X-position; in other words, it must become lax (given that RP has no tense vowels associated with single X-positions). This sequence of derivational events is depicted in (11) for *hear* (but ignoring the syllable onset):

(11)

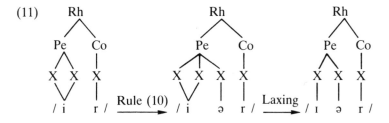

303

The rule of 'Pre-[ə] Laxing', spelled out in (12) below, is thus an automatic consequence of our conditions on phonological representations in English: given the conditions that govern the association of vowels with X-positions and that of X-positions with peaks in RP, this rule is the only way to prevent ill-formed syllables from surfacing.

(12) *Pre-[ə] Laxing*

$$\begin{bmatrix} -\text{consonantal} \\ +\text{tense} \end{bmatrix} \rightarrow [-\text{tense}] \ / \ \underline{\phantom{xxx}} \bigwedge^{\text{Pe}} [\ \text{ə}\ ]$$

This rule laxes tense vowels followed by [ə] provided they share a syllable peak. Note that in this formulation of the rule, forms such as *trachea* /trəkiə/, where [i] and [ə] occupy different syllables, are not affected.

We conclude this discussion of the distribution of [r] in RP with a summary of the derivational steps needed to produce *care*, *caring*, *tar* and *tarring*:

(13)

|  | care | caring | tar | tarring |
|---|---|---|---|---|
| a. Underlying: | / k e r / | / k e r / | / t ɑ r / | / t ɑ r / |
| b. Rule (10): | [ keər ] | [ keər ] | (*n/a*) | (*n/a*) |
| c. Rule (12): | [ kɛər ] | [kɛər ] | (*n/a*) | (*n/a*) |
| d. Rule (9): | [ kɛəɾ ] | (*n/a*) | [ taɾ ] | (*n/a*) |
| e. Surface: | [ kɛə ] | [ kɛər ] | [ tɑ ] | [ tɑr ] |

As was noted above, a full account of nonrhotic /r/ in terms of a generative theory would have had to include the derivation of lax vowels such as those in *bird*, *herd*, *church* and *butter*. Moreover, such an account should also address the problem of 'intrusive /r/', which is intimately connected with nonrhoticism (see sect. 9.3.2.1). We do not go into such details in this demonstration, which is intended to be a mere sketch of a possible derivation in a generative framework; let us instead review briefly the derivational devices that have been employed in this section. As in our account of [ŋ] in section 10.2.1 above, we have used the device of **rule ordering**, if in somewhat more intricate form: both Laxing (12) and /r/-Deletion (9) must be ordered after Centring Diphthongisation (10) – the former because it refers crucially to the inserted [ə], and the latter because the /r/ must not be deleted before it has had a chance to trigger Centring Diphthongisation. Note, however, that Laxing and /r/-Deletion are not ordered with respect to each other: neither rule makes any reference to the input or output of the other. The ordering of steps (c) and (d) in the derivation (13) above could have been reversed without adverse affects. Again, as in the case of the [ŋ] derivation, we have used a **deletion rule** (namely (9)); but there are two devices that occur here for the first time: an **insertion rule** – (10) – and a **feature-changing rule**, (12). No such rule occurred in the derivation of [ŋ]. Rule (4b), producing [ŋ] out of the archiphoneme /N/, did not actually change any features of the underlying /N/ but merely filled a blank in its feature specification: /N/ is characterised as a nasal without a place of articulation specification (recall sect. 8.5).

### 10.2.3 *The Vowel-Shift derivation*

Our final case study of generative derivations is concerned with vowel alternations of the type *serene* – *serenity*, exemplified in (2) above. This is one of the best known and also one of the most complex derivations ever proposed in the generative phonology of English. The account given here simplifies those found in the relevant literature in two ways. Firstly, this account will be couched in the representational framework familiar from earlier chapters of this book; the discussion will not include the different representational assumptions made in the literature but, rather, be strictly confined to the derivational aspects of such vowel alternations. And secondly, out of the range of relevant vowel alternations given in the (still incomplete) list in (2) above, we shall only discuss the two alternating pairs exemplified below:

(14)  a. serene – serenity  
   obscene – obscenity  
   appeal – appellative  } [i]–[ɛ]  
   metre – metrical  
   deep – depth  

   b. concave – concavity  
   profane – profanity  
   compare – comparative  } [e]–[a]  
   explain – explanatory  
   sane – sanity  

There is a two-way distinction between the members of both these pairs of vowels: in both pairs, the first member is tense and the second lax; and the first member is higher than the second. Thus, /i/ is [+ tense, + high, – low] while /ɛ/ is [– tense, – high, – low], and /e/ is [+ tense, – high, – low] while /a/ is [– tense, – high, + low]. (The long–short distinction that accompanies the tense–lax distinction in RP and GA is here irrelevant.) If we are to derive the members of each pair from a common underlier (which is not necessarily identical with either surface vowel) then we have to confront a fairly complex set of feature changes. Let us again first map out the path that our derivation will take and then discuss the details.

Let us assume, for the moment without discussion, that the vowel underlying the [i]–[ɛ] pair is /e/, [+ tense, − high, − low], and that the vowel underlying the [e]–[a] pair is [+ tense, − high, + low], here transcribed as /ā/. Note that none of the phonemic inventories of English discussed in chapters 3 and 4 above contained such a phoneme: this vowel can never surface without derivational changes to its feature composition. For the moment, this is not a problem; but it will be one later on. To derive [i] and [ɛ] (as in *serene – serenity*) from /e/ we first have to devise a rule that laxes the underlying /e/ in *serenity* but allows that in *serene* to remain tense; and a further rule, which we shall call Tense-Vowel Shift, must raise the vowel in *serene* from /e/ to [i] – without, however, raising the laxed vowel in *serenity*. Similarly, in *sane – sanity* the laxing rule must produce [a] from underlying /ā/ in *sanity*, whereas in *sane* the /ā/ must rise to [e]. Here is a summary of this derivation:

(15)

| | serene | serenity | sane | sanity |
|---|---|---|---|---|
| a. Underlying vowel: | /e/ | /e/ | /ā/ | /ā/ |
| b. Laxing: | *(n/a)* | [ɛ] | *(n/a)* | [a] |
| c. Tense-Vowel Shift: | [i] | *(n/a)* | [e] | *(n/a)* |
| d. Surface vowel: | [i] | [ɛ] | [e] | [a] |

Let us deal with the laxing rule first. What all the instances in (14) where Laxing must apply have in common (except for one: *depth*) is that the vowel in question is part of a trisyllabic foot – each time, the vowel that is to be laxed is followed by two unstressed syllables. We may formulate our rule as follows:

(16) *Trisyllabic Laxing*

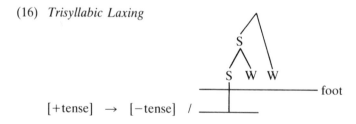

This rule will lax any underlyingly tense vowel that occurs in such a 'trisyllabic' context; but it does not affect vowels that do not occur in such contexts. Hence, the stressed vowels in *serenity*, *sanity* etc. are laxed, while their counterparts in *serene, sane* remain tense. In a full account, further rules would be required to serve this part of the derivation: we would not only require another laxing rule to deal with cases such as *depth*, but also rules that, conversely, turn underlyingly lax vowels into tense ones in certain contexts. We do not discuss these rules here but will briefly return to them later.

Turning now to Tense-Vowel Shift, we have to account for the derivations of /e/ to [i] and of /ā/ to [e]. The rules are given in (17) below, where (17a) handles the former derivation and (17b) the latter:

(17)   *Tense-Vowel Shift*

a.
$$\begin{bmatrix} - \text{ consonantal} \\ + \text{ tense} \\ - \text{ high} \\ - \text{ low} \end{bmatrix} \rightarrow [+ \text{ high}]$$

b.
$$\begin{bmatrix} - \text{ consonantal} \\ + \text{ tense} \\ - \text{ high} \\ + \text{ low} \end{bmatrix} \rightarrow [- \text{ low}]$$

We now have three rules: Trisyllabic Laxing (16), as well as the two rules of Tense-Vowel Shift (17a, b). The chart below illustrates their interaction in the derivation:

(18)

|  | serene | serenity | sane | sanity |
|---|---|---|---|---|
| a. Underlying vowel: | /e/ | /e/ | /ā/ | /ā/ |
| b. Laxing: | (*n/a*) | [ɛ] | (*n/a*) | [a] |
| c. Tense-Vowel Shift (a): | [i] | (*n/a*) | (*n/a*) | (*n/a*) |
| d. Tense-Vowel Shift (b): | (*n/a*) | (*n/a*) | [e] | (*n/a*) |
| e. Surface vowel: | [i] | [ɛ] | [e] | [a] |

Again, a specific order has to be imposed on the application of the three rules. Trisyllabic Laxing must apply first: the vowels in *serenity* and *sanity* must be laxed before Tense-Vowel Shift has a chance to apply to them. Moreover, Tense-Vowel Shift (a) must be ordered before Tense-Vowel Shift (b): if their order were reversed then the vowel in *sane* would shift twice: rule (b) would change it from /ā/ to [e]; and, being [− high, − low], this [e] would then go through rule (a) and *sane* would wrongly surface as *[sin]. This problem is avoided if the two rules are ordered as in (18) above.

An interesting question arises now: is there really only one way to account for this set of vowel alternations? Or is there an alternative? There is – one, even, that has considerably less abstract and therefore more plausible underliers. Consider the following derivation:

(19)

|  | serene | serenity | sane | sanity |
|---|---|---|---|---|
| a. Underlying vowel: | /i/ | /i/ | /e/ | /e/ |
| b. Laxing: | (n/a) | /ɪ/ | (n/a) | [ɛ] |
| c. Lax-Vowel Shift (a): | (n/a) | (n/a) | (n/a) | [a] |
| d. Lax-Vowel Shift (b): | (n/a) | [ɛ] | (n/a) | (n/a) |
| e. Surface vowel: | [i] | [ɛ] | [e] | [a] |

What is different here is the task performed by the two Vowel-Shift rules. While in our first account these rules raised tense vowels, their counterparts in this version of the derivation affect *lax* vowels by *lowering* them. The new rules, alternative to (17), are given below:

(20)  *Lax-Vowel Shift*

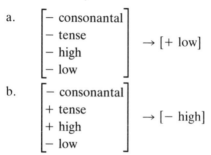

a.
$$\begin{bmatrix} - \text{ consonantal} \\ - \text{ tense} \\ - \text{ high} \\ - \text{ low} \end{bmatrix} \rightarrow [+ \text{ low}]$$

b.
$$\begin{bmatrix} - \text{ consonantal} \\ + \text{ tense} \\ + \text{ high} \\ - \text{ low} \end{bmatrix} \rightarrow [- \text{ high}]$$

Rule (20a) derives [a] from [ɛ] (*sanity*), (20b) [ɛ] from [i] (*serenity*). This appears to be only a minor change of derivational strategy; but its consequences are interesting. *Serene* now has an underlying /i/ and *sane* an underlying /e/, a rather more plausible proposition: the morphologically simple forms *serene* and *sane* now undergo no phonological rules – their underlying forms are identical with their surface forms – and the phonological derivations of *serenity* and *sanity* reflect the intuition that here the vowels change *because of* the attachment of *-ity*: this attachment triggers the laxing rule, whose output in turn undergoes Lax-Vowel Shift.

To evaluate these two alternative approaches to the *sane – sanity* problem, let us extend our data base for a moment. Consider the alternation found in the second vowels in *Canada – Canadian*. As in *sane – sanity*, we have an alternation of [a] and [e] here (although the [a] in *Canada* is subject to a reduction to [ə], not here discussed, for most speakers); what distinguishes the two pairs is that in *sanity* the underlyingly tense vowel (of *sane*) is laxed while in *Canadian* an underlyingly lax vowel (*Canada*) is tensed, by a Tensing rule that we need not formulate here. In (21a) below is a derivation involving Tense-Vowel Shift (17); in (21b) the alternative derivation involving Lax-Vowel Shift (20).

(21)  a.

| | | Canada | Canadian |
|---|---|---|---|
| | Underlying vowel: | /a/ | /a/ |
| | Tensing: | (n/a) | [ā] |
| | Tense–Vowel Shift (b): | (n/a) | [e] |
| | Surface vowel: | [a] | [e] |

  b.

| | | Canada | Canadian |
|---|---|---|---|
| | Underlying vowel: | /ɛ/ | /ɛ/ |
| | Tensing: | (n/a) | [e] |
| | Lax-Vowel Shift (a): | [a] | (n/a) |
| | Surface vowel: | [a] | [e] |

Here, again, either analysis accounts for the facts. As for our intuitive preference, however, the picture is reversed: while in *sane – sanity* the analysis involving Lax-Vowel Shift was the more attractive one in that it allowed the rather realistic underlying representation /sen/, here it is the analysis using Tense-Vowel Shift, shown in (21a) above, whose underlying representation is the more attractive one. The Lax-Vowel Shift alternative forces us here to represent the stressed vowel in *Canada* underlyingly as /ɛ/.

To make matters worse, the choice that we have to make involves not two alternative analyses but three. We might use Tense-Vowel Shift in both *sane – sanity* and *Canada – Canadian*. This seems preferable as regards the latter pair but unattractive as regards the former. Or we might use Lax-Vowel Shift in both pairs. This seems preferable in the former pair but unattractive in the latter. Or we might use Lax-Vowel Shift in the former and Tense-Vowel Shift in the latter! This would combine the attractive features of both analyses – realistic underliers in all cases – but there would be a price to pay: we would lose the generalisation that *sane – sanity* and *Canada – Canadian* are subject to the same phonological regularity. Our phonology of English would have to contain both pairs of vowel-shift rules – (17) *and* (20). The theory of Generative Phonology has for long rated the simplicity and generality of its rule systems above all else – if a generalisation can be made then it *must* be made, even at the expense of rather abstract underliers. What we found unattractive in the two derivations presented above has not been regarded as a problem by generative phonologists, who in the interest of simplicity–generality would have favoured either of the first two over the third possibility involving both Vowel Shifts.

### 10.2.4 *Constraining derivational power: free rides and derived environments*

Generative phonologies are powerful. Abstract underliers, feature-changing rules, rule ordering, deletion rules, insertion rules, reference to nonphonological information – such a battery of devices adds up to a phonological theory that seems able to account for almost anything, if in a way that is at times rather less than insightful. If we accept the assumption that the *sane – sanity* and *Canada – Canadian* alternations discussed above constitute a phonological problem – and recall that not all phonologists do – we are still faced with (at least) three different possibilities of tackling the problem, none of which is superior to the others in an objectively measurable way. There is hardly any point in producing highly formal derivations if the evaluation of competing derivations is then subject to vague notions such as personal preference. Talking of preference, what we would prefer is a more constrained theory – one that, rather than allowing as many alternative analyses of any given problem as an imaginative analyst may care to devise, permits (maximally) one analysis, ruling out any alternative analyses as unacceptable under the theory. This is a tall order; and here is not the place to develop such a theory. However, a few thoughts to this end are clearly called for. Restricting our discussion to the devices invoked in connection with the vowel-shift alternations, let us ask ourselves what caused this excess of possible analyses.

Clearly, the main problem lies in the fact that in Generative Phonology, as it stands, phonological rules are allowed to apply freely in morphologically simple words. To go back to *sane – sanity*, what made our first analysis unattractive was the fact that it derived *sane* [sen] from underlying [sān], through Tense-Vowel Shift, rather than taking the more realistic underlier /sen/ as its starting point. Given that *sanity* is (morphologically) derived from *sane*, the stressed vowel in *sanity* should be phonologically derived from that found in *sane*.

The problem is actually worse than it has looked so far. Consider words such as *play*, *name* and *frail*, all containing tense [e]. In any generative phonology of English that contains Tense-Vowel Shift (17), these words must be derived from underlying /plā/, /nām/, /frāl/ although they never engage in alternations of the *sanity* type that would warrant such an abstract analysis, where underlying forms differ from surface forms. And if we represented them as /ple/, /nem/ and /frel/ then Tense-Vowel Shift would produce *[pli], *[nim] and *[fril] unless we marked them as exceptions to this rule. As it happens, the vast majority of English words containing tense vowels would have to be marked as Vowel-Shift exceptions – vowel alternations only occur in a small, mainly Latinate, subsection of the vocabulary. This is the **free-ride** problem of Generative Phonology. To avoid large-scale exception marking for rules that are not fully productive, words are allowed to take 'free rides' through derivations. Such words then have underlying forms whose abstractness – that is, remoteness from the surface form – is not justified through any phonological alternations. Clearly, this is undesirable: Generative Phonology should not allow *play* to have an underlying representation other than /ple/

The Tense-Vowel Shift rule is not the only one of our rules to be beset with the free-ride problem. Lax-Vowel Shift faces similar problems in nonalternating words containing lax vowels. Moreover, consider again the rule of Trisyllabic Laxing, (16) above. This rule brings about the laxness of the stressed vowel in *sanity*; but if we leave it unconstrained it will also wrongly affect the stressed vowels in *nightingale, ivory, Oberon* etc. Moreover, the stressed lax vowels in words such as *camera, pedestal, pelican* etc. will be derived from underlyingly tense ones – /ā/ for *camera* and /e/ for *pedestal, pelican* – through free rides.

What our phonological theory needs is an automatic derivational constraint that blocks Trisyllabic Laxing in *nightingale* and *ivory* as well as ruling out the possibility of spurious derivation of the lax stressed vowels in *camera* and *pedestal* from underlyingly tense vowels. Going back to Tense-Vowel Shift, this constraint should rule out free-ride derivations such as *play* from /plā/, as well as reducing the number of derivational options available in *sane – sanity* and *Canada – Canadian*. Here is such a constraint:

(22)   *Derived-Environment Condition*

Feature-changing rules apply in derived environments only,

where a **derived environment** may be defined as an environment created by a morphological derivation or by a previously applied feature-changing rule (which will in turn have been subject to (22)). What does the Derived-Environment Condition do for us?

It constrains Trisyllabic Laxing in such a way as to permit the rule to produce the lax vowels in *sanity, serenity* etc., but to block its application in *nightingale*; moreover, the spurious derivation of the lax vowel in *camera* through Trisyllabic Laxing is ruled out. The 'trisyllabic' environment of the stressed vowel in *sanity, serenity* is brought about by the attachment of the morpheme {-ity} to the morphemes {sane}, {serene} etc. while in both *nightingale* and *camera* the trisyllabic environments are 'underlying' rather than 'derived'. For Trisyllabic Laxing, then, (22) makes exactly the right predictions within our corpus of data; but what about Vowel Shift, in its various forms and derivations discussed in section 10.2.3?

Let us take the original, Tense-Vowel Shift analysis first. This rule is barred by the Derived-Environment Condition from applying in *serene* and *sane*: these therefore cannot be underlyingly /sɪren/ and /sān/ respectively and the analysis given in (18) above is ruled out. On the other hand, Tense-Vowel Shift is not blocked in *Canadian* ((21a) above): here, a tensing rule turns the underlying /a/ of *Canada* into [ā]. We have not discussed this rule, but assuming its operation has to do with the attachment of *-ian*, we may also assume that the Derived-Environment Condition does not block it. Then Tense-Vowel Shift turns this [ā], which is not 'underlying' but 'derived' (through the Tensing rule), into [e]. Condition (22) thus blocks the undesirable derivation of *sane* from /sān/, but it does not interfere with the derivation of *Canadian* from /kanada/, which earlier we found to be more acceptable.

As for Lax-Vowel Shift, this rule is blocked exactly in those cases where its tense competitor is permitted, and, vice versa, it is permitted where Tense-Vowel Shift is blocked: Lax-Vowel Shift applies in a derived environment in *sanity* – (19) above – in that its input has been produced by Trisyllabic Laxing; but in *Canada* (21b) the rule is blocked.

Recall that at the end of our Vowel-Shift discussion in section 10.2.3, we were left with a choice between three possible analyses: that involving Tense-Vowel Shift throughout, that involving Lax-Vowel Shift throughout and that involving both. The last option is characterised, as we saw, by lesser simplicity–generality, but it has the advantage of operating from plausible underlying forms. The Derived-Environment Condition forces us to adopt this option. A generative phonology of English containing this condition is unable to produce the first two of the three options; and in a wider sense, such a phonology bans free rides, thereby severely constraining the choice of possible underlying representations in every morpheme of the language.

The story of derivational constraints does not end here; indeed, its end is to date probably unwritten. Further constraints have been proposed; and the one discussed here – the Derived-Environment Condition – has been shown to be in need of further refinement. As it stands, its blocking effect on phonological rules is not strong enough. Consider once again Trisyllabic Laxing. The Derived-Environment Condition correctly bars any application of this rule in the derivations of *nightingale* as well as *camera*; and – equally correctly – it allows the rule to operate in derived forms such as *sanity, serenity, appellative* etc. But it also permits (and therefore wrongly *predicts*) Laxing in *evenly, leaderless, laziness, nationhood* (but compare *national!*) and many other such morphologically complex forms, where in reality no laxing takes place. It would seem that certain morphological derivations produce environments for Trisyllabic Laxing to operate in while others – such as the attachment of *-ly, -less, -ness, -hood* – do not. If we assume that the difference in behaviour of *nationhood* and *national*, with regard to Laxing, lies in the nature of the morphological suffix, then our discussion should now shift into the area of morphology. We do not perform this shift in focus here; suffice it to say that recent Generative Phonology, in pursuit of the derivational constraints whose necessity should have become clear in this discussion, has indeed made this shift in focus. Concerned with the phonological regularities found within recurrent morphological units, a generative phonological theory that contains powerful derivational devices also needs derivational constraints; and these must not only themselves be powerful but also sophisticated in their reference to the nature of morphological units. This is the theory of **Lexical Phonology**: a recent variant of Generative Phonology notable for its close interaction between morphological and phonological derivations. However, rather than further mapping the history of derivational thought in phonological theory, let us now turn to the second ingredient of phonological theories: representations.

### 10.3 More on phonological representations

We noted earlier that the phonological theory pursued in the previous chapters of this book may be characterised as fairly unsophisticated on the derivational side. A possible way of remedying this shortcoming – if, indeed, it is to be considered a shortcoming – was suggested in section 10.2 above. As regards its representational aspect, on the other hand, our theory has been considerably more highly developed, recognising not only bundles of phonological features in linear order but also a hierarchy of higher-order phonological constituents: X-positions, syllables (with further internal structure), feet, words and phrases. These are fairly uncontroversial representational ingredients of most current phonological theories. Details differ; but rather than reviewing such differences in detail, let us return to a phonological unit that has been central to our concerns; yet our treatment of phonological representations has left it both poorly defined and – as we shall see – insufficiently structured: the segment.

### 10.3.1 *What is a segment?*

There is no straightforward phonetic answer to this question. In a 'string of segments' such as (RP/GA) *pain* [pʰeɪn], the boundaries between what we have been viewing as discrete units are by no means clear-cut; and the phonetic events occurring between these (rather fuzzy) boundaries are neither homogeneous nor equal in duration. Boundaries are blurred, for example, by the fact that the voicing of the vowel does not begin at the same time as the [p] is released (the phenomenon of 'aspiration'); moreover, the velum is lowered (resulting in the 'nasalisation' of the vowel) well before alveolar closure marks, in our conception, the onset of [n]. But where does the nasal 'segment' begin – with the onset of nasality or with the onset of alveolar closure? As for the content of each 'segment' (wherever we decide to place the boundaries), recall that the production of [p] involves a sequence of three events: the formation, holding and release of oral closure – three segments or one? And the vowel in *pain* is not only partially nasalised; it is also 'long' as well as, being in phonetic terms a diphthong, changing its quality during its production.

In this particular instance, the dissolution of segment boundaries and contents has been brought about derivationally in our phonological theory: representing *pain* underlyingly as /pen/ (each phoneme representing a bundle of features), we have treated aspiration and nasalisation as well as any long–short distinctions among vowels as redundant phenomena; moreover, we have represented the [eɪ] as an underlying monophthong. The heterogeneity of [p] we have ignored, except for noting that such stops may occasionally – and again allophonically – remain unreleased. However, this assumption whereby underlying representations are discrete and internally homogeneous feature bundles does not solve the problem: our phonological theory operates with discrete feature bundles throughout the phonological derivation, representing surface-phonetic forms inappropriately in basically the same way and enforcing the notion of 'segments' even in cases where phonetic phenomena such as the ones discussed above patently go against it.

This assumption of an essentially 'segment-based' phonological theory ran into a further problem when, in chapter 6, the X-tier was introduced into phonological representations. While in the absence of this device (for example, in underlying representations as we have defined them) any feature bundle may be identified as a 'segment', the X-tier makes such a simple definition impossible. Consider the following:

(23) a.   X    b.   X    c.  X   X

       [ n ]    [ t   ʃ ]    [ i ]

We have no problem identifying [n] (23a) as a single segment: here, one feature bundle corresponds to one X-position. But is an affricate – the association of two feature bundles with a single X-position, as in (23b) – two 'segments' or one? Is a 'long' vowel, a single feature bundle associated with two X-positions as in (23c), one segment or two? And are these important questions to ask?

Given the problems that the notion of the 'segment' faces in phonetic terms, the answer to the last question is probably negative: nothing hinges, in our representational framework, on our answers to the first two questions or, in general, on our decisions as to what building blocks of our phonological representations we call 'segments'. In a phonological theory that recognises a feature tier as well as an X-tier, the segment is an informal, ambiguous (if at times nevertheless quite useful) notion. In the following paragraphs, our discussion will remain focussed on feature bundles and X-positions – thereby retaining its concern with 'segments' even in the absence of an unambiguous definition. However, far from sharpening our understanding of the 'segment', this discussion will further undermine this notion.

### 10.3.2 *Features and the X-tier*

According to our previous assumptions, a given feature bundle may either be associated with a single X-position ((23a) above); or it may share an X-position with another feature bundle (23b); or a complete feature bundle may be 'spread' over two X-positions (23c). Any association of features with X-positions has always been assumed to hold for the *entire* feature bundle: neighbouring X-positions have been allowed to share an entire feature bundle; but if they had fewer than *all* features in common then their feature bundles were analysed as entirely separate. Consider the following examples:

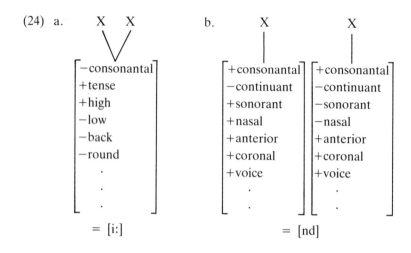

(24)  a.    X   X                    b.        X               X

$$\begin{bmatrix} -\text{consonantal} \\ +\text{tense} \\ +\text{high} \\ -\text{low} \\ -\text{back} \\ -\text{round} \\ \cdot \\ \cdot \\ \cdot \end{bmatrix}$$

$$= \text{[i:]}$$

$$\begin{bmatrix} +\text{consonantal} \\ -\text{continuant} \\ +\text{sonorant} \\ +\text{nasal} \\ +\text{anterior} \\ +\text{coronal} \\ +\text{voice} \\ \cdot \\ \cdot \end{bmatrix} \begin{bmatrix} +\text{consonantal} \\ -\text{continuant} \\ -\text{sonorant} \\ -\text{nasal} \\ +\text{anterior} \\ +\text{coronal} \\ +\text{voice} \\ \cdot \\ \cdot \end{bmatrix}$$

$$= \text{[nd]}$$

In (24a) we have two X-positions, each of which is associated with the features characterising [i]; but rather than representing this configuration in terms of two identical feature bundles – therefore as [ii] – we have allowed these X-positions to share one bundle. In (24b) we have again two X-positions. Both of these are associated with [+ consonantal, − continuant, + anterior, + coronal, + voice] etc.; but since they differ in terms of sonorancy and nasality, their *entire* feature matrices are kept separate in our representation. Returning to the vexed question of boundaries between 'segments', (24a) expresses the fact that no phonetic divide occurs between the two X-positions; but (24b) states that while there is a point in the production of [nd] at which [+ sonorant] changes to [− sonorant] and [+ nasal] to [− nasal], the same point is also of significance where consonantality, voicing, anteriority etc. of [nd] are concerned. Clearly, this makes no phonetic sense.

In phonological terms, a representation such as (24b) above implies that for any two neighbouring X-positions not sharing a feature bundle, the identity of certain features and the difference of others is entirely accidental: partial identity of feature bundles has no representational consequences. That this implication is unsatisfactory can be shown with respect to phonotactic constraints as well as allophonic rules of English. Here are some examples.

Obstruent sequences not containing syllable or morpheme boundaries (and in some cases even containing morpheme boundaries) must agree in terms of voicing: such sequences must be either voiceless throughout (as in (25a) below) or voiced throughout (25b):

(25)  a. still    *[sd zt]           b. shrubs  *[bs pz]
      spill    *[sb zp]             adze    *[ds tz]
      skill    *[sg zk]             Bloggs  *[gs kz]
      text     *[ksd kzt gst] etc.   loves   *[vs fz]
      lisp     *[sb zp]             loved   *[vt fd]
      flask    *[sg zk]
      laughs   *[fz vs]
      laughed  *[fd vt]

A phonotactic constraint as pervasive as this one, holding in onsets as well as rhymes, surely cannot be treated as an accident. An 'obstruent sequence' should clearly be characterised as a single phonological unit, with recurrent behaviour, rather than as an accidental concatenation of two feature bundles both of which contain the feature [− sonorant]. The 'recurrent behaviour' of such a unit is its identity in terms of voicing. Below is a statement of this generalisation – further calling into question any notion that the feature bundle represents the 'segment'.

(26)

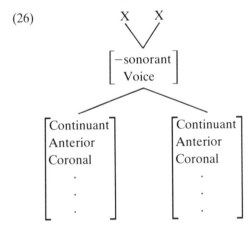

Any feature not specified in (26) is freely variable (although there may be further constraints that are irrelevant here). The important point expressed in (26) is that obstruent sequences, if assumed to be phonological units of the form given here, *must*, rather than may, agree in voicing: a structure such as this one does not permit voicing disagreement. A structure such as this one, then, correctly reflects the obligatory voicing agreement in such sequences in English while a sequence of two separate feature matrices would fail to express this obligatoriness. Of course, both matrices might contain the specification [− voice], or both [+ voice]; but the representation would also allow two further (but ill-formed) possibilities.

Another phonotactic constraint in English which is equally poorly expressed in terms of entirely separate feature bundles involves nasal-plus-stop 'sequences' not containing morpheme or syllable boundaries: in any such sequence, the nasal's place of articulation must agree with that of the following stop.

(27)  think       *[ŋg ŋp ŋb ŋd ŋt]
      camp        *[mb mk mg md mt]
      mint, bend  *[nb np nk ng]

Some further regularities may be identified in such cases: [mb] cannot occur in the syllable rhyme but is possible if divided by a syllable boundary (*amber*); [ŋg] behaves similarly in most accents of English; and [ŋ] may possibly be derived from underlying /ng/ or /nk/ (see section 10.2.1 above). Ignoring such possibilities of further refinement, we may state the relevant constraint as follows:

(28)

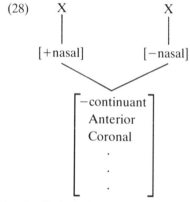

Within the limits of the data given in (27) above, any nasal-plus-stop 'sequence' must have the form (28). Notice that the only feature that is nonredundantly sequential in such a 'sequence' is the nasality specification. Redundantly, the sonorancy specification will also be sequential ([+ sonorant] following from [+ nasal], [− sonorant] from [− nasal]; the voicing specification is redundantly 'plus' in the [+ nasal] slot but either 'plus' or 'minus' in the [− nasal] slot. What we have in (28) is, once again, the simplest possible expression of the basic generalisation contained in the list (27): in a sequence of the form '[+ nasal]–[− nasal]', where both are [− continuant], features referring to places of articulation *must* be the same. Note again that the alternative representation involving two entirely separate feature bundles would fail to predict this fact of English phonotactics: in such a statement, any two corresponding feature specifications may or may not be the same; and even if we specified all place features identically the representation would still allow for a number of nonidentical alternatives which cannot exist in English.

Let us, finally, turn to some allophonic rules. We noted in our discussion of assimilatory processes in English (sect. 8.2.2 above) that such processes are governed in English by a single principle (namely, that assimilations are *anticipatory*, such that segments anticipate features of following segments rather than carrying features over from preceding segments); and we formulated this principle schematically as follows:

(29)  $/X/ \rightarrow [+ F] / \underline{\quad} [+ F]$

But this statement is unsatisfactory on several counts. Firstly, it does not have the status of a rule, given that its input, its output, the effected change as well as the environment in which the change happens are not fully characterised. Example (29) is merely the general scheme which assimilation rules adhere to. Secondly, as a scheme it is, in the light of the representational refinements we have just discussed, inappropriate. Given the possibility for X-positions to share certain features while not sharing others, we would wish to characterise assimilation as the spread of features onto the preceding X-position, rather than the copying of features of the second matrix into the first matrix, as our earlier formulation (29) suggests. Apart from resulting in a more elegant and, in phonetic terms, more sensible statement, this would also express an important point made in section 9.4: assimilation is an instance of **structure simplification** in connected speech: a given X-position loses part of its own featural specification, sharing instead the corresponding part of its right neighbour's specification. Let us accordingly reformulate the Assimilation Principle as in (30) below, where [E] and [F] stand for 'specifications of corresponding features':

(30)  *Assimilation Principle*

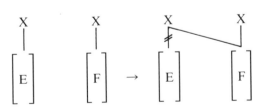

Thus, the [− nasal] specification of a given X-position may be 'delinked' and replaced by a linkage with the [+ nasal] specification of the right-hand neighbour. This is a 'nasal assimilation': [hãnd]. Or, an X-position may delink one or more of its place of articulation features and, again, link with those of its right-hand neighbour instead. Voicing assimilations may be expressed in the same way: compare *of* [ɒf] *course* and *of* [ɒv] *all*. Note that (26) and (28) above are static wellformedness conditions, which no phonological representation is allowed to violate, while (30) is a scheme for a set of possible phonological *rules*: in the course of a phonological derivation, a given feature (or set of features) underlyingly linked with a given X-position may be delinked and replaced by the neighbour's feature(s). As we saw in chapter 8, such rules may be optional.

It is possible, of course, to eliminate rules of this form from the phonology (thus dispensing with part of the derivational side of the phonology) and to reformulate them as 'permitted but nonobligatory configurations' (to avoid the term 'optional wellformedness conditions'), as in (31) below. This is an aside here, intended to point to the possibility that enrichments of the representational side of phonological theory may make some (or perhaps even all) of its derivational side superfluous. Again, the success of such a strategy will depend on the assumed scope of the phonological component of the grammar – recall some remarks on this subject in section 10.1 above. We do not pursue such questions here, but note, merely, that the derivational and representational sides of phonological theory are perhaps not quite as independent of each other as has so far been implied. Here is the statement of a 'permitted configuration' that may replace the Assimilation Principle (30) – note that the term 'assimilation', implying a process, is no longer applicable here:

(31)  *Permitted configuration*

where 'F' again stands for 'certain features'. But *what* features? Example (31) and its derivational counterpart (30) still fail to specify the range of possible assimilatory phenomena in English – in representational terms, the range of features that might be implicated in (30)/(31); they represent a principle rather than a clearly defined rule, or set of rules, and are in that respect (if not in representational terms) no better than the formulation (29). Is any feature as likely to be involved in assimilatory processes as any other?

### 10.3.3 *Do feature matrices have structure?*

The question that arose above, in connection with assimilatory processes, may be rephrased in more general terms. Are feature matrices unstructured, such that features may be listed in random order, any two features being as related (or as unrelated) to each other as any two others are? Or does a feature matrix have an internal structure? Such an internal structure might have the form of **submatrices**, whose members are more closely related to each other than they are to the members of other submatrices; evidence for such internal structure of feature matrices would be, for example, the recurrent involvement of whole submatrices in phonological generalisations. If phonological generalisations can be shown to involve recurrent groups of features then these groups should have the status of phonological units in our analysis – the status of submatrices in the feature tier. Does a feature matrix, then, look like (32a), as so far we have been assuming it does, or like (32b) below?

(32)   a.   b.

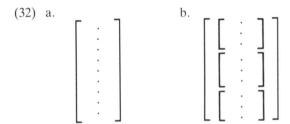

The feature matrix in (32b) is divided into submatrices, which in turn contain the features. In this example we happen to have three such submatrices; but if the proposal of such structure is adopted then we have to decide how many submatrices there are and, of course, how the set of features that we have been using is to be divided up among them.

When we developed our feature system in chapters 4 and 5 above, the possibility of submatrices was not considered. But by not assuming the presence of any structure within the feature matrix we failed to acknowledge in our phonology the fact that in *phonetic* terms, features do indeed fall into distinct groups. We had seen this as early as in chapter 1, where we had distinguished four distinct processes in the production of speech sounds: the **initiation, phonation, oro-nasal** and **articulation** processes. Of these, we may safely ignore the first: as we saw in chapter 1, the only type of initiation that is systematically used in the production of English speech is one of a pulmonic egressive air stream; this process is therefore not subject to featural distinctions in English. But the other three processes are clearly phonologically relevant in English: within the phonation process we have distinguished [+ voice] and [− voice]; within the oro-nasal process we have the distinctive feature [Nasal]; and within the articulatory process the rest of our features, further subdivided into 'place' and 'manner' of articulation. But, again, is such a grouping of features into submatrices *phonologically* relevant? And is *this particular* grouping the one most appropriate to the expression of generalisations? Given that the set of features used in our phonology is not precisely that used in the phonetic descriptions of chapter 1, the different processes might similarly be in need of revision.

Some evidence has, in fact, accrued in the preceding chapters for groupings of this kind. In particular, we have seen that the various features specifying places of articulation frequently function together in phonological generalisations. Certain sequences of the form 'nasal plus stop' must have the same place of articulation – recall (28) above. Place of articulation features are typically involved in assimilatory processes (along with nasality and voicing). Quite commonly, phonological generalisations in English and its history are conditional on two adjacent segments having 'the same place of articulation' or 'different places of articulation', without any *particular* place of articulation being specified. Note that such a recurrent condition cannot be stated satisfactorily unless features, or groups of features, are allowed to spread over two X-positions (recall the arguments given in sect. 10.3.2 above), and unless the recurrent nature of this group of features is expressed in terms of a 'Place' submatrix. Without such a unit, the representational theory makes the false prediction that the 'Place' group of features is merely a random subset of the whole set of features, no more recurrent in phonological generalisations than any other random subset of features. Is there, then, a submatrix 'Articulation', as was suggested in chapter 1, or are 'Place' and 'Manner' distinct submatrices? Probably, they are distinct: place and manner features rarely function together in phonological generalisations: unlike the place features, those specifying manners of articulation have, as we saw in chapter 6, a mainly classificatory function relevant, for example, in the statement of syllable templates. Indeed, it is a recurrent condition in certain phonological generalisations that place features must be the same but manner features different, or vice versa. For example, it is an important phonotactic constraint in English that two identical consonants ('geminate consonants') cannot occur adjacently in the same syllable. Rather tentatively, then, we may suggest that feature matrices have something like the following structure:

(33)
$$\begin{bmatrix} [ & \text{Manner} & ] \\ [ & \text{Place} & ] \\ [ & \text{Phonation} & ] \\ [ & \text{Oro-nasality} & ] \end{bmatrix}$$

All except [Manner] are likely to be involved in assimilatory processes. That does not mean, of course, that we have established the distinctness of the [Phonation] and [Oro-nasality] submatrices here; nor can we claim purely on the basis of English assimilations that either of them is distinct from the [Manner] submatrix. (Assimilation may in any case, depending on speech style, tempo etc., be more far-reaching than we have acknowledged: recall the discussion of connected speech in chapter 9.) And as we have seen, the mere fact that they were treated as distinct in our rather informal phonetic discussion in chapter 1 has no strong implications regarding our phonological grouping of features.

Having seen the type of argument that may lead to the establishment of submatrices in phonological representations, we do not pursue this line of enquiry any further. But we are, at least, left with the strong possibility that phonological theory should allow for representations that are more highly structured than those used in the earlier chapters of this book were. Indeed, recent phonological theory (under headings such as **Dependency Phonology** and **Autosegmental Phonology**) is notable for such an interest in (and proliferation of) representational devices, to some extent at the expense of derivational devices, and in particular concerning the structure of 'segments' – whatever those are.

### Suggested reading to chapter 10

Section 10.2   On Generative Phonology, abstractness etc. see Lass (1984: ch. 9), Sommerstein (1977: chs. 6, 9) and Durand (1990: ch. 4). Chomsky and Halle (1968) is the classic major work in this theory; on the vowel-shift derivation for tense vowels see their chapter 4 (summarised in Durand 1990: ch. 4); also Halle (1977), addressing the problems posed by the feature [Tense]. The rule of Lax-Vowel Shift, and much of the argument in section 10.2.3, are due to McMahon (1990).

Section 10.2.4   On free rides see Zwicky (1970); on the theory of Lexical Phonology and the Derived-Environment Condition (in the literature called

'Strict Cycle Condition') see Durand (1990; sect. 5.2), Kaisse and Shaw (1985), Kiparsky (1982), Mohanan (1986).

Section 10.3  For summaries of recent developments on the representational side of phonological theory see Durand (1990: chs. 7, 8), Goldsmith (1989). On Dependency Phonology, and different proposals concerning 'submatrices' (also called 'gestures'), see Lass (1984: chs. 6, 11), Anderson and Ewen (1987). For a more radical revision of phonological theory, which claims not to recognise the derivational dimension (nor, indeed, the phoneme or other forms of 'underlying' representations) see Kaye (1989).

# REFERENCES

Abercrombie, D. (1964) *English Phonetic Texts*. London: Faber and Faber.
(1965) Syllable quantity and enclitics in English. In D. Abercrombie, *Studies in Phonetics and Linguistics*. London: Oxford University Press.
(1967) *Elements of General Phonetics*. Edinburgh: Edinburgh University Press.
(1971) Some functions of silent stress. In A. J. Aitken, A. McIntosh and H. Pálsson (eds.) *Edinburgh Studies in English and Scots*. London: Longman.
(1979) The accents of Standard English in Scotland. In A. J. Aitken and T. McArthur (eds.) *Languages of Scotland*. Edinburgh: Chambers.
Abramson A. S. and L. Lisker (1970) Discriminability along the voicing continuum. In B. Hála, M. Romportl and P. Janota (eds.) *Proceedings of the Sixth International Congress of the Phonetic Sciences*. Prague: Academia.
Agutter, A. (1988) The not-so-Scottish Vowel Length Rule. In J. M. Anderson and N. Macleod (eds.) *Edinburgh Studies in the English Language*. Edinburgh: John Donald.
Aitken, A. J. (1981) The Scottish Vowel-Length Rule. In M. Benskin and M. L. Samuels (eds.) *So Meny People Longages and Tonges: Philological Essays in Scots and Medieval English Presented to Angus McIntosh*. Edinburgh: Middle English Dialect Project.
Anderson, J. M. and C. Ewen (1987) *Principles of Dependency Phonology*. Cambridge: Cambridge University Press.
Anderson, J. M. and C. Jones (1974) Three theses concerning phonological representations. *Journal of Linguistics* 10: 1–26.
Anderson, S. R. (1985) *Phonology in the Twentieth Century: Theories of Rules and Theories of Representations*. Chicago: University of Chicago Press.
Bailey, R. W. and M. Görlach (eds.) (1982) *English as a World Language*. Ann Arbor: University of Michigan Press.
Bauer, L. (1983) *English Word Formation*. Cambridge: Cambridge University Press.
Bauer, L., J. M. Dienhart, H. H. Hartvigson and L. K. Jakobsen (1980) *American English Pronunciation*. Copenhagen: Gyldendal.
Bell, A. and J. Bybee Hooper (eds.) (1978) *Syllables and Segments*. Amsterdam: North-Holland.

# References

Bronstein, A. J. (1960) *The Pronunciation of American English*. Englewood Cliffs NJ: Prentice-Hall.

Brown, G. (1990) *Listening to Spoken English*, 2nd edn. Harlow: Longman.

Catford, J. C. (1977) *Fundamental Problems in Phonetics*. Edinburgh: Edinburgh University Press.

(1988) *A Practical Course in Phonetics*. Oxford: Clarendon Press.

Chen, M. (1970) Vowel length variation as a function of the voicing of the consonant environment. *Phonetics* 22: 129–59.

Chomsky, N. and M. Halle (1968) *The Sound Pattern of English*. New York: Harper and Row.

Classe, A. (1939) *The Rhythm of English Prose*. Oxford: Blackwell.

Clements, G. N. and S. J. Keyser (1983) *CV Phonology: a Generative Theory of the Syllable*. Cambridge MA: MIT Press.

Couper-Kuhlen, E. (1986) *An Introduction to English Prosody*. London: Arnold.

Cruttenden, A. (1986) *Intonation*. Cambridge: Cambridge University Press.

Dauer, R. (1983) Stress-timing and syllable-timing reanalyzed. *Journal of Phonetics* 11: 51–62.

Davidsen-Nielsen, N. (1978) *Neutralization and Archiphoneme: Two Phonological Concepts and their History*. Copenhagen: Akademisk Forlag.

Durand, J. (1990) *Generative and Non-Linear Phonology*. Harlow: Longman.

Fallows, D. (1981) Experimental evidence for English syllabification and syllable structure. *Journal of Linguistics* 17: 309–17.

Fischer-Jørgensen, E. (1975) *Trends in Phonological Theory: a Historical Introduction*. Copenhagen: Akademisk Forlag.

Fry, D. B. (1979) *The Physics of Speech*. Cambridge: Cambridge University Press.

Fudge, E. (1969) Syllables. *Journal of Linguistics* 5: 253–86.

(1984) *English Word-Stress*. London: Allen and Unwin.

(1987) Branching structures within the syllable. *Journal of Linguistics* 23: 359–77.

Fujimura, O. (1979) An analysis of English syllables as cores and affixes. *Zeitschrift für Phonetik, Sprachwissenschaft und Kommunikationsforschung* 32: 471–6.

Giegerich, H. J. (1985) *Metrical Phonology and Phonological Structure: German and English*. Cambridge: Cambridge University Press.

(1986) Relating to metrical structure. In J. Durand (ed.) *Dependency and Non-Linear Phonology*. London: Croom Helm.

Gimson, A. C. (1989) *An Introduction to the Pronunciation of English*, 4th edn, revised by S. Samsaran. London: Arnold.

Goldsmith, J. (1989) *Autosegmental and Metrical Phonology*. Oxford: Blackwell.

Halle, M. (1977) Tenseness, vowel shift and the phonology of the back vowels in Modern English. *Linguistic Inquiry* 8: 611–25.

Halle, M. and G. N. Clements (1983) *Problem Book in Phonology*. Cambridge MA: MIT Press.

Halle, M. and J. R. Vergnaud (1987) *An Essay on Stress*. Cambridge MA: MIT Press.

Halliday, M. A. K. (1970) *A Course in Spoken English: Intonation*. Oxford: Oxford University Press.

Harms, R. T. (1968) *Introduction to Phonological Theory*. Englewood Cliffs NJ: Prentice-Hall.

Hawkins, P. (1984) *Introducing Phonology*. London: Hutchinson.

Hayes, B. (1982) Extrametricality and English stress. *Linguistic Inquiry* 13: 227–76.

(1984) The phonology of rhythm in English. *Linguistic Inquiry* 15: 33–74.

Higginbottom, E. M. (1965) Glottal reinforcement in English. *Transactions of the Philological Society* 129–42.

Hoard, J. E. (1971) Aspiration, tenseness and syllabification in English. *Language* 47: 133–40.

Hogg, R. and C. B. McCully (1987) *Metrical Phonology: a Coursebook*. Cambridge: Cambridge University Press.

House, A. S. (1961) On vowel duration in English. *Journal of the Acoustic Society of America* 33: 1174–8.

Hughes, A. and P. Trudgill (1987) *English Accents and Dialects*, 2nd edn. London: Arnold.

Hyman, L. (1975) *Phonology: Theory and Analysis*. New York: Holt, Rinehart and Winston.

(1977) On the nature of the linguistic stress. In L. Hyman (ed.) *Studies in Stress and Accent* (Southern California Occasional Papers in Linguistics, 4). Los Angeles: Department of Linguistics, University of Southern California.

Ingria, R. (1980) Compensatory lengthening as a metrical phenomenon. *Linguistic Inquiry* 11: 465–95.

IPA (1949) *The Principles of the International Phonetic Association*. London: Department of Phonetics, University College.

Jakobson, R. and M. Halle (1964) Tenseness and laxness. In R. Jakobson, *Selected Writings*, vol. I. S'Gravenhage: Mouton.

Jones, C. (1976) Some constraints on medial consonant clusters. *Language* 52: 121–30.

Jones, D. (1977) *Everyman's English Pronouncing Dictionary*, 14th edn. London: Dent.

Kager, R. and E. Visch (1988) Metrical constituency and rhythmic adjustment. *Phonology* 5: 21–71.

Kahn, D. (1980) *Syllable-based Generalizations in English Phonology*. New York: Garland.

Kaisse, E. and P. Shaw (1985) On the theory of Lexical Phonology. *Phonology*

*Yearbook* 2: 1–30.

Kaye, J. (1989) *Phonology: a Cognitive View*. Hillsdale NJ: Erlbaum.

Kenyon, J. S. (1958) *American Pronunciation*, 10th edn. Ann Arbor MI: Wahr.

Kenyon, J. S. and T. A. Knott (1953) *A Pronouncing Dictionary of American English*. Springfield: Merriam.

Kiparsky, P. (1982) Lexical morphology and phonology. In The Linguistic Society of Korea (ed.) *Linguistics in the Morning Calm*. Seoul: Hanshin.

Knowles, G. (1987) *Patterns of Spoken English: an Introduction to English Phonetics*. Harlow: Longman.

Kreidler, C. W. (1989) *The Pronunciation of English: a Course Book in Phonology*. Oxford: Blackwell.

Ladd, D. R. (1980) *The Grammar of Intonational Meaning*. Bloomington: Indiana University Press.

Ladefoged, P. (1971) *Preliminaries to Linguistic Phonetics*. Chicago: University of Chicago Press.

(1982) *A Course in Phonetics*, 2nd edn. New York: Harcourt Brace Jovanovich.

Lass, R. (1976) *English Phonology and Phonological Theory*. Cambridge: Cambridge University Press.

(1984) *Phonology: an Introduction to Basic Concepts*. Cambridge: Cambridge University Press.

(1987) *The Shape of English: Structure and History*. London: Dent.

Leben, W. (1980) A metrical analysis of length. *Linguistic Inquiry* 11: 497–509.

Lehiste, I. (1977) Isochrony reconsidered. *Journal of Phonetics* 5: 253–63.

Levin, J. (1983) Dependent levels of representation: the skeletal tier and syllabic projections. *GLOW Newsletter* 10: 52–4.

(1985) A metrical theory of syllabicity. PhD dissertation, MIT, Cambridge MA.

Liberman, M. and A. Prince (1977) On stress and linguistic rhythm. *Linguistic Inquiry* 8: 249–336.

Lisker, L. and A. S. Abramson (1971) Distinctive features and language control. *Language* 47: 767–85.

McClure, J. D. (1979) Vowel duration in a Scottish dialect. *Journal of the International Phonetic Association* 7: 10–16.

McMahon, A. (1990) Vowel shift, free rides and strict cyclicity. *Lingua* 80: 197–225.

(1991) Lexical phonology and sound change: the case of the Scottish Vowel Length Rule. *Journal of Linguistics* 27: 29–59.

Milroy, J. (1981) *Regional Accents of English: Belfast*. Belfast: Blackstaff Press.

Mobärg, M. (1989) *English 'Standard' Pronunciations: a Study of Attitudes* (Gothenburg Studies in English). Gothenburg: Acta Universitatis Gothoburgensis.

Mohanan, K. P. (1986) *The Theory of Lexical Phonology*. Dordrecht: Reidel.

O'Connor, J. D. and J. L. M. Trim (1953) Vowel, consonant and syllable: a phonological definition. *Word* 9: 103–22.

Prator, C. H., Jr. and B. W. Robinett (1972) *Manual of American English Pronunciation*, 3rd edn. New York: Holt, Rinehart and Winston.

Poldauf, I. (1984) *English Word Stress: a Theory of Word-Stress Patterns in English*. Oxford: Pergamon Press.

Pullum, G. K. and W. A. Ladusaw (1986) *Phonetic Symbol Guide*. Chicago: University of Chicago Press.

Roach, P. (1973) Glottalization of English /p/, /t/, /k/ and /tʃ/: a reexamination. *Journal of the International Phonetic Association* 3: 10–21.

(1982) On the distinction between 'stress-timed' and 'syllable-timed' languages. In D. Crystal (ed.) *Linguistic Controversies: Essays in Linguistic Theory and Practice in Honour of F. R. Palmer*. London: Arnold.

Romaine, S. (1978) Postvocalic /r/ in Scottish English: sound change in progress? In P. Trudgill (ed.) *Sociolinguistic Patterns in British English*. London: Arnold.

Selkirk, E. (1980) The role of prosodic categories in English word stress. *Linguistic Inquiry* 11: 563–605.

(1982) The syllable. In H. van der Hulst and N. Smith (eds.) *The Structure of Phonological Representations (Part II)*. Dordrecht: Foris.

(1984) On the major class features and syllable theory. In M. Aronoff and R. T. Oehrle (eds.) *Language Sound Structure: Studies in Phonology Presented to Morris Halle by his Teacher and Students*. Cambridge MA: MIT Press.

Siegel, D. (1979) *Topics in English Morphology*. New York: Garland.

Sommerstein, A. (1977) *Modern Phonology*. London: Arnold.

Stanley, R. (1967) Redundancy rules in phonology. *Language* 43: 393–435.

Treiman, R. and C. Danis (1988) Syllabification of intervocalic consonants. *Journal of Memory and Language* 27: 87–104.

Trubetzkoy, N. (1939) *Grundzüge der Phonologie*. English transl. by C. Baltaxe (1969) *Principles of Phonology*. Berkeley: University of California Press.

Vennemann, T. (1972) On the theory of syllabic phonology. *Linguistische Berichte* 18: 1–18.

Wells, J. C. (1982) *Accents of English*, 3 vols. Cambridge: Cambridge University Press.

(1990) *Longman Pronouncing Dictionary*. Harlow: Longman.

Wiik, K. (1965) *Finnish and English Vowels*. Turku: University of Turku Press.

Wood, S. (1975) Tense and lax vowels – degree of constriction or pharyngeal volume? *Lund Working Papers in Phonetics* 11: 55–107.

Zwicky, A. (1970) The free ride principle and two rules of complete assimilation in English. *Papers from the Sixth Regional Meeting, Chicago Linguistic Society*. Chicago: Chicago Linguistic Society.

# INDEX

*This index indicates pages where subjects/terms are defined or discussed in some detail.*